CHINESE ELITES
AND POLITICAL
CHANGE

Harvard East Asian Series 96

*The Council on East Asian Studies at Harvard University,
through the Fairbank Center for East Asian Research,
administers research projects designed to further
scholarly understanding of China, Japan, Korea, Vietnam,
Inner Asia, and adjacent areas.*

CHINESE ELITES AND POLITICAL CHANGE

Zhejiang Province in the Early Twentieth Century

R. Keith Schoppa

Harvard University Press
Cambridge, Massachusetts,
and London, England
1982

Publication of this book has been aided by a grant
from the Andrew W. Mellon Foundation

Library of Congress Cataloging in Publication Data

Schoppa, R. Keith, 1943–
  Chinese elites and political change.

  (Harvard East Asian series; 96)
  Bibliography: p.
  Includes index.
    1. Chekiang Province (China)—Politics and government.
2. Elite (Social sciences)—China—Chekiang Province.
I. Title. II. Series.
DS793.C3S3   305.5′2   81-7075
ISBN 0-674-12325-5   AACR2

for Beth

Acknowledgments

The list of those to whom I owe various debts in the preparation of this book is long. My teachers at the University of Michigan guided, supported, and challenged me at different stages of the project: Albert Feuerwerker first suggested Zhejiang as a research area and gave me continual support and encouragement; Ernest Young always asked the hard and significant questions; and Chang Chun-shu first encouraged my study of local history. My debt to G. William Skinner is obvious: I have benefited not only from his important theories but also from his willing advice and criticism. I am also deeply grateful for Philip Kuhn's support and suggestions at various stages of the project.

I wish to thank the participants of the Modern China Project at the University of Chicago in 1978–1979, especially Tsou Tang, David Strand, Susan Mann Jones, Ch'en Yung-fa, and Guy Alitto, for their ideas and advice. I am grateful to Mary Rankin, Andrew Nathan, and Thomas Rawski for their comments on an earlier manuscript on Zhejiang. Wan Weiying of the University of Michigan Asia Library and Paul Ho and James Cheng of the University of Chicago Far Eastern Library offered invaluable assistance.

The Valparaiso University Research Professorship that I held for two consecutive years (1976–1978) provided me with release time and sufficient stipend to proceed with the research. For this award, I thank the University's Committee on Creative Work and Research. In the Valparaiso University Department of Geography, I am grateful to Kenneth

Keifenheim for drawing the maps and to Alice Rechlin and Richard Hansis for their assistance on a number of problems.

It has become customary to include one's spouse at the end of the list, and in this case too it is the last but the most important acknowledgment. The many hours she spent typing, retyping, and editing the manuscript would alone entitle Beth to my deep gratitude. But even more significant were her understanding and sense of perspective. Finally, thanks to Kara and Derek, who never understood why I spent so much time in my study but always provided me with a change of pace and a fresh perspective.

Contents

CONTENTS

Tables

Maps

Note on Romanization

With a few exceptions, this book uses the *pinyin* system of romanization. For those Zhejiang cities that were treaty ports—Hangchow, Ningpo, and Wenchow—I use the postal system romanization by which they are most well-known. In discussing the *prefectures* of which these three were capitals, however, I use *pinyin:* Hangzhou, Ningbo, and Wenzhou. All other place names are rendered in *pinyin,* as are personal names except for Sun Yat-sen and Chiang Kai-shek, the forms of which are well known in Western writings.

PART ONE

The Context of Elite Activity

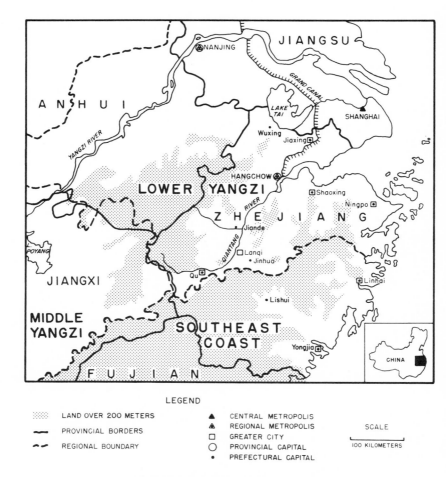

LEGEND

▒ LAND OVER 200 METERS	▲	CENTRAL METROPOLIS	
— PROVINCIAL BORDERS	▲	REGIONAL METROPOLIS	SCALE
⌐⌐ REGIONAL BOUNDARY	□	GREATER CITY	
	○	PROVINCIAL CAPITAL	100 KILOMETERS
	•	PREFECTURAL CAPITAL	

1. Zhejiang province and surrounding area

1

Elites and Political Development:
The Historical Context

Constructing a strong, viable nation-state has been a crucial goal of the twentieth-century Chinese revolution. Viewed superficially, the nation-building process has been discontinuous, interrupted at times by struggles among various elites over the strategy and tactics for attaining this goal. For example, researchers have usually interpreted the years 1913 to 1927 as a glaring discontinuity—a period when political disintegration temporarily held in abeyance the nation-building effort.[1] One thesis of this book is that such an interpretation overlooks significant developments that occurred at lower levels of the polity.

Generally those who offer that interpretation have explicitly or implicitly treated various elites as the betrayers of the 1911 revolution and either the purposeful or the inadvertent destroyers of the Republic. These researchers have often viewed early-twentieth-century elites stereotypically, as little more than caricatures: the self-seeking militarist, the corrupt bureaucrat, the well-intentioned but ineffectual reformer, the besieged or exploitative bourgeoisie, and—most notable of all—the conservative landlord and the local bully–evil gentry amalgam. Until elites and their roles are more clearly understood, the development of the Chinese nation and the nature of twentieth-century politics and society will also remain unclear.

Late Qing Dynasty Elites and Their Roles

The mid-eighteenth century is generally recognized as the apex of state strength and prosperity in imperial China. By the early nineteenth century, demographic trends and economic and social problems had brought the state into a marked political-administrative decline. Within another half century, internal rebellions and the onslaught of Western imperialism had exacerbated the deterioration. This precipitate decline acceler-

3

ated several trends among social and political elites that had begun to develop in the seventeenth and early eighteenth centuries.

Recent scholarship has suggested that in the performance of public functions in China a "long-term secular trend from official to private responsibility" began in the early seventeenth century: local gentry (civil service degree-holders) and nongentry elites began to assume responsibility for funding and managing public projects in place of officials who had previously directed such concerns.[2] Flourishing commercialization of some areas in the eighteenth century gave rise both to a growing private sector and to the public sector's increased reliance on private mechanisms and processes—as in the partial dependence of government tax officials on private grain merchants and shippers.[3]

The trend toward private responsibility for public functions accelerated in the early nineteenth century when the mushrooming rate of population growth and increasingly serious fiscal problems contributed to a "general breakdown of public functions."[4] No longer able to provide many administrative services and unable to absorb the proliferating gentry into legitimate civil service posts, the government allowed increasing local elite involvement in quasi-administrative functions. Upper gentry (holders of *jinshi, juren,* and regular *gongsheng* degrees) and lower gentry (holders of *shengyuan,* purchased *gongsheng,* and *jiansheng* degrees) began to participate in the collection of various taxes and, by mid-century, in the management of militia units. In addition many lower gentry became involved in subbureaucratic functions as clerks and runners in county yamens.

The reconstruction roles assumed by local elites, generally called gentry-managers (*shendong*), in the wake of the Taiping Rebellion (1850–1864) were part of this long-term trend. It has been shown that in some areas these reformist elites moved into the sponsorship and management of Western-style schools, hospitals, and newspapers in the last decades of the nineteenth century.[5] In short, throughout the nineteenth century, as an array of problems forced the government to withdraw from a primary role in many local concerns, area elites participated more energetically in their management. Studies delineating this trend have generally dealt with relatively highly commercialized areas,[6] and it seems likely that this trend existed more clearly in areas of substantial commercialization than in those that were less commercialized.

In the eighteenth century internal trade increased and the first important commercial links to Europe were established. The mid-nineteenth century brought to already thriving areas increased foreign trade and modern transport in the form of steamships and steam launches.[7] This growing commercialization affected the outlooks and roles of elites in the rich plains and coastal areas. Distinctions between gentry and nongentry elites blurred as upper and lower gentry became increasingly involved in commercial affairs. By the turn of the twentieth century, many gentry had commercial interests.[8] Since wealthy nongentry merchants adopted gentry life-styles as they participated in local reconstruction and reform, it seems clear that late Qing commercialization hastened the end of the centuries-old ideological separation of gentry (*shen*) and merchant (*shang*).[9] Near the end of the nineteenth century, growing involvement with foreign nations and the effects of the unequal treaty system made elites in areas subject to Western influence conscious of national problems. The reform efforts of gentry and nongentry elites in the last decades of the century were aimed in part at strengthening the nation to withstand the continuing Western pressure.

In sum, the substantial expansion of local elite (gentry and nongentry) roles in traditional and modern spheres had by the twentieth century created an increasingly assertive elite population in commercialized areas. Less commercialized areas tended to see neither the growing awareness of national issues nor the changes and shifts among elites and elite roles. With the Qing dynasty reform efforts (1901–1911), the abolition of the civil service examination (1905), and the end of the monarchy (1912), the first years of the century brought important changes to Zhejiang's elites in all areas.

Elites and Political Development

This study analyzes sociopolitical elites and political change in Zhejiang province during the first three decades of the twentieth century. Within the considerable strictures of the sources, it examines the social backgrounds, spheres of activity, and patterns of recruitment, careers, and decision making of local and provincial elites, that is, those who controlled public policies through their performance of political, social, and economic leadership roles. This elite population specifically includes (1) those who held actual leadership posts in various elite institutions: self-government bodies, ad hoc political associations, and politically significant professional associations (chambers of commerce, and education, agriculture, and lawyers' associations); and (2) those who played crucial roles in particular noninstitutional decisions or in managing crisis situations.[10] This analysis reveals that for elites these years were not simply a period of aborted national goals, but rather a time of substantial political transformation and development.

Because the term "political development," like "modernization" under which it is sometimes subsumed, has often been inadequately defined and normatively perceived, it is essential from the start to clarify my use of the term.[11] Political development in general occurs in a social system, defined as a unit of components (for example, individuals, groups, institutions, local political units) linked over time. The level of development refers to the interdependency and complexity of a system's components at any point in time.[12] At its simplest, the process of political development is the transition from primary to composite and complex political structures and phenomena. Around primary kin, patron-client, and brokerage relationships evolve more differentiated and institutionalized structures. This evolution does not mean the displacement or diminution of the primary by the complex. In Zhejiang, primary phenomena remained dominant features amid increased sociopolitical variety and differentiation.

By elite political development, I mean the increase in the political interdependency and complexity of elites, their associations and institutions.[13] The process of political development itself was neither spatially nor temporally uniform during the early decades of the twentieth century, and it did not spring from the same source in all areas of the province. This differentiation in development can be effectively analyzed by classifying provincial counties into ecological zones based upon indicators of economic development. Differential elite political development markedly shaped local and provincial politics in these years and thus is crucial to an understanding of the period's political dynamics. In the longer term, it is significant because subsequent regimes—the Guomindang, Japanese (in some areas), and Communist—either had to build on the elite structures, experiences, and processes that had developed in various zones or had to deal with their specific consequences. Five interrelated aspects of elite political development indicate political differentiation across ecological zones.

The Significance of Elite Institutionalization. The traditional Chinese state, suspicious of local elite political potential, had controlled the elites' institutional roles. Perhaps best known is the curtailment of degree-holders' participation in the leadership of decimal hierarchies (*baojia* and *lijia*) structured for purposes of surveillance and taxation. The crisis of the Qing administration, however, provided these elites with an opportunity to move into greater political roles. With continuing internal deterioration and increasing foreign pressure, the Qing dynasty, in the last decade of its search for wealth and power, sponsored the establishment of elite institutions at provincial capitals and at county (*xian*) and subcounty levels: self-government bodies and various professional associations (*fatuan*)—chambers of commerce (*shang hui*), education associations (*jiaoyu hui*), and agricultural associations (*nong hui*).[14] These institutions promised to fulfill two desiderata for the court: to control the localities more effectively by co-opting elite political roles under official auspices; and to provide organs for carrying out reforms and policing new or important professions without large financial outlays.

For the local elites, however, these government-sponsored institutions offered greater promise of local initiative and autonomy. They provided a framework in which elites met and deliberated on a multitude of local and occupational concerns. That they were organized at a time of debate over national directions and goals meant discussions of national issues as well. The revolutionary organizational change cannot be overemphasized. The context of elite actions had changed markedly: the government had underwritten local elite political involvement in quasi-governmental organizations. The politicization of Chinese society had leaped forward by government edict.

The establishment of elite institutions through which items on the political agenda are decided and by which public functions are performed is only one aspect of elite institutionalization. Two other features are crucial in gauging the level of political development. First is the development of elite identity with the established institution: elites begin to see themselves as part of the institutions that have been given political power. Second, these elites begin to see the institution itself as a major political actor, capable of seeking redress, impeaching wrongdoers, working for sundry goals. This sense of institutional integrity and power is the most significant of the three, having considerable political import.

The Increased Importance of the Public Sphere in Functional Responsibilities. As the late Qing and the early Republican governments attempted to rationalize and reorganize political space through the introduction of new state forms to the locality, elite roles began to shift. Those public works and welfare functions that had come increasingly into the private sphere since the early seventeenth century began to be transferred to the public sphere, either under direct government supervision or in various specialized public institutions, many of which were sponsored by the government. The first years of the twentieth century saw the reversal of the secular trend evident since the late Ming dynasty and the beginning of the trend toward greater governmental control and responsibility that was seen in Guomindang blueprints and that culminated under the Communist regime.

It is noteworthy that this trend continued in the midst of the alleged disintegration of China in the early Republic. My study of local self-government reveals substantially stronger local government control over elites in the early 1920s than in the late Qing dynasty. Such an important trend remains hidden if one looks only at national affairs. My exploration of local and provincial politics and society is undertaken on the premise that assertions about national trends and developments can be made with a measure of certainty only after careful subnational analysis. In the case of Zhejiang, local trends indicated fundamental political change, despite apparent chaos on the national level. In the less developed zones the long-term trend to the private sphere did not appear so clearly, and the co-optation of the private by the public sphere thus was less a factor.

The Significance of Voluntary Sociopolitical Associations. One of the central ideas in the turn-of-the-century writings of the political thinker Liang Qichao was the concept of "grouping" (*qun*). Liang criticized cultural attachments based on "territory or biological relatedness or occupation" as divisive, and he regretted the lack of civic groupings, which might foster the integration of the Chinese into a "cohesive and well-knit political community."[15] His comments indicate recognition of the crucial role of sociopolitical collectivities in political development. Groupings provide structures for social and political horizontal linkages with the consequent potential for greater social cohesion.[16] They serve as interest groups for the attainment of specialized political and social goals. If organized on a hierarchically cumulative basis, they provide a framework for vertical integration, fostering interdependency at different levels of the polity.

In imperial times, the chief voluntary associations were native place associations and guilds, which (contrary to Liang's opinion) contributed significantly to political development in the early twentieth century. Following the formation of bureaucratic factions at the end of the Ming dynasty, the Qing state had been continuously on guard against other types of voluntary elite associations with political potential. Only in the mid-1890s did elites begin to lose their own wariness of association and join political study groups to promote their visions of change. As Frederic Wakeman has suggested, reformers "felt justified in arguing that clubs, societies, and parties were all just as necessary to human development as lineage or neighborhood solidarity."[17] Voluntary associations sprang up in the last decade of the Qing dynasty, enlisting men and women in solving local problems and in dealing with national political issues. The coming of the Republic accelerated this organizational and associative revolution, whose extent was dependent on the level of economic development.

Increased Elite Participation in Political Processes. This aspect of development is, in one sense, simply the concomitant of elite institutionalization and the establishment of voluntary associations; but it has important dynamics that should be stressed. Participation changed the nature of elites by tending to multiply social and political identities. A man like Shen Wenhua of Jiaxing county was no longer simply a wealthy lineage-based gentry-manager performing in a private capacity those public managerial functions that his status permitted. In the midst of organizational development, Shen became a prominent member of specialized institutions that broadened and differentiated his identity: he was the head of the education association and of the anti-opium bureau; a leader in associations to renovate Chinese society and to prevent local encroachments by foreign companies; and the head of the county assembly.[18] Shen retained his all-important private ties and identities, and his new institutional and political identities meant that he also related within an institutional context to other elites and institutions.

As organizational participation increased, so did the possibility that politically significant cleavages, as well as new elite linkages, would develop. Participation brought elites more sociopolitical complexity while it tended to increase the complexity of sociopolitical space. The results were nothing less than the remaking of elite society. The potential degree of elite participation as measured in the number of potential linkages to other components of the social system varied from zone to zone. Shen Wenhua obviously had more opportunities for political and social participation in different organizations and processes in the relatively developed county of Jiaxing than did elites in backwater areas.[19]

Increasing Elite Identification with Particular Political Space. Chinese elites had always identified themselves with their family's native place. Although this identification was primarily sociocultural, native place ties had important political potential. Such ties provided linkages to others from the same county, prefecture, and province. In the early twentieth century the establishment of new, specifically delimited subcounty districts for self-government and education enabled elites to make conscious decisions on the political-administrative disposition of their home areas.

At the same time, elite identification with province and nation emerged in the oft-stated concern for nation building. Strong national feeling had begun to develop at the end of the nineteenth century,[20] and in the first years of the twentieth, students in Japan and reformers returning to their native places spoke of making the locality and province the foundation of the nation. The political history of Zhejiang in this period is in part an account of the interplay of the loyalties to nation, province, and locality. In this regard, the correlations between level of economic development and strength of identification with specific political space are again significant.

An Overview of Early-Twentieth-Century Zhejiang Political History

Britain's initial failure to act on an 1898 concession to construct the Shanghai-Hangchow-Ningpo railroad had led the Beijing government to annul this grant in 1905. After Zhejiang elites had founded and registered their own railroad company, Britain pressured Beijing to reopen negotiations in the summer of 1907. Elites, primarily those in the most developed areas, exploded in protest. Caught up in the nationalism of the pre-1911 years, they demanded control of their railroad. Although Beijing eventually concluded a loan agreement with the British, it stipulated that the company's control and management remain in Zhejiang hands. In 1910, when Britain forced the removal of the company's director, certain elites once again reacted bitterly.[21] The establishment of Qing-sponsored professional and (after 1909) self-government institutions in which local and provincial elites discussed political issues facilitated these nationalistic outbursts.

The process and significance of the 1911 revolution varied in different areas of the province. For the more developed sectors, the years immediately after the revolution have been called the liberal republic, a period of civilian elite openness to new social and political ideas and structures.[22] But by 1914 there were increasing indications that the pre-1911 nationalistic elite fervor was temporarily spent. President Yuan Shikai's February 1914 abolition of all self-government bodies—from the provincial assembly to county and subcounty organs—snuffed out the major institutions of elite expression until they were reestablished in the 1920s. The immediate beneficiaries of the 1911 revolution on the provincial level were the new military elites. Although the military was not, as in some other provinces, a continuously dominant force in Zhejiang politics, it played a significant role throughout the early Republic. Table 1 provides a list of military and civil governors from 1911 to 1927.

The beginning years of the Republic saw the revolutionary military coalition splinter into factions on the basis of military academy ties. By the summer of 1912, the regime of Jiang Zungui and his fellow Japan Army Officers Academy graduates had come to an end amid recrimination and assassination. Military Governor Zhu Rui, a graduate of the Nanjing Military Academy, began his administration hailed as the hero of the Zhejiang forces that took Nanjing during the revolution; however, he and his close associate Civil Governor Qu Yingguang supported President Yuan in the "second revolution" of 1913 and in Yuan's aborted monarchical attempt in 1915 and 1916. From late 1914, when Zhu was incapacitated by illness, the government was in the hands of Qu, who was increasingly accused of maladministration and corruption. The Zhu-Qu regime was overthrown in the growing anti-Yuan movement in the spring of 1916, with Zhejiangese graduates of the Baoding and Zhejiang military academies seizing power. When graduates of these academies turned on one another, the coalition collapsed; as a result, in January 1917, Beijing sent Yang Shande to bring Zhejiang under firmer control.[23]

This seizure of power by outside forces did not immediately engulf the

Table 1.
Zhejiang military and civil governors, 1911–1927

Military	Civil
Tang Shouqian (November 1911–December 1911)	
Jiang Zungui (December 1911–August 1912)	
Zhu Rui (August 1912–April 1916)	Qu Yingguang (September 1912–May 1916)
Qu Yingguang (April 1916–May 1916)	
Lü Gongwang (June 1916–December 1916)	Lü Gongwang (June 1916–December 1916)
Yang Shande (January 1917–August 1919)	Qi Yaoshan (January 1917–June 1920)
Lu Yongxiang (August 1919–September 1924)	Shen Jinjian (June 1920–October 1922)
	Zhang Zaiyang (October 1922–September 1924)
Sun Chuanfang (September 1924–February 1927)	Xia Chao (September 1924–October 1926)
	Chen Yi (October 1926–December 1926)

province in the fire of warlord struggle: until the late summer of 1924, Zhejiang escaped military action. During his tenure, Yang Shande showed little interest in warlord machinations. The strong-willed Civil Governor Qi Yaoshan actually dominated provincial politics. Qi, who had at one time served on the staff (*mufu*) of Zhang Zhidong, set out to build Zhejiang into his own power base, challenging Zhejiangese in positions of civil power and antagonizing new-style elites by his staunch conservatism. Impeached twice by provincial assemblies, he was removed from office in June 1920.[24]

Yang's successor, Lu Yongxiang, was an active supporter of the national military figure Duan Qirui. Following Duan's defeat by Zhili forces in the summer of 1920, three of the four provinces bordering Zhejiang were controlled by Lu's enemies.[25] The severe threat of war with Jiangsu dissipated after both provinces' military leaders pulled back. By 1922, however, Zhili power had expanded over northern and central China so that Zhejiang provided the only obstacle to the clique's complete control of the Lower Yangzi area. Sun Chuanfang completed the conquest of Zhejiang in September 1924. For the first time the province was controlled by a militarist strong enough to warrant national attention. By late 1925, with Sun's victory in Jiangsu, Zhejiang found itself one of a group of provinces governed from Nanjing.

Zhejiangese civilian and military elites who had seen provincial control disappear into Beiyang hands in early 1917 witnessed the evolution of the harsh realities of militarist control. Strong provincial feelings born in 1917 gave rise over the next decade to several elite attempts to establish provincial autonomy and to protect provincial integrity through military means and constitutional efforts. In the years after the 1924 war, Sun suppressed elite political initiatives, and hopes for provincial autonomy flickered. They were snuffed out with the success of Nationalist forces in early 1927.

2

The Four Zhejiangs

Zhejiang is the smallest Chinese province, in area approximately the size of the state of Indiana.[1] Its size, however, has not insured geographical integrity. From the beginning of its recorded history, geographical and ecological differences were translated into political division in the states of Wu and Yue. Wu extended into four modern prefectures—Jiaxing, Hangzhou, Huzhou, and Yanzhou; the rest of present-day Zhejiang made up Yue. (See Map 2 for the prefectural delineations.) These basic divisions are often referred to respectively as western Zhejiang (Zhexi) and eastern Zhejiang (Zhedong).[2] In this conception, Zhexi comprises the three northernmost prefectures on the Yangzi alluvial plain as well as the basin of the Qiantang River, which flows into Hangchow Bay. The terrain of Zhedong ranges from areas of rolling hills to steep mountains, from which numerous streams flow into Hangchow Bay and the East China Sea.

Recent writers have used the major division—Zhexi and Zhedong—in a purely topographical sense, calling the three northern, generally level prefectures (Jiaxing, Hangzhou, and Huzhou) Zhexi and the remaining eight prefectures, dominated by hills and mountains, Zhedong.[3] In this model, Zhexi's economic interests closely parallel those of southern Jiangsu. Traditionally marked by large landholdings (some extending up to several thousand mu) and crossed by numerous waterways for transportation and irrigation, Zhexi produced two crops of rice annually (generally providing a sufficient supply for that area's high population density) and some of the finest silk in the world.[4] In contrast, landholdings in mountainous Zhedong were both smaller and less fertile, necessitating the importation of rice.[5]

This division of the province into Zhexi and Zhedong does not, however, provide an adequate framework for analyzing elites and their functions in a period of political change and development, for it fails to con-

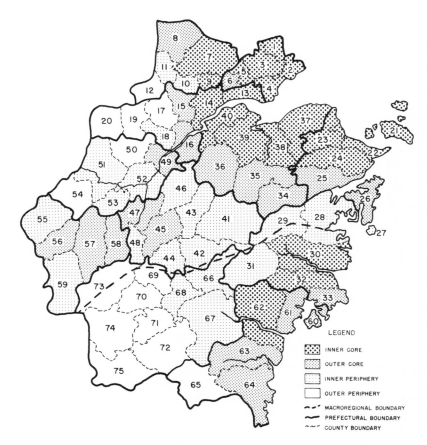

2.   Zonal distribution of Zhejiang prefectures and counties

Key to Map 2

County	Map Number	County	Map Number
Anji	11	Shouchang	53
Changhua	20	Songyang	70
Changshan	56	Suian	54
Changxing	8	Suichang	73
Cheng	35	† Taiping	33
* Chongde	6	Taishun	65
Ciqi	23	Tangqi	48
Deqing	9	Tiantai	29
Dinghai	21	Tonglu	49
Dongyang	41	Tongxiang	5
Fenghua	25	† Wenling	33
Fenshui	50	Wukang	10
Fuyang	16	Wuxing	7
Haining	13	Wuyi	44
Haiyan	4	Xianju	31
Hang	14	Xiangshan	26
Huangyan	32	Xiaofeng	12
Jiande	52	Xiaoshan	40
Jiangshan	59	Xinchang	34
Jiashan	1	Xindeng	18
Jiaxing	3	Xuanping	69
Jingning	72	Yin	24
Jinhua	45	Yiwu	43
Jinyun	66	Yongjia	62
Kaihua	55	Yongkang	42
Lanqi	47	Yuhang	15
Linan	17	Yuhuan	60
Linhai	30	Yunhe	71
Lishui	68	Yuqian	19
Longchuan	74	Yuyao	37
Longyu	58	Zhenhai	22
Luoqing	61	Zhuji	36
Nantian	27		
Ninghai	28	Prefecture	Map Number
Pinghu	2	Jiaxing	1–6
Pingyang	64	Huzhou	7–12
Pujiang	46	Hangzhou	13–20
Qingtian	67	Ningbo	21–27
Qingyuan	75	Taizhou	28–33
Qu	57	Shaoxing	34–40
Qunan	51	Jinhua	41–48
Ruian	63	Yanzhou	49–54
Shangyu	38	Quzhou	55–59
Shaoxing	39	Wenzhou	60–65
* Shimen	6	Chuzhou	66–75

* Before 1912 Chongde County was called Shimen.
† Before 1912 Wenling County was called Taiping.

sider substantial intraregional differences and the effects of economic and social change upon an area's environment.[6] Man acts within a specific spatial context. It is obvious, however, that humans do not simply interact with the natural environment but also with artificial environmental features—for example, commercial exchange patterns, technological advances, and institutions to facilitate, mediate, and direct change. The natural and artificial environments affect sociopolitical elites and social structures and are in turn altered by these changed elites and structures.

Classification of Social Ecological Zones

An essential first step, therefore, is to classify the spaces in which elites act and with which they interact, a classification based on both natural and artificial environmental criteria. William Skinner's regional model, based upon population density, is an appropriate initial framework for delineating broad spatial zones in which the interdependent variables of the "ecological complex"—population, the natural environment, technology, and socioeconomic structures—exhibit variance in degree or kind.[7] These zones are basically categories of economic development, by which I mean the process of economic transition from the simple (lower population density, lower degree of occupational and managerial specialization, lower level of technology, and higher degree of local economic self-sufficiency) to the composite and complex (higher population density, greater degree of specialization, higher level of technology, and spreading local and extralocal commercialization).[8] The level of development is obviously always relative, never absolute.

As in the traditional paradigms, by Skinner's model the province is divided into two regions, which comprise portions of the relatively more urbanized Lower Yangzi region and of the less urbanized Southeast Coast.[9] The province contains both core and peripheral areas from each macroregion. Skinner posits a continuum of urbanization, shading off in "concentric gradients" from the highly developed regional core to the less developed periphery.[10] A study of Zhejiang's seventy-five counties in the two macroregions supports the general accuracy of this continuum concept.[11] However, for a systematic analysis of elites and their political and social structures, this conception is inadequate: it is too vaguely and insufficiently differentiated to represent a range of elite structural types, allowing only polar types to be presented clearly and offering description only in terms of broad social and political parameters.

To rectify this lack of differentiation, I constructed a range of differentiated development zones as a framework for analyzing variations in elites and their political structures and behavior. To provide hypotheses about the number of zones and their delimitations, I first rank-ordered counties on the basis of each of three quantitative indicators of development: population density; highest postal ranking of county seats or of nonadministrative towns; and a financial institution index, determined by the number of pawnshops and native banks per population.[12]

The relationship between population density and commercialization, an important aspect of development, has been frequently noted. In areas of high density, commercialization is facilitated. Costs for the delivery of goods and services are lowered, and increased economic and occupational specialization is fostered.[13] In a society largely untouched by modern communication and transportation, population density helps determine the "degree of connectedness" and capacity for interchange within that society. Modern transportation destroys this relationship between development and population density.[14] But in Zhejiang before 1920 only Skinner's core area had been affected by modern (rail or steamer) transportation. Population density thus can be taken as an indicator of potential socioeconomic linkages.[15]

I have used the postal ranking system as a surrogate measure of the commercial development of a county's urban centers.[16] As Skinner points out, businessmen used the postal services more than other groups.[17] Lin Chuanjia's 1918 gazetteer of Zhejiang indicates the strong correlation between level of business activity and level of postal service.[18] Another more direct statistical measure of each county's economic development is its number of financial institutions per population, specifically native banks (qianzhuang) and pawnshops, which were capable of supporting commercial enterprise and fostering development. The very few modern-style banks were not included, as they were located only in major metropolitan areas before 1929.[19] The index obtained for each institution (based upon native banks and pawnshops per population) was combined into one financial institution variable.[20]

Three marked breaks in the statistical rankings of county population density and financial institutions suggested four hypothetical development zones. Ordering the postal rank designation into four classes, I proceeded to scale each county for each variable; counties with designation 111 are at the core extreme, those with 444, at the periphery extreme.[21] Summing the totals of each variable's ranked class (one through four) enabled me to set the limits for each zone (see Appendix B). The counties included in each hypothetical zone are listed on Table 2 and delineated on Map 2.[22]

The hypothetical nature of the four zones is underscored by the paucity of quantitative data, specifically the availability of only three variables. The zones serve as somewhat arbitrary boundaries that are used to analyze intraprovincial political systems "in something like the manner that an ecologist designates any localized set of organisms and their environ-

Table 2.
Zonal classification of counties

Inner core	Outer core	Inner periphery	Outer periphery
Yin	Lanqi	Lishui	Songyang
Hang	Qu	Anji	Changhua
Shaoxing	Xiangshan	Qingtian	Taishun
Jiashan	Yuhang	Yongkang	Suian
Haining	Jinhua	Ninghai	Xuanping
Pinghu	Fuyang	Jiangshan	Xiaofeng
Zhenhai	Cheng	Xindeng	Yunhe
Yuyao	Luoqing	Yiwu	Yuqian
Jiaxing	Ruian	Wukang	Longchuan
Haiyan	Zhuji	Tiantai	Fenshui
Ciqi	Longyu	Pujiang	Suichang
Xiaoshan	Chongde	Dongyang	Jingning
Tongxiang	Wenling	Kaihua	Qingyuan
Wuxing	Fenghua	Wuyi	Linan
Huangyan	Xinchang	Xianju	
Dinghai	Pingyang	Jiande	
Linhai	Changshan	Nantian	
Yongjia	Tonglu	Tangqi	
Deqing	Yuhuan	Jinyun	
Shangyu	Changxing	Shouchang	
		Qunan	

ment as an 'ecosystem.' "[23] They are significant because my research into early-twentieth-century politics and society bears out the hypothesis. There were four Zhejiangs, rather than three or five or nine, because four different political and social configurations emerge from an empirical study of the historical data.

The Inner Core

The zone of highest development is designated the inner core. Its twenty counties contained the highest-level central places and over 44 percent of the province's population.[24] With less than 24 percent of the provincial land area, this zone is almost identical to the areas assigned by Skinner to the "core."[25] Thus, the relative developmental pattern in Zhejiang into the 1920s seems to have remained the same as in the 1890s (the period delineated by Skinner). The inner core includes parts of the greater city trading areas (and prefectures) of Jiaxing, Huzhou, Shaoxing, Ningbo, Taizhou, Wenzhou, and the area around Hangchow. (See Appendix A for a delineation of the units of analysis in this study.)

Ningpo was one of the ports opened to the West in the Treaty of Nanjing in 1842. Abundant water transportation routes facilitated its commercial success in external and internal trade. Its tie to Shanghai and the commercial and banking network that resulted have been well documented.[26] By 1913 Ningpo was connected to Shaoxing via the Ningpo-Cao-e section of the Shanghai-Hangchow-Ningpo railway and by the 1920s to Hangchow by bus from the Baiguan terminal on the Cao-e River.[27] Navigable streams and sea routes linked Ningpo directly to the counties that it served as prefectural center (see Map 3). Ningbo entrepreneurs sometimes collaborated with their Shaoxing counterparts in commercial undertakings in both Zhejiang and Shanghai. Shaoxing merchants played a major role in many areas, most notably on the Hangchow commercial and business scene.[28]

A high degree of commercialization and horizontal elite mobility also marked the inner-core portions of Hangzhou, Huzhou, and Jiaxing. Hangchow, the provincial capital and regional metropolis, became a treaty port after the Treaty of Shimonoseki in 1895. Like Ningpo, it was favored with excellent communication facilities. The Grand Canal linked it to major centers; steam launches and junks sailed frequently between Hangchow and Shanghai, and after May 1909, the railroad linked these cities. The main channel from the interior of the province to Hangchow was the Qiantang River, the largest in Zhejiang; fed by several important tributaries, it connected the capital to the economic centers of Quzhou and Lanqi in Zhejiang and Huizhou in Anhui. The Qiantang network also made Hangchow the principal commercial and financial center of Shangrao in Jiangxi province.[29] Jiaxing prefecture (at the main city of which a Maritime Customs station was established in late 1896) and Huzhou prefecture contain some of China's most productive rice and mulberry areas. Crisscrossed by waterways and bordering Lake Tai, they were linked to Shanghai by rail and regular boat service.[30]

The major urban center in the Zhejiang portion of the Southeast Coast was Wenchow. Located at the mouth of the Ou, Zhejiang's second largest river, Wenchow became a treaty port in the 1876 Treaty of Chefoo, but great success as a modern commercial center eluded it. Internal trade was sluggish: the Ou River, despite its tributaries in southern counties, was too shallow in many places to facilitate commerce. Because of the proximity of Ningpo and Shanghai, trade with the West was slow. In regional trade, Wenchow suffered as a satellite of Ningpo.[31] Both qualitative and quantitative indicators suggest that the degree of development in Wenchow (Yongjia county) was less than the Lower Yangzi core. Statistical indicators place it at the lower end of the inner-core spectrum.[32]

Linhai and Huangyan counties in Taizhou prefecture experienced commercial development as entrepôts between Wenchow and Shanghai. Connected in the Republic by daily steam launch service on the Ling

3.   Zhejiang river systems

River, the Linhai county seat and Haimen, its most important market town, exported tea and citrus fruits. Haimen and Huangyan were connected to Shanghai by weekly steamers.[33] The level of development in both counties, as in Yongjia, was less than that of the Lower Yangzi inner core.

The Outer Core

The second zone is the outer core. Many of its twenty counties (with 26 percent of the land and 31 percent of the province's population) were contiguous to the inner core, generally permitting relatively easy overland travel to that zone. Most of the significant urban centers were located on important rivers like the Qiantang, Ou, Cao-e, or one of their major tributaries. Attracting regional merchants, these centers served as important commercial entrepôts, handling large quantities of exported goods (tea, hams, wood products, vegetable tallows, and citrus fruits) and imported commodities (silk and cotton goods, kerosene, and salt). River traffic between the core zones was by sailboat or, by the 1910s, steam launch; passenger boat service operated at least from the years of the early Republic.[34] Of the four prefectural capitals outside of the inner core, two—Jinhua and Quzhou (Qu)—were located in this zone.

The Inner Periphery

The two outer zones shared a general lack of involvement with the core zones. The inner periphery's twenty-one counties (with 30 percent of the land and 17 percent of the province's population) were not, however, like the primitive backwaters of the least developed outer periphery. Inner-periphery centers were generally located on minor tributaries of major rivers or occasionally branches of these tributaries. Streams were navigable, although sometimes shallow, rapid, and passable only in spring and summer. Traffic was normally restricted to bamboo rafts, which carried exports of tea, paper, and soybeans, and imports generally confined to essential commodities. Because of the contiguity of these areas to the outer core and their location at the headwaters of important streams, merchants from outside the province, but generally from within the macroregion, were not unusual; many counties had one center with a merchant guild (*huiguan*).[35]

The Outer Periphery

The fourteen counties of the outer periphery were mountainous with little arable land. They had great difficulty in developing any continuous interchange with more developed counties. Most were located in remote areas, and although they contained 21 percent of the land area, they had only 7 percent of the province's population. If navigable streams existed, they were often too rocky or rapid for vessels other than small rowboats; in such cases, it took from ten days to two weeks to reach inner-core centers. Many counties did not have navigable streams; overland travel, however difficult, was the only alternative. Commercial and social intercourse with areas even in fairly close proximity was often curtailed. Large areas in counties like Xuanping and Jingning did not even contain standard market towns.[36] Most counties were without financial institutions, and some had no postal service.

Aspects of the Model

Patterns of Zonal Configuration

Although Map 2 reveals a general concentric gradience of outer zones from the inner core and a general zonal geographic contiguity, these features are not necessary in the model. For a number of reasons, certain counties appear in one zone when their geographic locations might first have suggested otherwise. The general correlation of higher economic development in counties along important rivers is evident in the stretch of outer-core counties along the Qiantang basin. As one nears the headwaters of the river, outer-core counties become predictably less regular. Tangqi county, for example, with only ten kilometers of river flowing through it, had no important upper-level markets. The outer-core status of Qu and Changshan counties comes not only from their importance as commercial entrepôts between Jiangxi markets and the Qiantang basin but also from relative economic prosperity due to ample natural resources, including extensive areas of arable lowland. Qu, the prefectural capital of Quzhou, was the greater city in the urban hierarchy of central places along the upper reaches of the Qiantang.

In the general sweep of outer-core counties along the Qiantang, however, Pujiang and Jiande appear as inner-periphery counties. Pujiang is an upland county with no direct connection to the Qiantang; it contains headwaters of rivers flowing in three different directions. The essayist Cao Juren, a native of Pujiang, noted that difficulty of travel prevented even many local elites from ever journeying to Hangchow, a mere 120 miles from the county seat.[37] The zonal placement of Jiande at first glance appears even more anomalous. The capital of former Yanzhou prefecture and located near the juncture of the Xinan and Qiantang rivers, this county had a low level of economic development because of its topography and location between more important economic centers. Over 90 percent of the county's land area was mountainous, one of the highest proportions of mountains to plains in the province. Agriculturally poor, Jiande also had little commercial activity. It was situated on the Qiantang between Tonglu, which flourished during the Republic, and Lanqi, a greater city in the urban central place hierarchy. Jiande's development languished in the face of the prosperity of the two other centers.[38]

Qunan is an inner-periphery county among outer-periphery counties along the Zhejiang-Anhui border. It is located on the Xinan River, which connects the upland basin of Huizhou (Anhui) to the Qiantang basin and the Hangchow regional city trading system.[39] Macroregional and subregional divides help pattern many of the peripheral counties. Peripheral counties embrace the divide between the Lower Yangzi and the Southeast Coast macroregions. The Lower Yangzi's first-order subregionalization reveals three economic regions centered on Shanghai, Hangchow, and Nanjing. The peripheral counties on Zhejiang's northwest border are located on the natural divide between the subregions centered on Hangchow and Nanjing. The counties on Zhejiang's southern border are located near or on the divide between the two northern subregions of the Southeast Coast—the basins of the Ou-Ling and Min rivers. Portions of counties like Changhua in the northwest and Longchuan and Jingning in the south were economically oriented to trading systems centered outside Zhejiang.[40] The trade of Qingyuan county in the south was completely oriented to the Min rather than to the Ou-Ling system.

The Unit of Analysis

The use of the county as the unit of analysis is the least satisfying aspect of the model. It is immediately obvious that whole counties are not themselves uniformly urban or rural. Intracounty gradations of development have much influence on elite institutions and political development: marketing areas, both congruent and noncongruent with townships (*xiang*), vary markedly in their degrees of development. In an ideal research world where there was no dearth of evidence, this study could be made on the basis of marketing communities; unfortunately, such data are unavailable. Even though county level data itself is not abundant, it is more widely available; and I would argue that analysis of the county units offers a general view of the pattern of development. Moreover, wherever possible in the following analyses of county politics, I have delineated intracounty degrees of development in order to provide as accurate a context as possible for the study of early-twentieth-century political change.

The Mode of Economic Development

The mode of development inherent in this model is the evolutionary extension of economic and technological patterns, first via natural routes and methods and, later, with the extension of transport technology, via artifical ones. Two points can be made about this process. First, there is no *inevitability* about its uniformity or extent. The peripheries did not have the concentration of resources necessary to experience some of the changes of the core zones. In addition, the development of the core zones may have fed to some extent on the underdevelopment of the peripheries. Furthermore, processes of economic development and decay were found alongside each other in the same zones and counties. Urban centers on water routes, for example, were often overshadowed by new centers along rail lines. Particular local situations could produce stagnation in the midst of development. Economic development was, in short, uneven; and a uniform process of designated economic development stages for all areas was not inevitable. A second aspect of the developmental process is the general relativity of developmental change among the four zones. Zdravko Mlinar and Henry Teune have contended that "the higher the level of development, the higher the rate of developmental change."[41] Changes experienced by rapidly developing outer-zone counties—such as the outer-core county of Lanqi—were still less than changes in inner-core counties.

This model does not preclude other modes of development. Other forces besides the economic and technological dynamic can stimulate or intervene in processes of economic development; direct and indirect political intrusion is a prime example. The demands of the military, for instance, may result indirectly in economic development. The best case in point is in the coastal county of Xiangshan (outer core) where a military base was built in 1913. This military construction, including modern communications facilities, prompted some incipient industrialization and expanded commercial development, which in turn led to interest in developing the territory near Sanmen Bay in the 1920s.[42] At times political intervention is direct, and attempts are made to extend or accelerate the development of technology and commercial processes in areas unlikely to experience them through gradual change. In the case of Zhejiang, the provincial government in the 1910s took an active role in trying to extend modern economic developments to the outer zones. In sum, economic development can come not only through the natural growth of a regional economy but also through the intervention of outside political forces, with either direct or indirect impact on local economic development.

The Dynamics of Political Development

In my use of the zonal model, there is an implicit correlation between economic and political development. That correlation is empirically verifiable, although it is imperfect and should not be taken to mean that both types of development necessarily proceed spatially or temporally in tandem or in uniform developmental paths.[43] The specific political effects of the Shanghai-Hangchow-Ningpo railroad on Jiaxing county offer an example that underscores the basic correlation. Completed in 1909, this railroad cut across the county near the East Gate of the walled county seat and directly through the town of Wangdian about ten miles to the south. Within a year, this development fostered a changed economic environment in the county seat and market town, which, in turn, brought new political issues and problems. In Wangdian, the increased commercial activity and its associated problems quickly led town elites to petition for more policemen. When thirty men were added at a cost of three thousand cash (*jin*) a year, a loud protest to the county officials came from nonnative pawnshop owners who were to be taxed heavily to pay for the additional policemen. The coming of the railroad to Wangdian thus stimulated political participation in the petitioning and protest by the town's elite, increased the presence of government-paid functionaries (police) in local affairs, and aggravated an antagonism, apparent in the area since the Taiping Rebellion, between natives and outsider merchants.[44]

In the county seat, the increased commercial activity near the train station contributed to rivalry between rich businessmen for the construction of inns and the widening of streets to facilitate trade—projects that brought merchant elites into contact with officials. This planned construction also stimulated protests from shop owners and home owners who were to be displaced.[45] As the population in the southeastern part of the city increased, petitions came to the magistrate to allow the establishment of schools, a process that called for direction from the government-sponsored education office and increased local taxes for funding.[46]

More dramatic was the railroad's overall effect on city and county economic and political patterns. Before the railroad, the center of Jiaxing's commercial life was its northern section, near the Grand Canal. The railroad's arrival created a competing commercial center, with substantial political ramifications. Previously Jiaxing sent tax grain to Shanghai via canals and streams; during shipment, the grain had been hostage to various extortionate practices that invariably left the amount on arrival considerably short. In the winter of 1909–10, the tax grain was sent by rail instead, arriving *in toto* at a much earlier date. Within a few months after its inaugural run, the railroad thus overcame a situation long inimical to government fiscal processes. Because of this success, certain merchants built warehouses near the station for the future handling of tax grain, which added to the growing prestige of the new commercial center.[47]

Over the next decade, the two centers became increasingly competitive. Although self-government and other elites planned and established rickshaw and telephone companies to link the centers physically, this economic competition substantially restructured county and county-seat politics. As merchants played greater roles in inner-core politics, economic rivalry contributed to the formation of a southern faction based on the new prosperity brought by the railroad and a northern faction linked to the erstwhile commercial superiority of the water routes.

Economic development, however, is only one stimulus of political development. Indirect political stimulation from events such as the provincial takeover by outside military forces in 1917 and the May Fourth (1919) and May Thirtieth (1925) episodes is another. News of these events energized elite opinion in certain zones, inspiring elite identification with province and nation, stimulating the establishment of associations, and involving the elite in political goals. Such stimulation obviously depended largely on the development of transportation and communication facilities. Direct political intervention can be seen in state attempts to apply to all administrative units regulations to reorganize political institutional space. Government-sponsored self-government bodies and professional associations in the last years of the Qing dynasty facilitated such elite political development.

3

Common Organizations in the Four Zhejiangs

Elite participation in various social and political organizations facilitated the development of personal linkages within the locality and with those at different levels of the economic and state administrative hierarchies. It also stimulated identification with differentiated and specialized institutions.Traditional associations—native place associations and guilds—and institutions sponsored by the government in the early twentieth century, common to all the province, were at once both the context for elite activity and the actors themselves.

Traditional Elite Organizations

Native Place Associations

One of the more remarkable features of Chinese culture was the strong sense of one's geographic origin and of mutual ties to natives of the area.[1] The Chinese writer Cao Juren has contended that such ties were the mortar (*gaoyao*) of politics, providing some of the strongest social linkages, which were often utilized in time of trouble as a ready network of support.[2] Institutionalizing the strong sense of spatial origins, native place associations facilitated and reinforced connections among administrative and commercial elites.[3] Urban institutions, they were located primarily in the core zones, but merchant associations (*huiguan*) were also sometimes found in urban centers in the peripheries.[4]

The zonal distribution of native place associations in Hangchow in 1932 reveals several important aspects of zonal relationships and social change (Table 3). The outer periphery had only one native place association in the regional metropolis by the early 1930s, reflecting this zone's almost complete lack of involvement with higher urban centers. Inner-periphery counties had some associations, but the largest numbers came

Table 3.
Zonal distribution of Zhejiang native place associations in Hangchow, 1932

Inner core		Outer core		Inner periphery		Outer periphery	
Ningbo	lHt[a]	Xinchang	t	Shouchang	lHt	Songyang	h
Wenzhou	t[b]	Fuyang	lHt	Yongkang	t		
Shaoshu	tong jiji	Fenghua	t	Ninghai	t		
(4 branches)		Zhuji	t	Tiantai	t		
Shangyu	lHt	Jinhua	h	Dongyang	t		
Siming	Yiyanglu	Fuyang	h	Ninghai	h		
Taizhou	lHt	Xiangshan	h				
Taizhou	h[c]	Wenling	t				
Haining	t	Changshan	t				
Ciqi	h						
Siming	h						
Linhai	lHt						

Source: Jianshe weiyuanhui diaocha Zhejiang jingji suo, comp. *Hangzhou shi jingji diaocha*, vol. 2, pp. 986–987.
   a. *Lü Hang[zhou] tongxianghui* (association of same place residents at Hangchow).
   b. *Tongxianghui* (same place association).
   c. *Huiguan* (*Landsmannschaften*).

from the core zones.[5] Most counties of the inner core were, in fact, oriented in economic matters primarily to Shanghai and only secondarily to Hangchow. The absence of associations in Hangchow from Jiaxing and Huzhou prefectures and their component counties reflects their greater commercial orientation to Shanghai, the macroregional capital.

A significant feature of the native place tie was its "hierarchically cumulative nature."[6] A Chinese was born into an administrative state hierarchy (township, county, prefecture, province) and an economic central place hierarchy (standard, intermediate, central marketing communities, and so forth). Lower levels of the hierarchies could be subsumed under higher levels. Sojourners could thus be associated with both county and prefectural associations. Prefectural associations enabled the county sojourner to participate in organizations with concerns beyond the county unit, thus facilitating elite orientation to higher-level structures and their concerns. In addition, the support of component county associations by prefectural associations promoted linkages among elites at these levels, contributing to a sense of elite integration that promised joint action on common problems. For example, in 1910 the Taizhou association supported the Huangyan county association in a bitter controversy over salt production; and in 1912 the Shaoxing association took the part of the Shangyu county association in lobbying for control of local social disorder.[7] These developments were less possible in the inner periphery: in

Hangchow only two county associations, from Ninghai and Tiantai, had prefectural associations to which they were hierarchically subordinate.

An era of increasingly rapid economic change, the early twentieth century witnessed the formation of many new associations. The Huzhou association in Shanghai, for example, grew rapidly.[8] New associations from Ningbo and Shaoxing were founded in important nonadministrative market towns like Haimen and Puyuan, as well as in major administrative centers.[9] In the last years of the Qing dynasty and the first years of the Republic, outer-core and inner-periphery counties established their initial associations at Hangchow or at their prefectural capitals.[10]

The new associations were not designated by the traditional *huiguan (Landsmannschaften)* nomenclature but were called *tongxianghui* ("same place association") or *lü Hang tongxianghui* ("association of same place residents at Hangchow").[11] Table 3 shows that Taizhou and Ningbo prefectures (the latter known also by the historical designation Siming) and Fuyang and Ninghai counties each had more than one association, but that only one was called *huiguan*. It is probable, as Susan Mann Jones suggests in her study of the Ningbo clique *(bang)* in Shanghai, that elites from these prefectures and counties formed the associations with new designations to circumvent domination by more entrenched elites in the traditional associations *(huiguan)*.[12] In the Shanghai case, the new associations, open to "traders, artisans, workers, and students," were quickly co-opted by the old elite leadership. It is difficult to say whether the same thing occurred in Hangchow, but indirect evidence suggests that the *huiguan* leaders may have indeed come to play inportant roles in the new organizations.[13]

It is certain from their functions that most native place associations, like those studied by the Gallins in Taibei in the 1960s, served primarily elite interests.[14] While they facilitated the handling of sojourning elites' concerns, they also offered considerable financial support for such native place needs as building schools and public works and undertaking reconstruction following natural disasters.[15] They formed networks through which local needs could be supplied by tapping distant sources. In 1922, for example, after devastating floods, Zhuji's county associations in Hangchow, Ningpo, Shaoxing, Shanghai, and Tianjin funneled funds back to the county.[16] Interceding with the provincial government for the benefit of local communities was also an important association role. Whether the intercession came for disaster relief, mediation of local controversies, or management of local crises, the associations were active brokers.[17] Associations also lobbied local official and nonofficial elites for specific community action. The Fenghua association in Ningpo sent telegrams and letters to county officials on the importance of installing a school board for the proper functioning of education.[18] In another example, the Shaoxing workers' association in Shanghai protested the Shaoxing assembly's ending of subsidies to a women's normal school.[19]

Apparently only one native place association assumed a direct political provincial role: the Jin-Qu-Yan-Chu Association, named for the first characters of its respective prefectures. Many associations, however, provided forums for the discussion of national and provincial issues, especially before the 1911 revolution, during various military crises, and during the 1920s debates over provincial constitutions.[20] These political discussions, together with the political brokerage roles, contributed to the politicization of sojourning elites; associations became vehicles for elite political involvement. When they returned to their communities, these elites probably became conduits by which national and provincial political ideas and concerns reached the county level.[21] Thus, associations based upon local attachments were by no means antithetical to the development of loyalties to and concerns about higher levels of the polity.[22] Their territorial hierarchical character also suggests that they served as integrating mechanisms for sociopolitical elites. In these ways, native place associations were positive vehicles in the political development of early-twentieth-century China.

Guilds

Occupational organizations (*huiguan, gongsuo,* and after new government regulations in 1903-04, *gonghui*) were concerned primarily with insuring the occupational welfare of the member businessmen. Few guilds became directly involved in political affairs; on the whole, the establishment and functioning of guilds is a better indicator of economic development than of political change. However, guild heads often became leaders of the government-established chambers of commerce that dotted the urban landscape by the early 1920s and that were clearly strong political forces. Occasionally guilds also assumed parapolitical local roles.

Peter Golas has suggested that beginning in the eighteenth century, guilds became less tied to the concept of native place and that various nonelite economic groups formed organizations to put forth their own interests.[23] At least until a rash of unionization in the 1920s, however, native place ties often remained a strong determinant in guild formation. Jiaxing bean curd makers, for example, formed two separate guilds in the late 1910s: one for those hailing from Jiaxing, the other for those from Shaoxing.[24] Zhuji natives. bemoaned the fact that most businesses in Zhuji were managed and apprenticed by Shaoxing men.[25] Like native place associations, some guilds also evidenced a nested territorial hierarchy, encompassing subordinate administrative and probably marketing units.[26] The Jiang-Zhe-An (Jiangsu, Zhejiang, Anhui) Silk Association was formed to lobby for silk industry reform and economic goals.[27] "All-

Zhejiang" associations were founded for the pawnshop, silk, and tea industries.[28] Prefectural silk and cocoon hong associations, including members from their component counties, met often in Jiaxing and Huzhou.[29] In Fenghua, merchants from all eight townships contributed to the building of a township merchant guild (*baxiang huiguan*) to facilitate trade.[30] In troubled economic times partly brought on by political turmoil, such territorial linkages provided a framework for joint meetings and correspondence that most likely contributed to a sense of occupational unity. Such contact probably heightened the political awareness of businessmen, some of whom became active in chambers of commerce.

Some guilds went beyond direct commercial roles, becoming involved, for example, in educational projects by the 1920s. In 1923 the Hangchow Silk Guild established a newspaper reading room, an athletic field, an English course, and a commercial night school with the declared purpose of promoting industrial education.[31] The Jiaxing cigarette industry guild also established a night school in 1923.[32] Occasionally guild roles, though prompted by economic concerns, had political overtones. In Xiaofeng and Anji counties, for example, the Bamboo Merchants Guild, established in the late Ming dynasty, became primarily concerned with police functions, protecting bamboo shoots and timbers from being stolen during peak harvesting seasons.[33] On Daishan Island in Dinghai county, fishing guilds assumed governmental responsibilities in ending the frequent "wars" among fishing fleets hailing from different areas.[34]

In short, guilds took on parapolitical roles, promoted social and economic change, provided individual leaders for other local organizations, and fostered extension of occupational concerns and values beyond single urban centers to larger spatial units. Recognizing the political potential of strong guilds, the government continued the traditional state policies toward commercial organizations by restricting and directing their formation and functions. For example, it refused salt merchants permission to establish their own guild; and, after 1930, it gave Guomindang county bureaus licensing power over newly formed guilds.[35]

Government-Sponsored Institutions

Local Self-Government Bodies, 1910-1927: An Institutional Survey

The sharp contrast between the Qing concept of self-government as an institution for elite control and various political theorists' ideas of self-government for elite mobilization remained a continual source of tension throughout this period.[36]

Qing Self-Government, 1909-1911. As called for in the Qing constitutional reforms, the establishment of local self-government began in 1909 on the county level with the organization of two offices. The self-government affairs office (*zizhi shiwu suo*) directed the process of establishing county and subcounty organs, particularly the census, districting, and elections. The self-government study office (*zizhi yanjiu suo*) trained census takers and dispatched lecturers to popularize the self-government effort.[37] The directors of both offices were trained at the provincial capital by self-government organization offices (*zizhi chouban chu*) and were appointed by the provincial governor. The directorships were limited to those holding the franchise—males over twenty-five with at least one of the following qualifications: a *gongsheng* degree at minimum, a middle-school education, three years of teaching experience, service as a specified class of official, or ownership of business or land worth more than 5,000 *yuan*.[38] Self-government involvement was obviously limited to the social and economic elites.

For those men who qualified as voters on the basis of commercial or landed wealth but who were illiterate, short reading courses were established by the education promotion office (*quanxuesuo*), charged under the Qing reforms with initiating and supervising plans for local school development.[39] The establishment of these short courses underlines the close linkage between the development of education and self-government. In Haining zhou, the director of the self-government affairs office was concurrently the director of the education promotion office. Over 55 percent (twenty-six of forty-seven) of the self-government leaders in Haining towns and townships were connected with education, serving as school founders, principals, or teachers.[40] When higher taxes to pay for self-government reforms led to outbreaks of violence in 1911, both self-government offices and schools were targets. As early as 1910, vitriolic verbal attacks were directed against the Jiashan county self-government and education promotion offices for attempting to arrogate undue power.[41]

County seat, town, and township councils were elected by the third lunar month of 1911 for two-year terms. County seat and town councils had twenty to fifty men; township councils, six to eight. These councils in turn chose the executive boards of the county seat and town (generally six members) and the township manager and his assistant. Municipality, market town, and township councils and boards were meeting in the core zones and in most counties of the peripheries by the late summer of 1911.[42]

Early Republican Self-Government, 1912-1914. A crucial institutional development for counties in all zones was the establishment of county assemblies (*xianyihui*) and executive boards (*canyihui*) by late 1912 and early 1913. Composed of twenty men who elected their own chairman and vice-chairman, the assembly chose a four-man board (chaired by the magistrate) to administer its decisions.[43] In all zones, the executive boards from 1912 to 1914 seem to have played only a minor role. Three of the eighteen gazetteers that included information on assemblies fail even to mention the boards, an indication of a less significant role. Newspaper accounts indicate that executive boards were only rarely involved in decision making; in some inner-core counties, the magistrates also seemed subordinated to the assertive assemblies.[44] Both assembly and board coexisted with those subcounty bodies that had been established before 1911, and inadequate delineation of function between county and subcounty bodies led to frequent disputes over authority.[45] On the whole, assemblies played key roles in the local political structure. Some became so assertive, especially after their power was threatened following the suppression of the second revolution in 1913, that the Hangchow government responded with curt reprimands or orders of abolition.[46]

The Co-optation of Self-Rule (zizhi) by Official Rule (guanzhi), 1914-1922. When Yuan Shikai abolished all self-government bodies in a move to tighten state control in February 1914, he promised new "self-government" regulations. Promulgated in late 1914, these regulations stipulated that each county magistrate appoint an upright gentry-manager (*zheng shendong*) to serve as county self-government deputy (*zizhi weiyuan*), who would oversee with his assistant the management of county funds and all public matters. County deputies held their positions for approximately one to three years and were, in many cases, former county assembly leaders.[47] In addition, a new "self-governing ward" (*zizhiqu*) to replace the haphazard township system was established, and its magistrate-appointed deputy was often the same man who had served as Qing township manager (*xiangdong*).[48] In reality the county magistrate firmly controlled the new self-government apparatus. The elite, frustrated by increasing magisterial authority, continued to try to assert themselves.[49] An overwhelming outpouring of accusations against newly empowered magistrates underscored their discontent.[50]

Following the demise of Yuan and provincial governors Zhu Rui and Qu Yingguang in the spring of 1916, elites demanded the restoration of assemblies. Despite orders to the contrary, five former county assemblies convened.[51] Specific orders from Beijing to the military governor to dissolve these assemblies ended their two-month rebirth.[52]

Self-Government in the 1920s. After northern forces seized the province in early 1917, local elites continued to demand a permanent reinstitution of representative bodies.[53] Although the Beijing government in September 1919 authorized the establishment of county assemblies, it was dilatory in setting down new election regulations.[54] Not until late 1920 could Hangchow begin to effectuate the new plan; new assemblies were not elected until late 1921, with sessions beginning in 1922.[55] The assemblies were to meet for a term of three years, with new elections to be held in late 1924. Because of the dislocations wrought by the 1924 war, however, assemblies elected in 1921 continued to meet into 1926. Apparently only two counties (in the outer core and inner periphery) functioned for long periods without these elite bodies.[56]

In addition to the ten-man assembly (a 50 percent reduction in size from the first assembly), an executive board (*canshihui*) was established. Headed by the magistrate, it had six other members: two chosen by the assembly and four appointed by the magistrate. Of the latter four, one served as an assistant (*zuoli*), apparently functioning as secretary, and one served as treasurer (*nayuan*).[57] This system differed notably from that which operated between 1912 and 1914 by considerably weakening non-official elite power—primarily through giving the executive board, controlled directly by the magistrate, preeminent power. The board had been relatively unimportant from 1912 to 1914; but in the 1920s, at least in part as a function of increased magisterial power, it became the major county administrative body. County finances were completely controlled by the board. Although the assembly made decisions on taxes and budget allocations, the board decided when and if to execute many of its decisions.[58]

Relations between assembly and board were strained in many counties. Frequently boards refused to accept assembly budgetary decisions; some disagreements flared over institutional arrangements.[59] In Jiaxing, frustration over the board's failure to execute its decisions led the assembly to abolish itself.[60] The 1920s model of local self-government was more internally antagonistic than its post-1911 predecessor. From 1912 to 1914, assembly-board antagonism was not apparent. But in the 1920s, conflicts of magisterial-board executive power and assembly legislative authority reverberated across the province. In an institutional sense, official rule (*guanzhi*) had co-opted elite proponents of self-rule (*zizhi*). This institutional development can be seen as a harbinger of the bureaucratization of the local scene attempted by the Nanjing government in the 1930s.[61]

Professional Associations (*Fatuan*)

Fatuan ("associations established by law") were nontraditional elite institutions with quasi-administrative functions. Established by the Qing and early Republican governments to regulate burgeoning professions (business, banking, and law) and to further modern education and agriculture, these bodies owed their inspiration to similar foreign organizations. The regulations establishing chambers of commerce in 1903, for example, reflect this foreign connection: chambers were to perform various managerial and mediational functions in the local economy "in addition to the duties discharged by the chambers of commerce *in foreign countries.*"[62] Government promulgation of the other *fatuan* followed:

education associations (1906); agriculture associations (1907); lawyers' associations (1912); and bankers' associations (1915).[63] In all matters they were subordinate to the government, which regulated their establishment, their structure, and the formation of any auxiliary organizations; government approval was even required for the convening of larger than customary professional association meetings.[64] Like self-government bodies, these associations were perceived by the government in part as control mechanisms over local elites.

Of the *fatuan,* only chambers of commerce and education and agriculture associations were established throughout the province. More than was the case with self-government bodies, their actual dates of establishment in each county were dependent on local conditions. Chambers of commerce in particular (and to some extent the other associations) exhibit variability across development zones in date of establishment and in functional importance.

Chambers of Commerce. Although their formation received much impetus from Western models, chambers, which were established in most inner-core counties by 1906, developed from the guild structure. According to codified regulations in 1914 during Yuan Shikai's centralization efforts, four fifths of the boards of directors of both general chambers (in larger cities) and regular chambers had to be guild members.[65] Although government regulations did not make chamber membership mandatory for local firms, the perceived occupational advantages stemming from larger federated organizations composed of various wholesale and retail businessmen insured chamber growth. Guild leaders from interests like silk, rice, pawnshops, and native banks often assumed chamber leadership. Their place in the hierarchy of local elites depended in large part on the locality's degree of development.

Gazetteers make it evident that counties in the peripheries did not have sufficient commercial activity to warrant the early establishment of chambers of commerce. In the outer core chambers were formed, on the average, more than a year after the modal date for the inner core; in the inner periphery, they were established almost three years later; and in the outer periphery, almost twelve years later.[66] To study zonal differentiation through variables other than date of formation, I have analyzed chambers through the reports of Japanese investigators.[67] Because of inconsistent reporting techniques, the number of members cannot be accurately gauged.[68] However, the number of board members, the number of meetings per month (probably of the board alone), and the expenditures and income for 1915–16 can be charted for each zone (Table 4).

With the exception of the median number of board members in the outer core, there is a decline in all four variables as one moves from inner core to outer periphery. One striking aspect of these figures is the very

Table 4.
Zonal comparisons of Zhejiang regular chambers of commerce, 1915–16

Zone	No. of board members		Times met per month		Income[a]		Expenditures[a]	
	Mean	Median	Mean	Median	Mean	Median	Mean	Median
Inner core	25.52	24	4.25	4.5	1,768.1	1,400	1,859.8	1,440
Outer core	24.92	27	3.6	3.0	677.2	750	735.2	795
Inner periphery	21.0	20	2.4	3.0	576.0	467	643.0	517
Outer periphery	15.0	17	2.0	2.0	371.0	233	392.7	295

Source: *Shina shōbetsu zenshi: Sekkō-shō*, pp. 739–792.

a. in *yuan*.

low budget of chambers even in the core zones. Income came generally from membership dues and in some counties from occasional excise taxes; the chambers were not fiscally subordinate to the county assembly. Except for the three general chambers in Hangchow, Ningpo, and Wenchow, which spent 7,612 *yuan,* 6,047 *yuan,* and 2,784 *yuan,* respectively, the low revenue and expenditures suggest that in the mid-1910s, chambers' functions may have been limited largely to brokerage roles and were probably dependent upon contributions for local development projects.

Inner-core chambers were in the forefront of nationalistic activity, from the railway controversy of the late Qing period to the post-May-Fourth era of boycotts and constitution making.[69] The Hangchow and Ningpo General Chambers of Commerce were leaders of the 1919 general strike and supported frequent measures to uplift the production of Chinese goods to compete with foreign products.[70] Although chambers in the outer zones did not exhibit such nationalistic spirit, other occupation-related functions and roles, such as protesting commercial taxes and forming defensive militia, were similar across zones.[71]

Education Associations. The key local educational institution, the education promotion office, was charged with initiating and supervising plans for school development. The initial aim of education associations (*jiaoyu hui*) was auxiliary: to foster the idea of education and, specifically, to popularize the modern school system.[72] The Jiaxing association, organized in mid-1911, for example, set up an education research office to deal with educational standards and a physical culture association to stir martial spirit. It also sponsored a township school federation to set standards for the multitude of private schools being established.[73] The founding dates for education associations differed less across zones than those for chambers of commerce primarily because the associations were not so dependent upon economic development. Even so, as with the establishment of agriculture associations, a general spatiotemporal pattern of formation is evident. Established in the core zones before the 1911 revolution, the education associations were generally not formed in the peripheral zones until several years into the Republic.

Educational expansion presented many problems, not the least of which was the necessity of setting some guidelines and standards for educational quality. It was reported that in the late Qing period as many as three hundred schools had been established in a single township of Zhuji.[74] A school in Huzhou reportedly had twenty students and eight teachers.[75] A rough survey of school construction according to gazetteer records in the decade from 1911 to 1920 shows that between 40 and 50 percent of all construction occurred between 1912 and 1914, with more than that average in the core zones and less in the counties of the peripheries.[76] To help standardize the burgeoning modern school system on a provincial basis, a Federation of County Education Associations (*jiaoyuhui lianhehui*) was founded in mid-1914.[77] It was the first such permanent federation to be formed in Zhejiang during the Republic, uniting in a permanent body county educational elite representatives from throughout the province. This federation and a provincial education association met frequently until 1927. Among the *fatuan,* education associations were the most politically progressive, becoming attuned rapidly to national issues and moving in the forefront of political and social change. From before the 1911 revolution into the mid-1920s, education associations at every level of the polity and in every zone took positions on national goals and crises, taxes and economic concerns, and the meaning and mechanisms of self-government.[78]

County associations were composed primarily of county school principals and teachers. The education promotion office played a major role in association activities until its abolition in the educational reforms of 1923. Its successor, the education bureau (*jiaoyu ju*), became the center for reform efforts in many counties. The bureau and the association often enunciated student demands vis-à-vis officials and more conservative educational elites in matters of curricula, coeducation, and the powers of principals.[79]

Agriculture Associations. The existence, roles, and accomplishments of agriculture associations are the most irregular of all *fatuan,* varying according to county and to time. In Jiaxing, for example, before the 1911 revolution, the agriculture association was one of the most active organizations. Meetings in 1910 reportedly attracted about one hundred leaders who discussed agricultural problems ranging from conservancy to insect pests. In February 1910 managers were elected for each township to look into problems of rice hoarding by merchants and to control the price of rice. (In other inner-core areas, these functions were usually undertaken by chambers of commerce.) In early 1911 the association organized an auxiliary body to deal with insect pest control, a problem that only worsened throughout the early Republic.[80] By mid-decade, however, the association had few funds, receiving support only from public monies meted out parsimoniously by the county assembly and self-government deputies. By 1918 it was bankrupt.[81] The agenda of its spring meeting in 1920 indicates that its concerns had shrunk to its own internal administration.[82] When the county had to grapple with a disastrous worm borer plague in the mid-1920s, an emergency organization was established; and the agriculture association played no important role.[83]

Although the paucity of sources prevents the documentation of such a precipitate decline of agriculture associations in other counties, it is certain that the financial problems that plagued the Jiaxing association beset others as well. In the outer zones, financial considerations were partly responsible for the late establishment of the associations (not until the mid-to-late 1910s) and their short lives (often only two or three years).[84] The degree of an association's involvement in local affairs rested on particular county circumstances and elites, not generally on its position in a certain development zone. The Dinghai association (inner core), for example, was an active force in the island county's reforestation, a task undertaken by self-government deputies in Xindeng (inner periphery).[85] Zhuji (outer core) had an active association of 160 members in 1915 and an experimental farm of over ninety mu; in contrast, Fenghua (outer core) had an association that was only nominally agricultural, spending its funds on a newspaper reading room and a building for social affairs.[86]

Differences in functions and import notwithstanding, in all zones the agriculture association was clearly an organization for elites. The Luoqing association became primarily a landlords' rent collection agency.[87] In most cases, the associations' functions were more related to general issues of local development (for example, reading rooms and road building) than to any specific agricultural interests.[88] It is not surprising that ad hoc organizations were established to deal with specific problems like insects and conservancy, and it is noteworthy that even in the inner core the institutionalization of the agriculture association lagged far behind that of other new elite organs. The landed elites continued to exercise private control of matters relating to this basic economic resource.

PART TWO

The Sociopolitical Ecology
of the Four Zhejiangs

Introduction

The hypotheses on elite trends set forth in Chapters 4–9 were derived in part from a systematic analysis of the leadership of township and county self-government organs. Self-government leadership provides an important general index of socially prominent and politically powerful local elites: men of primary local significance usually headed these bodies themselves or were related to the leaders. These institutions existed in all counties with approximately the same number of elites involved in each; they provide three different data sets (late Qing and early Republican subcounty bodies, and county assemblies from 1912 to 1914 and from 1922 to 1927) that allow observation, within the constraints of the sources, of institutional elite trends over time. References in this section are often made to the statistics in Tables 5 to 8, which detail the social and functional backgrounds of these elites in each zone and elite (individual and kin) continuity between self-government sessions.

Because various gazetteer lacunae and inadequacies make self-government statistics highly tentative, they are useful primarily in providing hypotheses on the social dynamics of early-twentieth-century politics. Study of non-self-government elites in gazetteers and other sources (including newspapers, governmental reports and communications, and memoirs) leads me to believe that these hypotheses can be largely substantiated and that self-government elite analysis provides a reasonably accurate means of getting at functional elites in general. In any case, this analysis is imbued with a healthy measure of tentativeness. Appendix C contains more detailed description of methodological and source-related considerations concerning self-government data.

Table 5.
Composition of inner-core self-government bodies

Characteristics of elites	Subcounty leaders, 1911–1914	First session county bodies, 1912–1914	Second session county bodies, 1922–1927
Degree-holders	23.4% (49)	13.9% (16)	7.7% (4)
School graduates	1.4% (3)	5.2% (6)	7.7% (4)
Both degree and graduate	0	1.7% (2)	1.9% (1)
Elite family connections as only status indication	25.4% (53)	20.9% (24)	7.7% (4)
Functional elites without degrees, diploma, or family ties	14.8% (31)	11.3% (13)	30.7% (16)
Nongentry or graduates, no elite family ties or functional roles other than self-government	32.1% (67)	42.6% (49)	34.6% (18)
Experience beyond locality	7.2% (15)[a]	8.7% (10)[a]	15.4% (8)[a]
Continuity from:			
Late Qing subcounty bodies	—	21.8% (19)[b]	5.6% (2)[c]
First session county bodies	—	—	38.5% (20)
Total	209	115	52

Sources: For subcounty leaders: *Deqing xianzhi,* passim; *Yuyao liucang zhi,* passim; *Zhenhai, xianzhi,* passim; *Zhenhai xinzhi beigao,* passim; *Haining zhou zhigao,* passim; *Ganzhi fulu,* passim; *Puyuan zhi,* passim; *Shuanglin zhenzhi,* passim; *Wu-Qing zhenzhi,* passim; and Chen Xunzheng, comp., *Yinxian tongzhi renwu bian,* passim. For first session bodies: *Deqing xianzhi,* passim; *Dinghai xianzhi,* passim; *Yuyao liucang zhi,* passim; *Zhenhai xianzhi,* passim; and *Zhenhai xinzhi beigao,* passim. For second session bodies: *Deqing xianzhi,* passim; *Dinghai xianzhi,* passim; *Zhenhai xianzhi,* passim; and *Zhenhai xinzhi beigao,* passim.

a. Percentages do not total 100% because of overlap in this category with degree-holders and school graduates.

b. Percentage based on 87 men (Dinghai county gazetteer contains no subcounty membership).

c. Percentage based on 36 men for reason listed in note b.

Table 6.
Composition of outer-core self-government bodies

Characteristics of elites	Subcounty leaders, 1911–1914	First session county bodies, 1912–1914	Second session county bodies, 1922–1927
Degree-holders	—	20.0% (14)	12.5% (7)
School graduates	—	7.1% (5)	12.5% (7)
Both degree and graduate	—	1.4% (1)	16.1% (9)
Elite family connections as only status indication	—	20.0% (14)	14.3% (8)
Functional elites without degrees, diploma, or family ties	—	11.4% (8)	17.9% (10)
Nongentry or graduates, no elite family ties or functional roles other than self-government	—	38.6% (27)	23.2% (13)
Experience beyond locality	—	5.7% (4)[a]	28.6% (16)[a]
Continuity from:			
Late Qing subcounty bodies	—	—	—
First session county bodies	—	—	10.7% (6)
Total	—	70	56

Sources: For first session bodies: *Qu xianzhi,* passim; *Xiangshan xianzhi,* passim; and *Xinchang xianzhi.* For second session bodies: *Xin Fenghua,* "diaocha," pp. 55–56; *Qu xianzhi,* passim; and *Xiangshan xianzhi,* passim.

a. Percentages do not total 100% because of overlap in this category.

Table 7.
Composition of inner-periphery self-government bodies

Characteristics of elites	Subcounty leaders, 1911–1914	First session county bodies, 1912–1914	Second session county bodies, 1922–1927
Degree-holders	23.1% (31)	20.2% (19)	12.3% (7)
School graduates	2.2% (3)	2.1% (2)	35.1% (20)
Both degree and graduate	0	0	0
Elite family connections as only status indication	11.2% (15)	10.6% (10)	17.5% (10)
Functional elites without degrees, diploma, or family ties	28.3% (38)	47.9% (45)	31.6% (18)
Nongentry or graduates, no elite family ties or functional roles other than self-government	31.3% (42)	19.1% (18)	5.3% (3)
Experience beyond locality	3.7% (5)[a]	6.4% (6)[a]	10.5% (6)[a]
Continuity from:			
Late Qing subcounty bodies	—	48.0% (36)[b]	20.5% (8)[c]
First session county bodies	—	—	5.3% (3)
Total	134	94	57

Sources: For subcounty leaders: *Lishui xianzhi,* passim; *Shouchang xianzhi,* passim; and *Xindeng xianzhi,* passim. For first session bodies: *Lishui xianzhi,* passim; *Shouchang xianzhi,* passim; *Tangqi xianzhi,* passim; and *Xindeng xianzhi,* passim. For second session bodies: *Lishui xianzhi,* passim; *Shouchang xianzhi,* passim; and *Tangqi xianzhi,* passim.

a. Percentages do not total 100% because of overlap in this category.

b. Percentage based on 75 men (Tangqi county gazetteer contains no subcounty membership).

c. Percentage based on 39 men for reason listed in note b.

Table 8.
Composition of outer-periphery self-government bodies

Characteristics of elites	Subcounty leaders, 1911–1914	First session county bodies, 1912–1914	Second session county bodies, 1922–1927
Degree-holders	36.3% (70)	30.9% (38)	19.8% (19)
School graduates	1.0% (2)	3.3% (4)	22.9% (22)
Both degree and graduate	0	4.1% (5)	8.3% (8)
Elite family connections as only status indication	17.1% (33)	19.5% (24)	19.8% (19)
Functional elites without degrees, diploma, or family ties	16.6% (32)	15.4% (19)	24.0% (23)
Nongentry or graduates, no elite family ties or functional roles other than self-government	25.9% (50)	22.8% (28)	5.2% (5)
Experience beyond locality	0	9.8% (12)[a]	29.2% (28)[a]
Continuity from:			
Late Qing subcounty bodies	—	17.2% (17)[b]	25.0% (20)[c]
First session county bodies	—	—	13.5% (13)
Total	193	123	96

Sources: For subcounty leaders: *Changhua xianzhi*, passim; *Songyang xianzhi*, passim; *Suian xianzhi*, passim; and *Xuanping xianzhi*, passim. For first and second session bodies: *Changhua xianzhi*, passim; *Jingning xianxuzhi*, passim; *Songyang xianzhi*, passim; *Suian xianzhi*, passim; and *Xuanping xianzhi*, passim.

a. Percentages do not total 100% because of overlap in this category.

b. Percentage based on 99 men (Jingning county gazetteer contains no subcounty membership).

c. Percentage based on 80 men for reason listed in note b.

4

Inner-Core Elite Career Bases and Patterns

Although no man's career can illustrate all the features of inner-core elite structures and politics, the career of Chen Zaiyan (1876–1927) of Shaoxing is highly suggestive of major patterns. A businessman involved in the tea and silk trade, Chen generously supported his lineage; he helped his younger brother attain a modern school education; and he supplied substantial amounts of money for community school and relief projects in the early years of the century. After the 1911 revolution, Chen moved into a more specifically political arena when he was elected to the county assembly and board.

In 1918 Chen was elected to the provincial assembly, but his eyes were never far from his local constituency. He was a voice for local merchants in the assembly, arguing for reduced commercial exactions, specifically in the hated *tongjuan* or commercial transit tax (the postrevolutionary *lijin*) and in levies for river patrol boats. After his tenure as provincial assemblyman, he returned to Shaoxing to serve as head of the chamber of commerce and played a major role in relief work following the devastating floods of 1922. Continuing to lead the county in initiating and funding public works, he mustered local elites (*shishen*) for action when a breach in the Shaoxing-Xiaoshan seawall precipitated a flood in 1926. He died in Shanghai, where he had gone for medical treatment, one week after Chiang Kai-shek's purge of the Communists in April 1927.[1]

Chen's life covered little more than half a century; but in terms of political and social developments for inner-core elites, this was a momentous period. This chapter and the next two probe aspects of inner-core elite career and political structures and offer a view of political and social change in the first three decades of the twentieth century. The following patterns, reflected in Chen's career, are important aspects to consider: the role of lineages in elite careers and local affairs; career patterns of eminent local elites, especially the attraction of higher urban centers for public and private careers; the participation of local elites in new organizations; and the blurring of traditional distinctions between gentry and merchant classes.

The Lineage as an Elite Base

Sources do not permit determination of the economic foundations of elite power in each zone. Commercial wealth was relatively more important in core zones than in peripheral. But elites in the core zones, which contained the richest agricultural land, also derived their status from landed wealth. Some clues to the basis of power can be gained by looking at the important Chinese institution, the lineage (*zu*), which, following Maurice Freedman, I define as a "permanent organized group" tracing "patrilineal descent from one ancestor."[2]

Sources and Comparison of Lineage Strength

Lineages in the inner core produced more functional elites and were wealthier and more famous than those in any other zone, a phenomenon that underscores the postulated correlation between lineage strength and rich agricultural and commercial areas.[3] Especially well-known are those of Jiaxing (immortalized by Pan Guangdan) and Shaoxing, which produced an abundance of genealogies apotheosizing the prefecture's lineages.[4] Lineage cohesion and power depended primarily upon collectively held land (the ancestral estate) and secondarily upon funds produced by commercial activity. Both sources of wealth made possible lineage security, providing an economic undergirding that traditionally allowed lineage members the wherewithal to study and take the civil service examination and an economic hedge against hard times. My study of gazetteers from all zones indicates that ancestral estates were most significant parts of the zonal landscape in the inner core and, to a lesser extent, the outer core. In the peripheral zones, despite their extensive genealogical coverage, gazetteer editors apparently did not deem the estates significant enough to include; there is evidence of small lineage estates, however, in at least one inner-periphery county.[5]

Available information from the core zones indicates estates ranging in size from twenty to almost two thousand mu. The inner core generally was marked by a higher proportion of large estates than the outer core, a pattern suggested by Table 9. Some lineages also had substantial reserve cash funds from land and probably commercial interests.[6]

Economic power was often translated into political clout. Very wealthy lineages (which I will call great lineages) in the inner core and, to lesser extent, the outer core dominated the county political scene, providing the bulk of political elites and overshadowing less imposing lineages in cer-

Table 9.
Size of lineage estates in sample counties of the core zones

Yuyao (inner core)		Xiangshan (outer core)	
Lineage	Mu	Lineage	Mu
Xie	1,400+	Ou	1,800+
Xie	1,695	Shen	50+
Wang	589	Jiang	—
Zhou	800+	Zheng	80+
Ma	600+	Chen	600+
Feng	324	Hu	20
Xie	735+		

Sources: *Xiangshan xianzhi*, 16:34a–b; *Yuyao liucang zhi*, 16:1a–5a.

tain marketing areas and villages. Great lineages in this period generally had one or more of these characteristics: ownership of more than one hundred mu of land; conspicuous evidence of wealth; production of many sociopolitical elites; and a sphere of activity ranging from ancestral native place to the county and beyond. Elites from great lineages had a wide range of interests and qualifications.

The profile of great lineages is evident from a perusal of Zhenhai and Deqing gazetteers. In Zhenhai there were at least ten important lineages that were highly degreed, had early graduates of modern schools, and counted among their members officials and important merchant-entrepreneurs. These lineages were involved to some degree in virtually all significant county undertakings. Eight of the ten had at least one and usually more members in the late Qing and early Republican self-government bodies. When one considers that these lineages also had their "representatives" in newly established professional associations, it is apparent that there was considerable functional integration among these elites. As many as six or seven men from one lineage were sometimes active in county affairs.[7] In Deqing county a similar picture emerges, with five or six great lineages providing the bulk of county-level leadership. In the late Qing dynasty they built schools, served in agriculture and education associations, headed the militia, and promoted sericulture and assorted public works. In Deqing, self-government membership was clearly subordinate to other endeavors: most of the great lineage oligarchy disdained direct participation.[8] Lineage domination in an area was often further solidified and enhanced through intermarriage of the most important lineages: several examples are the powerful Cao and Li lineages and Sheng and Xie lineages of Zhenhai, and the Chu and Shen lineages of Jiaxing.[9] Marriage strategies promoted local lineage strength and continuity into the Republican period.

Other, less powerful lineages played not insignificant roles in inner-core county affairs. They owned small ancestral estates that enabled them to dominate their marketing areas (sometimes congruent with the township). The Yang and Shao of Lihaisuo in Shaoxing, for example, held eighty-five and sixty-plus mu respectively.[10] The Yang dominated all public functions—charity, defense, school construction, public works, fire fighting—from at least the turn of the century into the 1920s. They were aided by the Du family (with which they had intermarried) and the Shao family. Area politics was marked by alternating periods of cooperation and competition among these various lineages and in some cases within lineages. Yang lineage power, which outranked that of the Dus and Shaos, came from degrees, land, and, by the 1920s, involvement in Shanghai banking.[11]

Lineages and Modern Developments

Lineage solidarity and significance were not generally diminished by the forces of economic modernization that were transforming the inner core and to a lesser extent the outer core in this period. In fact, lineage resources provided the means for many elites to adapt to modern changes: funds previously used for the civil service examination now enabled students to travel to Hangchow, Shanghai, or Tokyo for modern training. The Zhang lineage of Yin county specifically designated its civil service examination fund to be used for students to study abroad.[12] Other lineages used funds to construct modern schools. The Gaos of Jiaxing used over 4,000 yuan in 1910 to build an impressive Western-style school.[13] The Qian and Wang lineages of the West Lake area of Hangchow built primary schools in 1920 to train their young in modern-style education.[14]

In the core zones the lineage often promoted and facilitated reform and change. In Yuyao county an anthrax vaccination center and a drug-dispensing bureau were established by lineages with ancestral estate funds.[15] The provincial government recognized the role of lineages in local development: in late 1920, at the request of the Jiaxing magistrate, the civil governor honored Sheng Bangbian for contributing to the community in establishing an estate (yizhuang) to support his lineage.[16] The lineage institution was frequently copied even where strong lineages did not exist. On the island of Daishan in Dinghai county, six lesser lineages had formed the Six Surname Association (liuxing gonghui) in the Jiaqing period (1796–1820). These lineages agreed to contribute monthly cash for sacrificial offerings, with the extra to be set aside for purchasing land. By 1924 they had built up an association estate of more than forty mu and a savings reserve of over 2,000 silver cash. The money was used for educational assistance to association members and the construction of an association center.[17]

Occasionally modern economic developments had adverse effects on lineage strength. Puyuan, a central market town on the border between Jiaxing and Tongxiang counties, had been an important silk-weaving center since the late Ming dynasty. The town began to decline economically after the Taiping Rebellion's devastation, and prosperity finally collapsed in the twentieth century as a result of at least two developments. The introduction of steam filatures in Wuxi shifted merchant interest from Huzhou to Jiangsu, and Puyuan's former role was supplanted by the Jiangsu town of Shengze. Puyuan's decline was also hastened by competition from the nearby central market town of Wangdian, which grew rapidly in the early Republic because of its location on the Shanghai-Hangchow-Ningpo railway.[18] There is evidence that this economic decline undercut the position of local lineages, especially those prominent in the silk industry.[19]

The very dynamics of development sometimes led to the weakening of local lineage strength. A case in point is the Zhu lineage in Yin county.[20] A great lineage, it had a three-hundred mu ancestral estate with a school. After 1911 its ambitious and qualified elites began to leave their native place for careers beyond the locality. Within a decade the school closed and some lineage lands had to be sold. Although the lineage reinstituted the school in 1935, other local reform efforts failed because of lack of ability and initiative on the part of those less-qualified elites who had remained in the locality. In 1933 lineage members donated a motorized water pump to the lineage fire-fighting association. It sat idle, however, because of lineage leaders' ignorance about its operation. The drain of qualified elites from their native place was a feature of developmental dynamics in the inner core that had important implications for the local community.

As a person becomes more sophisticated (that is, develops more organizational allegiances and specialized personal credentials), there is a tendency for him to shift his focus to social and political levels of greater complexity, levels of greater diversification and variety.[21] Charles Tilly points to this development-participation nexus with regard to communities that vary "in the extent and type of their external involvements. Cities grasp the outside world hungrily, while villages timidly extend their antennae."[22] The more Zhejiang's inner core developed, the more its better-qualified denizens tended to move to higher levels in the system. This did not necessarily mean that outward-bound elites had no relations with native place affairs, but they did not participate in day-to-day political and social situations. In their place were less-qualified kin: a lower-degreed brother or a nondegreed son or a nephew with purchased rank. For example, Li Kangguang and Dai Yan, both *shengyuan* and chairmen of their township councils in Yin county, had brothers with upper degrees serving outside Zhejiang in official positions.[23] For the lineage it might mean, as Ho Ping-ti has noted, that a " 'less distinguished' branch of a lineage would ordinarily be 'left behind' to manage property."[24] In some cases, this led to the weakening of lineages on the local scene, at least in terms of their elites' domination of local political functions. On the whole, however, lineages remained the crucial social collectivity, in many cases directing local change and making elite accommodation to change more possible.

Elite Career Patterns

Level of Development and Career Mobility

The correlation between higher levels of development and tendency to gravitate to higher spheres in the system helps explain what first appears to be an anomaly. Sources indicate that inner-core counties produced more degree-holding elites than counties in the outer zones. Xuanping county (outer periphery), for example, produced only two *jinshi* (one of them a military *jinshi*) and three *juren* in the entire Qing dynasty (1644–1912).[25] By way of contrast, inner-core Zhenhai produced twelve *jinshi* and eighty *juren* in the Guangxu period (1874–1908) alone.[26] Yet there tended to be more upper- and lower-degree-holders in self-government roles in the outer zones.[27]

Inner-core upper gentry, as shown in Table 10, tended to seek careers outside their home areas. Except for Xiangshan county (outer core), *gongsheng* degree-holders from the core zones were more likely to serve outside their county than those from the peripheries. *Juren* degree-holders in all zones tended to serve outside at some point in their careers; but inner-core *juren* generally did so until their retirements, whereas outer-core *juren* tended to serve outside for shorter periods, with large segments of their careers spent as local functional elites.[28]

In sum, career patterns of mobility were at least in part dependent on the level of economic development of an elite's native place.[29] More degree-holders served as self-government elites in the outer zones than in the inner core because of the tendency of highly qualified inner-core elites to go beyond native place. This trend was also enhanced by the lesser importance attached to self-government membership in the inner core: many lower-degree-holders there probably chose not to participate. In the political complexity of the inner core, especially with the early de-

Table 10.
Upper-degree-holders of the Guangxu period and spheres of subsequent political roles, 1900–1920

Zone/counties	Juren				Gongsheng			
	Total	Out of county	In county	No political role[a]	Total	Out of county	In county	No political role[a]
Inner core								
Zhenhai	80	10 (12.5%)	10 (12.5%)	60 (75%)	83	15 (18.1%)	12 (14.5%)	56 (67.5%)
Outer core								
Qu	4	1 (25%)	—	3 (75%)	50	14 (28%)	8 (16%)	28 (56%)
Xiangshan	7	5 (71.4%)	1 (14.3%)	1 (14.3%)	35	2 (5.7%)	8 (22.9%)	25 (71.4%)
Inner periphery								
Shouchang	1	1 (100%)	—	—	35	2 (5.7%)	11 (31.4%)	22 (62.9%)
Outer periphery								
Changhua	0	—	—	—	27	2 (7.4%)	7 (25.9%)	18 (66.7%)

Sources: *Zhenhai xianzhi*, passim; *Zhenhai xinzhi beigao*, passim; *Qu xianzhi*, passim; *Xiangshan xianzhi*, passim; *Shouchang xianzhi*, passim; and *Changhua xianzhi*, passim.

a. Some degree-holders in this column may have died before the period under consideration.

velopment of professional associations, self-government organs were simply one institution among many.

Lower Elites

Lower-Degree-Holders. I have hypothesized that elites who remained in the localities were often less qualified than those who left. The analysis of these lesser elites—lower-degree-holders and self-government types without recorded social or other functional credentials—is made difficult by the lack of adequate sources. A substantial portion of the latter category of self-government elites probably held unrecorded lower or purchased degrees—a hypothesis based on the two most complete gazetteers in this regard (from Suian county and the town of Shuanglin) and on fragmentary evidence from other counties.

Of the 83 percent of Suian's total 111-man county seat and township councils whose social background can be identified, 72.8 percent (sixty-seven) held lower degrees, and only 9.8 percent (ten) had upper degrees.[30] In Shuanglin, of twenty-eight council and board members, 39.2 percent (eleven) were *shengyuan,* and 10.7 percent (three) were upper-degree-holders. Although the Shuanglin gazetteer gives no information on *jiansheng,* purchased degree-holders or men of rank probably made up a substantial portion of those on whom social background information is not ascertainable (50 percent).[31] The available gazetteers from lower administrative units indicate that many whom the relevant county gazetteers did not attribute with these credentials, did, in fact, hold lower degrees.[32] In addition, sketchy biographical data from Yin and Zhenhai counties describes the lower and purchased degree backgrounds of county and board leaders.[33]

Available evidence neither conclusively supports nor disproves Ichiko Chūzō's assertion that the important self-government posts were "virtually monopolized by the lower gentry."[34] Of 532 leaders of the late Qing and early Republican subcounty bodies, 13.3 percent (seventy-one) held upper degrees and 15.8 percent (eighty-four) held recorded lower degrees: there were approximately the same number of upper-degreed as *specified* lower-degreed leaders. The number of leaders who held unrecorded lower degrees can never be determined. Certainly, however, many did not. Even in the richly detailed Suian gazetteer, which lists all lower and purchased degrees, 17 percent had no degrees, kin ties, or recorded function other than their self-government posts. In the inner core, this elite category remained a major part of self-government leadership from the late Qing dynasty into the 1920s, ranging from 32.1 percent to 42.6 percent of the total.

Self-Government Elites without Recorded Social or Other Functional

Credentials. Because of the nature of the sources, these elites can never be analyzed systematically; descriptions gleaned from many sources must suffice. It would be tempting, but not convincing, to place them in some ready-made (but little-analyzed) category like "agrarian bourgeoisie," "conservative local gentry," or the ever-popular *tuhao lieshen* ("local bullies and evil gentry").[35] It is clear, however, that they derived considerable prestige from some source, having been elected to subcounty councils and county assemblies and, in the case of the councils, selected by their peers to head them. Many practiced legitimate occupations and roles as doctors, merchants, shopkeepers, and, in the inner core, occasionally managers of modern industrial concerns.[36] Others were more traditional types: learned men without degrees; the illiterate shopkeeper whose prestige came from his acumen at settling local disputes; and the council member in a Shaoxing township whose only listed credentials were his filial piety and his renown as an arbiter are but a few examples.[37]

Among them were also men who had bought or bullied their way to power, often unaccompanied by traditional elite trappings. For example, in Yuyao county, the chairman and vice-chairman of a town council were kinsmen, the first nicknamed the Sea Dragon King whose greatest reputation was as a gambler, the second nicknamed the Gray Snake, notorious as a pettifogger.[38] In this same county was also a former bandit leader who used his newfound self-government power to assault yamen runners who had previously harassed him.[39] Throughout the core zones, there were frequent reports of gamblers, opium addicts, illiterates, pettifoggers, secret society leaders, and former bandits in the self-government bodies.[40] Counties in the core zones contained up to nine times as many self-government leaders without degrees or other accomplishments as the peripheries—a statistic I do not find substantively skewed in any zone because of gazetteer coverage.[41] Such a phenomenon indicates greater elite diversity in the core zones, the tendency of especially well-qualified men to seek a higher level of participation, and, perhaps, the relatively lesser significance that core zones placed upon self-government organs.

It has been suggested that the lower elites were the source of the infamous *tuhao lieshen* of the Republic.[42] The term was used indiscriminately to describe an enemy of any social background, however, ranging from landlord types to urban politicians to academics and returning modern school graduates.[43] This variety in social types suggests that the lower elites isolated as a group do not deserve this dubious distinction. Many lower elites had probably played an important role on the local social and political scene from at least the mid-nineteenth century on. But the significant difference from the past was that the Qing government had institutionalized their previously unrecognized position. This political legitimation of the lower elites was an important aspect of local political development.

Outer-Ranging Elites

Elites and Native Place in the Revolutionary Period. In the years before 1911, the tendency of highly qualified inner-core elites to migrate to more developed areas was partially reversed as some outer-ranging elites came home. Students with radical ideas returned from Shanghai, Beijing, and Japan. Reform-minded bureaucrats left their posts and returned home. Both groups perceived Qing policy as troglodytic and viewed the building of a modern nation-state on a firm local foundation as imperative. In some areas, especially Wenchow and Hangchow, the reforms wrought by returning elites were a continuation of earlier efforts in the 1880s and early 1890s—the establishment of Western-style schools, newspapers, and various reformist societies.[44] In others, like Linhai and Huangyan, they were the first attempts at local reform.[45] The reform ethic touched all levels of the inner-core urban hierarchy.[46] Returnees (most of whom were scions of great or at least important local lineages) were often joined by community leaders. Both groups were concerned with national matters; of twenty-two determinable town and township self-government leaders in Jiaxing, eighteen (82 percent) were leaders of voluntary patriotic organizations that sprang up in 1910 and 1911.[47]

After the revolution, however, the returnees in large part left, their local approach seemingly obviated by the monarchical abdication. In this sense, the revolution brought the reentry of many better-qualified inner-core elites into national careers.[48] Returned students were most apt to move beyond their localities. Self-government statistics suggest the post-revolution student gravitation to higher urban centers: the number of returned students participating in subcounty bodies dropped from a few to zero after the revolution. Men like Waseda University graduates Chen Zihao of Yin county and Zhu Xizu of Haiyan served in self-government and other reform capacities in the last years of the Qing dynasty but left in 1912 for official positions in Beijing and other provinces.[49] There was also an exodus of local elites who had no previous experience outside the locality. They were men like Xi Bingyuan of Deqing, a lower-degreed graduate of the Zhejiang Sericulture School, who had served only in local posts before the revolution but had a succession of positions in other provinces after 1912.[50] Various evidence suggests that in this regard at least, the 1911 revolution proved a liberating force for inner-core elite careers.

Generational Cohorts and Native Place Ties: A Hypothesis. This liberating effect also appeared in the tendency of younger men to remain outside without retaining close and continual ties to native place. The traditional outer-ranging elite had maintained an interest in his home community, assisting it and its denizens during his career and especially after his retirement. Cong Nengshu of Shaoxing, for example, who served in the late Qing dynasty as magistrate and circuit intendant in Jiangsu, maintained a constant interest in native place affairs including conservancy, relief, and charitable projects.[51]

On the basis of extremely fragmentary data, I have hypothesized that the strength of inner-core elite ties to native place correlates generally with different generational cohorts.[52] Outer-ranging elites who were born in the late 1850s and 1860s tended to maintain strong ties to their home communities during the Republic, assisting them during their careers and after their retirements.[53] The cohort of the 1870s seems transitional—some had little to do with the problems and projects of their native places and others were involved at times of local crisis.[54] For these generational cohorts, traditional native place concerns merged in the late Qing period into concerns for nation building on a local foundation.

Inner-core elites of the 1880s generation, however, tended to be little involved in local affairs.[55] Coming of age in the last Qing decade and gaining modern degrees then or in the early Republic, they were the revolution's children, accepting what it had to offer—career freedom—and not very interested in maintaining the close native place ties of their elders. They returned for important family occasions and to visit ancestral tombs, but the ideal of a returning gentry, performing various tasks for the locality, was dying.

Elites and Native Place in the 1920s

Another wave of returning native place elites with outside experience began during 1922–23. The bleak national situation led some of the older returnees to imitate the late Qing reformist program of rebuilding from the local level. For many of these elites, however, though they maintained ties to their communities, the focus was now on the province as unit in a political federation, not the township.[56] Younger modern school graduates returned to their native places, not like returned students in the late Qing period to remake the community in a multipronged thrust, but as specialists.[57] They were little connected to the older, more generalist local elites in interests or inclination, and, in contrast to the students in the postrevolution period, they tended to take part in self-government bodies. Products of the May Fourth ferment, these specialists were, like the earlier returned students, strongly nationalistic, and they often participated in parapolitical study societies or the reorganized Guomindang.

Clashes between some of the modern-trained specialists and older, generalist elites were frequent. Bitter rivalries developed between traditional types in county assemblies and returned normal- and middle-school graduates over the administration of modern schools. During the wave of educational reforms in the late 1910s and early 1920s, school boards had been set up to manage and oversee major middle and normal schools in each county. Returned recent graduates, many of whom had drunk the heady wine of May Fourth iconoclasm and resentment against the established elite, participated in the local education bureaus that frequently opposed nonofficial and official elites on issues of school board composition and functions.[58]

The local elites' resentment, however, extended not only to the new, specialized elites but also to some older pre-1911 reformist elites who undertook action in the localities. Chu Fucheng occasioned so much rancor in Jiaxing with his involvement in insect control efforts in the mid-1920s that the county assembly abolished itself partly in frustration over his role.[59] It is clear upon analysis that the relationships of outer-ranging elites to native place and to those who remained in the native place depended in large part upon national events to which these elites were largely oriented.

5

Inner-Core Elite Collectivities:
Social Groupings and Voluntary Associations

Historically, Chinese political and social philosophy has been concerned with social groupings. The most famous of these groupings, the scholar-gentry, peasant, artisan, and merchant, provided their members with a social identity beyond that of the lineage and family. The gentry and often, despite Confucian predilections, the merchants, were the elite strata. Shifts and changes in these and other elite social groupings were significant in early-twentieth-century local politics.

Gentry, Gentry-Merchant, and Merchant

The traditional Chinese gentry, civil service examination degree-holders, had seen their vehicle to elite status abolished by Qing decree in 1905. Various special examinations continued into 1911 to forestall elite disgruntlement in a period of national crisis. When the monarchy fell, however, this route to elite status was closed forever. It is not surprising, therefore, that the percentage of inner-core degree-holders serving in county self-government positions decreased from 23.4 percent in 1911 to 7.7 percent in the 1920s. In China's agrarian society, land traditionally provided most lineages or families with the wealth by which they could move into gentry status with a degree and into gentry functions with sums for local improvements.[1] As Chang Chung-li has illustrated, however, by the early nineteenth century, large numbers of gentry were involved in commercial activities from which they derived substantial income.[2] By the turn of the century, most gentry (*shen* or *shenshi*) in the core zones probably had some commercial interests.

Two members of the Zhenhai county gentry serve as examples.[3] Sheng Bingwei received his *jinshi* degree in 1880, and worked as an education official in Sichuan and Jiangxi. Returning home to care for his ill mother in the late 1890s, he set up county schools, helped in charitable projects, and organized militia bureaus. Active in the railway agitation of 1907 and increasingly involved in commercial matters, he continued to play important roles in local affairs until his death in 1931. Yu Ruchang obtained the *shengyuan* degree in 1872. With his formerly illustrious lineage in economic decline, he joined another *shengyuan* in establishing a market town business that served as a springboard for his local leadership in education, self-government, and management of civil disorder. Many other examples could be cited,[4] but the picture that emerges is of gentry families with strong mercantile resources initiating reform and performing traditional functions for their communities.

As the gentry became involved in the commercial realm, wealthy merchants, degreed or not, performed gentry functions alongside degree-holders. By the mid-nineteenth century, any functional distinction in the inner core between gentry and wealthy merchants had largely disappeared. The blurring of traditional social delimitations was evidenced etymologically in the designation "gentry-merchant" (*shenshang*) in the late nineteenth and early twentieth centuries. Historically this term has been used in two different ways. Sources from the late Qing dynasty into the 1930s frequently use *shenshang* to mean groups of gentry and merchants. Up to the 1920s, however, the phrase sometimes also referred to individuals, with "merchant" indicating career base and "gentry" serving as attribute.[5] When applied to individuals, it was often used (like the phrase "local bullies and evil gentry") without analytical discrimination, describing a perceived social type rather than an analytic category. Generally, "gentry-merchant" referred to merchants with purchased degrees or, more loosely, simply wealthy merchants performing gentry roles,[6] and I too use the term in this way. The functional roles were more crucial for designation to this category than the possession of degrees; these roles also distinguished gentry-merchants from merchants.

As with the gentry category, there are many examples of gentry-merchants. Ningpo and Shaoxing prefectures were peopled with many outstanding functional elites who began their careers as merchants and, after business success, purchased degrees.[7] There were also gentry-merchants like Zhou Wenfu, a nondegreed rich rice merchant of Yuyao, whose status came from his local roles in relief, charity, and public works in the 1880s and 1890s.[8] The gentry-merchant was influential in the economic and political arenas at all levels of the urban hierarchy.

The general merchant category included numerous distinctions in commercial scale as well as in nature and scope of functional activity. Of all commercial types, the gentry-merchant was the most politically influential. Perhaps more financially powerful but with little direct participation in the political sphere was the new (primarily compradorial) group of industrial capitalists who lived in Shanghai. They often participated in the economic development of their native places, like Zhou Shiying of Zhenhai, collaborating with gentry-merchants but playing little personal role in political affairs.[9]

With less economic and political power were merchants (including so-journers) who were involved primarily in local enterprises, generally lacking the resources to range throughout the zone, province, or region.[10] They held no gentry credentials and played no gentry roles in the late Qing dynasty. They were active in local guilds and chambers of commerce. Not included in this group are local shopkeepers, objects of taxation and often mass riots, who had a more limited range of resources and scope of activity than those in my designated merchant category.[11] Some merchants may have owned and perhaps managed retail shops, but such roles were exceptions.

My study of entrepreneurs in the city of Jiaxing during the last years of the Qing period underscores the functional distinction between gentry-merchants and merchants.[12] It reveals eleven gentry-merchants involved in many organizations and roles, and six merchants who participated in neither political organizations nor chamber of commerce leadership and who performed no recorded political and social functions. Yet these six merchants wielded substantial economic power in guilds concerned with shipping, wood products, fishing, and cotton goods. Although they were not recorded among political functionaries, their voices did not go unheard by the chamber of commerce or the gentry-merchants. They did not participate openly, however, in political decision making, at least until after the 1911 revolution. Instead, they offered the benefits that money could buy, underwriting local defense and charity.[13] In most civic responsibilities, gentry and gentry-merchant led and merchant followed.

Elite Social Groupings in Late Qing Self-Government

Local post-Taiping reforms were promoted and directed in large part by gentry and gentry-merchants.[14] In the last years of the Qing dynasty, these men moved quickly into self-government and professional association leadership positions where they frequently clashed with merchants and shopkeepers.

I have been able to determine from newspapers the names of twenty-one members of the Hangchow city council in 1910 and 1911. Sixteen (76 percent) were important gentry and gentry-merchants, fourteen of whom had interests in the rice, silk, salt, and banking industries.[15] In its two years of existence, the council had numerous clashes with merchants in the metropolitan area. Merchants from outside the city wall argued that the opportunity for business expansion, stimulated by the opening of the railroad from Shanghai, could best be seized by constructing a theater district in the West Lake area so that business could continue into the evening. Fearing the spread of gambling and prostitution, the council opposed the plan on the grounds that it would increase public disturbances. This debate dragged on into the Republic.[16] The council's plan to levy a boat tax brought protests from merchants in the nearby town of Jianggan who were themselves boat tax farmers, one of whom (nicknamed the "straw sandals pettifogger") was a township manager. In this case, entrenched suburban merchant interests clashed with a larger urban center's gentry and gentry-merchant leadership.[17] In the fall of 1911 the council's call for greater control of rice merchants indicated its distrust of some aspects of merchant activity.[18]

The interests of shopkeepers also were affected by decisions of gentry and gentry-merchant self-government bodies. In Xincheng, a central market town in Jiaxing, wineshop owners joined to thwart the imposition of a county self-government tax on wine by the cup.[19] In Shanyin county, when county self-government taxes were levied on certain commodities, shopkeepers in the town of Anchang responded by raising the prices of their goods. Nearby farmers, upset at the price hike and urged by some shopkeepers to "teach the self-government people a lesson," destroyed the council's meeting hall, two schools, and the home of a board member. The council and board demanded that reparations be made and punishments meted out. Although the results were not recorded, a reporter noted that shopkeepers and merchants contributed food and provisions to the farmers after their rampage.[20]

Late Qing self-government bodies, in short, did not represent merchant interests but rather the concerns of gentry and gentry-merchants, with the "gentry" aspect of gentry-merchant often seeming the dominant factor. It is clear also that one cannot speak of "*the* bourgeoisie" without distorting the complexity of local politics in the last years of the Qing dynasty. Different interests dependent upon specific occupation, scope of concern, and arena of activity within the urban hierarchy produced different goals.

Early Republican Gentry and Gentry-Merchant Public Roles

In the late Qing period, modern enterprises had been primarily joint undertakings of officials, gentry, and gentry-merchants.[21] My study of the managers and chief stockholding spokesmen of the Hangchow Electric Light Company (founded in 1908) and the Hangchow Telephone Company (established in 1909) indicates that gentry and gentry-merchants with ties to officialdom—not merchants—were the key developers.[22] When developmental interests beckoned in less developed zones, gentry and gentry-merchants attempted to establish mining companies in Anji in early 1910 and in Kaihua in 1911 (both inner periphery).[23] The 1911 revolution had a liberating effect for many inner-core elites: for the gentry and gentry-merchants it touched off a wave of developmental projects and demands that so-called official-merchant (*guanshang*) companies be turned over to them for full control.[24] The proliferation of these elite projects was aided by a liberal provincial government policy. Guidelines from Hangchow for the silk cocoon industry, for example, ordered officials to let the industry police itself.[25] A provincial bureau was established to promote mining.[26] The years 1912 and 1913 saw the establishment of cotton mills, electric companies, cement companies, new shipping firms, and silk factories in a wave of gentry and gentry-merchant activity.[27]

Men from these groups, which by the late 1910s and 1920s had become so intertwined that they were often referred to simple as gentry (*shen*), continued during the early Republic as local leaders at all urban levels. A sampling of meetings on crucial local and national issues in Jiaxing from 1910 to 1927—on prerevolutionary preparations in 1911; the controversy over the British-American Tobacco Company in 1912; the 1916 Association to debate national and self-government issues; and the crusade to defeat the rice worm borer from 1923 to 1927—reveals a fairly consistent gentry and gentry-merchant amalgam.[28]

Another example of their leadership continuity is seen in the Ningpo branch of the International Famine Relief Commission in the early 1920s, which contained forty-two members from Zhenhai—all but ten of whom were important gentry and gentry-merchants from the turn of the century.[29] Individually, they were the key Zhenhai functional elites, performing over 70 percent of all recorded local functions after 1911. The involvement of only two of the total in the county self-government bodies of the late Qing period and early Republic indicates these organs' relative lack of importance in this inner-core county.

The Rise of Merchants

The continued dominance of the gentry and gentry-merchant groups should not, however, overshadow the rise of the merchant stratum as local entrepreneurs with substantial political power.[30] Merchants emerged from the 1911 revolution with greater assertiveness. Although gazetteer sources are generally reticent on merchant status, some merchants were among those self-government figures in two categories: functional elites without degrees, diplomas, or recorded family ties; and those for whom only self-government roles could be found. The number for both categories increased from almost 47 percent in the late Qing period to 65 percent in the 1920s. These statistics suggest a greater merchant involvement following the revolution, an interpretation that is supported by circumstantial evidence. Self-government councils seem to have exhibited an almost mercantile bias after 1911. In Hangchow, city merchants and council jointly sponsored a cocoon hong in the city to stop the flow of money to nearby areas.[31] Merchant members of the Jiaxing city council were instrumental in the expansion of a rickshaw company running from the railroad station to the city's older commercial district.[32] Self-government bodies in Shangyu county petitioned for the abolition of the hated *tongjuan*, the object of bitter merchant attack from the early months of 1912.[33] The marked lack of merchant self-government tax protests in contrast to the large numbers of such protests before the revolution suggests an improved relationship between merchants and self-government bodies.[34]

There are other evidences of the postrevolution surge of merchant assertion. A highly symbolic episode with political overtones was the nationalization of the Shanghai-Hangchow-Ningpo railway. This symbol of nationalistic determination to retain economic sovereignty had fallen into financial difficulties. In the first years of the Republic, many of the original board members (who in 1910 had all been gentry and gentry-merchants) had moved on to national affairs.[35] When meetings were held in early 1914 to discuss the question of nationalization to protect the investors' interests, nineteen of the thirty men who play important roles were merchants in one or more enterprises. They were clearly different from the late Qing railroad elite. Two gentry-merchants spoke against nationalization, noting that the decision to nationalize would still be tantamount to handing the company over to foreigners. Yet nationalization was approved by a seven-to-one margin.[36]

In the early 1910s, merchants and farmers (*nongmin*) besieged the authorities for permission to set up cocoon hongs. Established raw silk and weaving interests, which were already hard-pressed by competition from the new silk filatures (which utilized the hongs), adamantly opposed uncontrolled proliferation of the hongs, arguing that inadequate regulation of the new industry was lowering the quality of the cocoons. The issue became a battle between would-be entrepreneurs, on the one hand, and industry gentry-merchants and established merchant hong owners who did not want competition, on the other.[37] Bureaucratic decisions before 1915 prohibited any new hongs, but over the next ten years the provincial assemblies liberalized the policy; in 1928 Chiang Kai-shek's government removed all restrictions.[38] This gradual liberalization points to the growing entrepreneurial spirit and the advances made by some nongentry merchants in the early Republic.

Merchants with no discernible gentry backgrounds tended to dominate the boards of companies established after 1914. For example, in Hangchow six powerful merchants established the Hualun Silk Factory in mid-1914 for the weaving of stockings.[39] In 1918 board members of the Hangchow telephone and electric companies included only one or two gentry-merchants.[40] The same pattern appears in the boards of a Jiaxing paper mill and the Jiaxing Electric Company in 1924.[41] Of eighteen telephone companies established in the inner core between 1915 and 1929, only two had gentry-merchant leaders. Merchants founded the Dinghai county electric and telephone companies in the mid-1920s.[42] A new generation of modernizers thus emerged by the mid-1910s and 1920s with fewer ties to the traditional elite of the past and to the pre-1911 gentry-merchant stratum.

These new entrepreneurs were found at all levels of the urban hierarchy. Merchants in the intermediate market of Xinhuang and the central market of Xincheng (Jiaxing county) established telephone and electric companies.[43] The powerful merchant Jin Yuanao petitioned the Zhejiang Industry Ministry for the right to establish an industrial complex at the central market town of Linpu in Shaoxing to manufacture paper, textiles, brushes, bamboo and wood products, and tiles.[44] Companies proliferated in the late 1910s and early 1920s. By the early 1920s insurance and real estate companies were established in the larger cities.[45]

Merchant enterprise inevitably led to greater political involvement. Establishing a business involved negotiations with officials about initial permission and various bureaucratic regulations affecting it. Setting up a modern enterprise made the owner liable to taxes, and by the 1920s, subject to strikes and political protests. It thrust him into the current of relations with the outside, as he procured machines from Shanghai or beyond and made contacts with native place organizations in large urban centers.[46] Political involvement and awareness were heightened.

Increased merchant visibility on the local scene is institutionally evident in the early Republican establishment of more chambers of commerce in nonadministrative towns. The government's 1917 regulation limiting them to two per county revealed its recognition of the potential power of chambers on the local scene. It refused to allow the formation of more than two even in counties, like Shangyu, that had several flourishing market towns.[47] In the mid-1920s inner-core towns circumvented this regulation by establishing branch chambers rather than their own discrete organizations.[48]

For example, Jiaxing county had no less than thirteen branch chambers by 1924.[49] They met frequently to discuss the economy and politics, exhibiting considerable political clout.[50] They blocked the 1920 appointment of a new self-government deputy because of his alleged antimerchant activities.[51] And they bitterly opposed and successfully forestalled official attempts to "reform" the collection of the house tax used for funding the police (believing that "reform" would lead to higher payments).[52] The county assembly was so dominated by silk merchants that in a forty-day period of its 1925 regular session it attained a quorum only three or four times because assemblymen kept returning to their silk businesses to deal with pressing problems.[53] The agenda of the chamber of commerce branch in the Jiaxing market town of Wangdian in early 1924 included not only business-related concerns but also items in regard to the town's sanitation, winter defense, and education.[54]

In many inner-core counties, chambers held paramount power. In Shaoxing by 1922 this *fatuan* had assumed the duties undertaken in most areas by county assemblies.[55] When war fears rippled over northern Zhejiang in 1923 and actual war engulfed it in 1924, the chambers arranged for defense and called for peace.[56] The provincial government recognized the power of the local bourgeoisie and its threat to official control: in the summer of 1925, the government ordered the circuit intendant (*daoyin*) to abolish within three days the merchant unions (*shang jie lianhehui*) that had sprung up in many counties.[57] Merchants and shopkeepers were significant participants in the general strikes and boycotts that punctuated the inner-core urban scene from 1919 on. Merchants inaugurated many enterprises in the early 1920s in order to "strengthen the country" (*fuguo*)—from the Yongjia lumber company and straw mat factory to the Yin county sugar mill.[58]

Yet the merchants seemed more openly self-interested than the old gentry-merchants. In June 1919, some merchants, citing possible economic losses, rebelled against the gentry-merchant head of the Hangchow General Chamber of Commerce, Gu Songqing, when he supported the general strike.[59] A crucial aspect of the rise of the merchants was a new sense of occupational specialization, illustrated by the appearance of commercial journals. Merchants were businessmen first; if a strong civic sense motivated a merchant entrepreneur, it was not generally of the all-encompassing gentry or gentry-merchant variety. In the past, merchants had hidden commercial objectives by leaving their native place to avoid the watchful eyes of local acquaintances or by masking these objectives through various guild-sponsored benevolent functions. By the 1920s they had begun to cast off such pretenses: Jiaxing shipping magnates, for example, simply refused to contribute to city-wide organizational relief effort, publicly citing their resentment over taxes.[60] Officials began to seek the advice of merchants who were company stockholders and board members.[61] Economic development and national need had helped make possible the rise of the specialized businessman-entrepreneur.

Modern-School Graduates

With the abolition of the civil service examination and the establishment of a modern school system in the last decade of the Qing era, the diploma and modern-school degree in large part replaced the traditional degree as the passport to career opportunities. A plethora of new schools were founded throughout the inner core: primary, middle, and normal schools; self-government institutes (*zizhi yanjiu suo*) in 1908 and in the early 1920s; special professional and occupational schools (*zhuanmen xuexiao*) covering fields like law, law enforcement, and industry; and universities and military academies. In addition, many schools offered short courses for those who wanted an inexpensive and less rigorous education.

Educational and Career Opportunities

Opportunities for upper-level education in the new educational system, like those in the traditonal system, were highly correlated with both zonal and personal prosperity and wealth. I have compiled county of origin lists for the 121 Zhejiang students in Japan in 1902 and 1903; for the 82 at Beijing University (*jingshi daxuetang*) in 1906; for the 52 at Qinghua University in 1917; and for the 306 at the Baoding Military Academy from 1912 to 1920.[62] Inner-core counties produced 81 percent (98) of the students in Japan; 80.8 percent (59) of the Beijing University students; 88.5 percent (46) of the Qinghua students; and 38.9 percent (119) of the Baoding cadets. More inner-core students attended Baoding in the beginning of the period from 1912 to 1920 than near the end (55.6 percent in the first class compared with 33.3 percent in the eighth), indicating a decreasing inner-core elite participation in military education over time. On the level of the individual, lists of graduates of upper-level schools from Zhenhai county and the towns of Wu-Qing and Puyuan indicate that between two thirds and three fourths of all graduates came from wealthy established lineages.[63]

Several aspects of Table 11, which suggests the types of educational backgrounds of early Republican elites and the career sphere made likely by specific academic credentials, are noteworthy.[64] First, students who are trained overseas became influential in teaching and the professions, and they rarely returned to their home province, much less their specific native place. Of 106 Zhejiang students who studied in the United States from 1909 to 1924, only ten (9.4 percent) remained in Zhejiang, seven of them in Hangchow. The remainder lived in various large urban centers, particularly Shanghai, Beijing, and Tianjin.[65] Second, of all types of provincial schools, law schools provided their graduates with the best credentials for higher sphere positions. Third, the modal educational background for local elites tended to be provincial and county middle and normal schools and below.[66] In addition, it is logical to assume that many local elites had some schooling at county and township level institutions that was not recorded.

Many men followed specialized careers based upon their education. Military academy graduates served in the modern army, the provincial forces (*xunfangdui* before 1911 and *jingbeidui* afterward), and the mari-

Table 11.
Types of education and probable career opportunities of early Republican elites

Type of schools	Most likely career positions	Equivalent traditional degree
Overseas, outside of Zhejiang	Professions, government service in Beijing or provincial administrative capitals	*Jinshi, juren*
Provincial law schools	County positions outside Zhejiang; judgeships in Zhejiang counties; tax bureau heads; some local elite county functions in education and self-government	*Jinshi, juren*
Provincial middle and normal schools	Lower bureaucratic positions, secretaries in ministries, tax collectors, school principals, and teachers, local functions in education, anti-opium; positions in Zhejiang county yamens	*Gongsheng* and below
County schools	Local elite functions, tax collectors, police assistants	*Shengyuan, jiansheng*
Military academies	Military roles, police chiefs	*Wujin, wuju*

time and riverine patrols; by the 1920s important principals and teachers were almost exclusively normal school graduates; law school graduates became involved in various areas of government; police schools turned out many men who served as county police chiefs.[67] Some of these professions deserve special attention for their roles in the early Republic.

The first decades of the century were a period of expansion for the profession of law. The traditional attitude toward men involved in litigation was strongly negative: those who were seen to profit from it—an official's private legal assistants (*muyou*) and pettifoggers—were treated with disdain. The issuance of new civil and criminal law codes in 1910 and 1912, respectively, and the necessity of training competent men to handle the new legal system led to the formation of law schools (*fazheng xuetang*) in many urban centers.[68] The Hangchow Law School short course graduated some eight hundred students from 1907 to 1910.[69] After the 1911 revolution, many private law schools sprang up, producing throngs of graduates, which led to demands for regulating schools and their curricula.[70] In many cases lawyers seemed little more than modern-trained pettifoggers. Peng Zuling, for example, son of a Qing dynasty salt official, was graduated from Zhejiang Law School. In two years as a legal officer in Cheng county, he established an infamous reputation as an avaricious inciter of litigation.[71]

To regulate the burgeoning legal profession, itself a symbol of the changing sociopolitical ethos, a new *fatuan*, the lawyers association (*lüshi hui*), was ordered established in 1912.[72] It remained a unique feature of the inner core into the late 1920s, with the exception of the Jinhua chapter (outer core) established in the late 1910s.[73] The Hangchow, Ningpo, Yongjia, and Jinhua associations met often to discuss major political and legal issues. Of the 146 members of the Hangchow association in 1919, at least 21 were among the most influential provincial elites, and many were early Guomindang party adherents.[74] Lawyers gravitated to larger urban centers; their spheres even in the inner core were largely circumscribed by urban level. Lawyers were employed by the Hangchow metropolitan city and township councils in a civil case as early as 1912.[75] By the 1920s Jiaxing chambers of commerce designated lawyers as permanent legal counsels.[76]

The problem of regulating and controlling police was more serious than supervising lawyers. Police touched the daily lives of local residents more than any other government force, keeping order, providing services, and collecting some taxes. Between 1907 and 1911 the provincial police school (*xunzheng xuetang*), with all its regular and short courses, graduated more than three hundred men, and there were between one and two thousand police school students in Zhejiang in 1913. The Zhejiang schools varied in their quality of training. As with lawyers, the government made attempts to control police proliferation by regulating the schools; but the problem was too widespread to be solved through such methods.[77] Police functionaries were omnipresent. Groups of merchants hired their own police; courts had their police for certain court functions; magistrates cultivated private police units.[78] These special police existed in addition to various government-mandated county and subcounty police. Local citizens (*gongmin*) repeatedly protested the activity of police assistants (*jingzuo*) who tended to assume the roles of traditional yamen runners, extorting the populace, accepting bribes, and promoting gambling.[79] The problems attendant to this police proliferation became more severe throughout the early Republic.

Military graduates in a military capacity played a much less pervasive and decisive role than police.[80] Disruptions of the peace sometimes brought units into action, and occasionally an officer was brought into official deliberations on matters of defense. But not until 1923 and after are there recorded indications of the military's direct involvement in local political affairs. In 1923, for example, the defense commissioner in Wuxing was made a leader of the new municipal government.[81] In late 1924 and early 1925, the commander of the Wenchow garrison vigorously opposed the appointment of a magistrate for Yongjia county despite orders that he not become involved in civilian affairs (*minzheng*).[82] But on the whole, except for periods of political turmoil (for example, the 1911 revolution and invasions in the 1920s by Sun Chuanfang and the Guomindang), local elites were little faced with a military presence in the councils of power.

Teaching offered normal school and other graduates career opportunities in an era of educational expansion. Many schools were ephemeral, primarily because of financial problems. Often they reappeared under a different name; some were converted in the 1920s from private primary or middle schools to commercial schools, underscoring merchant importance by that time.[83] Women's schools, established in large urban centers in the late Qing period, were among the most short-lived and were the first to feel the brunt of local economic problems: women's normal and law schools were generally closed or functioning weakly by the mid-1920s.[84] Teachers were in the forefront of revolutionary and reformist activity before 1911, in the May Fourth period, and in the era of local Guomindang organizations from 1923 to 1927.

Graduates of specific provincial professional schools—engineering, industrial, and agricultural—played no role on the local level until the 1920s and usually then only for specific projects. Engineers were hired for dredging and dike building; agricultural graduates were employed as entomologists; forestry graduates were assigned to reforestation projects.[85] Graduates of industrial schools had immense career oppotunities. A report of the first four years of the Zhejiang Industrial School (*gongye xuexiao*) (1920–1923) showed that of 820 graduates, 74.5 percent had jobs in pertinent industrial professions, and 10.7 percent had sought more education.[86] Like military graduates and modern lawyers, they were seldom seen on a continuous basis in most communities.

Throughout the early Republic journalism became increasingly important in fostering political ideas. Reformist officials and returned students had established newspapers and magazines in the inner core in the last decade of the Qing era. The halcyon days of newspaper journalism came in the first two years of the Republic when the threat of censorship did not loom so large as in the late 1910s and the 1920s. Xiang Shiyuan in his encyclopedic study of journalism in Zhejiang discusses the many short-lived newspapers that expounded various political positions in the 1910s.[87] Directed by the modern-school graduate elites, the wave of modern-style journalism was almost totally an inner-core phenomenon until the mid-1920s.

Developmental Elite Change

Xiang Shiyuan describes a pattern among journalistic elites from about 1900 to 1928 that is highly suggestive of general developmental elite changes in Zhejiang's inner core. Before the 1911 revolution, leading journalists were reformist-nationalists, intent on remaking the Chinese nation by ousting the Manchus and undertaking local reforms. For journalists, the 1911 revolution was a leap toward greater politicization. Politician-journalists formed newspapers to put forth the specific views of new political parties. In the press, the emphasis slowly shifted from the ideal of nationalism to the political process. After the 1917 seizure of the province by Beiyang forces, journalistic elites became the provincial politicians, speaking for political factions in provincial affairs.

The early 1920s saw the emergence of the professional journalist, who was not and had never been primarily a politician, either nationalist or provincial. The age of journalism as an avocation or as a support for another primary occupation was disappearing in the face of specialization. Commercial journals appeared in this period, putting forth the ideas of the merchant, as did education journals, which discussed educational reform. The military began to make its presence felt in journalism after Sun Chuanfang's 1924 victory; but it was not until after the Guomindang success in early 1927 that military domination of journalistic elites became complete.

This elite profile suggests that inner-core elites through the first years of the Republic typically were generalists, with both national and provincial interests. The primary focus of their political concerns narrowed from the nationalism of the revolution to the provincialism of the late 1910s.

Paralleling this attitudinal shift was the emergence of the professional specialist who rivaled to varying degrees the older, generalist elites. Merchants emerged from under the shadow of gentry and gentry-merchant, contributing substantially to local economic development. They were joined by new, functionally specialized graduates whose contribution varied from level to level of the urban economic hierarchy. Modern-trained teachers and police seemed most influential in local decision making and concerns. Confined mainly to larger centers until the early to mid-1920s, lawyers, military figures, journalists, and various professional groups were less significant local forces. Eventually in the increasingly politicized world of the 1920s, many of these specialists came to be dominated by or merged with military politicians. Xiang's profile highlights key aspects of inner-core elite development in these decades, especially the increasing differentiation, specialization, and politicization.

Elites and Voluntary Associations, 1900–1927

For elites in the early-twentieth-century inner core, social identity began to mean more than lineage base, social grouping, or occupational classification. As national events and government-sponsored institutions began to politicize many inner-core elites, voluntary associations brought them into groups, providing a forum for the exchange and reinforcement of ideas on national, provincial, and local issues. These associations facilitated the growth of new personal connections that served as bonds for various political activities. They provided the organizational basis for many community services and functioned as agents of change, mediating between primary kin and territorial groupings, on the one hand, and the state, on the other. Their importance for political development cannot be overemphasized.

The first thirty years of the century saw two periods when voluntary associations were formed in large number: 1907 to 1914 and 1916 to 1924. Both periods were ended by political suppression at the hands of government authorities—Yuan Shikai in 1914 and military bureaucrats Sun Chuanfang and Chiang Kai-shek in the mid-1920s. The society created by the halcyon years of association formation was viewed by some political leaders as socially untidy and potentially disruptive; they thus sought greater control over new social structures and processes.

Associations in the Revolutionary Era, 1907–1914

Voluntary associations as core zone institutions sprang up in the railway controversy of 1907.[88] Until 1912 their raison d'être was to further the nationalistic goal of strengthening and reforming China. The foreign threat was clear, symbolized by high-handed British action in 1907 and again in 1910 when they forced the dismissal of the railway director Tang. Ad hoc associations, joined by professional associations that had been established by 1910 in the inner core's major urban centers, responded with a telegraphic chorus of denunciations to the government.[89]

To strengthen the nation through the localities, branches of the National Martial Association (*guomin shangwu hui*) were established in 1911 in various inner-core counties by Shanghai representatives of the national organization.[90] The common themes at all the organizational meetings were nationalism, physical fitness, militia formation, and the need for association journals. Chambers of commerce followed the association's bidding by establishing militia units throughout the inner core.[91] The concern for personal physical fitness was new to Chinese elites. Although traditional elites had scorned the active physical life, the new elite concern with national physical strength led quite naturally to great interest in physical training and readiness. In the spring of 1910, Hangchow held the first Zhejiang interschool athletic meet.[92] Such meets not only emphasized physical training but fostered competition, elite identification with particular schools, and, most important, personal linkages among students.

The number of elites involved in the association is difficult to estimate, but certainly many participated: attendance at the organizational meetings reportedly ranged from over one hundred to over four hundred.[93] An association leader at Jiaxing argued that in the future the Chinese people's primary concern had to be the sovereignty of the nation rather than simply loyalty to the immediate family unit as in the past.[94] What he did not say was that organizations like this were redefining experientially the sense of collectivity in Chinese culture. Jiaxing women, excluded from professional associations and their advisory auxiliaries by strict regulations, formed a Women's Martial Association, arguing that men were too debauched to better society.[95] Amid the nationalistic excitement in the summer of 1911, reform groups were organized to ban opium and cigarettes and to encourage the production of Chinese goods to compete with foreign products.[96]

With the 1912 collapse of the monarchy and the disappearance of the "king's law," the political ethos of the past was shattered.[97] For elites in the inner core, the revolution was a license to proceed apace with the expansion of the organization ethic. The liberal republic (1912–1914) was one of the heydays of both political and nonpolitical voluntary associations. The most radical change from the late Qing period was the appearance of political parties or party-inspired organizations. By the spring of 1912, branches of half a dozen parties were established in administrative urban centers by returned students or political operatives from Shanghai. Many elites must have been touched to some degree by the rapid political organizing: newspaper accounts reveal that attendance at party meetings ranged from about fifty to six hundred, with many leaders of professional and nonpolitical associations participating.[98] In addition to their stance on the national situation, some parties pressed for such particular local reforms as establishing price limits on rice, building an orphanage, and sponsoring the opening of a textile factory.[99]

Nationalism continued to be a major dynamic in associations of the liberal republic. Perceived infringements on Chinese sovereignty ignited the founding of organizations to uphold Chinese rights. Leagues to reconquer Mongolia, which had fallen into Russia's orbit after 1911, formed throughout the inner core.[100] A British and American Tobacco Company agent's insistence on operating against regulations inside Jiaxing led to the founding of the Society to Protect National Sovereignty (*bao quanguoquan hui*).[101] Concerned as well with the work of nationalism were women's rights organizations: the Men and Women's Equal Rights Association, whose major goal was women's suffrage, was one of the foremost spokesmen of nationalism during the Mongolian episode.[102]

Reform associations proliferated. Starting with the premise that the polity and society should be restructured, many joined study societies focusing on constitutionalism, public rights, national livelihood, the role of law, and the tenets of republicanism. Some societies called for economic development.[103] Still others wanted to pull back the reins of what seemed to be rampaging change. A study society to preserve the "national essence" formed at Hangchow.[104] To improve society, the Organization to Foster Integrity (*shangyi tuan*) was founded at Jiaxing. Accepting as its members all but the unemployed, it met regularly at the hall (*minglun tang*) where tablets of local degree-holders and notables were kept.[105] Its title and meeting place suggest the ties between the new associations and the traditional gentry ethos.

Education-related associations flourished. Physical culture societies (*tiyu hui*) continued to be formed; schools organized special exercise departments, and physical fitness became an increasingly important aspect of school life.[106] One of the most important traditional elite social connections, the special tie to those who attained specific civil service degrees in the same year, was institutionalized in the new context of the modern school system with the 1913 organization of alumni groups in major inner-core urban centers.[107]

Interest groups as well as nationalistic reform-minded associations flourished in the liberal republic. In 1913 landlords in the Jiaxing area organized the Joint Agricultural Society (*tianye lianhehui*) to discuss methods of collecting rent from obstinate renters. They eventually established a rent collection bureau in a building attached to the yamen.[108] In the summer of 1912, forty county assembly representatives formed a federation to lobby for abolition of the onerous military tribute rice exaction (*caonan mi*) borne heavily by Zhejiang.[109] Other non-self-government territorial-based associations also brought elites together at higher levels of the administrative hierarchy than their native place. County elites, for example, were incorporated at the prefectural level in the Ningbo Public Property Bureau and the Federation of Jiaxing Merchant Militia.[110]

In sum, inner-core elites worked in an organizational context that differed markedly from a decade earlier. A multitude of voluntary and professional associations offered elites the opportunity to participate in political and social isues. With participation came extrapersonal goals with which to identify and structural linkages for the development of elite networks.

Yuan Shikai's abolition of self-government organs in 1914 inaugurated a period in sharp contrast to the organizationally vigorous liberal republic. Professional associations continued to meet, though the autonomy of at least the chambers of commerce was sharply restricted by new regulations.[111] Voluntary associations were repressed. There was a brief flurry of nationalistic organizing by students in the 1915 Twenty-One Demands episode with Japan, but it died away quickly.[112] Yuan Shikai's autocratic action, however, inadvertently stimulated the development of specialized organizations to deal with local and provincial problems. Self-government bodies, incarnating the new public ethos and symbolizing elite politicization, had remained generalist organizations, spreading their attention over a wide range of issues. After their abolition, many functionally specific institutions developed for managing conservancy problems, charity, and public works. Some were government sponsored or received government subsidies. Instead of men acting individually in these civic affairs (as was often the case before 1910), committees and organizations were established with regulations and officers to deal with everything from dredging a river and building a single bridge to providing grain relief in time of famine.[113] Even after the 1922 reestablishment of county self-government bodies, the new specialized organizations continued. They were not only evidence of the increasing functional specialization of organizations but also indicated efforts to routinize and regularize day-to-day civic activities. Although some elites continued to contribute large sums individually, the late imperial trend toward privately managed civic functions, as well as the idea of the generalist scope of action, was being overshadowed.[114]

Inner-Core Elite Associations, 1916-1924

In the wake of Yuan's demise in mid-1916, elites began a period of unprecedented organizational vigor. Although this period saw accelerated expansion of professional associations and the reestablishment of county self-government bodies, it is primarily notable for its explosion of voluntary organizations and meetings. The major impetus, as in 1907 and after the revolution, was nationalism. Following the May Fourth incident, merchant and student associations, patriotic societies, and all-interests' federations (*gejia lianhehui*) expressed the demands of various social groups.[115] As one crisis after another fell upon the nation in the 1920s, these organizations coalesced with professional association federations at large urban centers to produce an elite structure for nationalistic discussion and action.[116] Murders of Chinese students by Japanese in Fuzhou (1919) and Tianjin (1920); the infamously corrupt presidential election of Cao Kun (1923); the May Thirtieth episode (1925); and the Northern Expedition all prompted large meetings.

In addition, mass citizens' meetings (*guomin dahui*) were held during crises, reportedly attracting one to four thousand persons.[117] In the late Qing period, large local demonstrations for a specific purpose or goal usually occurred before the yamen.[118] Beginning in the late 1910s, the demonstration site was usually a modern school's athletic field.[119] In a symbolic spatial sense, public protest, nationalism, and the stress upon physical activity coalesced. More and larger athletic meets of primary and secondary schools at every level of the urban hierarchy were held in these years—one in May 1917, of Hangchow, Shaoxing, and Jiaxing middle schools, drew over two thousand participants.[120] These meets facilitated the formation of student linkages that were put to use in organizing nationalistic political demonstrations and rallies on these same athletic fields.[121]

In addition to primarily nationalistic organizations, this period saw three other important new organizational developments that will be detailed in Part Three. First, this era was marked by the formation of provincial political factions and coalitions. Second, major inner-core urban centers also saw the organization of branches of the new national Guomindang.[122] Third, organizations were formed that suggested the growing significance of the macroregional unit at a time of national political fragmentation. In 1920 northern Zhejiang and southwestern Jiangsu elites formed the Wu Society to discuss joint problems of the area.[123] In late 1922 both provinces' federations of county assemblies began joint meetings to discuss their potential roles in peacemaking and constitution adopting.[124] A Lake Tai Regional Self-Government Federation met for discussions in 1925.[125]

Earlier associational trends from the revolutionary era continued. Women's groups pressed for the expansion of female political roles, especially for the right to participate in the provincial constitutional process of the early 1920s.[126] Study societies to probe almost every conceivable topic formed in many counties.[127] In part they were stimulated by the

May Fourth ferment, which also spawned student organizations advocating social change, school self-governance, and military training.[128] Professional groups who had not yet organized began to do so: Hangchow police (1919), school teachers (1920), and middle school principals (1923).[129] In 1923 occupational federations for graduates of agriculture and forestry schools and for journalists were established.[130]

The inner core rapidly increased its contacts with the outside in these years. Well-known speakers like John Dewey and Rabindrinath Tagore spoke to student and study groups in large cities, and less-known speakers from Korea lectured in smaller cities on the death of that nation.[131] Inner-core elite organizations with foreign ties flourished. The YMCA in many cities and larger towns, the Red Cross with branches in some smaller towns, and the Ningpo branch of the International Famine Relief Commission are prime examples.[132] In sum, this veritable explosion of organizing and association suggests that inner-core elites as a whole were becoming more politicized, outward-looking, and conscious of specialized roles in a sociopolitical space that itself was becoming increasingly differentiated. Men and women joined associations to attain goals, to protest decisions, and for mutual edification.

Between 1924 and 1927, the increasing drive toward organization clashed with Sun's repressive policies. The more politically active organizations, including the Guomindang, were destroyed or strictly controlled, their leaders jailed and manhandled.[133] From mid-1927 the political-military regime of the Guomindang continued Sun's repression by trying to kill voluntary associationism, redirecting it instead to government-sponsored quasi-bureaucratic units. Professional and occupational associations were founded only with the government's promptings while the government viewed askance the formation of patriotic and study associations.[134] The days of completely voluntary associationism had passed.

6

Inner-Core Elites and Political Decision Making

One obvious way of assessing the goals of local elites is to study the political agenda that they set. Analyzing, in turn, various elite decision-making patterns in carrying out this agenda elucidates intraelite relationships, local power situations, and elite trends.[1]

The Magistrate and Local Elites

Because the management of local issues always included the county magistrate to some degree (if only in consultation), a survey of his role is essential for understanding the context and modes of decision making. The Qing magistrate had often been described as the parent-official (*fumu guan*) of the people, wielding an awesome amount of local power with his charge to oversee county order and tax collection.[2] The early Republican magistrate performed the same functions as his Qing predecessor except for his judicial roles in the years 1912–1914 and 1916–17 when county courts were in operation. Although general spheres of magisterial responsibility were the same throughout the province, the actual roles in relation to local elites differed from zone to zone.

In some inner-core counties following the 1911 revolution, the magistrate seemed subordinated to the county assemblies. The Yin assembly, for example, reportedly controlled the county magistrate; and the Jiaxing assembly successfully rejected an appointed magistrate.[3] Following Yuan Shikai's centralizing efforts in 1914, however, magistrates in all zones seem to have exceeded limitations in fiscal, judicial, and control functions. Inner-core elites continually railed against magistrates' misappropriating the taxes they levied or changing tax schedules for profit.[4] The complaints indicated that magistrates often spent minute amounts of the collected total for local measures and that tax monies found their way to the magistrates' own coffers.[5] The slaughter tax (*tuzaishui*), for example, was particularly abused by magistrates.[6] Judicial power returned to magistrates when local courts were abolished in 1914. Although courts were reestablished briefly in 1916 and 1917, magistrates in most counties retained chief judicial authority through 1927.[7] During these years, magistrates wielded this authority with a vengeance. Between 1914 and 1916 they decreed increasingly excessive punishments: Governor Lü Gongwang even had to forbid magistrates from ordering the death penalty on their own authority.[8] County elite accusations against magistrates stemmed from excessive and unfair penalties and the inevitable extortion in criminal and civil cases.[9]

Above all else, magistrates in the early Republic assumed police and control functions that surpassed their delegated authority. Under the new militia system established in 1914, the magistrates had the authority to direct units in times of crisis and to control the preparation of winter defense programs against bandit threats.[10] However, many magistrates went far beyond militia supervision. "Temporary police" units (*linshi jingcha*) of ten or more men, which had been established during the revolution in many counties, continued to exist under the magistrate's direction. In October 1916 Lü Gongwang abolished them; but funded by a special county tax, they were retained in most areas under different names. By late 1918 they had become the magistrates' private forces and a festering source of extortion. The provincial assembly voted to abolish them in late 1918, but there is no information on whether or to what degree this decision was carried out.[11] In the 1920s despite provincial orders to cease, magistrates also continued to add policemen to the mandated local force at their own discretion.[12]

Of all local levies (with the possible exception of the slaughter tax), the house tax (*fangzu*) levied for police elicited the greatest number of complaints. Elite perceptions of the importance of police for the protection of their interests, coupled with continuing evidence of police corruption and the rise of police occupational arrogance, caused great ambivalence toward police funding. When the Jiaxing magistrate announced increases in the house, tea, and wine taxes in mid-1923 to increase the number of police, county assembly and chambers of commerce wired protests to Hangchow.[13] When the decision was made simply to make the collection of the house tax more efficient rather than to increase it, elites continued to attack the plan as a mask for extracting as much as possible. The issue of police taxes erupted again later after a decision to upgrade the police office (*suo*) to a bureau (*ju*), a decision that increased police expenditures and consequently taxes.[14] The magistrate clearly controlled police issues; local elite organizations were at most advisory, and usually adversary.

The relationship between elite and magistrate was thus often antagonistic, but it was also symbiotic. Late Qing reformers viewed the close connection between local officials and "bad" gentry (*lieshen*) as a note-worthy feature of the local scene.[15] Magistrates worked closely with inner-core commercial and landed elites. Chambers of commerce were important fiscal allies. In Yin county, for example, the magistrate relied on the chamber to assist in funding the riverine police. In Shangyu, the magistrate, accused by gentry of misappropriation and maladministration, retained his post through his connections to important chamber elites.[16]

Despite the surfeit of local miscellaneous taxes, the primary levy in the Republic remained the land tax. Although it was forwarded to Hangchow and the national coffers, its surtaxes were used for local needs. The magistrate, therefore, had a great interest in assuring its scheduled collection from landlords, who did not remit their assessment unless their tenants paid the rents. Crop failures as well as high rents often made it impossible for tenants to pay in full. The lowering or suspension of taxes in the wake of natural disasters, which in turn theoretically relieved pressure on tenants, was fairly infrequent.[17] The result was that in many cases the magistrate and landed elite joined to compel rent payments.

Landlords in Shangyu in the last years of the Qing regime had collected no more than 70 or 80 percent of their stated rents. Following a summer typhoon in 1911, they established an agricultural affairs office (*nongye shiwu suo*) to compel the collection of 90 to 95 percent. The magistrate's refusal of relief to distressed tenants led to the burning of the yamen.[18] The landlords of the rich agricultural prefecture of Jiaxing had continual problems with renters and rent collection. Elites reportedly believed that the power of tenants had grown rapidly following the Taiping upheavals and that only a strong show of force could deal with recalcitrant tenants.[19] When Shimen county tenants banded together to seek official redress in the face of escalating rents in early 1911, the magistrate called for troops immediately.[20] Similar tenant actions marked the early years of Republic.[21]

The establishment of rent collection bureaus was a more common approach than summoning troops in dealing with this problem. Jiaxing and Pinghu county assemblies set up such bureaus to counteract a wave of tenant revolts in 1913. The Jiaxing assembly chairman also headed a federation of landlords (*tianye lianhehui*) to force rent payments at a time when the assembly was lowering taxes for property owners.[22] Although the provincial government closed the bureau several months later (as beyond the scope of county jurisdiction), it was reestablished by the magistrate and local elites in 1914, 1916, 1917, 1924, and 1926.[23] Attached to the county yamen and staffed by yamen employees, the bureau adopted various tactics: in 1913 rewards were offered for quick payment; in 1917 recalcitrant tenants were arrested. I have found only one account of a bureau affecting a large group of tenant households. A rent collection bureau was established in the intermediate market town of Wangjiangjing in January 1924 to deal with 1,046 tenant households in arrears. As a result of bureau action, 597 households paid 5,776 *yuan* by early August. In addition, 254 households had apparently been intimidated sufficiently to pay on their own. Thus, 81 percent of the tenant households behind in their rent payments had paid at least some additional money under direct or indirect bureau pressure.[24] During years when there was no formal bureau in an area, self-government deputies were sent to reason with recalcitrant tenants; in 1920, in Xincheng township (Jiaxing), this method fomented a riot.[25]

My research suggests that the inner-core magistrates were not as involved in "societal management" as the local elites. The magistrate's chief concerns were control of revenue and its collection and, later in the period, handling the problem of disorder. Instigation and direction of local projects in education, economic development, and social services were generally left to inner-core elites. Occasionally the magistrate initiated projects like school building or road construction as in Dinghai in 1912 and Zhenhai in 1913, respectively;[26] but in local development issues, the inner-core magistrate was often more of a consultant or underwriter of necessary funds, a role in sharp contrast to magisterial functions in other zones.

The Delineation of Subcounty Administrative Boundaries

The process of census taking and drawing boundaries between subcounty self-government districts was crucial to an area's elite and thus occasioned much dispute. The question of how much territory around a town or a county seat should be districted with the central urban area was an especially rancorous issue among inner-core elites.[27] The West Lake area of Hangchow (situated outside the city wall) balked at being incorporated into the city district, its elites arguing that Hangchow and West Lake interests differed and that its own interests could best be maintained by an autonomous district. It maintained its autonomy but at the cost of much ill feeling between both areas' elites.[28] The incorporation of contiguous townships into the town district of Shuanglin brought arguments and delay from township elites because the proposed districting disrupted the developed marketing pattern. In the end, Shuanglin elites prevailed.[29]

Detailed accounts of self-government districting in Shaoxing underscore various aspects of the process.[30] The city was divided into thirty-nine wards (*fang*), with each ward headquarters at a temple (*shemiao*), where such questions as relief and winter defense measures had previously been handled. Ward boundaries were not actually set; people could decide to which ward they belonged. The vague delimitations of intraurban boundaries were abandoned outside the city as elites (*shishen*) attempted to draw fixed boundaries, a process that stirred considerable animosity.[31] The sense of political boundaries in China had not been strong, and attempts to establish them at this time contravened some long-held orientations. For example, Tianyue, a densely populated township on the border between Shanyin and Xiaoshan counties, had traditionally been divided into three sections; but one section, even though a part of Shanyin, had always been controlled by Xiaoshan because of its topographical similarity (and probably marketing links).[32] Its incorporation under the self-government of Shanyin brought loud protests.

Marketing networks were the fundamental consideration in town and township districting. Because of marketing ties, a fishing village near the town of Anchang, although outside the rule-of-thumb distance (five or six *li*) for incorporation with a town, was included in the town district. On the other hand, when Anchang attempted to incorporate one village that was not economically oriented to the town (apparently for the purpose of controlling competition in a certain trade), the village elite refused. The dispute continued until the abolition of the self-government system in 1914. When the boundaries of Yangwang township were drawn, they included not only villages linked to the market of Yangwang but one village, Xiaoli, that belonged to the marketing system of Lufu township. Xiaoli had carried on a long-running dispute with other villages in Lufu township; and although Xiaoli was separated by hills from Yangwang, it asked to be part of the latter. The townships' elites engaged in a bitter dispute, with both claiming rights over the village. Lufu township, however, had marketing and topography on its side as well, and the county self-government office designated Xiaoli as part of Lufu.

Customs (*xiguan*) and elite preference were other considerations in Shaoxing's districting. For example, two small townships were formed from the same marketing system: despite topographical similarity and sparse population, their difference in customs led to separate districts. Another township contained villages whose market town was in another township because topography and similar customs tied them to the first. In yet another instance, a township that was basically a single marketing system included some extraneous villages. In some larger villages, elites called for and obtained separate townships for their villages, thus dividing marketing systems.

The self-government movement gave an area's elite the opportunity to make conscious choices about identifying its political and economic interests with a definite physical political space.[33] Choices were made to protect interests: preserving marketing or previous social orientation, preventing urban interests from encroaching on more rural areas, promoting the development of areas that shared common interests. In this sense, political boundaries were becoming more important in the inner core.

Roles of Local Self-Government Organs

The agenda of subcounty self-government before the 1911 revolution included traditional elite concerns: public works, charity, relief, public morals, and education. In late imperial society, these concerns were the sphere of individual gentry or nongentry elites; if ad hoc organizations were established to deal with specific problems, they were generally ephemeral. The government role was supportive, not primary. With the establishment of self-government bodies in 1910 and 1911, the control of these issues was taken from the private domain into the public sphere of government-established bodies, an important aspect of twentieth-century political development. In Shaoxing, for example, granaries for famine relief, operated in the Qing period through a land tax surcharge, had been managed by the Xu family of the city of Shaoxing. In 1911 the family turned over the responsibility to the city self-government council.[34] Similarly, the orphanage at the town of Qing (Tongxiang county), which had been established in the 1870s, was taken over by the township council in 1910.[35]

With traditional gentry roles increasingly transferred to the public sphere, the question of funding local conservancy, charitable, and defense projects became crucial. To provide in the public sphere what once had been provided by wealthy local elites, taxes were levied on various commodities—cigarettes, fish, meat, wine, bamboo, and tinfoil used in rituals—as well as on boats transporting the commodities to market.[36] This economically regressive taxation most affected nonelite consumers and merchants, whose protests often flared into violence: in Zhenhai and Jiashan in the early fall of 1911, schools and self-government offices were burned, and a Zhenhai township assistant was killed.[37]

The self-government organs saw themselves as upholders of traditional public morality in the new public sphere. The Jiaxing city council attempted to curtail the spread of prostitution and to halt what were called "lewd" practices at a nearby Buddhist convent.[38] Inner-core gentry and gentry-merchants seemed especially to see themselves as sustainers of the Confucian moral ethos through their support of education. The editor of the Ganpu (town) gazetteer (Haiyan county) contended that some elites supported education to counteract the effects of mercantile habits and customs from Shanghai that were pervading the area.[39] Prevailing beliefs that modern schools were a source of local development and a contribution to national strength also encouraged elite involvement in education.

After the 1911 revolution subcounty bodies concentrated much of their energy on modern developmental projects. With the exception of the metropolitan area of Hangchow where prerevolution councils and boards had set up streetlights and instituted street cleaning, late Qing subcounty organs did not undertake modern projects.[40] In 1912 and 1913, in contrast, these bodies began to establish electric light companies and telephone systems, modern clinics and pharmacies, loan agencies for aspiring apprentices and merchants, and educational institutions like newspaper reading offices to keep the interested abreast of political, social, and economic developments.[41] The councils of smaller urban centers, like Shuanglin, also became involved in instituting streetlights and a street-cleaning system.[42]

In Ningbo and Shaoxing, township postrevolution councils and managers began to assume control over difficult problems of conservancy, specifically flood control measures.[43] During the late Qing, in contrast, gentry-managers and lineages had directed these projects. To be sure, it was often the case that these same elites were now in township self-government organizations. But the framework was important, and the framework had changed; now self-government bodies were the legitimate parties in conservancy disputes. Angers flared in several counties when some local notables attempted to handle conservancy problems without going through the councils.[44] Township elites had quickly perceived government-legitimated councils as vehicles for realizing the interests of their locality. Traditional issues were becoming part of the public sphere as self-conscious elite politicization increased.

County assemblies, established in 1912, managed projects and deliberated over issues that involved more than one township and were thus beyond the purview of subcounty councils. There was, however, no clear-cut delineation between the roles of assemblies and the subcounty councils: both levied taxes, promoted education, and supervised public works, charity, and relief. Because the county assembly generally controlled the funds for the subcounty organs, numerous jurisdictional disputes erupted over fiscal matters. Clashes between assembly and city council over funding in Haiyan and Zhenhai counties are particularly notable.[45] In late 1913 Yin county and subcounty organs demanded that the civil governor rule specifically on the delimitation of their powers.[46] Evidence suggests that such political battles were a common feature of the inner core, indicating substantial awareness of the value and meaning of different political institutions.

There is no recorded evidence that either county or subcounty bodies expressed any nationalistic sentiment. When a Ningpo assemblyman proposed protesting Yuan Shikai's 1913 reconstruction loan, the assembly from this previously dynamic revolutionary center greeted his motion with silence, and the chairman suggested that it would be a grave move. When the same member raised the issue again, it died for lack of a second.[47] The only questions of national concern that attracted vigorous assembly discussion were the high rates of central government taxation on the counties.[48]

Self-government deputies from 1914 until assemblies were reestablished in 1922 were basically the magistrates' agents in investigating and advising on the wide spectrum of local issues that had previously concerned the assemblies.[49] Deputies served as the liaison between the local government and various elite organizations. The magistrate sometimes brought township deputies into joint session to discuss pressing county problems, forming a de facto county assembly.[50]

The roles of the second session county assemblies (1922 to 1927) differed in several ways from those of the first (1912 to 1914). The second assemblies coexisted with important specialized organizations—road, drainage, and sanitation committees, for example—that performed roles carried out by the first assemblies. As a result, in the 1920s the county assemblies and boards were primarily concerned with appropriating revenue rather than with managing specific programs.[51] This role obviously entailed their assent and implied some program supervision; in view of continual fiscal problems, the county board, in particular, exercised close control over local projects.[52]

Although educational concerns remained in the forefront of assembly action in both sessions, the specific issues varied. During the first session, the thrust was toward organizing and constructing modern schools, with the continual search for more funds plaguing all educational deliberations. Although expenses were still a major concern, the assembly's chief educational issue in the 1920s was control: keeping in check what were considered radical teachers and students; struggling with education bureaus and school boards for some measure of control over middle and normal schools; and stifling burgeoning school strikes precipitated by budget cuts.[53] The inner-core's obsession with the establishment of schools for modern national development had become in some counties a struggle to repress student protest and radical ideas.

County assembly and board nationalism of the 1920s provides an index of the growth of nationalism on the local level since the first assemblies, which had given little, if any, evidence of national concern. The second assemblies looked beyond the local scene to both province and nation, voicing repeated calls for a provincial constitution; calling for upholding the nation by resisting the fraudulent presidential election of

1923; and sending telegrams demanding prompt Chinese action in the face of the foreign aggression of the May Thirtieth incident.[54]

Local Expenditures and Political Priorities: The Case of Jiaxing

Governmental administrative processes and leadership attitudes about priorities can generally be surmised by analyzing the budgeting of public money. Budgetary information for the local governmental level in the early Republic is scarce, but I was able to find the Jiaxing county self-government budgets from 1918 and 1923 (see Table 12) and the county education budget for 1923.[55]

Table 12.
Jiaxing county self-government expenditures

Type of expenditure	1918		1923	
	Total in yuan	% of total	Total in yuan	% of total
Administration				
Salaries and operating costs	1,320	9.9	7,894	30.3
Census	2,314	17.5	a	—
Charity				
Orphanages	3,300	24.9	14,711	56.6
Poor children's home	1,000	7.5	2,188	8.4
Workhouse	960	7.2	(Abolished)	—
Burial	332	2.5	464	1.8
Relief grain	600	4.5	600	2.3
Education				
Subsidies; public lecture bureau	580	4.4	a	—
Agriculture				
Insect control	367	2.8	a	—
Cattle inoculation	155	1.2	150	.6
Public works				
Pavilion repair	1,000	7.6	a	—
Public wells	536	4.0	a	—
Other				
European war relief fund	800	6.0	—	—
Total	13,275	100.0	26,047	100.0
Annual surplus	7,061		2,140	

Source: *Shi Bao*, 1919/10/3 and 1923/11/21.
a. Not budgeted under self-government expenditures.

Self-government funds came primarily from a fixed 20 percent of the land tax surcharge; in addition, some counties levied new excise taxes or designated portions of existing excise taxes for self-government use.[56] Jiaxing's 1918 budget can be divided into five categories: administrative costs, charity and social welfare, auxiliary education expenses, agriculture, and public works. The 6 percent earmarked as the European war relief fund reflected the elites' willingness to appropriate local funds for nonlocal causes and the increasing cosmopolitanism of the inner core.

The largest percentage (46.6 percent) was devoted to charity and social welfare, including the county orphanage (*yuyingtang*) and poor children's home (*piner yuan*), the county workhouse (*pinmin xiyi suo*), relief grain, and burial expenses. Administrative costs of self-government, including deputies' salaries and the omnipresent early Republican census, took over one quarter of the total, with salaries and operating costs alone amounting to 9.9 percent. Public works (the repair of a famous pavilion and the digging of public wells) received 11.6 percent, followed by auxiliary education expenses (4.4 percent) and agriculture-related expenditures (3.9 percent).

Almost all of the county's education budget came not from self-government funds but from a set 40 percent of the land tax surcharge and a variety of local taxes: part of the house tax, a boat tax, and an amusement tax. In addition, some amounts were derived from rent on school-owned or former academy (*shuyuan*) lands. The education promotion office managed education funds. The first session assemblies had subsidized the education and agriculture associations, but by 1918 this fiscal connection was gone primarily because of lack of funds.[57] This ending of subsidies also suggests the tendency by the late 1910s for specific organizations to become separate from (and thereby narrow the initial scope of) self-government. This budgetary separation was made territorial in late 1923 when county education districts that had been congruent with self-government districts (*qu*) were differentiated in the establishment of discrete education districts (*xuequ*).[58]

Perhaps the most telling budgetary item is the small outlay for agriculture-related concerns. Jiaxing, one of the richest agricultural areas in China, was beset by continual conservancy and insect pest problems. Yet in 1918 the agriculture association, which theoretically should have overseen these concerns, was bankrupt. When it asked the magistrate for use of 20 percent of the self-government funds, he turned the matter over to the self-government deputies. The magistrate supported the deputies' decision that there were no extra funds to distribute (despite the more than 7,000 *yuan* budget surplus) and announced that the association should be self-supporting.[59] This episode reflects self-government disdain for the association's handling of agricultural matters. The deputies did allot 367 *yuan* for insect control, but this paltry sum provided little assistance given the severity of the problem; by 1923, even this meager amount was gone.

Between 1918 and 1923, the self-government budget almost doubled. The continuing inflation rate contributed to this huge increase to some degree,[60] but the startling budgetary growth far and away surpassed inflationary trends.

Sixty-nine percent of the 1923 budget went to charity and social welfare, with a small outlay for cattle vaccination being the only other non-administrative item. There were no provisions for education-related concerns, public works, or insect control (despite an even severer plague); and the county workhouse had been abolished. The local elites were supplying fewer services through self-government organs at a much higher cost to the county than before. Although assemblies and boards discussed many issues, the scope of their fiscal control was steadily shrinking, a trend in sharp contrast to the expansion of functional concerns among inner-core chambers of commerce during this period.

Even more remarkable was the portion of the budget designated for assembly and board administrative and operating costs: they amounted to over 30 percent of the total 1923 budget (compared to 9.9 percent in the 1918 budget). On the whole, the concurrent diminution of scope and the ballooning of expenditures suggests that local self-government in the 1920s became a much less positive exercise of elite power than in the first years of the Republic; increasingly these organs tended to exist for the profit of elites at the expense of those who bore self-government taxes. In September 1923 merchants in one township appealed to the magistrate to halt the collection of self-government excise taxes because self-government organs had simply stopped handling public concerns. The magistrate refused, saying that the tax, which had been collected for over a decade, was necessary. Letters of support for the magistrate's position came from assembly members who argued that if the tax were lost, self-government progress would deteriorate.[61]

The 1923 county education budget (41,523 *yuan*) was almost 60 percent larger than the total self-government budget (26,047 *yuan*). Management in education was much less wasteful than in self-government. In the former, only 8.2 percent of the budget was utilized in administration, whereas in the latter, 30.3 percent of the funds were so designated. The education outlays were for funding county schools, subsidies for township schools, scholarships, the Boy Scouts, and libraries. Whereas self-government operated in both 1918 and 1923 with a surplus, educational expenditures always seemed to outrun the income (in 1923 there was a deficit of almost 5,000 *yuan*).[62]

Issues and Modes of Decision Making

Inner-Core Natives Versus Outsiders

One of the seemingly intractable inner-core problems during the late Qing and early Republican periods was the animosity between natives (*bendi ren*) and outsiders (*keren*). Because of the strength of native place ties, relations between these two groups historically have been at best uneasy. Native elites jealously guarded what were perceived as native priorities, and established lineages provided much anti-immigrant leadership. Merchants by the nature of their trade were less condemnatory.

Following northern Zhejiang's near depopulation in the Taiping episode, immigrants flooded into the region from the overcrowded prefectures of Ningbo and Shaoxing and the poor agricultural counties of Taizhou and Wenzhou. Inevitably clashes of interest led to bloody fights and in 1883 to the slaughter of several hundred immigrants.[63] Subject to considerable discrimination, some immigrants at the dynasty's end engaged in banditry and opium cultivation to the dismay of native elites.[64] Continual eruptions of violence between natives and outsiders marked the early Republic.[65]

Many outsiders became economically powerful in the inner core, which no doubt fostered considerable native resentment. Immigrants reportedly controlled at least one third of the land in Jiaxing in 1912.[66] The county assembly's attempt to retaliate by levying an additional land tax surcharge per mu on immigrant-owned land led to bitter tax resistance.[67] Outsiders made many contributions to local economic developments. They funded the construction of bridges in the town of Wangdian (Jiaxing) and lighthouses in Dinghai.[68] The Ganpu gazetteer credits immigrants from Shaoxing with changing the local economy by introducing cotton and mountain yams, which flourished in the sandy soil, at a time when the Ganpu salt industry was in decline.[69]

Despite evidence that immigrants provided for public works improvements and played crucial roles in inner-core economic life, native elites persisted in holding to the stereotype adumbrated by Civil Governor Qu Yingguang in his 1915 reports: outsiders were lazy, shiftless, and untrustworthy.[70] Natives forbade immigrant participation in local governance and in militia organizations.[71] In some cases, native elites suppressed immigrant involvement in modern enterprises like electric and telephone companies. Despite the great need for linking the two major market areas in Jiaxing, local elites halted the mid-1914 efforts of outside merchants to initiate construction of a telephone company, preferring to wait until 1920 for its establishment by natives.[72] In 1921 in the town of Puyuan, an electric company established by outsiders floundered when natives showed little interest.[73] In short, outsiders in the inner core were often limited or controlled in their actions.[74]

In most inner-core counties, local elites were strong enough to resist outside control of local interests. In less developed counties, however, inner-core outsiders sometimes controlled a local economy. Ningboese control of many Wenchow businesses produced considerable antagonism. Ningbo managers and foremen arrived in 1913 to construct and supervise the Puhua Electric Light Company because the owners felt that "local men were not competent to manage the plant successfully." Incidents between Ningbo foremen and resentful native Wenchow workmen were commonplace.[75]

Issues of Conservancy

Water management issues were the most persistent and important of the inner core: obtaining sufficient drinking and irrigation water, insuring protection from flooded rivers and raging oceans, and securing the navigability of commercial lifelines. With the exception of the seawalls, whose mammoth construction required government support, individual elites traditionally handled these problems. They continued to play an important role in the early Republic, contributing funds and managing projects.[76]

After the 1911 revolution self-government organs emerged as important actors in water control issues. In conservancy work, the location of dikes was a critical matter: a dike built in one area might cut off an irrigation supply in another. The history of conservancy is thus marked by feuding and outright struggle. In Yin county, on the request of certain citizens, the self-government representatives of the city district and five townships organized in 1913 to repair an important dike; but one section (*du*) of a township objected to the plans. In an increasingly bitter exchange, the magistrate was compelled to send his deputies with the county assembly chairman to confer with the disputants.[77] The outcome was unclear, but the following aspects of the decision-making process revealed in this example are noteworthy: local initiation, the crucial role of subcounty self-government bodies, and the mediating role of magistrate and assembly chairman. At times, as in Zhenhai in October 1913, the magistrate initiated dike construction by calling together all township managers and councils, but in most cases, local elites launched conservancy projects.[78] The county assembly primarily fulfilled an appellate function in these issues, mediating and overseeing projects if subcounty bodies failed to handle the problem.

Reclamation projects often accompanied conservancy. Shaoxing prefecture with its numerous opportunities for reclamation was a target of individual wealthy elites; but, as in conservancy, self-government elites began to claim primacy of action on the basis of their government-established legitimacy. In the celebrated case of Lake Xiang in Xiaoshan

county, efforts of private entrepreneurs between 1903 and 1910 to develop the area were taken over by subcounty councils and managers in
1911.[79] Shortly before their abolition in 1914, township councils in Yuyao
county blocked the efforts of a powerful Shangyu county elite to manage
a reclamation project, contending that the project was within the
self-government purview. This case was complicated by the proposed de-
veloper's "outsider" status and the opposition of a powerful Yuyao native
in Shanghai who wanted to undertake the project himself.[80]

The trend for public institutions to initiate and manage water projects
advanced markedly in 1913 with the formation of the Northern Zhejiang
Conservancy Council (*Zhexi shuili yishihui*). Established by the provincial assembly with a stipulated tax base from silk, cocoon, and boat taxes,
the initial purpose of the organization was to oversee the dredging of the
canals of Jiaxing, Huzhou, and Hangzhou prefectures. These canals had
become almost impassable and could not be of optimal use in irrigation
because of silt and waterweeds.[81] Subordinate to the assembly and civil
governor and composed primarily of provincial assemblymen, the council decided which conservancy projects to fund and allotted monies for
each through an engineering office (*gongcheng shiwu suo*).[82] Its success in
overseeing many local projects encouraged inner-core elites from south of
the Qiantang estuary in Shaoxing and Ningbo prefectures to form their
own council (*Zhedong shuili yishihui*).[83] The councils' attempts to deal
with conservancy problems in an entire region helped broaden local concerns beyond the native place: canal systems north of Hangchow Bay
were seen as intricately related not only to each other but also to West
Lake at Hangchow and Lake Tai; rivers in Shaoxing were viewed as part
of the Sanjiang system.

In the 1920s the Northern Conservancy Council became less concerned
with designating projects and more involved in administering funds. Designation, surveying, and supervision of projects fell to a conservancy
committee (*shuili weiyuan hui*) composed mostly of engineers.[84] The parent council, like county assemblies, became more concerned with process
than substance, was torn by factions, and provided fewer services. Told
by the council that there were no more funds for dredging, Nanxun gentry in 1920 threatened to take the conservancy surtaxes they collected and
use the money for themselves, arguing that they saw no results from the
taxes sent to the council.[85]

The control of conservancy and reclamation in the first three decades
of the twentieth century moved from private gentry/gentry-merchant, to
self-government organs, to specific conservancy organizations, and finally to specialized committees composed of engineers and trained specialists. The next step of control, as illustrated in the Lake Xiang project
(even before the Guomindang takeover), was direct management by the

government bureaucracy.[86] Increased specialization, marked institution-alization in local affairs, and increased government involvement in local problems emerged as significant patterns in water management.

Charity and Social Welfare

Despite similarities to trends in conservancy, such as the early importance of subcounty self-government organs, the management of local welfare projects differed in significant ways. Generalist institutions remained important. County self-government organs in the late 1910s and 1920s generally retained budgetary controls over charitable projects. When charity boards were established, as in Hang county, they supervised the entire range of social services. In both boards and self-government bodies, elite disagreements over specific use of large sums of money led to prolonged struggles.[87] Chambers of commerce also played an important role in charitable relief. They and their member merchants were expected to contribute money for charity; merchants were repeatedly enlisted to sell grain at cost and to participate in rice distribution at times of famine.[88]

The government intervened in social welfare matters much more rapidly than in conservancy, ordering the establishment of county work-houses in 1913 and of charity bureaus (*yinli ju*) in 1915.[89] A closer look at county workhouses reveals the configuration of elite roles and policy in this area. The workhouses were designed to take paupers and vagrants off the streets and teach them a craft. Regulations called for a workhouse in each county seat and township, to be managed by the magistrate and county assembly, with a local leader designated head (*zhang*). Invariably one of the community's key elites, the appointed head met with self-government deputies to discuss local matters. Elite involvement with these houses was motivated not so much by humanitarianism as by the desire to keep the starving poor out of sight.[90] By 1924, in Hangchow, the workhouse—as a sign of the times—was headed by the military police.[91]

From the beginning, inner-core counties complained of insufficient funds for workhouses.[92] Workhouse residents could remain for twenty-two months if they so desired. Of the manufactured products' sales, 60 percent were for public use; the remainder could be retained by residents to start their own businesses.[93] With the severe money shortage of the 1920s, county assemblies one by one abolished or sharply curtailed the houses' functions. A detailed Jiaxing assembly investigation in 1923 reported that though twenty-eight apprentices were registered, there were actually only eighteen men on the premises and at most twelve or thirteen of these were apprentices. Of the latter, only six were weaving and three or four working with rattan; the rest were doing nothing. In light of this report and because Jiaxing's paper mills supplied "alternative work," the assembly abolished the institution.[94]

Despite the involvement of the government and other local institutions in charity efforts, social welfare services continued to depend largely on voluntary contributions. Native place associations frequently provided aid not only to their members but also to their local communities.[95] Voluntary associations like the Ningpo branch of the International Famine Relief Commission contributed mightily.[96] Large amounts also came from theatrical productions staged for general charity and at times of specific disasters.[97] Welfare management remained a hybrid of traditional and modern approaches. Perhaps the very broad, generalist nature of charitable undertakings precluded the specialization evident in other areas of local concern. The government intervention indicated the necessity of prodding local elites to fulfill traditional functions in the midst of new situations.

The Battle against Insect Pests

Beginning in the last years of the Qing dynasty, rice crops in Jiaxing and Hangzhou prefectures began to be attacked by an extraordinarily destructive pest, the rice borer. Severe infestation began in 1923 with losses for six counties (Jiaxing, Jiashan, Pinghu, Haiyan, Haining, and Hang) estimated at 40 percent of the crop.[98] Within two years, the borer spread to Shaoxing, Ningbo, Wenzhou, and Taizhou. Because of the plague's severity in Jiaxing prefecture, government and local elites there made major efforts to curb it.

In the late 1910s self-government deputies had allotted paltry sums in a largely ineffectual effort to educate farmers in pest control. In early 1924 on the advice of a Hangchow-appointed commission of specialists from the provincial agricultural school, the Zhejiang Entomological Bureau was formed at Jiaxing. It performed both scientific and educational services: investigating crop damage and prescribing methods of destroying the pest; and delivering lectures, publishing and distributing leaflets, and exhibiting insect specimens in different stages of growth.[99]

Concurrently, Jiaxing elites initiated an association devoted to combatting the rice borer (*chuming hui*). Notably, elites did not try to utilize the county agriculture association, which had become impotent by 1918. Nor did the county assembly become the leader of the anti-insect campaign—although the assembly did vote to spend over ten thousand *yuan* for the cause in 1924. Rather, the association was an ad hoc organization initiated by the nationally known Jiaxing elite Chu Fucheng. Chu headed preparations for the establishment of a permanent bureau (to be open daily and manned by one or two members) and an association, which would meet periodically and whose primary function was educative. He invited thirty-four elites representing all of the county's self-government districts to join and appointed a head of research and publicists to spread the antiborer message.[100] Local elites, students, teachers, and officials were all mobilized in the fight. The campaign was a mixture of local elite initiative and government-supported specialists' efforts. Both depended on popularizing the problem through various kinds of publicity and on mobilizing the energies of the area's populace.

The campaign utilized two primary methods to destroy the pest—collecting the eggs before they hatched, and attracting moths with lamps and killing them at night. In 1924 the Haiyan government issued twenty thousand lamps, one for every ten mu of land, to the county's farmers. In 1926 the Jiaxing government issued fifty thousand lamps. One or two men from each village directed the placement of the lamps over wooden tubs of oil and water into which the moths would fall; volunteers verified the correct use of the lamps on nightly inspections. In 1926, when Jiaxing self-government funds were sharply curtailed, the county government funded the extensive effort with an additional land tax surcharge. Farmers were given rewards—medals, letters of commendation from the magistrate, and presents of meat, wine, and money—for turning in either unhatched eggs or dead moths.[101] The methods reportedly were successful in mitigating the effect of the borers.

In place of established institutions, specialists and ad hoc organizations provided much leadership in this crisis. The mammoth effort depended not only on government support but also on the voluntary participation of the local populace and almost certainly required voluntary contributions. Like conservancy and some charitable efforts, the antiborer campaign reflected the trend toward functional specialization and differentiation and the tendency for the public sphere to supplant the private in the management of local issues.

7

Outer-Core Political and Elite Structures

Students from outer-core counties who studied in inner-core schools often returned to reform their native communities. A Fenghua county student, returning for a visit in 1922, was appalled to find that people in his native township believed that the emergence of the rightful Son of Heaven would solve local and national problems. Assuming a relationship between economic and political development, he suggested that such political ignorance could be overcome through better means of communication and transportation.[1] A returning Jinhua graduate, in contrast, promoted direct political development in his native place by establishing in 1923 his own village self-government system (*cun zizhi zhi*) with two deliberative bodies.[2] Whatever the means, outside-trained modernizers and inner-core developers looked upon the outer core as an area for development.

Elite Career Patterns and Trends

The Lure of the Inner Core

The absence of late Qing subcounty self-government data for outer-core elites precludes a definitive analysis at that level and for that period.[3] Examples suggest that in the late Qing period the outer core, like the inner, experienced the return of some reform-minded officials and students who were determined to build a nation on the foundation of locality.[4] Less like inner-core patterns was the greater tendency for returnees to remain in or retain close contact with their native places in the first years of the Republic. Elites in the outer core probably had fewer qualifications and sociopolitical attributes than inner-core elites and were therefore unable or unwilling to compete in more developed areas. Whatever the explanation, there are many examples of returnees who chose to remain.[5]

The lure of the inner core for especially well-qualified and ambitious outer-core elites remained strong, however. Men like Jiang Ruiqi, chairman of the first Jinhua County Assembly, were drawn to the inner core: Jiang became head of the Hang county workhouse in 1914.[6] In particular, large numbers of modern-trained students spent their careers outside their home areas. A 1922 listing of Fenghua county graduates of the Fourth Provincial Normal School at Ningpo from 1915 to 1922 provides evidence for this trend.[7] Of seventy-eight graduates, only twelve (15.4 percent) remained in their native county whereas fully 78.2 percent (sixty-one) took positions outside. Of those who left Fenghua, 90.2 percent (fifty-five) remained in inner-core counties (Yin, Zhenhai, and Ciqi) of their native prefecture of Ningbo; four (6.6 percent) went to Shanghai and one each, to Hankou and Beijing. Because the eleven provincial normal schools (except for the First Provincial Normal School, at Hangchow) were less prestigious than provincial middle and professional schools, it is probable that graduates of the latter enjoyed even more mobility out of their home areas than did normal-school graduates.

Elite Patterns in the Late 1910s and 1920s

Although there were notable changes among inner-core elites immediately following the 1911 revolution, self-government statistics suggest that marked changes among elites in the outer core did not come until the late 1910s and 1920s. Besides the decline in degree-holders, there were striking differences between the composition of the first assembly and that of the second in the outer core: the percentage of modern-school graduates leaped from 8.5 to 28.6 percent; those with experience beyond their home communities jumped from 5.7 to 28.6 percent (some of these were older official types returning home); those whose only identification was as a member of an elite kin group dropped from 20 to 14.3 percent; and although the cases are few, only 10.7 percent of the first assembly members or their families served in the second assembly, in contrast to 38.5 percent in the inner core. The accuracy of this small degree of continuity is buttressed by similar figures from the peripheries. If the 1911 revolution had less immediate impact on outer-core elites, it can be argued that the changed political circumstances it fostered made possible the outer-core elite shifts later in the decade.

In the early 1920s modern-trained specialists and some influential official elites returned to remake their localities. Some graduates became local specialists, like Beida agriculture student Yu Linsen who established an experimental farm in his native county of Tonglu, or the Qu county graduate of a forestry school who supervised (and in his ignorance ruined) his county's model forestry station.[8] Others returned to more generalist roles, including participation in self-government. Returning officials usually assumed self-government roles and more generalized leadership functions. Lu Zhongyue of Zhuji, for example, returned from his service as magistrate and national assemblyman to become a county assembly member, the head of a county road association, and (as some 1920s inner-core returnees) a member of the provincial constitutional assembly.[9] Zhuang Jingzhong of Fenghua—businessman, bureaucrat, provincial assemblyman, and educator—returned to head relief efforts, to serve as chairman of the county assembly, and also to be elected to the constitutional assembly.[10]

The seventeen-man Fenghua County Assembly provides an example of the mix of modern graduates and returning officials in the 1920s outer core.[11] As groups, officials and graduates each made up 47.1 percent of the assembly. Only 11.8 percent (two) had served in the first assembly. This small carry-over underscores the aforementioned low degree of continuity between the two assemblies. The ages of the assemblymen ranged from 26 to 62 with the average being 42.8 and the median, 42. Half of the assembly members were born before 1880 (the range being from 1860 to 1878) and half after 1880 (the range being from 1886 to 1896). Recalling Andrew Nathan's contention about the differences between the cohorts of the 1860s and the 1870s and those of the 1880s and 1890s, one can interpret at least this county assembly as a forum of men with two distinct historical life experiences. In addition, their social background and career experiences differed sharply. Five of the eight graduates were from the younger cohorts while all of the degree-holders were above the median age. Of the eight former officials, only two were younger than the median age. Although there is no record of assembly deliberations that might indicate relationships among assemblymen, this assembly and probably others of the outer zones tended to represent more a meeting of generations than did inner-core assemblies; fewer older elites seemed to serve in self-government leadership positions in the inner core. Counties in the outer zones, undergoing incipient developmental change, tended to develop more elite factions and cliques based on degree of receptivity to change than did the inner core.[12]

In these less developed zones, merchants as a distinct, politically involved group were less notable than in the inner core. Qu county's early modernizing developments in agriculture, education, and self-government as well as the later establishment of modern industry were led by a talented group of gentry and gentry-merchants.[13] Similarly, in Zhuji county it was not the merchants, as in the inner core, who supplied the leadership for electric light companies in the county seat and in the major market town of Fengqiao, but gentry and gentry-merchants.[14] In Jinhua, gentry-merchants pooled their capital in early 1920 to establish an automobile firm.[15]

Modern-Trained Elites and Their Occupations

Law and Journalism. Of the newly important professions that played significant roles in the Republican inner core—law, journalism, police, and military—the roles of the first two were greatly diminished in the outer core whereas those of the last two reflected the same inner-core pattern. The only lawyers' association of the outer core was located in Jinhua, the only place outside of the inner core where a court functioned in the early 1920s.[16] Traditional legal methods held sway in outer-core counties like Zhuji, where it was reported in 1925 that there were some two hundred old-style pettifoggers and only seven new-style lawyers.[17]

Journalists also played a lesser role in the outer core. Jinhua county in the Qiantang basin had seen the establishment of a reformist newspaper, the *Xin Bao,* which ran briefly in 1904. But after its collapse, there were no newspapers until the publication of the *New Jinhua Weekly* (*Xin Jinhua xunkan*) in 1918.[18] Local authorities quashed the 1913 effort of the Lanqi education association to publish a newspaper, contending that its title, which included the characters for Chinese Republic (*Zhonghua minguo gonghe*), was too inflammatory.[19] In the main, outer-core counties waited until the May Fourth period to experience the rise of modern journalism—some ten to twenty years later than in the inner core. A Lanqi daily published one small sheet beginning in 1918 or 1919, but it lasted only six months.[20] A Zhuji newspaper, the *Zhuji Peoples' News* (*minbao*), began publishing in September 1919. The voice of liberal students condemning the ways of established county elites, it was opposed in 1921 and 1922 by a county elite newspaper, the *Yiwu ribao.*[21] Only after the success of the Guomindang in 1927 did other counties of the outer core, such as Fuyang, Yuhang, and Pingyang, establish newspapers, which served then primarily as party organs.[22] The slow modernization of the legal profession and the retarded development of modern journalism helped to perpetuate a more traditional outlook in the outer core.

Control-Related Occupations. In contrast, police touched the lives of outer-core citizens as closely as in the inner core. The problems of insufficient funding, police corruption, and insufficient manpower at times of crisis appeared continually in outer-core counties.[23] The 1923 county budget of Zhuji reveals that the police budget made up more than one third (33.8 percent) of the total, only slightly less than the greatest outlay for education (35.4 percent)—an indication of the importance attached to police functions.[24]

In the 1920s the police and judicial officials of the late Qing period were nostalgically viewed as having been positive forces on the local political scene. There may have been some truth in this, for police officials in the last years of the Qing dynasty were generally drawn from influential local elites who, like the 1910 Zhuji police chief renowned for flood relief work, were of the traditional gentry mold.[25] By the 1920s some unscrupulous *shengyuan* and *jiansheng* made careers serving as police officials in one county after another.[26] Commentators on the Zhuji situation noted that many became police assistants (*jingzuo*), who were notoriously corrupt; that many had no previous experience (graduates of modern police schools tended to gravitate to the inner core); and that they linked themselves to unscrupulous gentry in a pattern reminiscent of the hated yamen employees of an earlier day.[27]

In such an environment, lower-level judicial functionaries also tended to proliferate. A magistrate's legal maximum number of judicial assistants (*chengfa li*) and judicial police (*sifa jingcha*) was six and eight, respectively. Records indicate that by 1921 and 1922, Zhuji's magistrate had twenty-four assistants and thirty-four police. This rapid proliferation of yamen functionaries was a result in part of the surge of litigation precipitated by pettifoggers. Civil and penal cases settled in the county ranged from just over four per day in early 1920 to over twenty-three per day in mid-1923.[28] Whether other zones had similar police expenditures and expansion of control-related subbureaucratic functionaries cannot be determined because of a lack of sources. Protests from all zones over police proliferation, corruption, and expense, however, indicate that the situation was probably similar elsewhere.

Just as in the inner core, the military per se did not generally play a continuous role in local political affairs until 1924. When crisis threatened, troops were dispatched and stationed at the key cities, Lanqi and Qu, on the Qiantang River.[29] Inner-core garrisons dispatched military companies to assist local militia units in handling disturbances in notoriously unstable counties like Zhuji, Cheng, and Xinchang.[30] Only after Sun Chuanfang's seizure of the province in late 1924 did the military become more extensively involved in daily affairs. Military headquarters, for example, were set up in late 1924 at the economically influential Jiangxi Guild in Lanqi.[31] Military exactions and extortion from 1924 to 1927 became a way of life, affecting outer-core economics and livelihood.[32]

In sum, although the outer core failed to experience some of the modernizing aspects of the inner core, it shared in full the problems of the 1920s—first the expansion of the police and, by the middle of the decade, the continuous military presence.

Voluntary Associations

Outer-core organizational development also lagged behind that of the inner core. The barometer of commercial activity, the chamber of commerce was established in outer-core counties on average more than a year after inner-core chambers. Although government-ordered education and agriculture associations were founded about the same time as in the inner core, in most outer-core counties, prerevolution organizing was limited to self-government organs and professional associations. Following the revolution, the associative movement became more evident in the outer core. Fenghua elites founded some small political parties in 1912 and organized meetings to discuss local issues.[33]

It was not, however, until the May Fourth period that outer-core elites experienced the explosion of voluntary associations that their counterparts had in the inner core. Study societies such as the Jinhua County Industrial Study Society blended an interest in science and economic development.[34] Many counties had political and education study societies, among them, Zhuji's Qingshan Club and Yu Society; Xiangshan's 1923 Club; and Fenghua's Yan Society.[35] In this period, as in some inner-core counties, township elites formed agriculture and education associations.[36] Fenghua elites set up conservancy bureaus for individual townships and the county as a whole.[37]

By the 1920s three other types of associationism had become common in the outer core: athletic meets, alumni associations, and occupational organizations. The first two provide another index of the time gap between inner and outer core. The first all-county athletic meets in the outer core were held in late 1919, some nine years after their institution in the inner core. Inner-core counties had generally established athletic fields by the mid-1910s, but in the outer core even relatively developed Qu county did not have one until 1926. Inner-core alumni associations were formed by 1913, whereas Zhuji's earliest was established in 1924. Evident in Zhuji's particularly rich record of organizations was the formation of county-wide occupational federations (for example, teachers, ironworkers, and shopkeepers) and education associations.[38] Such umbrella organizations indicated the development of a wider degree of territorial association among certain groups.

County Politics and Political Structure

The Roles of Self-Government Organs

In the few years of their existence (1910–1914), outer-core subcounty self-government bodies emerged as locally recognized, legitimate political and economic actors. For example, although the construction of a bridge in Xiangshan county was of great importance for communications, the township council lacked sufficient funds to build it. After a member of the local gentry, who attempted to raise the money by subscription, began to build the stone bridge, township people (*xiangmin*) forcefully opposed the project because it was not directed by the council.[39] The considerable legitimacy accorded the council in township affairs indicates the extent of the acceptance of new political institutions and the transfer of previous concerns of private responsibility into the public sphere. The Zhuji modern-style gazetteer, in a similar vein, relates how a medical clinic, privately established in 1902, was taken over by the county seat council in 1910.[40] Subcounty bodies initiated and managed some modern changes. Zhuji's thirteen township councils founded a federation to supervise the spending of a newly levied educational tax.[41] After the revolution some of these councils established small model factories, paralleling the interest in economic development seen in postrevolution inner-core subcounty self-government.[42]

Evidence suggests that, despite some rather expansive reports of the range of issues and local import of the first and second county assemblies, these bodies in the outer core realized little of the institutional power of inner-core assemblies.[43] Their institutionalization was weaker partly because they allocated far less of their financial resources for actual public projects and more for salaries of assemblymen and other administrative expenses. While administrative expenses took 30.3 percent of the total 1923 self-government budget in Jiaxing, in Fenghua these expenses took 68.3 percent and in Zhuji, 72.3 percent of the self-government budget. The huge percentage allotted to administration lends credence to the claim of the editors of the *Zhuji gaiguan* that the self-government organs were institutions of local elite aggrandizement.[44] Although it may have meant considerable self-enrichment for the assembly elite,

Table 13.
Outer-core county expenditures

Expenditure	Zhuji (1923)		Fenghua (1922)	
	Yuan	% of Total	Yuan	% of Total
Self-government	10,428	19.6	6,853	24.0
Education	18,872	35.4	11,986	42.0
Public works, miscellaneous	6,008	11.3	2,250	7.9
Charity	—	—	7,474	26.2
Police	18,016	33.8	—	
Total	53,324		28,563	

Sources: *Xin Fenghua*, "diaocha," pp. 1–29; *Zhuji gaiguan*, "Zhuji gaiguan," pp. 75–79 and 135–140.

this budgetary decision resulted in the assembly's having less *institutional* scope and power when it dealt with the wide range of local issues that required funding. More important, the growth of institutional assembly power was curtailed by the power of the magistrate and the county bureaucracy on the local political scene. The editors of the *Zhuji gaiguan* downplayed the role of the assembly, arguing that the magistrate made key decisions after informal conversations with those elites whom he invited into his inner circle as advisers—a perpetuation of late Qing practices.[45] The magistrate controlled the budgets for public works, charity, and education, in contrast to the inner core, where self-government and professional associations often controlled or contributed to funding for some of these concerns.

The Magistrate and Local Elites

In the less developed zones, the magistrate played a greater role in initiating local projects than local elites;[46] and magistrates in outer zones took a greater role in issues of societal management than their counterparts in the inner core. For example, in 1898 the magistrate in Qu county established an agricultural affairs bureau to advance sericulture in the southern townships. This short-lived institution was followed by the 1902 establishment of an agriculture society (*nongwu hui*). By 1908, under the magistrate's direction, this society had taken over the investigation and direction of irrigation projects in order to uplift the area's agriculture.[47] In Zhuji county in the early 1920s, the magistrate initiated the county road association and called together wealthy gentry to organize relief programs and defensive measures.[48]

A particularly detailed case study of bridge building in Luoqing county reveals considerable local elite initiative but substantially more official control than was often apparent in the inner core.[49] A citizen (*gongmin*) named Zheng, concerned about a dangerously decrepit wooden bridge between Luoqing and Yongjia counties, called together gentry (*shenshi*) from both counties at the end of 1918. The convocation decided to build both a new bridge and a dike, chose Zheng to head the project, and set up another meeting to plan financing. The second meeting debated three ways to finance the construction: a land surtax paid in kind, a cash surtax, and subscriptions from rich households and merchants. When elites opposed the tax solutions, Zheng appealed to the circuit intendant, who directed the magistrates of both counties to take over the projects. This action probably led to the increased taxation opposed by the elites.

At times elites sought the magistrate to arbitrate in stalemates in local decision making. In a 1913 dike-building case in a Fenghua township, a citizen persuaded the gentry and elders (*shenqi*) of several dozen villages to discuss means of financing the project. Some agreed to a proposed land tax surcharge; others did not. Computation showed that the project could not be built with only the amount levied on those who agreed. The instigator then asked the magistrate to reduce the land tax on farmers who agreed, but not on others. The magistrate reportedly consented.[50] In short, whether the magistrate initiated an action, stepped in on his own accord, or was brought in by the elites themselves, he usually played a more crucial role in outer-core decision making than in the inner core.

Local elites in the core zones had increasingly gained more autonomy from bureaucratic control since the early nineteenth century. By the late Qing period and the first years of the Republic, inner-core elites had come to the fore, initiating and leading many public functions. The editors of the *Zhuji gaiguan* contended that by the last years of the monarchy, the powers of outer-core local elites and magistrate were balanced.[51] Certainly the relationships often were not friendly. Magistrates sometimes found organized assembly elites obstreperous. Elite disgruntlement with the magistrate led to many impeachments: of fifty-two recorded formal impeachments from 1911 to 1927, the two core zones produced thirty-four (eighteen in the inner and sixteen in the outer), over 63 percent of the total.[52] Relationships between magistrates and the local populace were not improved by the magistrates' short tenures: it was reported in Zhuji that magistrates in the 1920s, well aware that they might be shuffled to another post, attempted in almost commercial fashion to capitalize on their position for financial gain.[53]

County Budgets as an Index of Differentiation

The extant budgets for Fenghua (1922) and Zhuji (1923) and for the inner-core county of Jiaxing (1923) point to differences not only between but also within zones. The most detailed categories for comparing inner- and outer-core county expenditures are self-government and education. The budget for these two items was more than twice as large in Jiaxing (67,570 *yuan*) as in the outer core (Zhuji, 29,300 *yuan* and Fenghua, 18,839 *yuan*). Per every ten thousand inhabitants, the sums amounted to 1,602 *yuan* in Jiaxing, 555 *yuan* in Zhuji, and 846 *yuan* in Fenghua.[54] Because the budgets of Fenghua and Zhuji each provide different information, an item-by-item comparison is impossible. (See Table 13.)

Not included formally in Zhuji's budget were charitable expenditures, an absence that may be suggestive of Zhuji's degree of development. In Jiaxing, in contrast, charity was included in the self-government budget; in Fenghua, it was a county government expense. This budgetary differentiation suggests that both Jiaxing and Fenghua had largely transposed the previously private concerns of orphanages and relief into the public sphere. In Zhuji, on the other hand, orphanages and relief were still primarily the responsibility of the private domain. Through computation of the private orphanage expenditures scattered throughout other sections of the Zhuji gazetteer, it is apparent (if the figures are complete) that far fewer monies were spent for orphanages in that county (12.9 percent of total expenditures) than in Fenghua (26.2 percent).[55] Zhuji, perhaps more than other core counties, had to devote an inordinate sum for police. Such budgetary differences between the two counties underscore Qu Yingguang's 1915 report that Fenghua was a rapidly developing prosperous county marked by cooperation between official and gentry, whereas Zhuji was an unstable county plagued by natural disasters and litigation.[56]

The Outer Core and Other Zones and Spheres

Relations with the Inner Core

Qu Yingguang concluded in his 1915 reports that twelve of the fourteen outer-core counties he investigated were making rapid strides toward or on the brink of development. Qu included in his definition of development better transportation facilities (new shipping routes and better boats), the establishment of model sericulture and agriculture stations, plans for modern industry, flourishing trade, and school construction. In most cases he attributed these advances to joint official-gentry (*guanshen*) action.[57] In general, however, the instigators of outer-core economic and political development came from the inner core and beyond the province. For powerful inner-core private entrepreneurs and the provincial government, the outer zones offered opportunities both for investment and for building the nation into a strong base from which to compete with foreign nations.

Inner-core counties, with the exception of Yongjia (Wenchow), had few mineral resources besides salt, small deposits of coal, and nonmetallic sedimentary deposits of limestone and clay. The mountainous outer zones had substantial ore deposits—iron, copper, zinc, silver, manganese, tin, molybdenum, cobalt, and antimony—as well as nonmetallic deposits of coal, alum, and fluorite.[58] The outer zones became targets for inner-core development of these resources. The hills of Zhuji, for example, contained large quantities of coal, zinc, and silver. In the late Qing dynasty, Hangchow and Shanghai entrepreneurs brought British and German mining engineers to inspect the mining areas, but the mining of coal and silver failed because of inadequate transportation routes and lack of capital.[59] Similarly, in Qu county, Hangchow and Shaoxing merchants attempted but failed to develop coal mines in the 1880s.[60] In the early Republic, mining entrepreneurs generally seemed to be headquartered in the inner core. From scattered information, I have compiled a list of eighteen mining entrepreneurs with coal, silver, and fluorspar interests in the outer zones. Of these, eleven (over 60 percent) came from inner-core county bases, especially Hang, Yin, and Dinghai; some of the remainder may also have been from the inner core but their residential bases cannot be determined.[61] Because of the huge outlays of capital and the risks involved, mining attracted only very wealthy businessmen.

The provincial government from the first months of the Republic played a key role in encouraging interested businessmen to develop these resources. In May 1912 the Hangchow government rejected efforts of Tonglu and Jiande merchants to open a silver mine on the premise that the plan did not fit in with the larger scheme of provincial development.[62] Provincial government elites jealously guarded their own opportunities vis-à-vis the outer zones. Early in 1913 the government established a provincial mining bureau that began to encourage inner-core entrepreneurs to set their sights on the former prefectures of Quzhou, Yanzhou, and Jinhua—all composed of counties located only in the three outer zones.[63] The Ouhai circuit intendant in 1918 advertised the iron deposits of outer-zone counties to Shanghai and Hangchow entrepreneurs, beckoning them to develop the mineral resources.[64] In early 1920 Zhejiang's industrial commissioner made the same area a target for mining and forestry development.[65] My impression on the basis of sketchy evidence is that not until the mid-1920s did local outer-core merchants—like Ye Zhengrong of Qu and Tang Ermin of Zhuji—begin to develop local mineral resources on a larger scale.[66]

The provincial government encouraged not only extractive industry in the three outer zones, but by 1917 it also pressed for industrial manufacturing, particularly in key centers like Jinhua and Lanqi, the stated goal being the preservation of Chinese sovereignty.[67] Beginning in 1915 with Qu Yingguang's recommendations, it frequently proposed model sericulture, agriculture, and forestry farms.[68] Government action to foster industrial and agricultural development in the outer zones was the harbinger of more complex rural projects in the late 1920s and 1930s. The government policy encouraged the return of fervent student reformers such as the aforementioned Tonglu and Qu county graduates who established experimental farms.

Although local gentry and gentry-merchants initiated and funded some industrial and agricultural projects, outsiders also participated in these developments.[69] The prosperous Anji-Changxing Timber Company was directed by two nonnatives, one of whom was a national assembly member and the other, Zhejiang's industrial commissioner.[70] Anhui merchants, probably from Huizhou, came to Lanqi annually to gather and oversee the preparation of candied dates (*zao*) for export. Setting up temporary facilities at local temples or halls, they bought dates from county farmers and distributed them to poor women in the county seat for preparation. These outsiders controlled preparation, prices, and marketing; local merchants did not participate.[71]

Sometimes inner-core elites paternalistically directed outer-zone affairs: in 1918 an entrepreneur from Linhai proposed the establishment of and regulations for model experimental sugar farms in three counties of the outer zones.[72] At times outside investors became local leaders in outer-core counties. Zhuang Jingzhong, sometime adviser to Zhejiang's military governor and head of the Zhejiang finance ministry, operated a lumber company in Yuhang county; after several years he became chairman of the county's agriculture association, even though he was a native of Fenghua.[73] Nonnative merchants in Qu worked with local gentry-merchants in public works projects, were instrumental in local merchant associations, and were often included in political discussions. They did not, however, become directly involved in self-government bodies or professional associations other than chambers of commerce.[74]

But what was seen by inner-core elites as development was sometimes interpreted by elites in the outer zones as subjugation and exploitation. The editors of *Zhuji gaiguan* railed against Shaoxing (inner core) outsiders who managed and were apprenticed in most of the shops in Zhuji's county seat. They asserted that Zhuji had become a mere "colony" (*zhimin di*) of Shaoxing and expressed the hope that county merchants and workers controlling their own bank could soon manage the county's economic development. The problem, they pointed out, was the decline of native-controlled commerce and wealth.[75] The same attitude had developed among Wenchow natives when they were subjected to Ningpo entrepreneurs (Wenchow, it should be recalled, was at the less developed end of the inner-core spectrum). Local elites bitterly protested the intrusion of outside mining entrepreneurs into Cheng, Jiangshan, and Changxing counties in 1918 and 1919.[76]

Both natives and outsiders, of course, could theoretically profit or benefit from the projects described. But given the great significance of native place ties and accompanying differences in dialect and customs, tensions were unavoidable. The native elites' resentment did not develop into full-blown policies of discrimination, however, as it did in the inner core. Nonnative merchants sometimes worked synergetically with outer-core natives in public affairs. Sufficiently detailed sources do not exist to indicate the extent to which the outer zones experienced Zhuji's sense of being colonized by those from more developed areas. It is probably true that while inner-core elites saw development in a positive aspect—developing the nation while enriching themselves—elites of the outer zones were more ambivalent. The latter appreciated the greater involvement of the locality in higher networks of trade and the general expansion of local

economies but were dubious about dependency on or subjection to outsiders.

The Christian Missionaries

One outsider group that seemed to cause greater problems in the outer
core than in other zones was foreign missionaries. The China Inland
Mission, Church Missionary Society, and the American Baptist Missionary Union had established missionary stations in most inner- and outer-
core counties by the 1870s.[77] Missionaries were most numerous in the
inner core, but newspaper and gazetteer sources indicate few serious
problems in that area. Disputes frequently broke out over mission land
purchases; but, perhaps because of the consular presence in Ningpo,
Hangchow, and Wenchow and the ease of transportation from these cities
to the outlying inner-core areas, they were usually settled peaceably.[78]
The outer core was farther removed from Western political power and
at the same time less accustomed to the presence of foreign outsiders.
Native-missionary relations in the outer core were complicated by the
outer-core counties' frequent subjection to bandit attacks from the less
developed inner periphery. Antimissionary disturbances often tended to
accompany other problems of social disorder.

Qu county had a substantial missionary presence: eleven Catholic
churches (all but three established after 1901) and five Protestant
churches. Foreign missionaries had built mountain retreats west of the
county seat in 1905 and 1920, causing fear among county elites that the
area would become a second Moganshan, the famous retreat for Shanghai area and inner-core missionaries northwest of Hangchow.[79] In the
summer of 1900 Qu was the target of secret society bandits aroused by
news of the Boxer Rebellion. Word of the approaching bandit forces ignited a riot in which the magistrate, missionaries, and local converts were
slain. Although the bandits' attempt to take Qu failed, both their campaign and the urban rioting suggests the connection between social unrest
and antimissionary activity.[80]

Similarly, in Xiangshan county in 1906, an uprising motivated by a
personal vendetta and greed took on an antimissionary tone. A local
Christian convert had antagonized Buddhist nuns by wanting to establish
a modern school at the nunnery. The nuns in turn indicated to one Zhang
Xiaojin, a *wusheng* degree-holder, that Christianity was destroying China
and must itself be destroyed. Zhang subsequently joined with the
Ninghai bandit Wang Xitong, acting under the Boxer slogan "Support
the Qing; destroy the foreigners." A bandit army of over four hundred
men demanded money from a convert with whom Zhang had been involved in litigation, burned a church, and captured several missionaries
before troops in the county seat finally halted the action.[81]

Zhuji county also had its Boxer-inspired movement in 1900, but it is more notable for its continual struggles with missionaries over property and property rights. Beginning in 1893 when a dispute between the Church Missionary Society and a Buddhist monk flared into violence, the bitterness continued past the revolution into two major incidents in 1914 and 1916. In both these incidents, the missionaries were pitted against the local elites who, in the first case, tried to protect land designated as school property from being taken by the church and, in the second, tried to obviate the sale of public lands to the church. The Zhuji elite won the first battle. In the second, the powerful Hangchow missionary D. Duncan Main, who had his own record of land grabs in the capital, pressured local officials to accede to the church's demands.[82] Although these episodes were not violent, the rancor of Zhuji elites extending over several decades was a notable feature of the local scene.

The Spread of Nationalism

Antimissionary incidents can be seen not only as social disturbances ignited by the presence of foreign outsiders but also as evidence of xenophobic nationalism. Elites in the outer core during the first three decades of the twentieth century were increasingly brought into a world beyond their locality—to the province and nation.

Some outer-core elites in the prefectural capitals of Jinhua and Qu were involved in the railway controversy in 1907. Through statements of support and some purchase of stocks, military men, students, merchants, and gentry in these cities evidenced strong antiforeign feelings. Some outer-core county native place organizations in Hangchow and Shanghai met to protest the proposed British loan.[83] The number of outer-core elites politicized by the railway episode is difficult to determine, but far fewer outer- than inner-core elites were involved.

Widespread national awareness in outer-core counties began only in the wake of the May Fourth incident and in the periodic antiforeign outbursts between 1920 and 1925. School strikes and commercial boycotts marked many outer-core counties—Lanqi, Jinhua, Yuhang, Ruian, and Zhuji—in the months following the 1919 demonstration.[84] Elites organized citizens' meetings (*guomin dahui*) and voluntary associations to promote Chinese products.[85] A Zhuji county organization to encourage the use of Chinese products put up posters advocating the boycott of Japanese goods, and its student members watched incoming boats day and night to prevent the unloading of such imports. At the newspaper reading center in the county seat, elites erected a monument on which were inscribed the Twenty-One Demands, as a reminder of national humiliation.[86] Other outer-core counties became involved in later nationalistic demonstrations: Fuyang in late 1919 and in the wake of the May Thir-

tieth incident, Tonglu and Xinchang.[87] Student speakers from Shanghai
visited outer-core counties in the Qiantang basin to relate personal descriptions of the May Thirtieth episode. In response, students and merchants collected money and gave dramatic presentations to raise money
to send to Shanghai.[88] Professional associations were also highly active.
The Zhuji Education Association, for example, planned (but never
achieved) the establishment of a textile mill to strengthen the county's
contribution to the national welfare.[89] Following the May Thirtieth incident, professional associations in many counties denounced imperialists
and called for boycotts.[90] In marked contrast to their quiet roles in the
1912 to 1914 period, most outer-core county assemblies also debated national and provincial issues, vigorously protesting the May Thirtieth tragedy.[91]

In sum, the outer core evidenced several major developmental patterns
that differentiated it from the inner core. They include the slower development of the economy, voluntary associations, and nationalism; the
shift in functional elite types in the late 1910s and early 1920s rather than
with the revolution; the importance of officials vis-à-vis local elites in initiating and managing community affairs; and the evolution into a target
for inner-core and Shanghai entrepreneurial endeavors.

8

Inner-Periphery Political and Elite Structures

Qu Yingguang's reports of 1915 repeatedly noted the newly flourishing or potential prosperity of the outer-core counties; for the inner periphery, in contrast, he pictured rusticity, poverty, and disorder and offered the hope that government-elite cooperation could eventually effectuate positive change.[1] Although the inner periphery shared certain development patterns with the outer core—for example, the time differential in developmental indicators, the timing of the early Republican changes in functional elite types, the relative functional roles of magistrate and elites, and the exploitation by outside developers—there were also important differences in career patterns, elite interaction, the political agenda, and specific organizational strength.

Inner-Periphery Elite Patterns: The Liu Lineage of Qingtian County

Many of the patterns of inner-periphery politics and elites in the late Qing and early Republican periods are suggested by the Liu lineage from Nantian township in southwestern Qingtian county.[2] The Lius lived in the small, fertile rice-producing area around Nantian Mountain for over five centuries. Their genealogy traces twenty generations and includes an occasional upper-degree-holder and many lower-degree-holders. The obviously approximated rounded numbers of degree-holders in some generations probably indicate periods of lineage decline when genealogical record keeping fell into disarray. The lineage seems to have had considerable strength and prosperity from approximately early in the Qianlong reign (circa 1750) to the early Daoguang period (circa 1830). There was then half a century of decline, followed by the temporary rejuvenation of the lineage in the 1880s. The lineage evidently prospered until the early

1930s, when lineage solidarity weakened. That the Liu lineage took new life at a time of considerably county instability and political change indicates its ability to accommodate itself to change and to seize new opportunities.

Of three Liu brothers in the late nineteenth century, only one held a degree (*shengyuan*). All were involved during the Tongzhi and Guangxu periods in their township's defense, particularly against local bullies (*hao*) and bandits rampaging from mountain lairs following the autumn harvests. To protect the Nantian area, the Qingtian magistrate in 1885 reestablished the *baojia* system. Elites from the Liu lineage assisted in setting down the local *baojia* regulations. Thus, the handling of the chief inner-peripheral issues in the last years of the Qing period—defense and control—came at the initiative of the magistrate, not the Lius themselves; and the magistrate's method was not militia unit formation but the imposition of the traditional surveillance system.

In the early twentieth century, the nine sons and four grandsons of these three brothers moved into modern functions in subcounty self-government bodies and the construction of modern schools. The lineage produced the township manager and assistant (the foremost subcounty self-government positions from 1910 to 1914) and two township deputies between 1914 and 1924. In addition, three were involved in the establishment and expansion of the township primary school in 1908 and 1913. The linkage of self-government and education was readily apparent spatially: the lower floor of the school served as the self-government office.

Among the sons and grandsons, there were five lower degrees (*shengyuan* and one purchased *gongsheng*) and one upper degree (a regular *gongsheng*). The large number of degrees compared to the previous generations is indicative of the lineage prosperity, which also enabled seven of the thirteen to go outside of Qingtian for modern school education. One joined the early-twentieth-century student exodus to Japan and studied at Hōsei University. The other six were graduated from the Zhejiang Military Academy between 1905 and 1908. The Japanese-educated grandson was later elected to the Qing provincial assembly and served as magistrate after 1912 both inside Zhejiang and out, bringing renown to his lineage. Of the six military graduates, three became military officers—two served at the Ningpo garrison and one in Zhejiang's First Division—one served as adviser in the office of Zhejiang's military governor in the early 1920s; and one became chief of police at Ningpo, after serving as a deputy defense commissioner in the 1910s.

Nantianshan, the Liu lineage home, was not economically advanced. It did not have a postal agency until 1935. Of its ten schools in 1932, seven were established after 1927. Not until 1930 did the county education bureau "recognize" the township school by appointing a principal. The township had no medical facility until 1935. In these ways it was typical of the inner periphery, where modern forms began to be adopted only in the late 1920s and 1930s. The Liu lineage had moved much more rapidly into the modern sphere. Moving from typical gentry leadership functions to roles in self-government and education to provincial civil and military careers, the Lius represent the transformation of a lineage and its sphere of action within a generation. The history of this lineage suggests certain characteristics of the inner periphery during the late Qing and early Republican periods: the primacy of defense and control concerns; the importance of the military as a source of career mobility; the role of the magistrate in relation to local elites; and the lateness of development.

Elite Career Patterns and Trends

Inner-periphery gazetteers are surprisingly silent on ancestral estates. Most prosperous lineages probably had land as a basis of their wealth, though holdings were substantially less than in core zones. The Liu lineage almost certainly owned an estate. Muramatsu Yuji describes the Hu lineage of Yongkang county, which in the mid-nineteenth century had an estate of over one hundred forty mu.[3] Townships located along or near river routes contained the most significant lineages in the counties.[4] Those townships in more mountainous areas without direct access to riverine arteries generally gave little evidence of lineage strength. Poor and underpopulated, they supplied few elites: of the total recorded 155 Tangqi county elites in the early twentieth century, the three townships (out of ten) without linkages to the county's rivers supplied only 13.[5] The functional elites of the poorer townships came from many different families.

An analysis of Shouchang, Lishui, and Tangqi counties also reveals that important trade centers (especially entrepôts on major streams or on county borders) and their townships contained no major, politically dominant lineages.[6] Instead these areas seem to have had a more flexible elite structure with greater opportunities for individuals or parvenu families to play important local political roles. A plotting of the native places of the 155 Tangqi elites shows that Tangqi's two major nonadministrative market towns produced only 2 functional elites for the period from 1900 to 1927. Many of the powerful elites and lineages, however, hailed from peri-urban areas: villages within a ten-kilometer range of these towns were the homes of 57 recorded county elites. Most strong lineages in riverine valleys of inner-peripheral counties (and the other outer zones as well) probably had some commercial interests that bolstered their economic power.

* * *

An analysis of political and economic functions, as pointed out in Appendix C, shows that between 73 and 85 percent of all recorded non-self-government functions in the peripheral zones were performed by self-government elites or their kin. An analysis of political elites in these zones can thus be made quite definitively on the basis of self-government data.

Of the four counties with detailed gazetteers, only one man in the late Qing subcounty self-government bodies had previous experience outside the county.[7] There was apparently no return of native sons from official positions or schools abroad in the late Qing period comparable to that in the core zones. The area produced fewer officials, having fewer degree-holders than the more prosperous zones. Furthermore, there were not many students from the inner periphery studying outside: of those 121 Zhejiang students in Japan in 1902 and 1903, only 5 (4.1 percent) were from this zone, and of the 73 at Beijing University in 1906, only 4 (5.5 percent) hailed from these counties. The only exception that I have found to this inner-peripheral pattern is Lishui county, which was the capital of Chuzhou prefecture. Its administrative status compensated in part for its sluggish economic development. A center of government, it was more likely to have offered government scholarships to interested youth and to have drawn to it some reform-minded late Qing officials. Sun Shouzhi, a *jinshi* county education official who returned to Lishui in 1910 to assist in educational reform, is an example of the latter. Several returned students in the last decade of the Qing joined in establishing the famous revolutionary front, the Utilitarian Cotton Cloth Mill; many of them were teachers at the prefectural middle school and a county primary school.[8]

As in the outer core, changes in elite types do not seem to have occurred at the time of the revolution. That 48 percent of the first county assemblymen had served in the late Qing subcounty self-government bodies suggests greater elite continuity over the watershed of the revolution than in the core zones. Like in the outer core, opportunities began to open up in the late 1910s and early 1920s. Almost 95 percent of the second assembly had been neither members nor relatives of members of the first assembly. Some of these men were probably gentry-merchants, like the Lishui industrialist Mao Guanfeng; others were men like Lishui's Zhu Yishi, whose credentials are unknown (these composed about 5 percent of the total).[9] Over 35 percent of all members were graduates returning from schools outside the county—from the former prefectural capitals as well as Hangchow, Shanghai, and Beijing.[10] Of these, 55 percent (eleven) were graduates of law schools in Hangchow and Shanghai; 35 percent (seven) were from prefectural and Hangchow normal and middle schools; and the remainder were from professional schools, primary schools, and institutes. The outward gravitation of elites experienced by the core zones was sharply curtailed, if not reversed, in the peripheral zones: more modern graduates played political roles in the inner periphery than in other zones.

In these counties, the diploma or certificate was as much the passport to something approaching traditional gentry status as it was the passport to new specialized functions in the core zones. The power attainable by overseas returned students was especially substantial. Liu Tingxuan of Lishui, for example, was graduated from Waseda University. He chose to remain in Lishui, heading the education association in the 1910s and 1920s, serving as head of the education promotion office in the late 1910s, building schools, contributing capital for an iron foundry in 1923, and serving on the county board in the 1920s. Letters from Liu and the head of the education association in 1918, Fu Tinggui, reveal that Fu (who did not have a modern-school education) and others felt considerable resentment toward Liu's leadership.[11]

The greater tendency for outer-ranging elites to return to their native places here than in the core zones was apparent not only with students but older-style elites as well. Of those Qing provincial assembly members, for example, whose Republican careers can be determined, two thirds of the men from the inner periphery (eight of twelve) spent at least part of their subsequent careers active in county affairs.[12] This compares with one third (six of eighteen) in the inner core and 36 percent (five of fourteen) in the outer core. (Two of four from the outer periphery whose careers can be determined returned to their home counties.) Similarly, in the 1920s, older elites with official experience returned to their counties for functional leadership roles.[13]

The reasons for the general return of highly qualified elites are hard to gauge. Many were certainly touched by new ideas of nationalism, specialization, and industrialization during their urban-based education. Idealist impulses to remake their locality provided a potent reason to return home. Others undoubtedly returned for family reasons, to carry on the lineage or to reflect well on the family name by their new credentials. Some may have been motivated by the fact that with modern credentials and experience beyond their native place, they could enjoy considerable prestige and power in their locality. The essayist Cao Juren, writing of his home county of Pujiang, notes these motivations. He describes one participant in the Hangchow revolution who instead of joining the provincial government like many of his peers, returned to his home to become an autocrat, in Cao's words, a local emperor (*tuhuangdi*) whose reputation was based largely on his experience and associations in the inner core.[14] In another example, former provincial assembly member Wang Binghao refused to relinquish his control of his home county of Xindeng; he was subsequently dislodged in mid-1912 by the military forces of the Hang-chow government.[15] The awe with which local people treated those who had returned from Hangchow or Shanghai indicates the possible psychological underpinnings for tiny satrapies.[16]

Gentry and Gentry-Merchants

Inner-periphery gazetteers suggest that, despite the predominantly noncommercial cast in these counties, gentry-merchants often became important county leaders. Some like the Zhou family of Xindeng were wealthy merchants who performed many charitable and political functions in the county.[17] Yuan Zhicheng of the same county, who accumulated his wealth in the late nineteenth century, had immense power, becoming an assistant of sorts to the magistrate in the last fifteen years of the Qing. He built schools, headed militia units, served in the subcounty self-government, and headed the agriculture association. His business had brought him into Hangchow where he and three other Xindeng elites in 1906 leased a building for the county guild.[18]

Unlike the core zones, modernizers from the late Qing period through the 1920s were solely gentry and gentry-merchants. No reported indigenous merchants became significant in economic development. Degreed members of the Tan family of Lishui established the textile factory that served as a revolutionary front in 1904 and the purely economic enterprise of a soft mat factory in 1924. The initial investment in the county electric company in 1919 and a match company in 1924 came from lower degree-holder and chairman of the chamber of commerce Zheng Baolin. The capital for the Pusheng iron foundry in 1923 was raised by Liu Tingxuan, a returned student from Japan; and a cement factory was organized by a lower-degree-holder who had served as township manager in the late Qing period.[19] The lack of development in the peripheral zones of a strong merchant group without traditional elite trappings or functional patterns was in part the result of both the lack of commercial prosperity in general and the greater traditionalism that rewarded gentry credentials and favored continuity of leadership.

Political Structure: County Oligarchs and the Magistrate

Self-government elites or their kin dominated the local functional elite scene in the periphery. On the face of it, one might conclude that self-government bodies were important local institutions; yet their importance was more apparent than real. Patterns of elite actions point to the institutional weakness of self-government bodies. In Xindeng county, at least 26 percent of those serving in late Qing councils served in different townships' Republican councils or in the county assembly representing other townships. Concurrently held assembly and township positions make it highly unlikely that elites resident in the county seat actually returned to their native place for township posts. The township councils in Xindeng in all likelihood existed only nominally—consisting of designated groups of highly respected and powerful elites who probably met informally as in the past. Some men in Xindeng were also designated to serve simultaneously in different self-government positions: Hong Xicheng was at once a member of the Qing provincial assembly and of the county seat council. Although the extent of Xindeng's fluidity of representation is not seen in other counties, other isolated cases point to a similar lack of institutionalization. For example, in Shouchang county, Chen Shanying served concurrently as chairman and vice-chairman of two different township councils.[20] The townships contained only standard market towns and villages; therefore the lure of urban centers, important market towns, or the county seat does not explain the arrangement. A more likely hypothesis is that Chen was oriented in native places and interests to two different trading systems in whose institutions he served. The new administrative units bound him no more than county administrative boundaries prevented certain townships from being naturally oriented to a different county.

The lesser degree of self-government institutionalization is also suggested by the careers of some of the most powerful men in Xindeng county. Involved in many spheres of activity, Wu Baosan, Hong Xicheng, and Yuan Zhicheng served (at least nominally) in the late Qing bodies but in no subsequent ones.[21] It is as if these men "tested" the new organs but found such institutionalization of their roles superfluous. Powerful elite avoidance of self-government service (only one of these men had kin in the assembly); fluidity of representation; and the gravitation of elites to the county seat indicate, in contrast to the core zones, only marginal acceptance of the institutionalization of elite functions in bodies identified by county and subcounty administrative units.

The political structure of the peripheral zones was marked by a small county oligarchy (often of eight or fewer men) with immense importance in a wide range of activity: there was much less individual diversity in county leadership than in the core zones.[22] The oligarchy came from strong lineages or rich, newly risen families, almost all of whom played important roles from the late 1890s into the 1920s and perhaps beyond. This resulted in a marked continuity on the county political scene. In Xindeng a five-man oligarchy not only assisted the magistrate, becoming involved in all essential community measures, but also provided links to the inner core, being connected to the county guild in Hangchow.[23] The

Shouchang oligarchy included four multifunctional elites, some with linkages to the inner core, and an Anhui merchant.[24] The oligarchy in Lishui county found its source not in lineages but in a specific pre-1911 revolutionary coalition of secret society members, bandits, students, and self-government elites. Persisting in county leadership circles well into the 1920s, this oligarchy was represented in county self-government bodies, sent men to provincial assemblies in Hangchow, and served in official county posts (from which, before their arrest in 1914, some of the group became quite wealthy by embezzling public funds).[25]

Available sources make it impossible to determine whether or how often each county oligarchy ever met as a group. In important matters such as community defense or public works of county-wide significance, the magistrate called on them for counsel and assistance. Each county oligarchy generally had links to more developed areas; often all of the group had such connections. The political structure in the inner periphery was not an open one; in the wealthy townships, one or two lineages dominated, and in the county a small oligarchy of highly qualified elites held dominant power. The influx of graduates in the 1920s did not substantially change the oligarchical picture in any county, for most of these returned elites seemed to concentrate in one or two areas.[26] Their range of activity was generally limited compared with that of the oligarchical elites; despite their significant roles, they usually remained supporting elites for the magistrate and oligarchy.

In light of both the oligarchy and the weakness of the early self-government institutions, an important question is whether those bodies developed into stronger institutional forces in the 1920s. Circumstantial evidence—specifically, the increasing degree of dispute over institutional regulations—indicates that institutional consciousness probably began to develop by that time. When organizations grapple with issues of regulations, they are often working out institutional arrangements and demarcations. Form and process become crucial concerns. Constant institutional wrangling can, of course, bespeak a lack of power, with energies exhausted in meaningless disputation. But it is interesting that in the core zones, questions of process and regulation played a crucial role in first session assemblies, whereas in the inner periphery they did not become important issues until after 1922.[27] For example, the Tiantai County Assembly was reportedly in turmoil in late 1923 because proper internal election procedures had not been followed.[28] In mid-1925, in a slap at official regulations, the same assembly refused to elect a chairman, choosing instead five members to serve as a board of deputies (*weiyuan*) to direct the assembly.[29] Disputes between assemblies and boards were prevalent in all zones but seen especially notable in the inner periphery in such counties as Wuyi, Qingtian, Tiantai, Lishui, and Qunan.[30] During elections for the constitutional convention in 1924, five of eight requests to Hangchow for rulings on procedural issues came from inner-peripheral counties (one came from the outer core and two from the outer periphery).[31] These counties' concerns perhaps suggest a growing consciousness of institutions and their functioning in the 1920s.

The magistrate was a more powerful force in the initiation and control of local affairs than in the core zones where individuals or groups of elites tended to initiate similar projects. The magistrates in Lishui and Pujiang, among other counties, organized and directed local elite oligarchies in the traditional undertakings of education, charity, and public works in the late 1910s and 1920s.[32] The number of recorded impeachments of magistrates in the province from 1911 to 1927 suggests that less antagonistic relationships existed between magistrates and county elites in the peripheries than in the core zones.[33] Of fifty-two impeachments, the inner periphery produced ten (19.2 percent) and the outer periphery, eight (15.4 percent). This relative quiescence among county elites suggests, if not always good relationships, at least more steady symbiotic ones.

Fatuan Institutionalization and Roles

The inner-peripheral setting of closed oligarchical leadership and magisterial control stunted the institutionalization of professional associations. Chambers of commerce were established in the inner periphery approximately three years later than in the inner core. On the whole, individual native and outside gentry-merchants seemed more important than the institution. Whereas economic development and increasing functional differentiation in the core zones promoted the growth of powerful chambers, the lack of economic development in the inner periphery prevented such institutionalization. The situation in Lishui, probably the most economically developed inner-periphery county, is a case in point. The Lishui police had petitioned Hangchow for subsidies to aid in the establishment of an electric power company. An inspector for the provincial government's bureau on electricity reported in late 1919 that the county's stagnant commercial situation did not warrant such a company. Police insistence, however, forced the inspector to recommend its establishment.[34] Local bureaucrats thus played the crucial role in this economic development.

The agriculture association was as weak an institution as in other zones, existing primarily as another framework for the same elites who served in assemblies and other professional associations.[35] I have found no evidence of its initiating agricultural improvements. Magistrate and key county elites, not the association, participated in agricultural decision making. The self-government deputy, not the association, for example, established and managed the two Xindeng county nurseries (*linchang*).[36]

Of the professional associations, the education association had the strongest sense of institutional power, and it fostered local change in many counties in the 1920s. Composed mostly of returned students, it tended to maintain linkages to the inner core. Kept abreast of political concerns in more developed areas by their former inner-core classmates, these new elites were more aware of national political issues than established inner-periphery elites.[37] In the early years of the 1920s, students became involved in moves to direct their education: strikes and meetings in Yongkang, Dongyang, Lishui, and Wuyi were undoubtedly stimulated by an awareness of similar events in the core zones.[38] Education associations led the May Thirtieth protests.[39] Nationalism became an inner-periphery concern only in the mid-1920s, again underscoring the general lag behind more developed zones.

Apart from secret societies, modern-style voluntary associations were rare in the counties of this zone at least until the mid-1920s when the education linkage to the inner core fostered some voluntary meetings.[40] A Wuyi county women's federation formed to discuss female representation in elected bodies, a reflection of similar core activities.[41] Some public works associations were organized.[42] Although more voluntary associations probably existed in these counties, they are unrecorded; it is difficult to avoid the conclusion that the inner periphery saw fewer and less specialized organizations than the core zones and that those that existed were more ephemeral and less likely to become permanent institutions.

The Shouchang gazetteer documents in detail the organizational "revolution" that occurred after the Guomindang victory in 1927. Stimulated by the government, shopkeepers, clothing makers, and bamboo workers organized. There were councils for the management of public property, for rewriting the county gazetteer, and for reconstruction.[43] Like the Qing professional associations, these were government sponsored and thus differed from the plethora of voluntary organizations in the core zones. This proliferation of organizations in the late 1920s and 1930s indicates that political development, as it had throughout the early years of the Republic in the peripheries, evolved primarily through government sponsorship and promotion. The stimuli for political change in these counties were, in sum, the provincial and local governments and the linkages of returned local students to the core zones.

The Political Agenda

The Control of Social Disorder

The chief issue in the inner periphery, affecting all else, was order: coping with bandits and robbers, lineage vendettas, and the seemingly uncontrollable gambling society (*huahui*) that spawned violence and instability.[44] County police were expected to handle the last two problems with the occasional assistance of local elite-managed militia units.[45]

Banditry can be divided into two types, seasonal outbreaks and more organized continuous brigandage. It was a recurring problem in all zones especially at times of crop shortage and natural disasters. In the inner core, however, it was quite sporadic and generally confined to certain areas—along the border with Jiangsu, along the silk routes on the southern shore of Lake Tai, and in three Shaoxing counties, Xiaoshan, Shaoxing, and Yuyao, at the lower end of river valleys emptying from the outer zones. Banditry tended to be most severe and pervasive in the outer core and inner periphery. The greater development of the outer core often attracted inner-periphery brigands who used their home counties as a base for attacks. For example, Tiantai and Xianju bandits often attacked Zhuji (outer core) residents with the assistance of Zhuji charcoal burners and kiln workers.[46] The counties of the peripheries also served as a haven for bandit regrouping. In the early 1920s, followers of a particularly vicious defeated Zhuji bandit fled to the peripheral counties of Anji and Xiaofeng where they swelled the ranks of already dissatisfied bamboo cutters and charcoal burners.[47]

The magistrate and local militia units directed the seasonal defense.[48] But in more highly organized disturbances, the magistrate relied on units of the provincial troops (*jingbeidui*) that were under the command of the civil governor. Scattered in various counties in the outer zones where there were no regular modern-trained troops, these forces had the primary job of supplementing local forces.[49] Hangchow also established special defense commissioners (*hujunshi*) for the Jia-Hu area and the eastern part of the province, especially the outer-zone counties of Taizhou.[50]

Like traditional bandit organizations, bandit groups in the early Republic copied the political forms of elites and elite governments.[51] They also mimicked the titles and slogans of nationalistic political parties of the inner core. Groups calling themselves the Citizens' Progress Society, Loyalist Party, and National Salvation Association raked outer-core and inner-periphery counties.[52] An organized army of seven thousand under bandit leader Zhou Yongguang marched under the revolutionary banner of Sun Yat-sen in August 1914 with the title of "Zhedong anti-Yuan army."[53] Reminiscent of the White Wolf in northern and central China, Zhou ranged throughout the middle-zone counties, spreading destruction and at least the nomenclature of republican nationalism.

Eliminating the cultivation of opium, which was widespread throughout the outer core and inner periphery especially in county border areas, was another control-related concern.[54] Although a few of the specially appointed anti-opium commissioners in 1912 and 1913 used rewards to encourage the extirpation of opium crops, most commissioners relied on force. In Ruian in the fall of 1913, troops destroyed the homes of farmers who resisted the destruction of opium crops.[55] In Ninghai after farmers banded together to protect their opium, only a bribe prevented troops from carrying out an order to devastate the area and shoot the inhabitants on sight.[56]

Financial Difficulties and the Non-Control-Related Agenda

There was little money available for elite concerns that were not related to control.[57] Some inner-periphery counties were in desperate financial shape. The magistrate of Xianju reported in late 1917 that the county government was bankrupt.[58] The magistrate of Qunan simultaneously served as the *tongjuan* bureau head—an arrangement whereby some commercial tax monies could find their way into local coffers.[59] With the economies of these counties in disarray, monies for public affairs were severely limited. In the core zones where there was considerably more elite initiation of local projects, such a restriction of local government revenue might not have been so serious. But in the peripheries, the local government played the vital role in this regard.

Scattered evidence indicates that police expenditures were oppressively high. A telegram from more than three hundred Anji county citizens in late 1923 protested that the county could not bear the costs of "clearing the countryside" (*qingxiang*) as prescribed by Hangchow.[60] In 1924 Qingtian citizens protested the establishment of a new police branch, arguing that the area was too poor to support it.[61] Yet, understandably, elites continued to demand protection from disorder.[62]

Educational expenditures also brought protests. Qu Yingguang in 1915 reported that counties in the peripheries had few schools and students, a situation, he noted, that was retarding county development.[63] Whereas core zones experienced much turmoil over school construction in the last years of the Qing period, the greater uproar in the peripheries seemed to come in 1914 in the wake of a school census that many felt to be a harbinger of higher taxes.[64] The magistrate of Jiangshan, noting the lack of attendance at county schools, called a meeting of wealthy gentry and decided to open a new school for the poor. Not only did the solution not seem to fit the problem, but the school was supported, not by the rich gentry, but by a new tax on hogs and tung oil.[65] When the Pujiang magistrate assembled elites to discuss financing schools, they decided on an additional levy that the chamber of commerce and agriculture association protested as impossible to bear.[66] The Education Ministry in Beijing in late 1920 took the unprecedented step (at least for Zhejiang counties) of abolishing the exorbitant Wuyi county schools surtax that had been levied since 1912.[67]

A mapping of school sites in Tangqi county reveals that wealthy townships had many schools and poorer ones, few. Almost all the schools were located along rivers and streams and were clustered markedly in the northern half of the county, which contained the county seat and two large market towns.[68] The linkage between economic development and school construction indicates both the greater tax revenue available in prosperous townships (some townships, at least in the beginning years of the Republic, levied their own excise taxes) and the activities of lineage elites founding their own schools.

Money was obviously not the only consideration in elite decisions to build schools. Ideology and outlook also played a role. An analysis of the Tangqi information shows that the township that contained the highest number of degree-holders produced the fewest relative number of modern-school graduates and was among the slowest in establishing schools (it had only two before 1916: only two of ten townships were so slow). This case suggests itself as an example of traditional conservatism holding back accommodation to change. The township of the major county entrepôt was also laggard in building schools (constructing only two before 1916), perhaps because of mercantile disinterest in school construction. In any case, the paucity of schools in this important commercial township stands in great contrast to the far less wealthy townships that averaged almost five by that date. The township, on the other hand, with the highest number of graduates also built the largest number of schools by 1926. (One can imagine idealistic modern graduates returning home to run schools in their localities.)

Financial stringency also played a role in the development of charitable institutions and relief. Despite continual official demands for the promotion of county workhouses, counties could operate them only half-heartedly because of lack of funds.[69] In Tangqi the jail doubled as a workhouse, indicating a link between social rehabilitation and the curtailing of disorder in the instability of the inner periphery. Relief institutions ordered by Qu Yingguang in 1915 were short-lived.[70] Orphanages were inadequately funded by the elites and often required magisterial action.[71] In short, disorder and financial difficulties hampered the development of local projects.

Origin of Military Careers:
Outer Core and Inner Periphery

Although Zhejiang's military leaders and graduates came from counties in all zones, a striking aspect of provincial military elite production is the relatively large number hailing from the outer core and inner periphery. The three outer zones produced far fewer modern students than the inner core: only 19 percent of the Zhejiang students in Japan in 1902 and 1903; 19.2 percent of students at Beijing University in 1906; and 6 percent of Qinghua students in 1917. Yet the Baoding Military Academy statistics from 1912 to 1920 seen in Table 14 present a different distribution. Although the inner-core counties still produced more military graduates than any other single zone, 61.2 percent came from the outer zones, with most of these hailing from the outer core and inner periphery. In comparison to the paltry 6 percent (all from the outer core) attending Qinghua approximately in the same time period, the strength of these zones in military cadet production is all the more striking.

Furthermore, an analysis of graduates after the sixth class produces the following distribution: inner core, 31.7 percent; outer core, 27.5 percent; inner periphery, 27.5 percent; outer periphery, 5 percent. By the late 1910s the outer core and inner periphery were producing increasingly more military cadets than the inner core. In rate of increase, the inner periphery was outstripping the others. I would hypothesize that if records for Zhejiang provincial military schools were available, the numbers from the two middle zones would outstrip the inner core and that the inner periphery would rank first in production of these elites. Even by 1912, the inner periphery was producing more of the provincial military elite than might be expected. Of twenty-three key revolutionary and post-revolutionary military officials, at least eight came from the inner core and seven from the inner periphery.[72]

The reasons for the high inner-periphery production of military elites can only be hypothesized. In a society becoming increasingly oriented to the military, education at a military academy promised a career away from one's native place. The Zhuji gazetteer suggests that the county's

Table 14.
Distribution of Zhejiangese Baoding Military Academy graduates

Class	Inner core	Outer core	Inner periphery	Outer periphery
Class 1	5 (55.6%)	2 (22.2%)	2 (22.2%)	—
Class 2	14 (41.2%)	9 (26.5%)	6 (17.6%)	5 (14.7%)
Class 3	58 (41.4%)	55 (39.3%)	23 (16.4%)	4 (2.9%)
Class 4	—	—	—	—
Class 5	4 (100%)	—	—	—
Class 6	24 (29.6%)	26 (32.1%)	25 (30.9%)	6 (7.4%)
Class 7	—	—	—	—
Class 8	10 (30.1%)	5 (15.2%)	18 (54.5%)	—
Class 9	4 (66.7%)	2 (33.3%)	—	—
Total	119 (38.8%)	99 (32.2%)	74 (24.1%)	15 (4.9%)
Per 100,000 inhabitants	1.35	1.67	2.02	1.05

Source: *Baoding junxiao tongxunlu,* passim.

increasing number of young boys who entered military academies at Hangchow in the late Qing and early Republican periods came from poor agricultural backgrounds and that the military offered an escape from the peasantry.[73] However, the social mobility hypothesis fails to explain why military schools rather than other types (which also offered mobility) attracted such a relatively greater proportion of men from the two middle zones. I suspect that these men, growing into adulthood in the unstable, disorderly atmosphere of these counties and being familiar with the efforts of their elite kin to establish defense and order, may have had a greater psychological predisposition toward military careers.

In the 1920s, until 1926 and 1927, the three outer zones were subjected to severe military exactions; the inner core largely escaped the heavy hand of the military until then—with the exception of the 1924 war with Jiangsu. From 1923 to 1926 all areas of the three outer zones were faced with roving troops making extortionate demands, impressing local men into their forces, and looting with impunity.[74] In such a militarily charged environment, life as a soldier may have seemed quite profitable and exciting. The importance of military careers among outer-zone elites posed a strong counterweight to the inner core's domination in the civilian career spheres.

The Role of Outsiders

The inner periphery shared with the outer core not only endemic banditry and the propensity for supplying military elites, but it was also the target of inner-core elite entrepreneurial interest. In addition, two types of more permanent outsiders played important roles in many inner-periphery counties: nonelite immigrants who had fled from rebellion or catastrophe in their native areas; and merchant elites, mostly from outside Zhejiang, who played important local roles. The first group increased tensions in counties where poverty already blighted the scene. In the jaundiced eye of Qu Yingguang, intractable immigrants caused many of the problems in these counties. Reports suggest that they were often more than willing to participate in social disturbances.[75] Sources, however, do not indicate the intensity of resentment seen in some core counties against such outsiders.

It is initially surprising to find extraprovincial merchants significant in underdeveloped local economies, but this phenomenon was not exceptional in the two peripheries. There is not a single pattern for inner-periphery counties. In Lishui and Xindeng counties, outside merchants apparently played no important role. Where they did so seems to be determined by specific county location and geography. Noteworthy are the patterns of Tangqi and Shouchang, both targets via the Xinan River of

Anhui merchants in the Lower Yangzi region. In some counties a market town was more flourishing than the county seat. Of these, Tangqi county seems alone in the extent of separation of mercantile from political centers. The chamber of commerce was established in Luofou, one of the two market towns near the Qu River, in 1907. Chamber of commerce elites all came from outside the county and five of seven came from Jiqi county in Anhui province; they performed no recorded political, social, or economically developmental functions for the county.[76] Logic would suggest that these elites were consulted by noncommercial elites; but there is no record of it, and the county seems anomalous in the extent of spatial separation of centers of political and commercial power.

In Shouchang, on the other hand, Anhui merchants played major roles in both economic and political developments. Of the five chairmen of the chamber of commerce in Shouchang, three were from Anhui and one of these served three terms. Unlike outer-core examples, this outside merchant elite played direct roles in noncommercial functions: they all headed militia and fire-fighting units throughout the period and one, Cheng Bingpan, was one of the county's functional oligarchs. From the middle of the Guangxu period until at least 1928, Cheng contributed great sums for public works and charity. There is evidence that he had purchased substantial land in the county. From 1911 through 1928 he managed militia units, winning a commendation from the civil governor in 1925.[77] Shouchang, which in the Republican period was not very prosperous, had in the late Qing period been linked closely to Lanqi county, an outer-core commercial center. This relationship explains at least in part the presence of outside merchants in this underdeveloped county.[78]

Inner-Periphery Themes of Development

Attacked in his Tangqi home by a group of straggling soldiers in the autumn of 1924, Hong Chenglu suffered injuries from which he never recovered, and he died in July 1926 at the age of forty-eight.[79] Certain aspects of his death and life are indicative of inner-periphery elite trends. His father, Hong Weiguang, a *lingsheng* degree-holder, had taken on the support of many in his lineage in the hard times following the Taiping destruction. The lineage home, along the Qu River between the county's two important riverine ports, had existed since the Song dynasty.

Chenglu, Weiguang's eldest son, became a *gongsheng* degree-holder in the late Guangxu period and also was graduated from the Beijing Law School (*jingshi fazheng xuetang*). While waiting for an appointment as magistrate, he lectured in a normal school and military academy. In the last years of the Qing dynasty, he headed a land reclamation bureau in Hebei. At the time of the revolution, he returned to Zhejiang where he was appointed to two county magistracies, the first in Lanqi in late 1911 and the second in Haining in 1914. His record in both was outstanding: rewards were showered on him from Hangchow and Beijing. He refused an appointment in Henan because of the illness of his father, who had been serving in the Tangqi County Assembly. Hong spent the rest of his career in Tangqi, devoting much time to supervising the county's new gazetteer project. As head of the education promotion office, he was in charge of the county's schools. He was also chairman of the county assembly from 1922 until his death.

Aspects of his background and career recall essential features of the political and social ecology of inner-periphery elites. Like the Lius of Nantianshan, Hong's base was a lineage, although his was apparently weaker than the Lius'. Like most politically significant lineages, it was in a river basin where both agricultural and commercial opportunities were available. Chenglu had one brother, who did not become a degree-holder or publicly significant. One can imagine Weiguang grooming Chenglu, described (perhaps stereotypically) as precocious, to carry on the family name. Like many inner-periphery elites, Chenglu was a transitional figure in that he attained a degree and also attended a modern school. His modern education and his teaching positions brought together the major educational thrusts of the early Republic: law school, normal school, and military academy. Even his position as head of land reclamation bespoke the concern for development evident in the inner core.

Typical of inner-periphery outer-ranging elites, Hong did not return to Tangqi in the late Qing period and came back to Zhejiang only after the revolution to take the magistracies. Membership in the county assembly passed from father to son, an obvious evidence of elite continuity. An official and a modern-school graduate, he returned to several important county functions in the 1920s, again typical of inner-periphery elite careers. He was apparently not one of the county's key elites (he had been outside the county for most of his career) in terms of range of functions and length of service. The political structure of inner-periphery counties was generally oligarchical; but Hong, because of the success in his career, obviously had the respect of the oligarchical county elites, for he joined the new elite types in limited leadership roles.

There is nothing in Hong's biography to indicate involvement in the concerns of nationalism—such as the railway controversy in the late Qing or the revolution or the May Fourth era. He may well have been a strong nationalist; however, evidence of a strong degree of nationalism among inner-periphery elites in general did not surface until the 1920s. Instead of national concerns, Hong seemed drawn to lineage and locality, reflecting the strong traditional cast of most inner-periphery elites. As coeditor of the county gazetteer, his main concerns were the sections on the devel-

opment of the county's borders and internal divisions, topography, transportation, and water conservancy—that is, space and its use within the
county context.

His mortal wounding by a wandering gang of soldiers recalls the instability of most of the counties of the inner periphery. Banditry and, by the
1920s, the scourge of military depredations were the bane of development
and the curse of the populace. Disorder had to be the obsession of the
magistrate, to the slighting of other concerns, in his important leadership
of local affairs. Elite goals became control and upholding traditions as the
defense against disorder. Modern changes made few inroads until the
mid-1920s.

9

Outer-Periphery Political and Elite Structures

Ouhai circuit, established in 1914, contained the former prefectures of Wenzhou and Chuzhou, all in the Southeast coast macroregion, with all four zones represented: one inner-core county, four outer core, three inner periphery, and eight outer periphery. A review of the published official papers of Huang Qinglan, the circuit intendant from 1918 to 1920, indicates a sharp distinction between the type and range of issues for the three inner zones and the outer periphery. Evident in Huang's admonitions, replies, and orders to magistrates and elites, issues in the three inner zones included public works, charitable efforts, police concerns, and (for the core zones) student demonstrations and the anti-Japanese boycott following May Fourth. The concern for developmental issues far surpassed the attention given to the various social issues of gambling, opium cultivation, and cattle rustling. In contrast, although occasionally responding on matters of public works, education, and agriculture, in the counties of the least developed outer periphery Huang concentrated on the bitter consequences of poverty, including widespread infanticide, wife selling, and grave digging.[1]

Qu Yingguang's 1915 reports on the outer-peripheral counties offer the same image: a people living largely untouched by any modern change, amid great rusticity and poverty, with a high degree of vagrancy.[2] The picture of the outer periphery, in obvious stark contrast to the inner core, is of a relative absence of social components.

The Diminished Meaning of Administrative Boundaries

The greater importance of natural borders over artificial boundaries was apparent in the daily lives of Zhejiangese at various times in all zones. Before the twentieth century, part of Tianyue township in Shao-

128

xing (inner core) was controlled by Xiaoshan county.[3] Changyue township in Shouchang (inner periphery) was commercially oriented to Lanqi (outer core).[4] Boundaries for self-government districts in the inner core seemed to take on a sense of authentic limits in the late Qing period, reflecting growing politicization. Scanty evidence from the outer core suggests that politicizing disputes over administrative districting developed only in the 1920s.[5] In contrast, administrative boundaries in the outer periphery had less relevance in political and social phenomena than those in the inner zones. This resulted at least in part from the location of outer-periphery counties on or near the topographical divides separating regional economies.

Xuanping county, for example, is on the watershed of the Lower Yangzi and Southeast Coast macroregions. Streams from four of its twelve townships flow toward the Qiantang River basin into Jinhua and Wuyi counties. The remaining townships drain into the Ou River basin, into the counties of Jinyun and Lishui. There was no integration of the former four townships into Xuanping. In its wood trade, one township was oriented to Jinhua, and the remaining trickle of county trade mostly traveled to the Ou River.[6] Of the county's oligarchical elite, none came from these four townships. In 1914 when bandits from Yongfeng township crossed into Baohe township, the people of Baohe sent pleas for help to Wuyi county rather than to its own closer county seat.[7] A writer in 1918 noted that most people in the county had no contact with the county seat during their lifetimes.[8] Only those townships contiguous to or situated on a stream flowing toward the county seat seemed to become involved in county affairs. Similarly, Changbei township of Changhua county, located on the subregional divide, had close ties to Anhui's Ningguo county through its meager tea trade. The poorest of Changhua's townships, it tended to send its students to school in Anhui, and it provided few important county elites.[9]

Township boundaries were also generally disregarded. When, in the early Republic, two Xuanping townships were found not to have the requisite population for provincial assembly election districts, each was promptly combined with another township. It was a completely artificial arrangement, with both new townships having no basis for cohesion.[10] Financial difficulties led two other townships to establish a joint township school, another example of the general unimportance of these internal county divisions in the primitive county situation.[11] Administrative boundaries became more than simply lines on a map only as inhabitants developed a sense of belonging to that particular unit. Generally, in the outer periphery, that development lay beyond the early Republic.[12]

Elite Structures and Careers: Patterns and Trends

Strong lineages generally thrived in rich agricultural and commercial areas. In the inner and outer cores, lineage strength correlated with wealthy counties; in the outer core and inner periphery, with prosperous river valleys. In the outer periphery, the same correlation obtains. Being wealthy is obviously a relative condition, and most townships in these counties had one or two lineages that tended to dominate them through a degree of wealth, which in the inner zones would not have been impressive. In the more prosperous townships of Xuanping and Suian, for example, one finds kin-based leadership in various townships.[13]

As in the inner periphery, the few relatively flourishing market towns (like Gushi in Songyang and Dongting in Suian) saw no kin-based domination. In most less prosperous townships, public functions were undertaken by men with a wide variety of surnames, with none dominating.[14] Some very poor and undeveloped townships were, however, controlled by kin-based elites.[15] This can probably be explained by the location of all these townships on the natural or administrative frontier. Those in Xuanping and Changhua had considerable problems with banditry. These border region kin-based groups apparently developed, at least originally, for defensive purposes. These findings and those from the other zones tend to corroborate the anthropological contentions that both prosperous local economies and the need for defense and protection were important factors conducive to strong lineage development.[16]

Elite Continuity

The salient characteristic of outer-periphery elites from the 1890s into the 1920s and beyond was their continuity. These counties had substantially more degree-holders in both the first and second assemblies than other zones. Continuity from late Qing subcounty bodies into the county bodies of the mid-1920s was greater than in any zone. There is no evidence of a large opening of political opportunities in the late 1910s and early 1920s, as in the outer core and inner periphery.

The continuity and domination of elites in a wide range of public activity is seen in individual careers as in lineages. Yu Shichang was a Xuanping lower-degree-holder. As far as can be determined, he did not come from a well-established lineage. Beginning in 1890, he participated in numerous public projects, founding a burial society and an orphanage, repairing the Confucian temple, and heading a militia unit, among other undertakings. He was head of the late Qing county seat board, a member of the county assembly, and head of the education promotion office. From 1917 to 1924, he was a county education deputy, and he served as a member of the county board of education in 1924 and 1925. For some three and a half decades, Yu was a county leader active in a wide range of affairs.[17] Pan Guanlan, a *jiansheng* degree-holder from Jingning county, began his recorded public activity as a bridge builder in 1897. His county career continued well into the 1930s in the sphere of self-government and public works.[18] Wang Dexing of Suian was a local leader before 1911 and served in the county seat council in 1910 and 1911. Involved in public works in the late 1910s and 1920s, he took a county education post in 1928 and headed a bureau to oversee educational funds in the 1930s.[19]

The best documented examples of career longevity come from Xiaofeng, whose county gazetteer was published in Taiwan in 1974.[20] Inasmuch as all other available gazetteers end by the 1930s, it is possible that other counties in the outer periphery also experienced such continuity. The Xiaofeng case is interesting because the entire reported county oligarchy continued its leadership from the early twentieth century into the 1940s. My analysis of inner and outer cores suggests that this pattern did not generally exist even into the 1920s in those areas; preliminary investigation into inner-core elites of the 1930s and 1940s, especially in Jiaxing prefecture, suggests that such continuity was rare.

In Xiaofeng county, Hong Dao, Wan He, Wang Lisan, and Ye Xiangyang played the major recorded county roles in education, self-government, public works, and industrial development. Their careers are instructive. Hong was the son of a gentry leader of the county reconstruction that followed the Taiping devastation. Involved in the 1911 revolution, he served on the county board from 1912 to 1914, organized schools, developed a coal mine, and supervised a forestry cooperative in 1936. Wang, a returned student from Japan, directed the 1911 county revolution. Involved in self-government, various cooperatives in the 1930s, and mining in 1939 and 1940, he devoted much time to schools from 1917 through 1941. Wan He and Ye Xiangyang were leaders of the county's two major factions. Wan, also a relative of an important post-Taiping county elite, had been involved in the 1911 revolution; he participated in educational reforms and self-government activity from 1912 until at least 1944 when he headed a temporary county board. Ye, whose ancestors were immigrants from Shaoxing, held a *gongsheng* degree; he served in the county assembly in 1912 to 1914, in the provincial assembly from 1921 to 1927, and on the county board in 1944. Instrumental in highway construction after World War II, Ye eventually fled to Taiwan, where he died in 1963.

Although the 1930s and 1940s are beyond the scope of this book, the course of these men's careers is perhaps suggestive of local political affairs beyond 1927. None of the men were involved in the rise of the Guomindang in the 1920s, either as recorded participants or as minor functionaries. The hiatus in their public careers from 1927 to 1936 ended when two became supervisors of cooperatives. The Xiaofeng data indicate that the traditional oligarchy became less prominent during early Guomindang control; following the Japanese takeover of the county, they reemerged as key county leaders.

The Oligarchy and the Magistrate

Although there is not such long-term evidence from other outer-periphery counties, an oligarchy controlling a wide range of public affairs was an important aspect of the political structure here as in the inner periphery. The Songyang oligarchy was composed of seven gentry and gentry-merchants with ties to long-established families.[21] The functional record of Xuanping's nine-man oligarchy reveals substantial control (under magisterial direction) of county affairs, as evidenced in Table 15.[22] Several points are noteworthy. Both degree-holders and graduates were represented; but three had no degrees or had not attended school, and two of the three did not come from strong lineage backgrounds. Though these men were less represented on Qing subcounty self-government bodies, both assemblies included eight of the nine. This suggests that in the outer periphery traditional elites were slow to see the potential of the self-government movement during the Qing period, but that these organs were then utilized in the Republic. Professional association leaders were chosen from these nine men, with four serving as agriculture association chairmen. Inasmuch as the magistrate called on the same men for a variety of functions, the institutions themselves seem less important than the men who composed them.

In militia control, educational functions, and public works, the range of the oligarchy is apparent. The assumption of minor bureaucratic posts in the county yamen by four of the nine points to a significant feature of the outer periphery: the interchangeability of yamen department functionaries and county elite. In no other zone have I found evidence of this degree of shuffling between county bureaucratic posts and generalist county elite roles. After men served in their native counties' yamens in the three inner zones, they did not move back to important independent local elite roles; often they used their specialized skills in similar minor posts in other counties.[23] In the outer periphery, however, a different pattern emerged. In addition to four of the Xuanping oligarchy, nine other important local elites—from one or more spheres of action—served one or more times in the county yamen. In Changhua, six functioned alternately as official and nonofficial elites with two of the county's oligarchical elite involved. In Suian, the number was twelve. In the outer-periphery counties, then, the line between official and nonofficial action was indistinct.

Table 15.
Xuanping county oligarchs with specific characteristics and roles

Background		Self-government		Professional associations		Roles	
Degree	4	Subcounty	3	Chamber of commerce chairman	1	Minor county officials	4
Graduate	2	1st assembly	8	Education association chairman	1	Public works	7
Strong lineage	7	2nd assembly	8	Agriculture association chairman	4	Militia heads	3
						School builders	4
						Education deputies	5
						Education promotion office head	1
						Head of workhouse	1
						Anti-opium head	1

Source: *Xuanping xianzhi*, passim.

Suian, Songyang, and Xuanping gazetteers indicate the magistrate's control of societal management and initiation of projects that in core zones were often handled by local elites. In Suian, the magistrate set up a county culture committee (*wenhua weiyuan hui*) in 1921; he initiated public works, personally overseeing the construction of a dike in the early 1920s; and he persisted in reopening the workhouse that had been allowed to close.[24] The Songyang magistrate inaugurated the first school athletic meets in late 1918.[25] Although Songyang had a number of modern-school graduates who had returned from outside, it remained for the magistrate to initiate this action: returning elites had fitted into the existing political ecology of the outer periphery. In Xuanping, the magistrate controlled the county orphanage, ordered the self-government bodies to oversee repair of dikes, and designated county elites to repair the Confucian temple. From 1917 to 1920, he sponsored the expansion of sericulture, sending the head of the agriculture association to Huzhou to buy seedling mulberry trees. The model mulberry field thus established was located next to the yamen.[26] Sections on public works and charity from outer-periphery county gazetteers provide a continual account of magistrates soliciting local elite contributions. The relationship of magistrate to outer-periphery elites may be seen as the continuation of the trend of less elite autonomy and initiative and greater control by the magistrate in the outer zones. Alternatively, involvement in the yamen itself may suggest an acute elite political awareness that county action was situated in the yamen; hence elites chose to be a part of it. Once inside the yamen, local elites could exercise greater control over the magistrate. This situation differed from the core zones where other institutions frequently vied with and occasionally transcended the importance of the yamen.

Elite Patterns in the 1920s

Two categories of self-government statistics from the 1920s suggest some changes in outer-periphery patterns. The number of graduates serving in native place organs leaped to 31 percent, a substantial increase surpassed only by the 35 percent serving in the inner periphery. In addition, the number who had spent time outside their counties increased by almost 20 percent from the first assembly period.[27] Many of these returnees were members of established kin groups who, by sending their students out, were showing the same tendency to accommodate themselves to the new political and social current as did similar elites on a greater scale in the inner periphery.

The distinct waves of returnees in the inner zones—before the 1911 revolution and in the 1920s—were not apparent here. The larger number of graduates and others with outside linkages in the 1920s had mostly returned throughout the first decade of the Republic, performing functions in the mid-to-late 1910s and then assuming self-government roles. There seemed to be no specific 1920s' influx of men who had been outside for lengthy periods. Outer-periphery graduates of schools in the inner zones tended to return to their native places. Men from Suian, Changhua, and Xuanping who between the late Qing period and the mid-1920s were graduated from a modern school outside their counties numbered fifty-one; seventy-nine; and fifty-eight, respectively. Of these, only 15.7 percent from Suian, 5.1 percent from Changhua, and 10.3 percent from Xuanping had careers outside their counties. Roughly between 85 and 95 percent of these counties' graduates returned—a sharp contrast to the core zones. The stronger degree of traditionalism in their backgrounds and the sense of local prestige and power offered by their credentials probably motivated their return.

Most students left to attend middle and normal schools. The number of military graduates was significantly decreased from those in the outer core and inner periphery, a trend suggested by the Baoding academy statistics. On a county-by-county basis, 8.6 percent (five) of Xuanping's graduates were military; 8.9 percent (five) of Jingning's graduates attended military academies. Neither Suian nor Changhua counties produced any military graduates.

The Political Agenda

From Qu Yingguang's viewpoint in 1915, the agenda for the outer-periphery counties included relief measures (specifically, public granaries and workhouses) and the stimulation of better methods of agricultural production.[28] The land in most of these counties was poor; income was meager. When bad crop years occurred (as in 1914 and 1915 following severe drought in many of the western Zhejiang counties), the ripple at the neck of the Chinese farmer (to use R. H. Tawney's famous metaphor) became a wave.[29] In such a situation, the goal of the counties in this zone became not so much "development" as subsistence and stability.

Qu and subsequent provincial leaders encouraged traditional local industry—paper manufacturing in Changhua, lumber and bamboo production in Yuqian and Xiaofeng, pottery making in Longchuan—for the invigoration of the local economy.[30] These admonitions brought little action, however. When local elites did attempt to act, as in Xiaofeng, there were few lasting results. In 1916 Wang Lisan opened a new paper mill that operated only two years because of the management's miscalculation of needed supplies.[31] In 1918 Wang attempted to establish an electric power company with old machinery purchased from the town of

Linghu in Wuxing (inner core); but the machinery worked for only two days and was never repaired.[32] Insufficient capital to overcome such difficulties was a continual problem.

The gulf between the most developed and the least developed zones is obvious both in the time differential in organizational establishment and in monies available for county needs. Chambers of commerce were founded almost twelve years later than in the inner core. Agriculture associations were begun later and existed a shorter period of time than in other zones.[33] County workhouses, envisioned as the hope of the wretched poor, operated only sporadically.[34] Both gross and per capita sums on Table 16 from scattered county budgetary data reflect the great disparities among zones and the penury of the outer-periphery counties.[35] Although the sums come from a range of four years, I do not think this substantially distorts the results. In the categories of self-government and education, the amounts spent per capita decrease greatly from the inner core.[36] A significant figure, indicating the greater attention to problems of disorder in the outer periphery, is the police expenditures. The two counties on which there is information spent more per capita than did Zhuji of the outer core, a comparison that is especially significant given that Zhuji was a notoriously unstable county and that its police expenditures probably far outran those of most outer-core counties. Xuanping spent more per inhabitant for police than for schools, a reversal of Zhuji's pattern and probably of the core zones in general.

Table 16.
Selected annual county expenditures, 1922–1926 (in *yuan*)

County	Self-Government		Education		Police	
	Gross	Per 10,000 inhabitants	Gross	Per 10,000 inhabitants	Gross	Per 10,000 inhabitants
Inner core						
Jiaxing	26,047	618	41,523	1,114	—	—
Outer core						
Fenghua	6,853	308	11,986	533	—	—
Zhuji	10,428	197	18,872	357	18,016	341
Outer periphery						
Xuanping	920	121	2,458	323	2,655	349
Jingning	c. 750	c. 64	—	—	—	—
Changhua	—	—	—	—	2,970	387

Sources: for Jiaxing, *Shi Bao*, 1923/10/31; for Fenghua, *Xin Fenghua*, "diaocha," pp. 1–29; for Zhuji, *Zhuji gaiguan*, "Zhuji gaiguan," pp. 75–79; for Xuanping, *Xuanping xianzhi*, 3:6a–b; for Jingning, *Jingning xianxuzhi* (reprint), pp. 207–210; and for Changhua, *Changhua xianzhi* (reprint), p. 154.

Many programs died or languished for lack of funds. The progress of education in Suian county was slowed by insufficient funds and consequently a shortage of teachers.[37] Faced with the same problems, Xuanping county attempted to train teachers in a county teachers' institute; but funds for the institute had to be taken from the county's primary school budget. Xuanping set up a newspaper reading room that was actually a gift of a rich elite from Longchuan county.[38]

The best example of both the financial crunch and the essential role of government in outer-periphery development involved Xuanping's workhouse.[39] Established as ordered by Hangchow in the beginning years of the Republic, it was headed by one of the county's oligarchs. The most successful of the three training sections taught dyeing; and its product, figured cotton cloth, was considered of high enough quality to be displayed at San Francisco's Panama Exposition in 1915. When another of the oligarchs became chairman in 1916, he attempted to expand the dye department; but he quickly ran into major problems: the lack of capital and an inability to reach a wider market. Then, in 1920, when the Hangchow government decreed that small towns like Xuanping did not have to establish workhouses, the county promptly stopped the whole project. In this case government orders stimulated what seemed to be a chance for economic development; but with government pressure gone, lack of local funds (and initiative) fated the project to extinction.

Insufficient revenues could lead directly to an inability to cope with social disorder, a continual outer-periphery problem. Bandits from Anhui, Jiangxi, and Fujian repeatedly attacked counties along the provincial borders.[40] Magistrates most often responded by marshalling militia units.[41] Sometimes local lineages like the Pan in Zhenwu township, Xuanping, organized their own militia to deal with local bandits (*tufei*) by getting subscriptions from rich households in the area.[42]

These counties especially felt the presence of marauding soldiers from surrounding provinces during the war scare of 1923, the Zhejiang-Jiangsu war of 1924 (and Sun Chuanfang's takeover of the province), and the Northern Expedition in 1926 and 1927.[43] Military extortions took huge sums, exacerbating the fiscal problems of the counties. In August 1924 Suian's county seat was faced with demands for 15,000 *jin*. The chamber of commerce chairman and a key county elite negotiated the demands down to 4,000 *jin*. But Suian's problems did not end there. In August 1926 remnants of armies defeated in Jiangxi in the Northern Expedition crossed into the county, demanding to be quartered in people's homes. Although the inhabitants of the county seat fled, the county board set up a reception area to offer needed supplies. When the soldiers left, they extorted 3,000 *jin*. In January 1927 the main army of the Northern Expedition passed through, impressing local men as porters and coolies for the attack on Jiande. Marauding military groups plundered the city again in September 1927 and November 1929.[44]

The county of Jingning on the Fujian border was the object of bandit raids from Fujian in the summer of 1927 and early in 1931. The latter raids, led by a former military man originally sent to crush the bandits, brought much loss of property and life. The county's plight was made more serious by the fact that in 1930 secret society uprisings, local bandit raids, and immigrant violence had left the economy in shambles.[45] Xiaofeng's border status led to its seizure in 1935 by remnants of Fang Zhimin's Jiangxi Soviet forces. When militia units were ineffective against the Communist troops, county government and elites fled to neighboring counties until Guomindang forces restored their control.[46] Outer-periphery counties experienced continual episodes of transborder banditry and military attacks. In the face of such depredations, the niceties of education, self-government, and modern development became rather meaningless.

The Role of Outsiders

Large numbers of nonelite immigrants heavily peopled such counties as Yuqian, Xiaofeng, Changhua, and Songyang.[47] Enterprising innerzone or Shanghai entrepreneurs paid little attention to the counties of the outer periphery. Most had few mineral resources to develop; and, if they did, transport facilities for carrying extracted minerals to the inner-core areas were poor or nonexistent.

Some outsiders, however, played important local elite roles despite the lack of developmental potential. Given the economic shortcomings of these counties, this phenomenon is difficult to fathom. The Suian gazetteer refers to that county's lack of involvement in commerce, noting that its chamber of commerce was not established until 1921 and that only by about 1930 did its own inhabitants begin to become involved in trade, chiefly in salt and tea. Suian had only one guild, from Jiande, the capital of its prefecture. Yet its chamber of commerce was headed by merchant outsiders mostly from Yi and Jiqi counties in the Anhui prefecture of Huizhou.[48] The specific commodities or interests of these men were not disclosed. In 1926, as the only evidence of their local noncommercial involvement, they joined with local elites who had an interest in business to establish a small electric plant.[49] The major river in Suian, the Wuqiangqi, connects the county to the Xinan River, which flows from Huizhou to Jiande. Thus, the Huizhou presence in the area is explicable, but the merchant activity in Suian in particular could not have been profitable. Local elites seemed willing to allow outsiders control of the economy, acceding to what appears to be simply an extractive operation.

Similarly, Huizhou merchants dominated Xiaofeng county businesses. Even though Xiaofeng's riverine linkage to Anhui is poor, in 1917 when the county chamber of commerce was formed, leaders and most members hailed from Huizhou. Whereas these merchants participated to some extent in Suian's industrial development, there is no indication that they did so in Xiaofeng county.[50]

Xuanping county's situation contravenes the accepted thought about natural trading systems and presents a completely different picture of the relationship between outsiders and natives than in other areas. The outsider merchant elites in Xuanping were from Jiangxi, which was not only in a different trading system but in a different macroregion. The county did not offer much commercial promise, for it produced only farm commodities. The reasons for their settling there and the nature of their commercial enterprises are not disclosed; but a Jiangxi guild was established at a rented pavilion, and these men became chamber of commerce leaders after its establishment in 1915.

The relationship of these Jiangxi outsiders to the native inhabitants was in developmental terms perhaps the logical culmination of the trend moving outward from the inner core. In the inner core, hostility and exclusion often faced outside merchants and residents. In the outer core, more symbiotic relationships existed between outsider and native, but they were laced with antagonism and resentment. In many counties of the inner periphery, outside merchants dominated trade and commercial organizations, participating in some counties with local elites in developmental projects. This pattern is also partially seen in Suian and Xiaofeng. In Xuanping, however, the Jiangxi outsiders were not only important mercantile elites but were also part of the county's political elite structure.[51] Wu Daonan and Wu Chengyu were active in public works fundings from early in the century, being charged by the magistrate to contribute to needed projects with other county elites. Wu Daonan, a gentry-manager, formed militia units in 1915 and was solicited for aid in 1924. Wu Chengyu joined Gan Shixin in the late Qing subcounty self-government bodies with Wu serving as board member and Gan, board vice-president. Gan was chairman of the county seat council in the early Republic, and his son was a member of the second county assembly. The integration of commercial and political elites and of nonofficial and official elites in Xuanping reemphasizes the picture of a small but persistent county oligarchy. The oligarchy's inclusion of outsiders may suggest a lack of county elite interest in commercial enterprise; a grudging elite acceptance of the ability of the outsiders and a recognition of the advantages of maintaining symbiotic relationships; or an almost primitive lack of emphasis upon cultural and political distinctions. The pattern was not duplicated in other counties that I have studied but may have existed in counties on the subregional divide between the Ou-Ling and Min basins.

The Beginnings of Political Development

In the first thirty years of the twentieth century, the counties in the outer periphery experienced few economic changes and no political changes sufficient to disrupt their oligarchical political structure. Most county oligarchs were from lineages based either in the few semiprosperous mountain basins or in frontier areas where defense necessitated lineage cohesion. Their interests in commerce were minimal; in this zone, the gentry-merchant hybrid rarely appeared.[52] In contrast to the inner periphery, few of the oligarchs had links outside the county. In Xuanping, for example, only two of the nine oligarchs had been beyond county borders for any period of time.[53] County political concerns were stability, order, public works, and economic subsistence. The most important person in the county was the magistrate, who initiated and promoted public projects.

Outer-periphery counties were highly undeveloped. Institutionalization of new organizations was slow; there was little specialization of functions; modern-style voluntary associations were, as best as can be determined, nonexistent. There was little sense of political identification with such administrative divisions as townships, counties, or province. The foreign pressure that had helped to politicize segments of elites in the inner zones was absent. Foreign missionaries did not generally expand into these counties until the twentieth century.[54] Awareness of national or provincial developments occasionally came via nonelites. News of the Boxer disturbances, for example, reached Suian through its native laborers at work in Qu county where antimissionary violence flared.[55] The frequent military depredations of the 1920s were a forced awakening of sorts to problems beyond the locality, but they were not generally politicizing.

The first decades of the century did, however, see certain agents of politicization from the outside. Late Qing political institutions established for the local elite, though not immediately successful as institutions, did provide the framework for greater awareness of political processes. The role of government in the establishment of common county institutions (some of which, like the workhouses, introduced new ways of handling old problems) and in the promotion of modern school system was also important. The magistrate was a crucial agent, stimulating interest in modern-style education, model agriculture experiment farms, and modern sanitation and medical techniques.[56]

The most significant nonofficial links beyond the county were modern-trained students, who brought ideas and specialized interests back to their native places. These were men like Pan Ding of Xuanping, graduate of Zhejiang's First Middle School in Hangchow and briefly head of the education department of the Lishui county government, who returned to Xuanping and dedicated himself to educational expansion and reform.[57] Or they were men like Changhua county's only graduates of Japanese schools, Fang Yinhua and Pan Bingwen, who after their return by 1906 wrote a lengthy essay, reprinted in the county gazetteer, encouraging modern study. Although most of their careers were spent outside the county, they were both from important lineages that provided county elites. It is logical to assume that some Changhua elites had at least a modicum of acquaintance with their Social Darwinist ideas.[58]

Sometimes returning students and county school students joined forces over local events. The Yuqian county historian described how students organized for the first time in the aftermath of a scandalous 1922 county board election.[59] Local issues also aroused a student protest and strike in Suian in the mid-1920s.[60] Zhu Wenxing and Fang Bingxing of Xiaofeng returned from school and established a county weekly newspaper. Although it published only seven issues, it provided the precedent for county factional newspapers, which began to be published in 1923.[61]

Xiaofeng county factionalism between Wan He's "Association" (xie-hui) and Ye Xiangyang's Youth League (Qingnian tuan) developed over conflicting personal interests and county programs. Both factional leaders served the county as representatives in Hangchow assemblies in the 1920s, and their linkages to Hangchow affairs seemed only to heighten bitterness and county wrangling. The choice of Ye's factional name indicates greater openness to the forces of change in the May Fourth period. Through this factionalism, concerns of national import became incorporated in local politics, adding a new dimension to old feuds. Such a process tended to increase the county elite's awareness of issues beyond the county.[62]

The continual elections for county assemblies, provincial assemblies, and constitutional conventions also brought the outer-periphery counties into the framework of greater political involvement. Although some outer-periphery counties, like Fenshui, were dilatory in convention elections, other counties showed great concern for following the letter of the election regulations.[63] Protest telegrams from Suian and Yuqian over the May Thirtieth episode indicate their incipient involvement in outside concerns through purposive political action.[64] In short, little by little the counties of the outer periphery were brought into the larger national arena. Although the involvement was shallow and tangential to local concerns, the framework for greater involvement was being constructed through new political dynamics.

PART THREE

Locality, Province, and Nation in Early-Twentieth-Century Politics

10

The 1911 Revolution

The white flags that flew from buildings in urban centers throughout Zhejiang in November and December of 1911 heralded a new political system. In efforts to understand the revolution's significance, historians have generally centered their attention on the revolution's instigators and their subsequent sociopolitical roles.[1] But apart from assertions of probable differences in the revolutionary leadership and the revolution's significance in coastal or riverine towns and cities, on the one hand, and the rural hinterland, on the other, historians have failed to place this important event in its spatial context.[2] Many have viewed the 1911 revolution in Mary Wright's undifferentiated image of a "rising tide of change"[3]— an image taken from the inner core and only the larger cities of the inner core, at that. Studying the 1911 revolution as it occurred in the context of local economic and political development brings debate over the revolution's meaning into proper spatial context and gives greater intelligibility and significance to what might otherwise be seen as a haphazard series of county seat coups. The zonal classification provides an important tool in elucidating the events of 1911 and their meaning.

The revolution in Zhejiang was, in general terms, a two-phase process: the key event for provincial politics came at the capital, Hangchow; it was followed by a series of coups (not directed from Hangchow) in county seats and larger nonadministrative market towns.

The Inner Core: The Hangchow Coup

The Hangchow coup, like other inner-core coups, was the work of an alliance of older reformist elites and returned students, dominated by modern military graduates. The New Army, born from the Qing regime's desire for military modernization, was built in Zhejiang around two regiments formed in 1905 and 1906.[4] One was led by an old-style military leader; the other by Jiang Zungui, a graduate of the Japan Army Officers Academy (*rikugun shikan gakkō*) who appointed to major posts graduates of his alma mater and of the Nanjing Military Academy.[5] Many of the New Army's minor officers had been trained at the Zhejiang Military Academy (*wubei xuetang*), founded in 1900. The higher career levels made possible by extraprovincial education were obvious.

As the New Army developed, secret revolutionary organizations—the Restoration Society and Tongmeng hui—made contacts with the army men and gathered converts to the revolutionary cause. Before 1907 the famous revolutionary Qiu Jin herself had brought a number of military men into the Restoration Society; and many men who had studied in Japan became associated with the Tongmeng hui. The sources for identifying individual affiliation with one or both of these societies are imprecise and often conflicting. It is probable, however, that many in the army were touched to some degree by the revolutionary message.

In 1909, two years after the executions of Xu Xilin and Qiu for their ill-fated revolutionary activity, a strictly military Restoration Society was revived in Hangchow; most members were soldiers from two regiments stationed near the capital. The three leading revolutionaries in the group were all returned military graduates: Zhu Rui, Gu Naibin, and Lü Gongwang.[6] Beginning in June 1911, the members of the society met to discuss the political situation. After news of the Wuchang uprising of October 10 reached Hangchow, they met several times to plan for the "restoration" (*guangfu*); revolutionary representatives from Shanghai attended most of the meetings.[7] The linkage to the macroregion capital is noteworthy. At the October 19 meeting, Zhu Rui introduced the provincial assembly member Chu Fucheng into the group, thus linking the New Army officers and the returned-student constitutionalists. Chu, a member of the Tongmeng hui, had been graduated from Oriental University (Tōyō Daigaku) in Japan and had returned to his home prefecture, Jiaxing, to lead in local reform activities.[8] The provincial assembly vice-presidents, Chen Shixia and Shen Junru, returned students from Japan, also participated in the precoup planning.[9] All three constitutionalists hailed from the inner-core prefectural capitals of Jiaxing and Ningpo.

By October 21 the governor's family had fled to Shanghai; most of the schools were closed; and the chaotic currency situation had thrown several thousand factory employees out of work.[10] In this supercharged atmosphere, the small group of New Army officers and returned graduates planned the coup and subsequent regime. They adopted the strategy of sending agents to join with long-time secret society leaders in Shaoxing and Jinyun in order to foment disorder and draw strong old-line military forces from Hangchow. This strategy reflected the previous decade's stillborn alliance between mostly inner-core returned students and some outer-zone secret society elites.[11] The revolutionaries decided that Tang Shouqian, the railway hero, should become the postrevolution military governor (*dudu*). They felt that as a provincial symbol, he could probably bring unity to diverse groups—gentry, merchants, and military; various military factions; and Restoration Society and Tongmeng hui partisans.

The New Army regiments and a so-called Dare-to-Die Corps led attacks on key public buildings on the night of November 4. The coup was successful, stimulating relatively little resistance.[12] Installing a stable new regime was more difficult. Lü Gongwang, New Army agent to the secret societies in Jinyun, was angered by the timing of the coup, believing that others had deliberately arranged it while he was away in order to keep him from the circle of power. Lü and fellow graduates of the Baoding Military Institute (*Baoding sucheng xuetang*) were further infuriated when they received only one insignificant position in the new government.[13]

Even more serious was the opposition that developed against the choice of Tang as military governor.[14] Early Restoration Society leaders like Wang Jinfa were furious, contending that Tang had supported the execution of Qiu Jin in 1907.[15] Other revolutionaries were repelled by Tang's decidedly moderate-conservative political stance. Like many Chinese leaders of the period, he was concerned about the possible interference of imperialists in Chinese affairs. In his first public statement he called for protecting the property and lives of foreigners and for harsh military justice for disturbers of the peace.[16] Some of the appointees to his military government scarcely seemed properly supportive of revolutionary politics. Zhou Chengtang, commander-in-chief of the army, had remained neutral to the revolution until the last moment. Gao Erdeng, the finance minister, though a member of the Tongmeng hui, was more enterprising entrepreneur than revolutionary.[17]

Most revolutionaries were antagonized by Tang's reaction to the Guilin affair. Guilin, the regimental colonel of the Manchu garrison, had been a leader in the railway movement and other reform activities where he had become friends with like-minded men like Tang and the president of the assembly, Chen Fuchen.[18] Although the garrison had surrendered on November 6, evidence came to light that Guilin and his son had hidden over two thousand rifles for a countercoup. Prompted by provincial assembly elites Chu Fucheng and Shen Junru, a temporary council (*linshi canyihui*) ordered the execution of both Manchus.[19] Tang, in Shanghai at the time of the execution, was extremely upset; his spontaneous reaction of sympathy for Guilin contrasted sharply with his recent excoriation of the Manchus and angered the revolutionaries.[20] Biting political opposition expressed through developing military factions led the increasingly bitter Tang to announce his resignation on December 13.

Tang's heavy reliance on returned students from Japan, pejoratively called imported goods (*bolaipin*) by many China-trained army officers, had spread dissatisfaction throughout the military ranks.[21] When he resigned to join the Nanjing government as communications minister, he supported his successor yet another of the returned students, Jiang Zungui, the key figure in the development of Zhejiang's New Army and the son of one of his best friends.[22] Most of the returned students from Japan were members of or had been associated with the Tongmeng hui whereas most of the other military leaders were members of the Restoration Society. Tang's choice of Jiang ignited a Restoration Society campaign to have its own man appointed military governor.

The candidate of many in the Restoration Society was Tao Chengzhang, who with Xu Xilin had founded the original organization in late 1904. After 1907 he had spent much of his time in Japan and Southeast Asia collecting money for use in the revolution. He returned to Zhejiang after the coup and served briefly in the council that sentenced Guilin to death. Tao then made his headquarters at Shanghai, gathering monetary support for the Zhejiang army's attack on Nanjing. There he met frequently with fellow society members Zhu Rui, Lü Gongwang, and Qu Yingguang.[23] Though there was some society support for Zhang Binglin and even for Wang Jinfa, who had been a major figure in revolutionary activities half a decade earlier, Tao quicky became the society's choice to succeed Tang.[24]

The nature of Jiang's and Tao's support is striking. Available sources suggest that Jiang's support came from inner-core elites—gentry, gentry-merchant, and student circles in Hangchow—and Zhejiangese gentry-merchants and merchants sojourning in Shanghai.[25] Tao's support, on the other hand, came partly from military men from outer-core counties in Jinhua, Quzhou, and Yanzhou. In light of the fact that most military officers were outer-ranging inner-core elites, it is interesting that most of the army's rank and file reportedly came from these three outer-zone prefectures.[26] Joining them in support of Tao were old-line provincial forces (*xunfangdui*) in Hangchow and some students at a Zhejiang military academy. Certain Hangchow merchants also called for Tao's leadership. Although their exact status and occupational specialty cannot be determined, they were not prestigious men: of twenty-five who supported Tao, none played any recorded roles in politics, public works, or the establishment of modern enterprises. In sum, Jiang was touted by those inner-core elites with linkages outside the province, whereas Tao's support came from traditional military types and those who were province-based and less notable.[27]

Because Tang held the strings of power and had chosen Jiang, there was no real chance that Tao could succeed him. An ad hoc committee of twenty-two unanimously rubberstamped Jiang's election in January 1912.[28] Public reaction in parts of Zhejiang was strongly negative. On January 14 an open telegram appeared in the Shanghai newspaper *Shi Bao* from Restoration Society figures pleading with Tao to return to Zhejiang to organize opposition.[29] On the evening of the same day, Tao was murdered in a Shanghai hospital. Chen Qimei, a Zhejiangese Tongmeng hui member who wanted to retain friendly leadership in the province and perhaps take over himself, apparently issued orders for the murder; the middleman who reportedly hired the killer was Chiang Kai-shek.[30]

Jiang Zungui had won the election but at a cost. His tenure as military governor, born in blood, was marked by continual factional feuding and punctuated by assassinations and revenge murders.[31] To make matters worse, Jiang seemed not much the revolutionary, appointing to office men who still supported the emperor. Such action gutted the support he had previously enjoyed among the province's Tongmeng hui chapters.[32] When he left office in August 1912, almost all the "imported goods" were also turned out of key provincial positions.[33] Zhu Rui, the hero of Nanjing whose triumphant return in May had seemed the only bright spot amid the political and economic ruins of the revolution, succeeded Jiang. The administration of Zhu (1912-1916), who hailed from the inner core, was characterized by the leadership of military elites who had been trained outside the province in Nanjing and Baoding. The Hangchow coup, in sum, was controlled by a group of New Army officers who utilized secret society ties and acted with reformist elites. Very quickly, however, this revolutionary coalition disintegrated into jealous factions intent upon destroying each other.

The Inner Core: Outside Hangchow

The counties of the inner core were, in general, the only ones prepared for the 1911 coups. Inner-core elites were involved in modern socioeconomic developments, with many links outward to Shanghai and beyond. In the years before 1911, the inner core had attracted outer-ranging elites who later became involved in nationalistic issues in their native places— the anti-American boycott of 1905, the railway movement, and national debt payment. They formed martial and reform organizations to deal with the "weak spirit" that many suggested had been characteristic of Chinese in the past. They spoke of building up the individual and the local unit in order to strengthen the nation.[34] Many of these reformers became revolutionaries. Important lineage-based gentry, gentry-merchants, and modern-school teachers, principals, and graduates began to form various organizations to serve as vehicles for revolutionary activity in the prefectural capitals, some county seats, and larger nonadministrative market towns. These men were joined in certain cities, especially Wuxing and Ningpo, by secret society members (Restoration Society and Tongmeng hui) and the New Army.[35]

Only in the inner core was there any sense of coordination in the hectic early days of November. Although the Hangchow revolutionary coalition did not direct any action elsewhere, a few prefectural centers did offer guidance to their counties. Ningpo elites sent representatives to four of the six counties in the prefecture to bring about or coordinate governmental changes; the two other counties sent a representative to Ningpo. It is impossible to tell if the decision for "restoration" (*guangfu*) in the four counties came before or after the Ningpo deputies arrived, but the cohesion of the prefectural unit is noteworthy. In early 1912 Ningbo elites from each county voluntarily organized an ad hoc prefectural council (*liuyi gonghui*) to deal with public affairs that remained unsettled in the wake of the revolution. This council was independent of the prefectural military government (*junzheng fenfu*).[36] In Wenzhou prefecture, elite representatives from each county gathered in the prefectural capital to discuss problems of defense and finance.[37]

The coup in Huzhou prefecture was ignited and directed not in Wuxing but in Shanghai, by Chen Qimei, a native of Huzhou, who had become Shanghai's military governor in early November. Interested in leading Zhejiang in the future, Chen had attended precoup military planning sessions in Hangchow.[38] In the days before the coups in Huzhou prefecture, Chen dispatched an emissary to already existing revolutionary groups to trigger the revolution.[39] Three months later, when financial and social chaos threatened the existence of the new prefectural military government, Chen sent his representatives and two companies of Guangdong soldiers to establish a new regime.[40]

In the inner core's administrative centers and in some of its larger nonadministrative centers where previous planning had occurred, the revolutionary elites and the general pattern of the revolution were thus often similar. In other inner-core areas, there was much more political indecision and social violence. In the town of Shuanglin (Wuxing county), the political actors and train of events differed sharply from those in many larger urban centers.[41] In Shuanglin the chief actors were merchants who were concerned about the loss to the town's silk industry if local order disintegrated. There had been no prerevolutionary establishment of militia units and no preparation for the political change. When news of the revolution in Wuxing reached Shuanglin, over one hundred of the town's businessmen met at the silk merchants' benevolent association to discuss militia funding. Using local *lijin* funds, they sent several merchants to Hangchow and Shanghai to purchase arms; in the meantime, they argued among themselves about who would lead the new militia units.

There were two subplots to this restoration drama. The first was a series of attempts by the head of the town's provincial forces military patrol to extort money from the merchants; he threatened to resign and leave a totally incompetent junior officer in charge. The second concerned the town board president who, arguing that all self-government functions should be assumed by the militia office, abolished the self-government organs. When Hangchow ordered their reestablishment, the board president fled to Shanghai, and a rump council and board called itself into session. In this episode, merchants, not gentry or gentry-merchants, played the key roles; and there was considerably more confusion and turmoil here than elsewhere about what was happening, what should be done, and who specifically should lead.

For elites in some inner-core counties of Shaoxing and Taizhou prefectures, the revolution only increased an already tense social situation. Both prefectures had suffered severe floods in the summer and early fall of 1911. There were reports that rice crops in Taizhou had been blown over by high winds and buried under several feet of mud and that Shaoxing's cotton crop was completely lost. In the wake of the revolution it was reported that some villagers had formed gangs, abducting the rich and looting their property. Such an extraordinary situation produced a different revolutionary elite experience from that in many other areas of the inner core. Some elites fled with whatever wealth they could take. Others reportedly began to arm their tenants in order to protect individual landholding and possessions.[42] This last report suggests that even in areas of social violence during the revolution, the dynamic was generally not class antagonism: landlords were not afraid to arm their tenants in an effort to rid the area of local bandit groups.

Thus there was no one overall inner-core revolutionary pattern. Local episodes varied in detail, and the degree of social turmoil depended on local conditions. In general, however, the inner-core coups of county-wide significance were directed by a coalition of leading gentry, gentry-merchants, and returned students, both military and civilian.[43] In most cases, the civilian revolutionaries had been involved in nationalistic activity and reform projects in the half decade before the revolution. Revolutionary organizations and militia units were often features of the inner-core counties long before the revolution. In many areas, there were important elite links beyond the inner core.

The Outer Zones

Rapid socioeconomic development, the spread of new and radical ideas, and expanding elite political participation and social linkages were, in the last years of the Qing, largely limited to the inner core. Historians surveying mainly this area have, not surprisingly, seen "a new world" and "a new society in the making."[44] But the inner-core population was less than half (44.5 percent) of the total provincial population. Elite structures and the sociopolitical ecology were markedly different in the outer zones; so too was the revolution.

There was little prerevolutionary preparation by modernizing elites in the outer zones. Word of the revolution led to impromptu decision making and considerable confusion. Events in some counties like Qu (outer core) and Jiande (inner periphery) seemed to repeat aspects of the coup in the inner-core town of Shuanglin: merchants met on their own or with self-government leaders to form militia units, to send for arms from inner-core urban centers, and to stave off military threats. In Jiande, merchants and self-government leaders asked Hangchow to permit the retention of the former prefect as head of the revolutionary government. When Hangchow agreed, returned students claimed the right to elect their own government leaders. Hangchow responded with a sharp condemnation of their action.[45] In Qu county, the chamber of commerce seized control in an attempt to name new government leaders and then was driven out by local provincial forces.[46]

In almost every county in the outer zones, the revolution ended in military seizure, notably not by New Army troops but by local militia units, old-line provincial forces, or bandit gangs.[47] These groups seemed to have little revolutionary motive other than seizing power and loot. In Tonglu county (outer core), as self-government leaders met to decide on a course of action, a unit of so-called righteous soldiers, probably local militiamen, marched into the county seat. They first demanded bribes from the self-government office and then insisted that they be selected as heads of the new government.[48] In Xiangshan county (outer core), area militia stormed the city, joined with police, and demanded money from the local elite—in the process, declaring "restoration."[49] An unspecified number of provincial troops entered the outer-core county seat of Longyu, declaring themselves for the revolution. The commander went directly to the yamen and demanded 400 *yuan*. His actions were discovered by his own troops, and they demanded equal payment; he refused, whereupon a destructive mutiny erupted. On the heels of this inglorious episode came an uprising of former yamen runners who knew that their fraudulent activities were at an end and whose demands on official elites to provide for them in the future had been rejected.[50]

In one outer-core county, Xinchang, the great bandit Zhou Yongguang launched a vicious attack on the county seat in the midst of elite deliberations on what course to follow.[51] As elites fled and small county militia units disappeared, Zhou entered the city, demanding recognition as a revolutionary leader.[52] In Luoqing county, another bandit leader tried to seize the opportunity for revolution. Taking advantage of the uncertainty spawned by the Hangchow coup and subsequent county elite decisions, Teng Huajin attacked the county seat. He was finally beaten back by provincial forces after local militia units failed to control him.[53] In short, in one county of the outer zones after another, the revolutionary denouement was the seizure of the local political scene by old-line military types, opportunistic bandits, or obstreperous local militia companies.

The other common revolutionary outcome in many of the counties of the outer zones was social chaos that sometimes lasted more than half a year. Upon receiving word of the revolution self-government bodies in the inner-periphery counties of Tangqi and Shouchang announced their support. But neither county could decide how to proceed with the revolution. Tangqi was unable to prepare for a new government until Hangchow sent military representatives in early 1912; in the interim, the county was raked by bandits and robbers.[54] Shouchang self-government elites had decided at the beginning of their revolutionary deliberations to establish defensive militia units. In the face of increasing outbreaks, however, fear heightened that the militia would not be able to handle any general uprising. The fear led to general immobilization and pleas to Hangchow in mid-December for help. An almost complete power vacuum remained until late February 1912 when Hangchow finally sent a military representative; during these three and a half months the Shouchang populace was at the mercy of bandits and robbers who plundered at will while a multitude of militia units floundered helplessly.[55]

Linan county in the outer periphery of Hangzhou prefecture felt the presence of bandits at least until mid-summer 1912, when its self-government bodies were still attempting to deal with the situation.[56] In the outer-periphery county of Xiaofeng, a *shengyuan* returned student from Japan, after contacts with the Huzhou military government, announced the end of the old regime. When he left to assume control in a neighboring county, however, the county government disintegrated. There followed an attempted military extortion, the flight of the wealthy, and a paralyzing county siege by erstwhile bamboo cutters and charcoal burners turned bandits.[57] Suian county (outer periphery) did not even get to the point of declaring support for the revolution. When word of the revolution reached the county seat, bitter rivalry erupted between county seat and township council elites. As the dispute spread, all order was destroyed. Rustics (*yumin*) and bandits (*tufei*) reportedly rampaged through the county.[58]

In most counties of the outer zones, effective defense became the key elite concern; and self-government leaders were often involved in setting up and leading militia units. Of the thirty-eight militia heads in Shouchang, for example, twenty-six had been Qing council heads or board members; of the four key militia leaders in Xindeng, three had served in the self-government movement. This situation contrasts with the inner core where in Deqing, for example, militia units were usually formed by elites other than self-government figures.[59] The local self-government bodies in the outer zones, composed of a traditional elite trying to retain property and control, were clearly forces for law and order, not change or development.

In two counties of the inner periphery, Yongkang and Lishui, violence erupted between loyalists and revolutionaries (in these cases linked to secret societies). In Yongkang, the Restoration Society leader Lü Fengqiao first led a military coup and then united secret society members in a so-called peoples' army (*minbing*), many of whom were hurriedly sent north to participate in the Nanjing expedition. After their departure, loyalist forces captured and executed nine Restoration Society members whose deaths, in turn, were avenged by a Restoration Society militia unit. Uninvolved county elites bitterly condemned the Hangchow government for not responding to calls for aid.[60]

In Lishui county, Lü had linked himself to radical returned students. The revolution there was instigated by a coalition of secret society members, returned students, and local self-government elites.[61] This merging of traditional local elites, some modern-school graduates, and secret society and bandit elites was unparalleled in other counties. Of nine legitimate elites who joined Lü's secret society forces in Lishui, four were returned students (three from Japan and one from the Zhejiang law school); two served in late Qing subcounty self-government; three served in county self-government of the 1920s; one was in the provisional provincial assembly from late 1911 to 1913; and four participated in the county's incipient industrial development in the 1920s. There was a comparable though somewhat less inclusive revolutionary coalition in Songyang (outer periphery).[62]

In both counties, the revolutionary coalition stimulated local opposition. In Songyang, after self-government elites were ordered to establish protective militia units, opposition developed from at least one powerful landlord.[63] The Lishui opposition was stronger and more persistent. An analysis of the four leading opposition elites there indicates only one major social difference in these antagonistic groups. Like the revolutionaries, the opposition's members came from important local lineages and were degreed and involved in self-government; but almost half the revolutionaries had experience in the inner core and beyond, whereas the opponents apparently had not been beyond their native place.[64]

The Meaning of the Revolution

For many Zhejiangese elites, even in the inner core, the significance of what happened in the fall of 1911 was not clear. The idea of a new order seemed very real to many—from the wealthy Nanxun silk merchants who fled to Shanghai with their wealth to the Ciqi city council, halted in the middle of elections by the revolution.[65] The question facing the merchants and the council (which postponed the elections until new regulations could be issued) was how much in postrevolution politics and society would be new and what the newness would entail.

For elites in the counties of the inner core, the revolution signaled considerable sociopolitical change. The Manchus were no longer a hindrance to national development. Building the nation from the local level now seemed less a necessity: political and career horizons broadened once more to include all the nation. Many who returned to reform the locality in the last years of the Qing left once more. The career lure of higher urban spheres beckoned those who had never before ventured from their native place. A spirit of newness infused these elites as "the liberal republic" was born—newness of opportunity, of possibility.

The horizons also widened for those who remained in their native places. If there was a prevalent sense of the absence of the "king's law" in the days following the revolution, there was also the reality of greater local elite control over community politics and society.[66] County assemblies and boards joined subcounty political bodies in an ever-widening network of elite political bases. It seemed the logical culmination of local elite sociopolitical trends since the mid-nineteenth century. New voluntary associations of myriad types and sizes created a sense that society itself could be restructured through local political action and through attention to laws and regulations. In the politics of many inner-core counties, the rising importance of merchants became increasingly obvious. The cultural apparel of the gentry, essential for the hybrid gentry-merchants, was discarded, as merchants began to act in more direct political ways for their specialized economic interests. In many areas, new political types found their ways into the political arena. The 1911 revolution was a momentous event for many inner-core elites.[67]

The "success" of the revolution ironically seemed to have temporarily weakened national feeling; the Manchus, after all, had been cast out. The conviction that the Manchus had been responsible for national degradation defused the issue of nationalism once the Qing dynasty was over. In the years immediately after 1911, county assemblies did not even give lip service to the nation. The willingness of elites to support the nationalization of the Shanghai-Hangchow-Ningpo railroad when such action still might mean foreign control contrasted sharply with the pre-1911 nationalistic outrage.[68] The passivity with which elites greeted the naming of Wang Shengsan as the province's commissioner of foreign affairs contrasted to the rancor with which Wang had been attacked as a foreign pawn in prerevolutionary days.[69]

The meaning of the revolution in the three outer zones is more problematical. Few gazetteers from these zones mention the revolution apart from defensive measures, and some not at all. The county elite historians' lack of interest in detailing the revolutionary process says much about perceptions of the event. Even though outer-core gazetteers like the *Zhuji gaiguan* failed to include coverage of the revolution, the editors did acknowledge some political discontinuity. They argued that a prerevolutionary antismoking campaign led by local leaders had relatively cleansed the county of the costly habit. But with the revolution, the British-American Tobacco Company was able to adopt the stratagem of sending samples of the best-grade cigarettes to the troops. Using the military as a base, the company once again began a wide dispersal.[70]

There are indications that an intangible sense of new forms and style stemming from the revolution penetrated at least to some areas of the outer core. The revolution reportedly encouraged Fenghua elites and commoners to impeach the head of the agriculture association for embezzling funds.[71] Similarly, when the magistrate of Cheng county maltreated a man accused in a lawsuit, the father of the accused remonstrated that the revolution had brought a change in the procedures of and relationships to government.[72] This sense of change was an important precondition for greater change: the outer-core elite opportunity structure did not open with the revolution but expanded gradually over the next decade and a half.

The peripheries, despite the presence of occasional returned students during the revolutionary events, seem to have lacked any lasting sense of new beginnings or evidence of important sociopolitical changes.[73] Ultimately, of course, the inner-core revolution affected the peripheries, not only through the new political system but also by eventually stimulating various shifts in elite careers and new elite relationships to the core zones. These shifts, however, did not generally occur until the 1920s or later. In the short run, the revolutionary spasms of social disorder and confusion rapidly spent themselves and stimulated only great elite concern for stability and, in cases, the greater solidification of the oligarchical control of county elites.

The inner-core revolutionary episodes were a significant sociopolitical milestone on the twentieth-century revolutionary road. Although the revolution in the outer zones provided some basis for later change, in the first years of the Republic it led primarily to the tightening of county elite oligarchies, if it had a perceptible effect at all. What in the inner core may have been a revolution emanating from a "rising tide of change"—asserting reformist and Han Chinese nationalistic ideals—was in the outer zones often a holding action by elites to prevent their demise in a wave of social disorder.[74]

11

Patterns of Nonofficial Elite Provincial Politics: Assemblies, Factions, and Coalitions

An episode in May 1920 suggests some significant aspects of early Republican provincial politics. Military Governor Lu wanted to initiate two provincial projects of economic development: a model silk-reeling factory and an officially sponsored East Zhejiang (*Zhedong*) fishing company.[1] Planning to propose these projects at a banquet for the provincial assembly, he first dispatched a subordinate to a powerful assemblyman, Xu Zuqian, to probe his reactions. Xu, who notably held no nominal assembly leadership posts, was hesitant about both proposals: the first, because such an undertaking had been unsuccessfully attempted during Qu Yingguang's administration (1912–1916); the second, because the Taizhou faction had its own plans for such a scheme. In the end, Xu agreed that lengthy discussions could probably overcome these problems; and the banquet with Lu's development overtures was held.

Besides the military governor's interest in provincial economic development, this episode is noteworthy for several reasons. First, the military's recognition of the assembly's role in decision making and its concern for the assembly's political sensitivity is revealed. The five provincial assemblies of the late Qing period and early Republic (the Qing assembly, 1910–11; the provisional assembly, 1911–1913; and the three regular Republican assemblies, 1913–14 and 1916–1918, 1918–1921, and 1921–1926) were crucial political actors. Second, though purely military factions were significant from the beginning of the Republic, Xu's concerns for the plans of the Taizhou faction suggest that various civilian coalitions and factions attained prominence in provincial deliberations by the late 1910s and 1920s. The civilian factions revealed the strength and political significance of traditional native place ties; and the civilian coalitions, the dynamics of developmental politics. Finally, in this episode, personal connections and approaches, not institutional mechanisms or structures, were the means facilitating the attainment of political goals.

158

Unfortunately, such personal approaches are are all too rarely recorded. Institutions and organizations were the framework in which personal ties operated to achieve political objectives.

Zhejiang Provincial Assemblies, 1910–1926

The Qing Assembly, 1910–1911

Under the traditional system's law of avoidance, civil service degree-holders could not serve as officials in their native province. The provincial assemblies offered a forum where men of talent could aspire to a new type of leadership. Table 17 provides a social background and functional profile of the men who served in the five assemblies.[2] Although the incomplete statistics mean that conclusions are tentative, the 51 to 74 percent of the assemblymen on whom background and functional information is available provides a good indication of the nature of individual assemblies and trends over time.

The Qing assembly (*ziyiju*) was composed primarily of traditional elites. Fifty-seven members (68.7 percent of those on whom we have background data) had traditional degrees; forty-two of these were upper degrees. There were probably more lower-degree-holders among the 25.9 percent on whom there was no background or functional data.[3] It was basically an assembly of provincial notables: at least 24 percent had served or would serve in official capacities at various administrative levels during their careers. No fewer than 8.4 percent became national legislators. Of the seventeen (20.5 percent) who were graduates of modern schools, twelve had attended school in Japan.

Despite the reformist temper of some of its leadership, politically the assembly was decidedly moderate to conservative, even if nationalistic in mood. Only 9.6 percent played some recorded role in the 1911 revolution either in Hangchow or their native places. The average age of fifteen assemblymen whose ages were ascertainable was 40.3 years (the range being from 31 to 54).[4] This obviously sketchy evidence suggests two observations on the historical life experiences that contributed to their outlooks. First, all the men had seen China lose two wars in the first three decades of their lives, in the 1880s to France and in 1895 to Japan. They had witnessed the imperialist power grabbing of 1898. Many were keenly aware of the plight of the Chinese nation and, as attested by assembly action, were strongly concerned with maintaining China's sovereignty. Individual assembly members worked in organizations devoted to repaying the country's debt, keeping Japanese merchants out of Hangchow, opposing the demands of medical missionary Duncan Main, and advocating the formation of militia for national defense. At least seven leaders in

Table 17.
Background and functions of provincial representatives, 1910–1926

Background and function[a]	Qing assembly	PPA	1 RPA	2 RPA	3 RPA	1924 constitutional convention
Degree-holders	57 (68.7%)[b]	3 (10.7%)	20 (24.4%)	8 (9.0%)	2 (2.6%)	9 (9.4%)
Degree and graduate	unknown	2 (7.1%)	8 (9.8%)	2 (2.2%)	1 (1.3%)	8 (8.3%)
Graduates	17 (20.5%)	1 (3.6%)	11 (13.4%)	15 (16.9%)	9 (11.8%)	21 (21.9%)
Particip't, 1911 revol.	8 (9.6%)	14 (50.0%)	18 (22.0%)	9 (10.1%)	5 (6.6%)	5 (5.2%)
Officials during career	20 (24.1%)	5 (17.9%)	17 (20.7%)	11 (12.4%)	4 (5.3%)	25 (26.0%)
National legislators	7 (8.4%)	5 (17.9%)	6 (7.3%)	10 (11.2%)	4 (5.3%)	12 (12.5%)
Merchants	3 (3.6%)	—	11 (13.4%)	9 (10.1%)	8 (10.5%)	10 (10.4%)
Journalists	2 (2.4%)	2 (7.1%)	4 (4.9%)	2 (2.2%)	10 (13.2%)	10 (10.4%)
Lawyers	2 (2.4%)	2 (7.1%)	3 (3.7%)	7 (7.9%)	11 (14.5%)	13 (13.5%)
No data available[c]	29 (25.9%)	10 (26.3%)	70 (46%)	63 (41.4%)	73 (49%)	53 (35.6%)
Total	112	38	152	152	149	149

Sources: For the Qing assembly, Zhang Pengyuan, *Lixian pai yu xinhai geming*, pp. 270–274; the PPA, *Minli Bao*, XT 3/11/24; 1 RPA, *Shi Bao*, 1913/1/12; 2 RPA, *Shi Bao*, 1918/7/31–8/7; for 3 RPA, *Shi Bao*, 1923/7–12 passim; constitutional assembly, *Shi Bao*, 1924/8–9 passim.

a. Certain persons may be included in more than one category.
b. Percentages throughout are based on the number for whom background data could be found.
c. Percentages are based on the total number in assemblies.

the railway company and antiloan movement of 1907 were elected to this assembly.[5] The assemblymen were, on the whole, ardent nationalists, concerned that Chinese rights were not being protected by the central government.

Yet these men were heirs of another historical experience. Most, having been born in the late 1860s and early 1870s, grew up seeing the scars and hearing the horrors of the greatest rebellion the world had known. Ho Ping-ti estimates that the Taiping Rebellion brought a 70 percent loss in the population of Hangzhou prefecture and a 67.7 percent loss in Jiaxing prefecture.[6] In August 1914, a reporter described the great devastation still apparent in the Yanzhou prefectural capital, where the "site of a [once] bustling, crowded [city] quarter" remained half a century later as desolate "grazing grounds."[7] The Qing assemblymen came from the learned class, which repeatedly discussed the rebellion in memoirs and local histories;[8] and they were members of the privileged classes, which stood to lose most from any social explosion. This common historical memory in part molded assemblymen's attitudes, stirring fears of a people mobilized but uncontrolled.

In 1910 and early 1911 elites accelerated militia formation for the stated purpose of building a strong nation. But in October 1911 the president of the assembly suggested that the first role of the militia was not to increase national strength but to preserve internal peace. Assembly members and other elite spokesmen in Hangchow agreed unanimously that if militia units were not carefully trained, disciplined, and controlled, they should not be given guns.[9] Simultaneously the assembly worked toward national sovereignty and warily monitored new developments at the lower levels of society.[10]

The Provisional Provincial Assembly, 1911-1913

Near the end of November 1911, the military government of Tang Shouqian ordered each prefecture to select four men to serve in a provisional provincial assembly (*linshi shengyihui*) (hereafter referred to as PPA).[11] Only thirty-eight out of a possible forty-four representatives made up the PPA, which first met on December 10, 1911.[12] The method of selection is not known, but fully 50 percent of those on whom data is available participated in the revolution, with 64 percent of those being members of the Restoration Society or the Tongmeng hui. Only three (7.9 percent) of the former 112-man Qing assembly served in this provisional assembly (see Table 18). The statistics indicate that five (17.9 percent) served later in national legislative organs—the largest percentage from any assembly—and that another five were officials outside their home areas.

The large proportion of revolutionaries and of those who sought

Table 18.
Overlap in provincial assembly attendance

	Qing assembly	PPA	1 RPA	2 RPA	3 RPA	1924 constitutional convention
Qing assembly	—	3 (7.9%)[a]	7 (4.6%)	2 (1.3%)	2 (1.3%)	8 (5.4%)
PPA	3 (2.7%)	—	7 (4.6%)	—	—	1 (0.7%)
1 RPA	7 (6.3%)	7 (18.4%)	—	24 (15.8%)	12 (8.1%)	13 (8.7%)
2 RPA	2 (1.8%)	—	24 (15.8%)	—	32 (21.5%)	10 (6.7%)
3 RPA	2 (1.8%)	—	12 (7.9%)	32 (21.1%)	—	12 (8.1%)
1924 constitutional convention	8 (7.1%)	1 (2.6%)	13 (8.6%)	10 (6.6%)	12 (8.1%)	—
Total in attendance	112	38	152	152	149	149

Sources: Same as for Table 17.
a. Percentages throughout are based on the total number in assemblies.

careers on the national stage suggests that this assembly was nationalistic and outward looking. Its pronouncements on Chinese rights vis-à-vis foreign powers and its insistence on national rather than provincial values further indicate nationalism as its hallmark.[13] The assembly agenda followed the pattern of its Qing predecessor: budgetary concerns, self-government programs, and public works.[14] Its longest-lasting legacy was in fiscal matters, with its institution of the *tongjuan* to replace the *lijin* and its abolition of the traditional military rice levy (*caonanmi*) that had been collected from the three northern prefectures.[15]

The Role of the 1911 Revolution as Seen in Assembly Profiles

Provincial assembly statistics suggest the importance of the 1911 watershed. The percentage of recorded traditional degree-holders dropped precipitantly from the Qing assembly and continued to fall to the low of 3.9 percent in the third Republican assembly (RPA), elected in 1921. A decline in degree-holders is not surprising, given the disappearance of degree opportunities after 1905. The sharpness of the decline is, however, somewhat unexpected. The more than 30 percent drop in this category from the 1910–11 assembly to the first RPA in 1913 and 1914 indicates an assembly much less dominated by traditional elites and more controlled by men who were perhaps less bound by traditional processes and experiences. The fact that almost 22 percent of the first RPA had actively participated in the revolution supports this hypothesis. Only 4.6 percent of the first RPA had served in the Qing assembly. After the revolution, many Qing assemblymen had gone beyond Zhejiang, become postrevolution provincial officials, or returned to their native places. A member in the first RPA was much less likely either to become a national legislator or to have an official post at some time during his career. He was also less likely to have participated in pre-1911 nationalistic efforts such as the railroad movement: 8.4 percent of the Qing assembly had participated in those events, whereas only 2.4 percent (two) of the first RPA representatives had done so.[16]

I was not able to find social or functional background data for between 40 and 50 percent of the members of the Republican assemblies. This contrasts with the 25 percent of those in the Qing assembly and PPA for whom such information is unavailable. These figures indicate the probability that more traditional lower-degreed and nondegreed elites—various types of local notables, landlords, and merchants—rose to provincial position following the revolution. The rise in recorded merchant representation from the Qing assembly to the first RPA (from 3.6 to 13.4 percent) corroborates this interpretation, pointing again to the increased merchant involvement following the revolution. Furthermore, 70 percent (seven of ten) of the merchant members in the first RPA came from the inner core, underscoring the fact that increased merchant involvement was primarily an inner-core trend.

The Regular Republican Assemblies, 1913–1927

The first RPA is the only one for which the native counties of all members are available. This information provides verification not only of zonal trends concerning mechants but other patterns as well.[17] The inner core alone contributed 42.9 percent of all traditional degree-holders to this assembly; at the same time, the outer zones had a much higher proportion of degree-holders in their local self-government bodies than did the inner core. These two trends seem to reemphasize the greater tendency of degree-holders from the inner core to gravitate to higher spheres of activity. The inner core alone also provided 55.6 percent of all those who had participated in the revolution, reflecting the inner core's role as the locus of revolutionary action.

Data on the ages of Republican assembly members are rare: I could find the ages of only four in the PPA and thirteen in the first RPA (these figures represent the same proportion of the respective assemblies). The small samples preclude a definitive interpretation; I include them as suggestive. The average age of the small provisional assembly sample was thirty-two; of the first RPA, thirty (the range in both samples was from twenty-two to forty-three). These averages are fully a decade less than the average of a similar sample of Qing assembly members. The small samples for all three assemblies suggest that different generational cohorts dominated the Qing assembly and the two early Republican assemblies. The average Qing assemblyman probably was born in the late 1860s and early 1870s, whereas the average Republican assemblyman from 1912 to 1914 was more likely to have been born in the late 1870s and 1880s. The 1860s and 1870s cohorts probably tended to be "traditional" and "transitional" in their retention of ties to native place, in contrast with the 1880s cohort, which was markedly less inclined to retain such ties. If these sketchy statistics are any indication of reality, the Republican assemblies were also much less tied to traditional views.

The first RPA's frequent clashes with Zhu Rui over national issues, particularly Yuan's independent loan action and the second revolution, reveal an assembly confident of its power. In 1913 the assembly advocated independence in opposition to Yuan's actions. When Zhu remained loyal to Yuan, several assemblymen including the chairman were forced to flee to Shanghai. The assembly itself desisted in its open defiance of Zhu and Yuan for fear of being dissolved.[18]

Xiang Shiyuan's implied model of modal elite evolution can be applied to profiles of the assemblies, with Qing assemblymen epitomized as reformist nationalists; the PPA and first RPA, as nationalist politicians; and the second and third RPA, as provincialist politicians immersed in factional and coalitional struggles. In the last two RPA's, moreover, there were more professional journalists, lawyers, and even military figures, also features of Xiang's paradigm of elites in the 1920s.

In the three RPA's, the percentage of merchants remained fairly stable; the large percentage for whom sources revealed no social or functional background data probably also included significant numbers of merchants. Decisions and deliberations in the last two RPA's support the view that merchant interests were among the assembly's primary concerns. The battle for liberalizing cocoon hong policy was led by the second RPA—an evidence of new merchant assembly elites vying with older established elites.[19] The vigorous assembly campaign to abolish the tax on advertising billboards instituted by Lu Yongxiang and increased by Sun Chuanfang points also to the strength of merchant interests.[20] In 1924 the assembly erupted in denunciation of an announced graduated tax on the capital worth of business establishments to pay for salaries for the third constitutional convention delegates. Although merchants had been in the vanguard of the constitutional movement, they threatened to oppose a new convention because of this tax. Every member who spoke in the assembly opposed it. The civil governor retreated hastily into the explanation that the tax was only in the planning stage.[21]

An intriguing assembly statistic is the decline in the number of graduates from the second to the third RPA, especially notable because one would expect a greater number of modern-school graduates in that assembly than in any other. I believe this decrease stems from the disenchantment of many recent student graduates with assembly service following the second RPA's post-May-Fourth actions. After sending telegrams opposed to the Shandong settlement and to the Beijing government's stand, the second RPA put aside its national concerns and concentrated on raising its own salaries forty *yuan* a month retroactive to August 1918, when it had been elected. The matter caused an immediate uproar; but despite popular protests and threatening demonstrations, the bill was passed with the overwhelming support of the largest faction (*pai*) in the assembly.[22] In the eyes of many nonassembly elites, assemblymen were arrogant and self-interested. By the third RPA, 24 percent had served in previous assemblies and were well accustomed to the salaries and perquisites that came with the position. When preparations for a fourth RPA were under way in 1924, an ad hoc group met to insist that in the new assembly there should be no "local bullies and evil gentry" (*tuhao lieshen*) elected for private gain.[23]

Like the first RPA, the second and third fought an almost constant battle with Zhejiang's military and civil governors. Continually at odds with Qi Yaoshan, the assembly impeached him twice and finally succeeded in having him removed from office in 1920.[24] The assembly's relationship to two forceful military governors, Lu Yongxiang and Sun Chuanfang, differed dramatically. Whereas Lu cultivated assembly support, fostering the development of an assembly faction to back him, the nadir of assembly fortunes came under Sun's regime. Sun sent military police to search the homes of assemblymen and arrogantly rejected assembly pleas to stop military impressment of civilians and halt an epidemic of military depredations on the populace. He argued that social turmoil came not from soldiers but "party men" (*dangren*).[25] It is little wonder that the assembly, already beset by quorum problems, atrophied into an impotent body.

Economic development issues dominated assembly sessions from 1918 to 1926: education subsidies and scholarships for overseas students, improvements in the silk industry, model factories and experimental farms, conservancy projects, and a lottery system for funding the construction of seawalls both north and south of Hangchow Bay.[26] But juxtaposed with this developmental thrust was a strong sociocultural conservatism. Assemblies rejected the idea of traveling lectures for the education of the poor; discussed stopping the spread of Bolshevism in schools (in this case symbolized by coeducation); condemned the use of phonetic Chinese; and demanded the reinstatement of local self-government for the purpose of better controlling and pacifying the people.[27]

Assemblies continued to take a nationalist position—on rumored secret treaties between Beijing and Tokyo in 1918, on the Shandong issue in 1919 and 1920, on the student shootings in Shanghai in May 1925, and on the attempts of Europeans in Zhejiang to purchase land.[28] They concerned themselves with major national issues from China's entrance into World War I to Cao Kun's presidential election in 1923.[29] Only after 1925 when assembly initiative was blunted by Sun's rule did it become less vocal on national issues.

The Republican assemblies, like their Qing predecessor, merged nationalism and sociocultural conservatism. To the Qing assembly agenda they added a greater concern for economic development. These three elements—national self-assertion, sociocultural conservatism, and economic development—would continue to dominate Chinese elite political programs into the 1930s and 1940s. Assemblies served as elite representative bodies and at their strongest point as able antagonists to the official elite. At the least, they were a provincial power with which officials had to reckon. The elite liberal parliamentary system operated into the 1920s in Zhejiang, checking official excesses and representing elite interest. The militaristic authoritarian methods of Sun Chuanfang doomed the system in 1925 and 1926; Chiang Kai-shek and the Guomindang dealt it the coup de grâce.

Nonassembly Provincial Elite Groups in the 1920s

In 1923 and again in 1925, the provincial assembly publicly voiced fear that its powers might be usurped by other elite organizations, specifically the Federation of County Assemblies (*xianyihui lianhehui*) and the Federation of Zhejiang Professional Associations (*Zhejiang ge fatuan lianhehui*).[30] Both federations were originally organized to work for self-government principles on the local and provincial levels because some elites felt that the provincial assembly was unable or unwilling to set self-government goals and work successfully to attain them.[31] In actuality, the two organizations became assembly competitors.

The Federation of County Assemblies

The Federation of County Assemblies, established in 1923, represented from twenty-seven to thirty-four counties.[32] One of its major concerns was the role of the provincial assembly in any new constitutional framework.[33] Primarily composed of counties from the core zones, the federation proposed the suspension of the assembly and in its place the establishment of an organ representing the will of the people (*minyi*).[34] In addition to its repeated proposals for a constitutional system, it discussed local problems: surtaxes, procedures for the omnipresent census, educational expenditures, and the role of the county board vis-à-vis the assembly.[35] Politically, it was decidedly progressive. The provincial assembly delayed any decision on the role of women in constitutional processes, whereas the federation agreed immediately to women's suffrage and participation in any constitutional convention.[36] It is noteworthy that many of the federation leaders were also members of the Guomindang.

Perhaps the most interesting aspects of the federation's work were its joint efforts with the Jiangsu Federation of County Assemblies. In 1924 federation leaders from both provinces began to join in discussions aimed at establishing lasting peace.[37] Meetings were held in Shanghai, with each provincial federation feting the other with banquets. Although war came six months later, the linkages that provincial elites had made led to continued communication. Following Sun Chuanfang's seizure of Jiangsu in October 1925, the two federations stepped up discussions on common issues other than peace.

In a December 1925 meeting, leaders of the federations issued a statement disparaging the artificial boundaries that the state had imposed between the provinces. They discussed joint action in conservancy projects, the restoration of self-government at the county level and below, and mutual economic concerns.[38] Such discussions reflected the increasing importance of the developmental macroregion for inner-core elites and echoed other Lower Yangzi elite activity, for example, the establishment of a Wu Society in 1920 and the Lake Tai Regional Self-Government Federation in 1925. Elite frustration in dealing with obstinate provincial regimes and the common sense appeal of parapolitical and political associations in handling common cross-boundary problems were notable features of the 1920s. They attest once more to the basically extralocal orientation of politically involved inner-core elites.

The Federation of Zhejiang Professional Associations

The Federation of Zhejiang Professional Associations was an inner-core organization of Hangchow-based elites and representatives from mostly inner-core county professional associations.[39] The federation, which in its 1923 meetings had 135 representatives from fifty-three associations, lobbied for self-government and provincial peace. It also debated many issues that emerged in the 1924 constitutional convention, took stands on national issues, and served as an advisory group for Lu.[40] Criticizing the provincial assembly as a haven for "local bullies and evil gentry," it too attempted to dilute the assembly's power.[41] In 1923 it proposed a provisional assembly (*linshi yihui*) as a substitute for the third RPA. The selection process outlined for this assembly evidenced some bias against the outer zones by weighting representation from inner-core counties more heavily.[42] This proposed assembly was never established. Politically, the federation was progressive, with major provincial professional associations leaning toward the Guomindang by 1924.

Provincial Political Patterns

Complex networks of traditional connections and the development of political factions based on these linkages marked the Hangchow scene in the early Republic. The broad contours of provincial politics were shaped by native place, specifically prefectural alignments.[43] Issues and factions became associated with particular native places or constellations of administrative units. Developmental dynamics were also significant in the formation of coalitions and in the general evolution of provincial politics.

Inner-Core Leadership Nodes and Competition

Inner-core counties and their elites dominated provincial politics into the 1920s. The nationalism of the railroad movement and the "rising tide of change" culminating in the 1911 revolution were basically inner-core phenomena. In the early years of the Republic, inner-core elites often treated the outer zones as areas ripe for economic development at the hands of the inner core. There was, however, no unified inner-core ruling coalition. Rather, four leadership nodes vying for provincial leadership emerged in the early Republican inner core: Zhexi (the prefectures of Hangzhou, Jiaxing, and Huzhou), Ning-Shao, Wenzhou, and Taizhou. In the evolution of provincial politics, Zhexi and Ning-Shao early played dominant roles while Taizhou and Wenzhou were secondary; in the 1910s, Taizhou emerged briefly as a key competing center.

Even a cursory survey of Zhejiang's politics reveals that Hangchow and Ningpo were competing centers. Hangchow, the province's administrative capital, was the political center of the Hang-Jia-Hu circuit and chief entrepôt on the Qiantang River. The close ties of the three prosperous northern prefectures to the capital insured their political role in provincial affairs. Ningpo, on the other hand, was without question the leading economic center of the province, tied closely to Shanghai and exercising control over the Shanghai financial world through its prefectural elites. Many Ningpoese openly contended that Ningpo should be the capital of Zhejiang.[44] As the center of merchant strength, Ningbo prefecture became the base for important tax opposition movements in the early Republic.[45] The center of considerable anti-Hangchow animosity and the site of the only garrison in a city strong enough to challenge the capital, Ningbo became the headquarters of repeated attempts to throw off Hangchow's leadership—in 1913, 1916, 1917, and 1924.[46]

In the 1880s and 1890s, Wenchow was the headquarters of a group of reformist scholars whose ideas were based on traditional statecraft notions and who looked askance at dependence on Western models. This coterie provided several eminent provincial leaders in the last Qing decade, among them the president of the Qing assembly, Chen Fuchen.[47] After the revolution, however, Wenchow contributed no significant provincial leaders nor did it play any but a subsidiary role in the formation of the factions and coalitions directing provincial affairs. This lack of contribution to provincial politics, the slowness of its economic development, and its reported greater traditionalism call into question the long-term practical effects of the late Qing reform group.[48]

At first glance, the Taizhou situation might seem similar. Only two of its six counties were inner-core (compared to only one of Wenzhou's six), and three were notoriously poor and socially unstable inner-periphery counties. Taizhou's economic development was slow even though Haimen (in Linhai county) and Huangyan were on shipping routes to Shanghai.[49] Despite its establishment of prerevolutionary reformist associations, it was not highly politically developed.[50] Its provincial political significance came via the emergence of a faction by 1918. Fragmentary evidence suggests that this faction may have had rice and opium interests as its economic base,[51] but there is little doubt that factional formation and continuity came from the strength of traditional connections and the spoils of political position, both official and nonofficial. A study of the origins of assemblymen in the first RPA shows that Taizhou prefecture supplied 23 percent of the entire assembly, sending more representatives than all of Zhexi and more than twice as many as Ningbo. It is most unlikely that election regulations, which called for each county to contribute members in proportion to qualified electors, were followed; in 1933 the very rich area of Zhexi, for example, had at least one and a half million more inhabitants than Taizhou.[52]

The source of such an apparent discrepancy in assembly representation may have been Qu Yingguang of Linhai county. The beginning of the Taizhou faction came with Qu's rise to power. Although his education was meager, he had taught geography at the Anhui Surveyor's School (*cehui xuetang*) when Zhu Rui was superintendent (*zongban*). According to one account, they swore themselves into brotherhood.[53] Qu later served as head of the provisioning office for Zhu's attack on Nanjing. During the summer of 1912, Qu was catapulted from secretary in the Zhejiang finance ministry to its head, and in the fall he became civil commissioner.[54] He held this position during the assembly elections. Qu's growing power in the Zhejiang government and his close links to Zhu lend credence to the hypothesis that Qu may have been behind the representational imbalance in order to bring Taizhou greater voice.

During Qu's years as civil governor, the strength of Taizhou natives in the provincial bureaucracy increased. A correspondent noted as early as mid-1913 that "the north of [Taizhou] has many links with the provincial capital."[55] When Qu became civil governor in Shandong in 1916, he reportedly appointed so many Zhejiangese that his power was headquartered in the Zhejiang guild.[56] Fellow Taizhou natives were especially hopeful of key Shandong positions.[57] Although specific information on Qu's early Zhejiang appointment methods is scant, he probably followed the same personnel procedures in Zhejiang as in Shandong.

Provincial Political Coalitions

The immediate stimulus for the organization of various coalitions in Hangchow politics was the blatant attempt at election fraud in the second RPA elections in 1918. The results of the election census released in early 1918 showed that of the three million Zhejiang residents with electoral rights (about 15 percent of the population), almost 75 percent were in the former prefectures of Taizhou and Wenzhou—and this did not include the electorate of Yongjia (the capital county of Wenzhou prefecture) and Tiantai. As the census results stood, the two prefectures were slated to hold 114 out of the 152 assembly seats.[58] The apparently rigged results appear to have been a power play by the inner-core areas of the Southeast Coast macroregion against the inner-core portion of the Lower Yangzi macroregion. When the census was retaken, the outcome was similar in prefectural representation to the first RPA (the representation of which was already weighted so that Taizhou and Wenzhou had 40 percent of the representatives).

Some of the early vocal opposition to the Tai-Wen electoral tactics came from the first RPA representatives from the Lower Yangzi macroregion prefectures of Jinhua, Quzhou, and Yanzhou. A study of assembly membership and action from 1909 until 1918 reveals domination by and for elites and elite projects in Zhexi, Ning-Shao, and Taizhou (in whose tow one often finds Wenzhou elites); the prefectures of the upper reaches of the Qiantang River, on the other hand, had little power and received scant attention in assembly deliberations.[59] These prefectures, all of whose counties were in the three outer zones, were quite evidently underrepresented in the first regular Republican assembly, at least compared to Taizhou; with greater population, these three prefectures had only twenty-four assemblymen as compared with Taizhou's thirty-five.[60]

In the midst of the turmoil over the 1918 elections, a representative from Duan Qirui's national "electoral machine," the Anfu club, visited interested elites in Hangchow.[61] He spoke especially to assembly elites from Jin-Qu-Yan and Taizhou in an obvious attempt to build support for the Anfu cause, for up to that point Zhejiang had remained neutral in the national contention between Duan and Feng Guozhang.[62] In the fall, Jiang Bangyan of Jinhua, former judicial official, member of the Anfu club, and in 1919 to become Zhejiang Salt Commissioner, made more contacts with Jin-Qu-Yan-Tai elites.[63]

The first indication of an emerging coalition from the four prefectures was the support by almost all elites from these areas (and Wenzhou as well) of the election of Zhou Jirong of Taizhou as president. Zhou was opposed by elites from Hang-Jia-Hu-Ning-Shao (hereafter HJHNS).[64] A coalition of outer-zone and less developed inner-core counties appears to have emerged in opposition to the most highly developed inner-core areas. Elites from economically deprived counties began to organize politically to compete with those who to that point had preponderant economic and political power. The Jin-Qu-Yan elites, eyeing Taizhou's political strength, linked themselves to that group; Taizhou, rebuffed in large measure by the HJHNS bloc in its assembly-stacking bid, hit upon the coalition as a method of regaining some of the strength it had lost in the retaken census. For all these elites, the linkage to a national faction must have been appealing.

Following the coalition's victory in the election of the assembly president and two vice-presidents, Jin-Qu-Yan-Tai elites, meeting with men from Wenzhou and Chuzhou, formed the Chenglu Club (*julebu*).[65] The rationale, as set forth by Jiang Bangyan, was that the nonexistence of provincial political parties was an obstacle to local self-government and the election of talented men to office.[66] He told the more than fifty men who attended the organizational meeting at the Pawnshop Guild Hall that the political club could now begin to assert the interests of its members.[67] Theoretically the group was open to all, but HJHNS elites refused to join. By April 1919 the HJHNS elites had formed their own political organization, the Society of Virtue (*liangshe*). It was composed in large part of the legal section of the assembly, which was dominated by inner-core elites, many of them lawyers. Being, in the main, former Tongmeng hui adherents and supporters of Sun Yat-sen, the Society of Virtue favored the government in Guangzhou. By early 1919 when the assembly's president (and Chenglu member) Zhou Jirong gave a banquet for assemblymen, relations between the two political clubs were such that the Society of Virtue members refused to attend.[68]

From this point until 1924, the essence of provincial politics was the competition between these and successor coalitions. They opposed each other in the salary increase fight in May 1919; in their responses to the May Fourth and student movement; in their reactions to the appointment of a civil governor in 1920 and again in 1925.[69] The Chenglu Club generally supported conservative social and political positions while the Society of Virtue championed more progressive ones.

Provincial Elite Coalitions and the Localities

Few assembly elites permanently resided in the capital, representing their native place in name only.[70] The majority lived in their native places and frequently returned.[71] An assemblyman wrote in September 1924 that fewer than forty assemblymen lived permanently in Hangchow (forty would have been only 26.8 percent of the total).[72] The assemblies elected in 1918 and 1921 were closely attuned to the problems of their respective counties. The primary concerns of the late Qing and provisional assemblies and, to a lesser extent, the first RPA were the concept of national and provincial status, law, and general development. The second and third RPA, in contrast, spoke more frequently about local problems—relief, alleged corruption, water conservancy, and social unrest. An example of this deep interest in native place affairs, two Shaoxing representatives returned home specifically for an important meeting of the county agriculture association.[73]

Most assembly elites, then, were not cut off from their locality or its problems. If only because they wanted to be reelected, most elites were concerned about their native place constituency. As elites joined provincial coalitions with linkages (however tenuous) to national political groups and as they returned to their native places and became involved in local political affairs, provincial and national concerns filtered down to county elites. County politics tended to be complex and highly partisan, with provincial elites often bringing outside concerns into the local political arena.[74] In many cases, personal animosity led antagonistic local leaders to espouse the opposite political viewpoints of the returning assemblymen. Newspapers frequently sprang up as voices of these factions, popularizing arguments on both sides of the issues and spreading information on national and provincial questions. Concerns about the New Culture movement in the wake of May Fourth eventually polarized the politics of such counties as Pinghu, Yongjia, and Linhai in the inner core; Zhuji in the outer core; Yongkang and Yiwu in the inner periphery; and Taishun, Xiaofeng, and Changhua in the outer periphery.[75] The importance of this phenomenon for elite political development cannot be underestimated. Elite identification with coalitions, factions, and issues altered the framework of or, at the very least, added new extralocal elements to the local elite political agenda.

Linhai county, base of the Taizhou faction, provides the most detailed example of this phenomenon. Although many Taizhou elites in Hangchow had joined the coalitional Chenglu Club in 1918, considerable rivalry existed among these elites: Zhou Jirong, for example, had bested fellow Taizhou native Zhou Shu in a bitter fight for the assembly's presidency.[76] In June 1919, with the Chenglu Club experiencing financial difficulties and signs that Jin-Qu-Yan elites were joining another coalition, Zhou Jirong began to curry favor with the founder of the Taizhou faction, Qu Yingguang, then governor of Shandong.[77] By the late summer of 1919, Zhou withdrew from the Chenglu Club and formed a purely Taizhou faction, the Public Inn (*gongyou*), which was funded by Qu Yingguang.[78] Through its own newspaper it vigorously opposed military governor Lu Yongxiang and supported a provincial constitution.[79] It was closely connected with the Sanmen Bay project, which planned agricultural and industrial development in the outer-zone Taizhou and Ningbo counties of Nantian, Xiangshan, and Ninghai.[80] So intimately were the project and Taizhou elites linked that when protests about the nature of the project arose, they were directed not to the provincial administrators but to Tu Tihua, national assemblyman from Taizhou.[81] With the decline of the faction, the project lost its strongest supporters and fell on hard times.[82]

The political positions of Zhou's faction were quickly transported to local Linhai politics where a newly formed opposing clique established its own newspaper at the county seat. The clique included those who were already Zhou's personal rivals, those who distrusted Qu Yingguang's role in Zhou's faction, and those who opposed Zhou's idea of a provincial constitution. A new local political configuration was thus crystallized by Zhou's factional activity at Hangchow. In addition, appearing in the county at about the same time was a group of elites supporting the New Culture movement, who opposed both Zhou and his opponents.[83] Within a few short years in the early 1920s, the framework of county politics had been transformed. Older issues remained, but new ones with provincial and national overtones contended for attention.

Each coalition politically mobilized elites from all four zones, though the Society of Virtue was dominated by inner-core elites and the Chenglu Club by those from the outer zones. In the second RPA, I have found only one man who belonged to a coalition that did not represent his native place.[84] For the third RPA, in contrast, an analysis of fifty-six coalition members whose native place is determinable shows that nine of the twenty-six (35 percent) belonging to the Peace Society (*pingshe*), the successor to the Society of Virtue, were from non-HJHNS prefectures; and that five of the thirty-one (16 percent) of the Weekly Association (*xingqihui*), the successor to the Public Inn, were from HJHNS prefectures.[85] Furthermore, some of these men were among the coalitional leaders. When the coalitions voted for third RPA assembly section (*gu*) assignments, they put up their own slates for leadership rather than agreeing to balance the leadership geographically as had been done in the second RPA.[86] As the coalitions were more geographically diverse, such balancing was unnecessary.

In the early 1920s coalitions based purely on native place networks began to decline. Although native place was still highly significant, greater coalitional geographic diversity suggests that issues and other personal connections began to play larger roles. Although personal ties obviously assumed great importance, I have found no evidence to suggest that they provided all the cohesion in the broad coalitions. Issues apart from native place ties, I hypothesize, were beginning to appear as important factors in some cases. In the third RPA, each more geographically diverse coalition set forth and became identified with proposals on the establishment of provincial self-government, delineating its own recommendations on constitutional procedures.[87] The debate at the 1924 constitutional convention, however, was generally formulated by geographically based coalitions; this suggests that purely issue-based groupings had not yet emerged as the essential political medium.

12

The Emergence of Outer-Zone Elites in Provincial Politics: The Jin-Qu-Yan-Chu Association, Political Ideals, and the Guomindang Victory

The upper reaches of the Qiantang River linked the inner core of Zhejiang to the Middle Yangzi macroregion, providing the path by which the Guomindang army advanced into Zhejiang during the Northern Expedition in late 1926 and 1927. All the counties in the three prefectures—Jinhua, Quzhou, and Yanzhou—along this path were in the three outer zones. Elites from these counties began to emerge in the 1920s as important leaders in provincial politics, playing significant roles in the 1924 constitutional convention and in the rise to power of the conservative Guomindang faction in the spring of 1927. An analysis of the developmental dynamics of the right-wing Guomindang triumph provides a sharper understanding of the political nature of the provincial Guomindang victory.

The Jin-Qu-Yan-Chu Association

Until the mid-1920s elites from Jinhua, Quzhou, Yanzhou, and Chuzhou controlled few provincial leadership posts and exercised little power in allocating provincial resources to their areas. Elites from these prefectures had provided the major source of support for Restoration Society leader Tao Chengzhang's unsuccessful bid for military governor in 1912. Because of their political underrepresentation and impotence, elites of the first three prefectures linked themselves to Taizhou and Wenzhou elites in the Chenglu Club. However, different goals and the establishment of the purely Taizhou faction, Public Inn, led to the coalition's collapse.

Perhaps because of the political weakness of these areas and their aborted attempt at coalition formation, in the last years of the 1910s a native place association, the Jin-Qu-Yan-Chu (JQYC) association, began to emerge as an important lobbying group and eventually a major force in Hangchow politics. Because this organization became highly significant in provincial politics in the mid-1920s, an analysis of its development and roles is essential, despite many source-related lacunae. It is difficult to date the association's founding. The first recorded meeting I have found was in May 1919.[1] Because recorded joint action by elites from these prefectures in the mid-fall of 1918 gives no indication of the association's existence, I hypothesize that it was organized in late 1918 or early 1919.[2] By late 1920 the association had become strong enough to purchase land for the construction of an association hall.[3]

Certain aspects of its establishment are noteworthy. First, it took the form of a traditional native place association, not a modern political club (*julebu*) or faction (*pai*), indicating perhaps a greater emphasis on traditional elite forms and attitudes. Second, it was the only joint prefectural native place association in Hangchow, with only Jinhua among these prefectures having its own prefectural native place association as well. Its joint nature immediately sets it apart on the provincial scene as atypical.[4] Third, it was a cross-regional association, made up of Jin, Qu, and Yan from the Lower Yangzi region and Chu from the Southeast Coast. The Chenglu Club was an unsuccessful attempt to bridge macroregional "boundaries" (interestingly, it was organized as a club not a native place association); the JQYC association, in contrast, did develop into a cross-regional force. Finally, all the counties in these four prefectures were located in the three outer zones. All other provincial prefectures had inner-core capitals and inner-core counties. The JQYC counties were marked by lesser economic development and political power, and they were the objects of inner-core elite development projects. This shared level of development and the sense of political subordination to inner-core elites apparently became important motivations in establishing the association.

The primacy of inner-core elite concerns over those of JQYC elites in the allocation of provincial resources is seen clearly in conservancy projects. The Northern Zhejiang Conservancy Council, established by the provincial assembly in 1913 to deal with canal dredging and irrigation promotion, was funded by specifically designated portions of silk, cocoon, and boat taxes from the Hang-Jia-Hu prefectures.[5] Elites from Ning-Shao had also organized their own council in late 1917 to deal mainly with flood control problems.[6] It was also funded through local taxes but received additional support from the government.[7] In both cases, the local taxes were channeled to Hangchow where the civil governor routed funds to specific council projects on the basis of provincial assembly action.[8]

The Tong River is the portion of the Qiantang between Tonglu and Jiande; it is shallow in places with many shoals. Elites from Jinhua, Quzhou, and Yanzhou favored its dredging to facilitate transportation between Hangchow and their home areas. Thus, headed by Hu Bingliu, second RPA representative from Yanzhou (Suian county), the Tong River Conservancy Council was established in 1918, like the others operating on local taxes to be allocated by the assembly.[9]

Whereas the assembly appropriated large sums for the Northern Conservancy Council (for example, 3,000 *yuan* for the construction of a single dike), the allocation for the whole Tong River project in mid-1920 was only 1,350 *yuan*.[10] This sum was especially exasperating in view of the favored inner-core elite development project at Sanmen Bay for which 2,000 *yuan* was appropriated for preliminary planning in 1920.[11] It was not a case of insufficient funding: the Lanqi chamber of commerce in June 1920 complained that 50,000 *yuan* had been collected for the project but that nothing was being done.[12] The Jin-Qu-Yan elites were simply too politically weak to effect assembly allocations. In December 1920, citing lack of interest and money, the provincial assembly abolished the Tong River council and—in an obvious show of disdain for these areas—took for its own purposes the taxes that had been collected for the project. Assembly election preparation costs for the third RPA had already reached almost 13,400 *yuan*; the Tong River taxes served as a source of these funds.[13]

At that point the JQYC association decided to take action. Meeting four days after the assembly decision to abolish the project, the association took steps to resuscitate it. Discussions included methods of funding, the possibility of getting soldiers for labor, and the potential involvement of Shanghai construction firms.[14] Although the eventual procedures are not recorded, the flourishing commerce of the towns along the river attest to the project's progress by 1923.[15]

By 1920 the association exhibited considerable solidarity of purpose, with elites from certain areas supporting the interests of those in the coalition from other areas. For example, the initiative to revive the Tong River project came largely from Chuzhou elites, men whose native places sent the majority of their trade down the Ou River, not the Qiantang. Reciprocally, in 1923 four of the five association men who lobbied Lu Yongxiang for better defenses against outside forces in the counties of Quzhou and Chuzhou were from Jinhua and Yanzhou.[16] Before Sun Chuanfang's entrance into the province in September of 1924, the association was again in the forefront, pressing for a stronger defense.[17]

The association built its strength on assembly elites, the military, and a few merchant-industrialists. A large group of military men headed by Ye Huanhua, Xu Zexun, and Xia Chao were crucial in the association's organization, purchase of property for an association hall, and defense lobbying. Ye and Xu were active military officers; Xia was head of the provincial police, becoming civil governor in 1924. Also instrumental in the direction of the association were Chen Huang, former factory superintendent in Shanghai, and Wu Zhiying, a silk entrepreneur involved in efforts to mechanize the industry.[18]

The JQYC association was again in the vanguard with its proposals for local self-government. Elites in the outer zones, in fact, seemed more insistent on the reestablishment of local self-government in the late 1910s and early 1920s than inner-core elites. Two thirds of the signers of an eloquent late 1919 plea for rule by the "people" (*minzhi*) as opposed to rule by officials (*guanzhi*) and for local self-government to protect the particularity of localities were JQYC assemblymen.[19] Although this could be interpreted as a cynical elite attempt to benefit from local taxes, it also indicates a growing awareness in the outer zones of the potential for achieving elite goals through political organizations. The JQYC association submitted a plan of its own for a preconstitutional convention census; unlike the provincial assembly's plan, it envisioned a system of specially appointed deputies to insure accuracy.[20] In the spring of 1924, the association, sponsoring meetings to discuss election procedures, wired every county assembly in its prefectures asking for elections on the basis of talent rather than bribes.[21] At the 1924 convention itself, the JQYC association elites played key roles.

The attempt to set down a provincial constitution in 1924 was the third such endeavor in the 1920s. The 9/9 constitution promulgated in 1921 and the "three-color" constitution of 1922–23 were never effectuated.[22] This third effort developed over the opposition of some inner-core elites and with the strong support of outer-zone elites.[23] The political and social positions taken by the convention's two coalitional blocs, the JQYC and the HJHNS groups, are of particular interest. Though some men from each area espoused positions set forth by the other area's elites, stands on the major issues generally followed this division. The power of Taizhou elites had shrunk dramatically from its heyday in the late 1910s. During the debate Taizhou and Wenzhou elites sided as often with the HJHNS bloc as with the JQYC group.

The composition of the 1924 convention compared with that of 1921 indicates that substantially greater power was allocated to county elites in 1924. The 1921 convention had had 207 men: 55 provincial assemblymen (26.6 percent), 75 county assembly representatives (36.2 percent), and 77 representatives of professional associations (37.2 percent).[24] In contrast, the 1924 convention had 149 members: 75 (50.3 percent) chosen by the county assemblies, 37 (24.8 percent) by the provincial assembly, and 37 (24.8 percent) by the professional associations.[25] In the actual elections, professional associations chose most of the national elite types. Since most of the provincial assembly choices were not men who had been active on the national scene, local and provincial elites composed over 75 percent of this convention. The voices of both convention blocs, then, more clearly represented local views than had those in the earlier convention.[26]

The elections of the convention's officers immediately indicated the nature of the rivalry of the two blocs, bringing into focus some of the sharp political and social divergencies between the inner core and outer zones. The elected chairman was Chu Fucheng, federalist member of the national assembly from Jiaxing (inner core). Chu had been a member of the Tongmeng hui before 1911 and in the 1920s was a member of the Guomindang. For first vice-president, the convention chose Ye Huanhua, longtime military figure from Qingtian (inner periphery), who had been a member of the Restoration Society before 1911. The balance between the two in regard to their revolutionary association affiliation, political orientation and status, and coalitional base is notable. In voting for the second vice-president, the JQYC candidate, Wang Tingyang, and the HJHNS candidate, Mo Yongzhen, each received fifty votes on the first ballot. Mo won on the second ballot by eight votes.[27]

The influence of native place in convention proceedings was evident from the start. There was considerable delay and controversy about the method of selecting personnel for the drafting committee. All suggestions assumed that the committee should be based upon native place criteria. At one point, a Shaoxing representative, Sun Shiwei, in an impassioned plea championed breaking the hold of native regions (*dapo quyu juyi*). But in the end, the drafting committee had almost equal representation from every former prefecture.[28] On many procedural matters and in some substantive debate (such as residency qualifications for the electorate), positions were taken without regard to coalition or native place.[29] But most crucial questions—the status of the province, the composition of the provincial assembly, the nature of the provincial executive, and the issue of local government—became identified with native place.

The basic political question raised by the drafting of a provincial constitution was the status of the province vis-à-vis the national political structure. The crucial debate centered on the issue of whether the province was concurrently both a self-governing unit and an administrative unit under central control.[30] The outer zones' JQYC bloc emphasized adherence to the national constitution, arguing that Zhejiang would eventually give allegiance to the central government; thus, the province in its constitution had to avoid colliding with the national government over administrative rights and duties. The inner-core HJHNS bloc, many of whom were Guomindang members, argued that Zhejiang's needs were paramount and that the province should be autonomous. Han Baohua, inner-core lawyer and in early 1927 a Zhejiang Guomindang official, endorsed the old pyramidal national political structure of township to national capital; but he contended that since there was no united central government, Zhejiang could not be its administrative unit.[31] The convention initially adopted the position of Han and the HJHNS, which was primarily a refusal to have any part of the current Beijing regime: Zhejiang was a self-governing province. On the surface, the arguments of the HJHNS coalition appear provincialist. But both positions—the HJHNS and the less openly anticenter stand of the JQYC bloc—were nationalistic, with the difference being the national government to which each was willing to owe allegiance.[32]

The 1924 war and the subsequent provincial power situation brought eventual acceptance of the JQYC position. In early October, the convention voted to frame a draft within the scope of the national constitution.[33] After the Zhili clique victory, the leadership of Cao Kun, the head of both the national government and the Zhili clique, more easily insured provincial cooperation and adherence to the 1923 national constitution. The latter stipulated that provincial self-government laws "shall not conflict with the Constitution and the national laws."[34] When the constitutional draft was promulgated on January 1, 1926, the section on provincial powers was identical to that in the federalist 9/9 constitution.[35]

The other major debated issues dealt with provincial and local institutions. Generally the JQYC arguments indicated a politically conservative stance: a centralized presidential provincial executive rather than a deputy system; some opposition to inclusion of a constitutional section on the people's livelihood (shengji); and the retention of the current provincial assembly powers.[36] In one issue, local government and elite roles, this bloc argued for either direct election of the magistrate (with right of recall) or adoption of a deputy-commission system of county government. (The HJHNS speakers, though less specific in their speeches, substantially agreed on this point.)[37] This more liberal position by the JQYC elites reflects the goal of greater autonomy for which some local elites had strived. These latter proposals can be cynically viewed as naked attempts by elites to control the locality for their own benefit; or they can be interpreted as evidence of growing elite politicization in attempting to grapple with existing local political problems through the manipulation of local institutions.[38] The HJHNS positions, in addition to their support of considerable local elite autonomy, included a deputy provincial executive; inclusion of a section on people's livelihood; and the granting to county assemblies the ultimate legislative authority should the provincial assembly block locally initiated proposals.[39] The final draft included all HJHNS positions except that of provincial status.

General coalitional conceptions of political goals and ideals thus emerged from the constitutional debate: the JQYC positions of loyalty to the central government, more centralized control at the provincial capital, considerable local elite political power, and an aversion to the state's role in social change; and the HJHNS stances of provincial autonomy, diminished central bureaucratic authority, local autonomy, and the instigative role of the state in social change. The views of neither coalition would be translated *in toto* to the tenets of post-1927 parties; but many of the JQYC positions that were not accepted at the convention would coincide with the ideals of the Guomindang faction that came to power in April 1927.

Provincial Guomindang Development to Mid-1927

The Formation of Guomindang Bureaus

As it developed in Zhejiang in the 1920s, the Guomindang was an inner-core phenomenon. Shen Dingyi, a native of Xiaoshan county (inner core), who returned from his trip to Moscow with Chiang Kai-shek in the late fall of 1923, personally organized the party bureau at Hangchow in April 1924.[40] That spring the first bureaus outside the capital were established in Pinghu county and at Haimen in Linhai county.[41] The first provincial party conference (*quansheng daibiao dahui*) was held in early March 1926 in Hangchow. Attending were thirty-seven representatives from thirteen party and branch bureaus. All but two of the represented counties were in the inner core; the two, Zhuji and Fuyang, were outer-core counties.[42] Not until after this conference did inner-core party members begin to make contacts with interested persons in the outer zones. For example, the Shouchang county bureau (inner periphery) was established late in 1926; the Suian county bureau (outer periphery) was formed at that same time by a Jiashan (inner core) party functionary.[43] In the formation of the party, as in other concerns, the outer zones were objects of inner-core elite initiative.

Factional dissension disrupted party affairs from the time of its organization. The Guomindang office established by Shen Dingyi generally attracted older Guomindang types who later became associated with the party's right wing. In the 1920s older elites returned to the inner core to remake the province as a first step toward federation. The older elites who were Guomindang members were generally late-Qing Tongmeng hui adherents; many of them had studied abroad and had been the beneficiaries of the 1911 revolution, serving in official or national legislative posts in the first decade of the Republic. Of twenty-one such men who served in the constitutional convention in 1924, twelve had been members of a proto-Guomindang Political Consultative Society formed in Hangchow in 1916. These men did not generally have the local perspective of the newer Guomindang provincial leaders; and they were resented by the newer elites.[44]

Another Guomindang party office established in Hangchow attracted younger revolutionaries, who generally became associated with the left wing of the party. All elected party leaders in March 1926 came from this group.[45] They were from the inner core, educated at modern schools in China or abroad, with careers predominantly in education, law, and journalism. Only two of twelve leaders had been involved in provincial level politics: Han Baohua and Cha Renwei, who both served in the 1924 constitutional convention; Cha had also been provincial assemblyman from 1921 to 1924. The others had been involved in founding county bureaus. This party elite group symbolized the modern-school educated, specialized, politicized inner-core elites of the 1920s.

The two offices bitterly opposed each other on matters of goals and strategy. The eclipse of the older group after 1925 came in large part because many left the province from mid-1925 until the Northern Expedition; provincial Guomindang activity was thus controlled by the left-wing elites. Zhejiang's representatives to the second session of the party's second plenum in Guangzhou were the leaders of the left wing, Ding Meisun and Xuan Zhonghua.[46] The Guomindang left wing supervised the establishment of party bureaus in the outer zones and bore the brunt of Sun Chuanfang's suppression in late 1926.[47]

The Establishment of the Workers' Association

Within two weeks of the founding of the Guomindang bureau in Hangchow in the spring of 1924, another Hangchow organization, the Workers' Association (*gongjie xiehui*), was established. Organized by elites from the outer zones, all of whom were members of the JQYC association, it would play a crucial role in the demise of the Guomindang Left in the spring of 1927. Unfortunately, material on this organization is scant. It was probably an outgrowth of the Dongyang (county) workers native place association (*Dongyang gongjie tongxianghui*), whose date of establishment I have been unable to determine. JQYC association elites met with Dongyang representatives and established the Workers' Association in late May 1924.[48] From the beginning, it was controlled by entrepreneurs in the weaving industry. Wu Zhiying, who drafted its charter, was a wealthy silk merchant active in efforts to mechanize the industry.[49] Dongyang natives were important in the Huzhou silk-weaving industry; and it is probable that Wu, whose native place is not determinable, was attempting to use the strength of the JQYC association (Dongyang is in Jinhua prefecture) to bring the natives under closer control at a time of increasing industry mechanization. It is also probable that Wu had ties to the older elites of the Guomindang. At the 1924 May Day rally in Hangchow, the two speakers to the workers groups (which included the Dong-yang workers native place association) were Wu and Shen Dingyi.[50]

There is evidence that the Workers' Association, meeting in the hall of the JQYC association and intimately connected to it, formed county branches over the next two years. For example, in Shouchang county (inner periphery) a Dongyang workers native place association was established in November 1924;[51] and in September 1925, in the outer periphery county of Xuanping (Chuzhou prefecture), a Workers' Association was established.[52] Described in the county gazetteer as a branch of the JQYC Workers' Association, its identity with the parent organization seems obvious. Its functions in the backwater county are, unfortunately, not delineated. But information on its founder, Chen Xiong, suggests that it was an elite organization established, like the early Republican rent collection agencies, by elites for the protection of elite interests. Chen, a graduate of the Zhejiang Law School, was an important leader in the county lumber business, chairman of the county education association from 1920 to 1924, and member of the county board.[53] The number of counties with Workers' Association branches in the JQYC area cannot be determined.[54] What is certain is that this association was an employer-run strongly paternalistic organization closely linked to the JQYC association elites.

The Victory of the Guomindang Right and JQYC Elites

With the advance of the Northern Expedition, the Hangchow General Labor Union (*conggong hui*), which had been established in 1926, became more outspoken in its demands for occupational reforms and workers' rights. Clearly under the leadership of the left-wing provincial party leaders, the union, at the end of March 1927, began to plan a union leaders institute to study "problems of organization and discipline, the role of unions and of workers' militias, propaganda methods, analysis of the capitalist system, and the role of the Chinese working class in the Chinese and world revolution."[55] Han Baohua, the head of the party's Workers' Bureau, ordered that newspapers edited by right-wing Guomindang men who opposed such objectives be closed.[56]

At this point, right-wing Guomindang members, military leaders, and businessmen-employers turned to the JQYC association's Workers' Association to lead an anti-union effort.[57] The new organization formed by these forces was called the Workmen's Federation (*zhigong lianhehui*). Headed by JQYC association leaders Tu Chenxiang, Zhang Hao, and Zhao Baisu, it met in the JQYC association hall.[58] The bulk of its strength was reportedly construction workers who were also members of the Dongyang workers' native place association.[59] Its purpose was to initiate the purge of the left-wing Guomindang provincial party leadership.

The Guomindang Right had thus linked its program to certain busi-nessmen-entrepreneurs and to elites from the outer zones' JQYC associa-tion.

A federation march sparked a labor union protest demonstration on March 31, 1927, during which fighting erupted between the two groups. Police and the military intervened and declared union worker militia units dissolved; this, in turn, prompted a general strike. The Guomindang right wing had anticipated the union's response, which they used as the pretext for the purge of current party leaders. On April 12, the purge began; all elected leaders of the Guomindang provincial committee of March 1926 were targeted for arrest. Most fled immediately, and the focus of the purge spread to county bureaus as well. Its work accom-plished, the Workmen's Federation was dissolved on April 14.[60]

The older generation of 1911 revolutionaries and elites from the JQYC area took the place of the ousted younger Guomindang left-wing elites. Of six provincial party leaders after the purge, all but one (Ruan Xing-cun) were returnees to Hangchow, men who had had no or only very little connection with provincial affairs for almost two decades. A list of the provincial government political affairs deputies reveals the same pattern. In addition, there is evidence that elites from the JQYC areas were well represented in the party and in government affairs: Chen Xihao of Dong-yang, who was instrumental in the purge, served as party political dep-uty into the 1930s; Wang Tingyang of Jinhua, a *jinshi,* official, provincial and national legislator, and head of the JQYC association, served as in-vestigative party deputy into the 1930s; Huang Weishi of Jinhua led the newly purged General Labor Union, being joined in the union leadership by others from his native place. Xu Baiyuan of Lanqi became the chief secretary of the provincial party bureau.[61] Evidence suggests that the Guomindang revolution enabled elites from the JQYC areas to emerge clearly in the circles of political power from which they had been largely excluded to that point.

The events of March and April 1927 saw the submersion of many of the younger leaders of the Guomindang Left, who hailed in large num-ber from the inner core. Most, if not all, had been Guomindang leaders in their native places. The period before 1911 had seen the return of outside elites to the core zones to rebuild the locality. The period of the early- to mid-1920s had seen the return of elites to localities in the three most de-veloped zones. The Guomindang revolution witnessed the return of out-side elites to many positions of provincial prominence. Men like Zhang Renjie, Ma Xulun, Jiang Menglin, and Chen Qicai had generally not been involved in provincial affairs for many years. Their return meant the submersion of a considerable degree of provincial and local elite initiative that had come from counties in at least the three most developed zones by the mid-1920s.[62]

The victory of the right-wing Guomindang in April 1927 may have symbolized the coalition of the military, of older elites whose political origins were linked with the Tongmeng hui, and of large numbers of elites from the outer core and inner periphery. Except for the greater emphasis placed on local autonomy by the JQYC bloc in the 1924 convention, the JQYC tenets of that time—emphasis upon loyalty to the capital, bureaucratic controls, and socially conservative goals—look very much like an outline of the eventual Guomindang program after 1928.[63] If this is the case, the Guomindang revolution was infused with ideas of late Qing nonofficial elite nationalism and the political and social outlook of many elites from the outer zones. Although it is emphatically not the case that all inner-core elites were progressive, many elites from the outer zones were less affected by the modern developmental changes of the inner core, were already used to more bureaucratic (magisterial) power over elite affairs, and were accustomed to the greater roles of police and military forces in controlling social disorder.

Conclusion

A cogent interpretation of early-twentieth-century Chinese society and politics must consider not only the highly urbanized sectors that have left the most abundant record but also those areas that were poorly developed. Until now, many scholars have tended to offer general interpretations of events and trends primarily on the basis of developments in relatively economically developed areas. They are intellectually replaying the tactics of reformers and politicians from the nineteenth-century self-strengthening reformers to Chiang Kai-shek: concentrating on developed areas to the neglect of vast, less developed territory. A view of the sociopolitical ecology of *all* areas brings important dynamics of elite structures and development into focus.[1] The zonal framework makes it clear that elite behavior and political development vary systematically through regional space from inner core to outer periphery.

Although all zones experienced the introduction of new institutions and consequent political processes in the first decades of the century, the degree of acceptance of institutions as legitimate political actors varied according to level of economic development. In the core zones, matters previously in the domain of private responsibility were increasingly transferred to the enlarging public institutional sphere; and newly established institutions came to be seen as important supervisory, mediational, and interest organizations in local affairs. In the peripheries, on the other hand, though oligarchical elites became involved in self-government bodies and professional associations, local politics retained a much more private character. Institutional identification was either nonexistent or in its earliest stages. The greater continuity of specific elites over time tended to deter any strong institutionalization of new specialized bodies; matters previously managed by informal groups of elites (usually under magisterial prompting) continued to be so handled.

The core-periphery division is less important than a progressive zonal

186

pattern in analyzing elite political roles and associations. In the late Qing inner core there was substantial integration in the leadership of political organs; but the increasing specialization and diversity after 1912 meant less elite integration and the development of more diversified politics. This zone witnessed a plethora of voluntary associations and developing interest groups capable of enunciating political, social, and economic goals and significant in linking elites in new organizational contexts. By the 1920s, those in specialized professions—both the newly self-conscious merchant stratum and the graduates of modern educational institutions—served alongside the old gentry and gentry-merchant strata. In this increasingly complex political, social, and economic environment, the county magistrate often deferred to local elites in the management of daily affairs. These trends became weaker the farther one moved away from the inner core. In the peripheries, strong oligarchical control and the close connection between nonofficial and official elites (even to the point of interchangeability of local elites with minor bureaucratic functionaries) provided a more tightly integrated, continuing leadership group than in the core zones. Fewer associations and specialized organs were established in the outer zones; when they were, it was generally later than in the more developed zones. A separate native merchant stratum was less important in the outer than inner core and insignificant in the peripheries. In the progression from inner to outer zones, the role of the magistrate loomed more significant, his supervisory scope over local affairs expanding and his leadership roles increasing.

Career patterns in each zone differed dramatically. Except for military cadets, the inner core provided the vast majority of those modern school students studying outside Zhejiang. Students and officials returned to reconstruct local society in the last decade of the Qing and again in the 1920s. Political opportunities expanded following the 1911 revolution. In general, many who emerged after the revolution continued in local political leadership roles into the 1920s. The outer core also saw students and officials return before 1911, but following the revolution, it experienced less of an exodus than did the inner core. Political leaders with more varied backgrounds tended to appear in the late 1910s and 1920s. The inner periphery had few pre-1911 returnees; but, as in the outer core, there was some opening of political opportunities in the late 1910s and 1920s. The continuity of elite leadership in the outer periphery from the 1890s into the 1930s and 1940s curtailed political opportunities. Those who did have training outside the county tended to return instead of seeking higher career spheres. Indeed, as one moves from the inner core to the outer periphery, the tendency increased for outer-educated or outer-ranging elites to return and remain in their native places for their careers.

The sense of identification with political-administrative units tended to become weaker in proportion to the distance away from the inner core. Subcounty self-government districting became a matter of serious dispute in the inner core; important market towns with county boundaries purposefully drawn through them (Wu-Qing and Puyuan, for example) continually wrestled with the issue of divided administrative county loyalty. Sketchier evidence suggests that newly drawn boundaries took on similar importance in the outer core at a later period; in Cheng county, for example, districting disputes became severe only in the mid-1920s. In the peripheral zones, however, county and subcounty boundaries seemed more ambiguous. Natural boundaries took precedence in many cases, and dual district representation in some self-government bodies suggests a lack of identity with specific administrative units. A stronger sense of political-administrative identity marked the core zones.

The more rapid growth of national and provincial feelings in the core zones also attests to this stronger sense of political identity. In the peripheries such identity did not develop until the 1920s and then, reportedly, only sporadically. The developmental pattern of such political identification underlines the obvious importance of transportation and communications facilities for the spread of political ideas.

Such marked political and social differentiation in the four zones resulted from the effects of different developmental processes on existing sociopolitical ecologies. Where economic development occurred via evolutionary change, as in the inner core, there were substantial early changes in elites and the social structure. Well-established lineages provided a base from which their elites could accommodate themselves to economic and political change, and new elites with strong occupational and specialized identities emerged to participate in developmental changes. Economic development stimulated structural alterations that gave rise to political interests and goals. Thus, the primary initial dynamic propelling the inner core toward political change before and during the early decades of the twentieth century was economic development. The elites of the inner core were primed to seize the new political institutions as opportunities for themselves and for the benefit of their interests. Political change wrought by the 1911 revolution markedly accelerated processes already under way, for example, the emergence of an increasingly important merchant class.

In contrast, in the outer zones, the primary initial dynamic of change was the penetration of the state in the form of government-sponsored institutions and processes into much tighter, less diverse elite oligarchical structures. Political penetration thus generally preceded economic development, which for most counties in the outer zones came long after the first three decades of the twentieth century. The political penetration did little initially to alter existing elite structures; similarly, the 1911 revolution either left untouched or strengthened local leadership. The incipient economic development that occurred in the outer core and inner periphery generally came at the hands of inner-core elites who looked upon these areas as sources of raw materials and investment opportunities. This policy (based in an inner core marked after 1912 by the growing power of merchant interests and a burgeoning capitalism) seems to reflect the pattern of structural economic imbalance between development zones described by scholars like Immanuel Wallerstein and Michael Hechter.[2] This imbalance itself provided much of the stimulus for the formation of provincial coalitions and factions and the increased politicization of elites from the outer zones, such as in the JQYC association.

An analysis of major provincial political events in these decades underscores the importance of differential development. The process and meaning of the 1911 revolution in the inner core, for example, differed substantially from that in the outer zones. In the 1920s the formation and direction of the Guomindang came from the inner core which, as in the pre-1911 period, was the source of radical ideas of change. Until the success of the Northern Expedition, the provincial Guomindang leadership promoted social change, espousing the tenets generally associated with the left-wing Guomindang. Unlike the 1911 episode, when many inner-core elites left native places for outside careers, the aftermath of the Northern Expedition saw the destruction of this elite: by mid-April 1927, the inner-core "revolutionary" aspect of Zhejiang's Nationalist revolution was dead. The Guomindang revolution in Zhejiang was co-opted by a coalition of pre-1912 revolutionaries (who returned after many years of absence) and social and political conservatives, many of them from the outer zones. Both these groups had previously experienced political displacement: the pre-1912 revolutionaries on the national scene (to which most of them had gravitated) by the Yuan Shikai and subsequent warlord-bureaucratic regimes; and the outer zones' elites by inner-core provincial domination. From its very beginning, the Guomindang regime in Zhejiang was an effort of those whom time had seemingly passed by and those whose native place ecology fostered bureucratic, military, and socially conservative approaches.

By the 1920s the outer zones became crucial targets and components of both the Guomindang and the Communist movements. Mao Zedong would base his rise on these outer zones—not (like the Guomindang) on their elites, but on nonelites who were not yet politicized. Although there is considerable evidence that inner-core nonelites had been brought into political processes of demonstrations and strikes by the 1920s, a similar politicization of nonelites in the outer zones had to await the Communist movement.

At its most general, the history of twentieth-century Chinese politics is the extension (however nonuniform and uneven) of the various aspects and processes of political development from the inner core to the outer zones and throughout the social structure—from elite groups into the nonelite sector. In a general way, 1911 brought Zhejiang's inner-core elites and some nonelites into the process; the 1920s nationalistic movements brought these groups and the outer zones' elites into the forefront of political change; and the Communist movement incorporated nonelites from the outer zones. The first decades of the twentieth century should therefore be viewed as an important initial stage in the politicization of Chinese society.

Appendices
Abbreviations Used in Notes
Notes
Bibliography
Glossary

The Units of Analysis

Whereas this zonal approach finds its inspiration in the regional-systems model that is based upon natural economic structures, the most common units of analysis in this political study are administrative: province, prefectures, counties, and townships. My research has shown that social and political identification of self and family came largely from political-administrative units. Taxes were paid and often assessed on a county basis; elections were held on county and prefectural bases. Native place associations of sojourning elites took their names from county, prefecture, and province: those units provided the structure for this important elite linkage.

My empirical study has revealed that such identification with administrative unit was not simply nominal; it was not hiding some transcendent political tie to natural economic units (trading systems). For example, prefectures, not greater city trading systems, are the appropriate framework for analyzing provincial political coalitions and alliances. Although many prefectural capitals were also greater cities, the territories encompassed by each prefecture and trading area were not coterminous. There were some counties or parts of counties that were administratively part of a prefecture but that were economically oriented to a greater city other than the prefectural capital. In every such case I have found, the political orientation of elites in areas oriented to different administrative and economic central places was to the administrative central place (the prefectural capital). Several examples are instructive.

Almost all of Ninghai and part of Tiantai counties (Taizhou prefecture) were part of the Ningpo greater city trading area; in fact, the macroregional "boundary" separated them from their prefectural capital. Yet when political factions and coalitions were established, they did not align themselves with Ningbo's faction: some of the greatest strength of Qu Yingguang's Taizhou faction came from these very counties. In the

Sanmen Bay project, to have been constructed in large measure in Ninghai, some of the strongest opponents hailed from Ningbo while Ninghai and Taizhou elites were its most vocal supporters. In sum, there is no evidence here of the political significance of the greater city trading area.

Although Yuyao elites were economically oriented to the Ningpo greater city trading area, in provincial politics its elites were spokesmen for Shaoxing causes (their native prefecture). Most of the trade from Pujiang flowed down the Puyang River through Zhuji to its greater city (and regional metropolis) Hangchow; but the political orientation of its elites was to its prefectural unit of Jinhua. In the development and functioning of the Jin-Qu-Yan-Chu association, political interests gave rise to a four-prefecture association which, highly contrary to what might be expected from the regional systems model, brought together elites from different macroregions. Their solidarity of purpose is noteworthy. When this association became a provincial political force in early 1927, elites from the prefectural capital (Jinhua) were in the vanguard, not those from the greater city of Lanqi (in Jinhua prefecture).

Taking the analysis to the subcounty level, a Shouchang township was economically oriented to Lanqi but contributed important elites to the Shouchang oligarchy. In the towns of Puyuan and Wu-Qing in Jiaxing and Huzhou, elites were forced to participate in different county politics by county boundaries that divided the towns. When self-government districts were established, elites often decided on districts that were not congruent with marketing areas.

Yet one more example from the higher levels of the economic hierarchy is also instructive. The three regional metropolises of the Lower Yangzi region were Nanjing, Shanghai, and Hangchow. Economically, part of Jiaxing fell within the Shanghai metropolitan trading system rather than in Hangchow's, while Huzhou fell within the Hangchow system. In the political world, however, the orientation was switched. Huzhou elites were closely involved in Shanghai affairs, whereas Jiaxing elites were key leaders in Hangchow politics.

I do not mean to imply that political and economic elites operated in two isolated worlds. Many times they were one and the same and, in any case, there was intercourse between them. The important consideration is that the regional systems model and central place theory does not answer every question. Where one would be foolhardy not to utilize it in issues of urbanization, demography, and economic structures, it would be equally foolhardy to apply every aspect of it to all questions. I do not believe that all assumptions or aspects of a model need be utilized (or even accepted) in order to realize the broad utility and suggestiveness of the model. Models provide insights and serve as tools, not straitjackets. Regional development models are based upon capitalistic, self-regulating markets and ultimately project megalopolis; yet such a model has been used to great effect in analyzing Chinese economy and society, even though it does not "fit."[1] The core-periphery aspect of regional analysis has been a significant intellectual tool in my zonal conception. The data reveal, however, that utilizing all aspects of the model as framework would be inappropriate for this analysis.

Finally, utilizing the county unit is not in the end very satisfying; intracounty differences in development obviously existed. Delving systematically below the county level to township or marketing communities is, however, precluded by lack of availability of subcounty data. I would argue that analysis of county units offers a general view of the pattern of development.

Data for County Classification

There is no one correct or completely satisfying method of classifying counties, given the paucity of statistical data. Alternative statistical methods to the one I have chosen, including factor analysis, were tried; but none of them produced a meaningful pattern of the variables. I believe that the method I have utilized has provided a logical and consistent patterning of counties. The following table indicates the variable values for each of the four classes.

Class	Population density per square kilometer	Financial institution index	Postal rank
1	316–750	4.37–12.09	1, 2
2	189–295	1.99– 3.84	3, 4
3	103–178	.14– 1.68	5, 6
4	0– 92	0	7, 8, 9

The divisions between categories in the population density and financial institution variables came from the most significant breaks in the continuous rank-ordering for each. The method for categorization of postal rank into four classes is described in note 21, Chapter 2.

In the classification of counties into four zones, those counties with a sum ranking of three to five were classified in the inner core; six to eight, in the outer core; nine to eleven, in the inner periphery; and twelve, in the outer periphery. The tables below give the raw data and ranking.

County	Classes	Population density	Postal rank	Financial institution index
		Inner Core		
Hang	1 1 1	750	1	8.13
Yin	1 1 1	462	1	12.09
Haining	1 1 1	525	1 (2)[a]	6.77
Shaoxing	1 1 1	446	1 (2)	8.31
Jiashan	1 1 1	481	1 (2)	6.81
Dinghai	1 2 1	358	2 (4)	6.60
Zhenhai	1 1 1	399	1 (2)	7.05
Xiaoshan	1 2 1	482	2 (4)	6.19
Pinghu	1 1 1	475	1 (2)	6.30
Ciqi	1 2 2	316	2 (4)	3.44
Jiaxing	1 1 2	393	1 (2)	3.84
Tongxiang	1 1 1	386	1 (2)	6.19
Huangyan	1 2 2	376	2 (4)	3.46
Deqing	1 2 1	376	2 (4)	8.11
Haiyan	1 2 1	342	2 (4)	4.37
Yuyao	1 1 1	447	1 (2)	4.51
Yongjia	2 1 1	197	1 (2)	5.77
Shangyu	1 2 2	424	2 (4)	1.99
Wuxing	1 1 1	319	1 (2)	6.83
Linhai	2 1 2	216	1 (2)	2.31
		Outer core		
Luoqing	2 3 3	295	3 (5)	.79
Lanqi	2 2 2	283	2 (3)	3.15
Zhuji	2 3 3	241	3 (5)	1.57
Ruian	2 2 3	269	2 (3)	.93
Wenling	1 4 2	526	4 (8)	2.34
Chongde	1 4 2	485	4 (8)	2.16
Yuhuan	1 4 3	321	4 (8)	.52
Pingyang	1 3 3	327	3 (5)	.15
Cheng	2 3 2	198	3 (5)	3.48
Jinhua	2 3 2	200	3 (5)	2.89
Xinchang	2 4 2	195	4 (8)	2.95
Xiangshan	2 2 2	191	2 (4)	3.35
Fenghua	3 4 1	178	4 (8)	11.25
Yuhang	3 3 1	160	3 (5)	4.45
Fuyang	3 2 2	154	2 (4)	2.81
Qu	3 2 1	137	2 (3)	5.00
Tonglu	3 2 3	106	2 (4)	.94
Longyu	3 3 2	154	3 (5)	2.32
Changxing	3 4 1	138	4 (8)	4.80
Changshan	3 3 2	110	3 (5)	2.35

County	Classes	Population density	Postal rank	Financial institution index
		Inner periphery		
Yiwu	2 4 3	290	4 (7)	1.24
Dongyang	2 4 3	215	4 (8)	.45
Jiande	4 2 3	72	2 (3)	1.67
Xindeng	3 4 2	112	4 (8)	2.24
Tiantai	3 4 3	175	4 (8)	1.58
Pujiang	2 4 3	189	4 (8)	.86
Jinyun	3 4 4	140	4 (8)	0
Anji	3 3 3	116	3 (5)	1.14
Lishui	3 3 3	103	3 (5)	1.68
Qingtian	4 3 4	92	3 (5)	0
Kaihua	4 4 2	53	4 (8)	2.62
Yongkang	2 4 4	264	4 (7)	0
Jiangshan	3 4 3	133	4 (7)	.37
Wuyi	3 4 3	108	4 (7)	1.06
Ninghai	3 4 3	124	4 (7)	.90
Xianju	3 4 3	106	4 (8)	.47
Wukang	3 3 4	111	3 (5)	0
Nantian	3 4 4	132	4 (8)	0
Tangqi	3 4 4	129	4 (8)	0
Shouchang	3 4 4	108	4 (8)	0
Qunan	4 4 2	83	4 (8)	2.09
		Outer periphery		
Songyang	4 4 4	81	4 (7)	0
Linan	4 4 4	86	4 (8)	0
Suichang	4 4 4	57	4 (8)	0
Xuanping	4 4 4	81	4 (8)	0
Qingyuan	4 4 4	45	4 (9)	0
Longchuan	4 4 4	45	4 (9)	0
Jingning	4 4 4	46	4 (9)	0
Changhua	4 4 4	54	4 (7)	0
Fenshui	4 4 4	60	4 (8)	0
Yuqian	4 4 4	64	4 (8)	0
Xiaofeng	4 4 4	75	4 (8)	0
Suian	4 4 4	84	4 (8)	0
Taishun	4 4 4	84	4 (8)	0
Yunhe	4 4 4	63	4 (8)	0

Sources: For population density, Guan Weilan, comp., *Zhonghua minguo xingzheng quhua ji tudi renkou tongji biao*, passim; for postal rank, *Shina shōbetsu zenshi: Sekkō-shō*, pp. 386–395; and for the financial institution index, *Zhongguo shiye zhi: Zhejiang sheng*, 9:28–68, 78–100; *Zhejiang caizheng yuekan*, 8 (February 1918): 59a–61a and 12 (June 1918): 54a–65a; *Zhejiang jinyongye gailan*, passim; and *Shina shōbetsu zenshi: Sekkō-shō*, pp. 796–881.

a. The number in parentheses is the original nine-class category rank.

Methodological and Source-Related Problems

I have gathered the names, roles, social backgrounds, and sociopolitical linkages of these elites primarily from a study of all applicable gazetteers and a day-by-day reading of the following newspapers: from Shanghai, the *Shi Bao,* from 1909 to mid-1927; the *Shen Bao,* from 1923 to 1927; the *Minli Bao,* from 1910 to 1913; and the *Zhonghua Xinbao* in 1917; and from Peking, the *Shuntian Shibao,* from 1921 to mid-1923. Zhejiang newspapers are not available for this period.

Other elite institutions besides self-government—chambers of commerce, education associations, agriculture associations—that could theoretically, perhaps, provide a comparable framework, varied greatly both in existence and in membership according to zone and county. Self-government elites are a good referent because generally anyone who claimed to be a local leader would become involved in or have a relative involved in self-government. In order to get a somewhat better estimate of the importance of self-government elites in the total picture of all elites, I made detailed studies of the counties (distributed in all zones) that have gazetteers from this period. In particular, I set out to determine the percentage of specified county *non*-self-government functions that were performed by self-government leaders or their kin. Included in this survey were the following functions in the period 1900 to 1927: heads of chambers of commerce; officers of education and agriculture associations; originators and heads of militia organizations; contributors to charity and relief; founders of schools; and initiators of public works, including irrigation projects, dikes, and dredging of waterways.

That study revealed that in counties with extant gazetteers in the two most economically developed zones from two fifths to more than half (the range is 42 percent to 56 percent) of all important non-self-government functions were performed by self-government elites or their kin.[1] In contrast, in counties of the two least economically developed zones between 73 percent and 85 percent of all major non-self-government functions were performed by self-government elites or their kin.[2] If the statistics err, they probably lessen the actual importance of self-government members and their kin. In some gazetteers, biographical and native place information is sparse, making it difficult to tell if same-surnamed men from the same township were related. In such cases, I have not included them as self-government kin even though, in fact, they may have been of the same lineage as a self-government member. Even with this possible deflationary error, the statistics indicate that in each zone there was considerable control of county political power in the hands of relatively small numbers of men connected to self-government either directly or through kin ties. When self-government functions are added to the statistics, they obviously only augment this control.

The statistics suggest that the functional scope of self-government-related elites was considerably greater in the less developed areas than in the more developed. A possible explanation for the weaker scope in the more developed areas was that a lesser emphasis was placed on involvement in self-government institutions. This phenomenon requires that more attention be given to *non*-self-government elites in the total picture of local functional elites. My analysis of elites in the core zones thus relies more heavily upon newspapers and non-self-government sections of gazetteers.

It would be appropriate to ask what types of men probably performed the other 44 to 58 percent of the local functions in the core zones. In all likelihood, they were men who shared the qualities of gentry and nongentry self-government elites: wealthy and strong figures, probably powerful merchants or imposing landlords. With wealth and prestige, they fulfilled their communities' needs for relief, public works, and defense. They were men like Lin Yonghuai of Xiangshan, a *lingsheng* degreeholder who served as head of the county agriculture association and the chamber of commerce and who built several county schools.[3] Or they were leaders like Kong Qingyi of Qu county, a gentry-merchant who headed the chamber of commerce; led in education and irrigation projects and in the anti-opium movement; and founded an electric company.[4] Or, as a last example, they were leaders like Zhang Yinhua of Xinchang, *shengyuan* and builder of schools.[5] The non-self-government functional elites were by every indication men of the same type, with similar backgrounds and scope of functions as self-government elites. In short, I contend that analysis of self-government elites provides reasonably close hypotheses about the nature of important county functional elites in general.

Several serious source-related difficulties, however, make self-government statistics tentative and useful primarily as a means of formulating hypotheses. For one, the percentage of counties producing gazetteers is far too small for reliable statistical conclusions about the population. Extant gazetteers cover from 24 percent (in the inner periphery) to 43 percent (in the outer periphery) of the total counties in particular zones. Nevertheless, I contend that *with other data* the statistics can be useful in surveying the social dynamics of local politics in the early twentieth century. The tables below indicate the zonal distribution of extant self-government data with the number of cases (men) involved in each.

Gazetteers from the inner core and the peripheries are richest in their inclusion and treatment of elites. Zhejiang's outer-core gazetteers provide poor sources for late Qing and early Republican subcounty self-government bodies. Fortunately, for the study of this zone at that time, two modern county histories written in the 1920s provide information to compensate in part for this lacuna (though only one has systematic treatment of self-government membership).

Late Qing and early Republican subcounty self-government leaders

Zone	County seats	Nonadministrative town	Townships	Men
Inner core	4	8	44	209
Outer core	1	—	2	7
Inner periphery	3	—	21	132
Outer periphery	4	—	31	184
Total	12	8	98	532

Sources: Same as for Tables 5-8.

First Republican county assembly membership, 1912–1914

	Counties	Men
Inner core	4	115
Outer core	3	70
Inner periphery	4	94
Outer periphery	5	123
Total	16	402

Sources: Same as for Tables 5-8.

Second Republican county assembly membership, 1922–1927

	Counties	Men
Inner core	3	52
Outer core	3	56
Inner periphery	3	57
Outer periphery	5	96
Total	14	261

Sources: Same as for Tables 5 to 8.

Two additional points should be noted. First, subcounty statistics apply to *leaders* of town and township self-government while the *entire* county assemblies are represented in the last two data sets. The risk of distortion in comparing these groups is not great, for those elected to the assemblies were generally the most qualified and active functional town and township elites who had themselves served as leaders of subcounty bodies. In terms of social background and functional analysis, I have found no evidence to suggest that leaders of township organs were not generally analogous to county assembly members.

Second, apart from the small number of extant gazetteers, internal source considerations increase the tentativeness in certain areas. Gazetteer coverage of elites and their backgrounds is often irregular in scope and depth. Often those very traditional degrees that are of great interest to the student of early-twentieth-century society—the *shengyuan* and *jiansheng*—are not included systematically. In cases where there was no systematic coverage in the gazetteer's section on degrees, I mined all its sections to garner information on these types. Yet it is certainly the case that some elites in two categories, those functional elites without recorded degrees, diploma, or family ties and those whose only recorded role was self-government membership, were lower-degree-holders. In all likelihood, the number of degree-holders in each zone should be increased as a proportion of the total; but, as there is no notable skewing in any zone due, for instance, to several county gazetteers having more or less than the usual lower-degree-holder coverage, I suspect that the increases would be relative.

In sum, I would contend that these source-related problems, though they make many conclusions tenuous, should not overwhelm and stifle empirical research and informed hypotheses. Even if these data are used primarily for producing hypotheses, that in itself is valuable given the virgin state of Chinese elite studies.

Abbreviations Used in the Notes

CEB	*Chinese Economic Bulletin*
CEJ	*Chinese Economic Journal*
CLIC	G. William Skinner, ed., *The City in Late Imperial China* (Stanford: Stanford University Press, 1977)
DC	*Decennial Reports,* 1912–1921 (Maritime Customs Service)
DZ	*Dongfang zazhi*
GG	Zhonghua minkuo kaiguo wushinian wenxian bianzuan weiyuanhui, ed., *Gesheng guangfu* in *Zhonghua minguo kai guo wushinian wenxian* (Taipei, 1962)
GS	*Gendai Shina jimmeikan* (Tokyo: Japan Ministry of Foreign Affairs, 1928)
JAS	*Journal of Asian Studies*
JSZ	Zhongguo kexue yuan lishi yanjiusuo disan suo, comp., *Jindai shi ziliao* (Beijing, 1954–1961)
MLB	*Minli Bao*
NA	National Archives, United States Department of State
NCH	*North China Herald*
OG	Huang Qinglan, *Ouhai guanzheng lu* (n.p., 1921; reprint, Taibei, n.d.)
QXLW	Qu Yingguang, *Qu xunanshi xunshi liangZhe wengao* (n.p., n.d.)
S	*Shi Bao*
SB	*Shen Bao*

Shina	Tōa Dōbunkai, comp., *Shina shōbetsu zenshi: Sekkō-shō* (Tokyo, 1919)
SS	*Shuntian Shibao*
SXZ	*Shaoxing xianzhi ziliao diyi ji,* 1937
TR	*Returns of Trade and Trade Reports* (China Imperial Maritime Customs)
X	xianzhi
XF	*Xin Fenghua,* 1922
XG	Chai Degeng et al., comp., *Xinhai geming* (Shanghai, 1956)
XGH	Zhongguo renmin zhengzhi xieshang huiyi quanguo weiyuanhui, ed., *Xinhai geming huiyilu* (Beijing, 1961–1963)
Z	zhenzhi
ZG	Zhuji minbao she, ed., *Zhuji gaiguan,* 1925
ZS	Shiyebu guoji maoyi ju, comp., *Zhongguo shiye zhi,* vol. 2, *Zhejiang sheng* (Shanghai, 1933)
ZW	*Zhuanji wenxue*
ZX	*Zhonghua Xinbao*
ZXB	*Zhenhai xinzhi beigao,* 1924
ZY	*Zhejiang yuekan*

Notes

1. Elites and Political Development

1. This view can be seen in most general studies of the period. See, for example, Immanuel C. Y. Hsu, *The Rise of Modern China,* 2nd ed. (New York, 1975), pp. 576 and 588; and James E. Sheridan, *China in Disintegration* (New York, 1975).

2. Yoshinobu Shiba, "Ningpo and Its Hinterland" in *CLIC,* p. 422. See also a description of this trend in Mark Elvin, "Market Towns and Waterways: The County of Shanghai from 1480 to 1910" in *CLIC,* pp. 441–473.

3. See especially Susan M. Jones and Philip A. Kuhn, "Dynastic Decline and the Roots of Rebellion" in *The Cambridge History of China,* vol. 10: *Late Ch'ing, 1800–1911, Part I,* ed. John K. Fairbank (Cambridge, 1978), pp. 109, 121–128, and 161.

4. Jones and Kuhn, "Dynastic Decline," p. 127.

5. See, for example, Mary Backus Rankin, "Local Reform Currents in Chekiang before 1900" in *Reform in Nineteenth Century China,* ed. Paul Cohen and John Schrecker (Cambridge, Mass., 1976), pp. 221–230.

6. See the two essays in note 2 above. In addition, most of the specific sites of active local gentry militia leadership in the mid-nineteenth century discussed by Philip Kuhn in his *Rebellion and Its Enemies in Late Imperial China* (Cambridge, Mass., 1970) coincide with regional cores delineated in G. William Skinner, "Regional Urbanization in Nineteenth Century China" in *CLIC,* pp. 214–215. The same is true of county elites in my earlier study, "The Composition and Functions of the Local Elite in Szechwan, 1851–1874," *Ch'ing-shih wen-t'i,* 2 (November 1973): 7–23.

7. Skinner, "Regional Urbanization," p. 228.

8. Personal communication with Philip Kuhn, June 3, 1978. An example is shipping magnate Zhang Rangsan of Ningpo, who is called a *shishen* in the sources. See *GG,* p. 117, and *S,* XT 2/7/8 and 1917/12/4. Dates of the *S* until December 1, 1911, are given according to reign title (*Xuantong*—XT) followed by lunar month and day.

9. For more general points on this development, see Wellington K. K. Chan, *Merchants, Mandarins, and Modern Enterprise in Late Ch'ing China* (Cambridge, Mass., 1977), pp. 39–63.

10. The methodological pitfalls of elite identification have been noted by many social scientists. See, for example, Robert D. Putnam, *The Comparative Study of Political Elites* (Englewood Cliffs, N.J., 1976), pp. 15–19; and Lewis J. Edinger, "The Comparative Analysis of Political Leadership," *Comparative Politics*, 7 (January 1975): 253–269. For the historian, biased sources could produce a skewed selection. Unrecorded brokers or advisers may have played more important local functions than "figurehead" power holders. I assume in this analysis that men recorded in the sources had more power (that is, more probability of controlling or influencing public policies) than others who were not recorded. For the concept of "power," see Putnam, *Comparative Study*, pp. 5–8; and Robert A. Dahl, *International Encyclopedia of the Social Sciences*, s.v. "Power."

The use of the behavioral strategy may be weak in that it does not indicate power wielders who were able to keep an issue from becoming part of the political agenda in the first place. With assiduous research and careful attention to the nature of particular political issues in specific locations, however, I believe the historian can surmount many of the inherent difficulties. It should be obvious that exact power relationships among historical elites will never be known because of source limitations. But the historian's role is to provide a vision of reality that closely approximates the actual elite structure. Awareness of methodological concerns can inspire care and a healthy measure of tentativeness; but, given the virgin state of the field of Chinese elite studies, these concerns cannot be allowed to overwhelm and stifle empirical research and informed conclusions. See Edinger's comments in this regard in his "Comparative Analysis," pp. 267–269.

11. On "political development," see Charles Tilly, "Western State-Making and Theories of Political Transformation" in *The Formation of National States in Western Europe*, ed. Charles Tilly (Princeton, 1975), pp. 601–638.

For criticisms of the concept of modernization, see Dean C. Tipps, "Modernization Theory and the Comparative Study of Societies: A Critical Perspective," *Comparative Studies in Society and History*, 15 (March 1973): 199–226. See also "Editorial Foreword," ibid., 20 (April 1978): 175–176.

For the fallacy of the tradition-modernity polarity in the modernization concept, see such works as Gerald A. Heeger, "The Politics of Integration: Community, Party, and Integration in Punjab" (Ph.D. diss., University of Chicago, 1971); and Lloyd I. Rudolph and Susanne H. Rudolph, *The Modernity of Tradition* (Chicago, 1967).

12. My definitions and approach rely heavily upon the work of Teune and Mlinar in the sociology of development. See Henry Teune and Zdravko Mlinar, *The Developmental Logic of Social Systems* (Beverly Hills, Calif., 1978); Mlinar and Teune, eds., *The Social Ecology of Change* (Beverly Hills, Calif., 1978) (hereafter referred to as *Social Ecology*); Teune and Mlinar, "Development and Participation" in *Local Politics, Development, and Participation*, ed. F. C. Bruhns, Franco Cazzola, and Jerzy Wiatr (Pittsburgh, 1974), pp. 136–159; and Teune, "Development and Territorial Political Systems," *International Review of Community Development*, no. 33–34 (1975): 159–172. The definition of the level of development comes from "Development and Participation," pp. 140–142.

13. In my conception, "political development" does not project an inevitable normative form of government at some end of an evolutionary developmental

road. Nor do I mean to burden such words as "complexity" and "interdependency" with normative meaning. This book concentrates on political development in elite society; it does not specifically treat the penetration of certain indicators of this development into the nonelite sector even though in highly commercialized areas some penetration occurred. For the relationship between elites and political development, see James J. Heaphey, "Spatial Aspects of Development Administration" in *Spatial Dimensions of Development Administration*, ed. James J. Heaphey (Durham, N.C., 1971), pp. 3–14; and Gerald A. Heeger, *The Politics of Underdevelopment* (New York, 1974), p. 8.

14. In the case of *nong hui*, branches were also to be set up in towns and villages. See H. H. Brunnert and V. V. Hagelstrom, *Present Day Political Organization of China* (Shanghai, 1912), pp. 68–70, 174–184, 358–359, 362–363, and 408–410.

15. Hao Chang, *Liang Ch'i-ch'ao and Intellectual Transition in China, 1890–1907* (Cambridge, Mass., 1971), pp. 95–100, 154–156.

16. See David Sills, *International Encyclopedia of the Social Sciences,* s.v. "Voluntary Associations: Sociological Aspects," for a discussion of the social import of voluntary associations.

17. Frederic Wakeman, Jr., *The Fall of Imperial China* (New York, 1975), p. 201.

18. *S,* XT 2/3/29; XT 3/1/17; 1912/4/2, 5/2 and 5/7; and 1913/7/21.

19. Teune and Mlinar, "Development and Participation," passim.

20. See Mary C. Wright, "Introduction: The Rising Tide of Change" in *China in Revolution: The First Phase 1900–1913,* ed. Mary C. Wright (New Haven, 1968), pp. 3–23.

21. For an overview of the railroad controversy, see my "Politics and Society in Chekiang, 1907–1927: Elite Power, Social Control, and the Making of a Province" (Ph.D. diss., University of Michigan, 1975), pp. 19–26. For the responses of elites see Mobei, *JiangZhe tielu fengzhao* (1907; reprinted, Taibei, 1968).

22. Ernest Young, *The Presidency of Yuan Shih-k'ai* (Ann Arbor, 1977), pp. 76–104.

23. For an extended account of these events, see my "Politics and Society in Chekiang," chaps. 3 to 5.

24. The biographical data on Qi come from *GS,* p. 938; and *S, 1917/1/12.* For Qi's actions, see *S,* 1917/2/26, 3/5; 1919/11/29, 12/10; 1920/3/23, 6/8–11, 13, 17.

25. For accounts of the national warlord situation, see Ch'i Hsi-sheng, *Warlord Politics in China, 1916–1928* (Stanford, 1976); and Wen Gongzhi, *Zuijin sanshinian Zhongguo junshishi,* 2 vols. (Taibei, 1962).

2. The Four Zhejiangs

1. George B. Cressey, "The Land Forms of Chekiang, China," *Annals of the Association of American Geographers,* 28 (1938): 274.

2. Zhang Qiyun, *Zhejiang sheng shide jiyao* (Shanghai, 1925), p. 66. Although the prefectural units were formally abolished in the early Republic, they continued to play a crucial role in the political considerations of official and nonofficial elites. They thus figure significantly in my account.

3. See, for example, Cao Juren, *Wo yu wode shijie* (Hong Kong, 1972); and Wang Ziliang, *Zhexi kangzhan jilüe* (Taibei, 1966).

4. Rhoads Murphey, *Shanghai: Key to Modern China* (Cambridge, Mass., 1953), p. 109. A mu is approximately one-sixth of an acre.

5. Cao, *Wo,* pp. 55–56; and Murphey, *Shanghai,* pp. 133 and 147.

6. For seminal and suggestive earlier work on historical sociopolitical ecology, see Charles Tilly, *The Vendée* (Cambridge, Mass., 1964); Juan J. Linz and Amando DeMiguel, "Within-Nation Differences and Comparisons: The Eight Spains" in *Comparing Nations: The Use of Quantitative Data in Cross-National Research,* ed. Richard Merritt and Stein Rokkan (New Haven, 1966); and Risto Alapuro, "Statemaking and Political Ecology in Finland" in *Social Ecology,* pp. 109–143.

7. Skinner, "Regional Urbanization," pp. 211–249. The phrase "ecological complex" appears in Leo F. Schnore, "Social Morphology and Human Ecology," *American Journal of Sociology,* 63 (May 1958): 620–634. I have changed the scope of some of the terms as described by Schnore, but these variables are crucial in the following analysis. See also the discussion in Carol A. Smith, "Analyzing Regional Social Systems" in *Regional Analysis,* vol. 2, *Social Systems,* ed. Carol A. Smith (New York, 1976), pp. 3–20.

8. The general definition of development comes from Zdravko Mlinar, "A Theoretical Transformation of Social Ecology: From Equilibrium to Development" in *Social Ecology,* p. 23. See also Skinner's delineation of these variables in "Regional Urbanization," pp. 230–236 and the discussion of urbanization in Tilly, *Vendée,* pp. 16–20.

9. See maps, pp. 214–215, in Skinner's "Regional Urbanization." It should be apparent from the start that my approach in this book is not strictly Skinnerian. I am considering only parts of two macroregions, parts that had been joined together with provincial boundaries for many centuries. Politically and administratively they were considered a unit. Skinner warns (p. 217) against considering only parts of macroregions in the analysis of urbanization. In analyzing political development, however, my research has shown that utilizing a provincial unit that provided the context for elite actions is the proper method of approach. Yet, as we shall see, Skinner's regional model and my corollary of it play a crucial role in the study of provincial political development.

10. G. William Skinner, "Cities and the Hierarchy of Local Systems" in *CLIC,* p. 282.

11. See Appendix A for discussion on the unit of analysis in this study.

12. In his delineation of macroregional core and periphery, Skinner uses population density as the sole variable. He has argued elsewhere ("Social Ecology and the Forces of Repression in North China," unpublished conference paper, 1979) that such a use minimizes the possibility of tautology. There is obviously redundant information in my three measures. Yet I feel that their use results in a more accurate gauge of development than any of the three used alone. The Spearman rank-order correlation between these variables is high: between population density rank and postal rank, .70; between density rank and financial institution rank, .74; and between postal rank and financial institution rank, .74.

If population density alone is used in ranking counties from most to least developed, the results are distorted: commercialized areas appear less "urban" than mountainous hinterland counties. The following is a rank-ordering of counties in the mid-range of development, according to population density: it indicates that this single variable could not adequately detail rank in degree of development. Density is per square kilometer.

Lanqi	283	Pujiang	189
Yongkang	264	Fenghua	178
Zhuji	241	Tiantai	175
Linhai	216	Yuhang	160
Dongyang	215	Fuyang	154
Cheng	209	Longyu	154
Jinhua	200	Jinyun	140
Yongjia	197	Changxing	138
Xinchang	195	Qu	137
Xiangshan	191		

In this ranking by population density, Yongjia, a greater-city and treaty port county, appears less urban than Yongkang, a county on the macroregional border; Pujiang is higher ranked than the highly commercialized county of Fenghua; and Jinyun, a backwater on the macroregional border ranks higher than Qu, where the important commercial greater city in southwestern Zhejiang is located. In short, deriving hypothetical development zones through population density alone is not possible; these statistics even cast doubt on the use of density statistics for detailing degree of urbanization.

Financial institutions and postal rank are the only two other variables that I have found existing in any systematic way for this period. I think that both provide important surrogate measures in lieu of other more direct measures of development (such as total volume of business per county). Financial institutions provide some index of commercialization and economic development. While population density and the number of financial institutions are available by counties, the postal rank designation is available for central places. There are some logical difficulties in applying this designation to counties, but I would argue that the measure does provide some measure of county business activity. There are obvious difficulties in using the county unit at all, inasmuch as intra-county gradations of development were certainly the reality. But the constraints of data availability preclude analysis on the level of subcounty or lower-level marketing systems. When used in conjunction with population density, these two variables "raise" counties like Linhai, Yongjia, Fenghua, and Qu properly above such mountainous hinterland counties as Yongkang and Jinyun in level of development.

In sum, although I recognize that certain problems exist in the use of these variables, I believe that for these years they provide a reasonably accurate picture of the level of development in Zhejiang counties. We are hostage to the lack of availability of data. It should also be recalled that the initial purpose of these variables was to produce hypotheses on the number and especially the delimitation of zones. Ultimately there are four zones because of the four kinds of sociopolitical ecologies that emerged from my research rather than from breaks in a statistical scale. I am indebted to William Skinner for his comments and assistance in the process of classifying the counties. His advice and criticism helped me deal with many problems.

13. Skinner, "Regional Urbanization," p. 232. When population density reaches a certain point, as Mlinar points out in "A Theoretical Transformation," p. 16, it may cease to be "an expression of the dynamics of socio-economic development" but "can as well 'contribute' to stagnation or even retardation." He cites as examples the cases of "overurbanization" in Calcutta and Bombay (fn. 11, p. 28). I am not aware of any area in Zhejiang in the early twentieth century that had reached such a point.

14. Mlinar, "A Theoretical Transformation," pp. 24–26. See also G. William Skinner, "Marketing and Social Structure in Rural China, Part II," *JAS*, 24 (February 1965): 195–228; and Lawrence W. Crissman, "Specific Central-Place Models for an Evolving System of Market Towns on the Changhua Plain, Taiwan" in *Regional Analysis*, vol. 1, *Economic Systems*, ed. Carol A. Smith (New York, 1976), pp. 183–218.

15. For population density, I have relied on the data in Guan Weilan, comp., *Zhonghua minguo xingzheng quhua ji tudi renkou tongji biao* (Taibei, 1956). Although these data relate ostensibly to the years 1938–1948 and thus may seem anachronistic, I believe they provide an accurate *ranking* for the early Republican period. Again, my concern is not specific interval-level population data but county *rank* according to population density. A 1933 county census, undertaken by the Ministry of Industry, is reported in *ZS* (*bian*) 1:12–25. The Spearman rank-order correlation between the 1933 and 1948 censuses is .99. I have chosen to use Guan's data rather than the 1933 data because his area figures are the most reliable for the period. Furthermore, no counties experienced extraordinary population increases or decreases during these years; nor were there important county boundary changes during this time. I feel satisfied that the ranking obtained from the 1948 data is a bit more precise for the early Republican period than the 1933 data. Though all census data from this period is suspect, we must work with the available data if we are to proceed with research into Chinese society.

16. See the directory of county postal services in *Shina*, pp. 386–395.

17. See Skinner, "Cities and the Hierarchy of Local Systems," pp. 347–349.

18. Lin Chuanjia, *Dazhonghua Zhejiang sheng dili zhi* (Shanghai, 1918), p. 306.

19. The only exception is Cheng county, which had a modern-style bank by 1924. See *ZS*, 9:7–13.

20. I am indebted to William Skinner for this suggestion. In deriving this index, I excluded those banks or pawnshops founded after 1925. During the first years of the 1920s many financial institutions were established by elites away from the core zones of the province, with considerable effect on economic and political development during the period under consideration. To include those founded after 1925 would have been misleading, for my analysis of local elites generally concludes by late 1925. Sources for the information on the financial institutions include *ZS*, 9:28–68, 78–100; *Zhejiang caizheng yuekan*, 8 (February 1918): 59a–61a; ibid., 12 (June 1918): 54a–65a; *Zhejiang jinyongye gailan* (Hangchow, 1947); and *Shina*, pp. 796–881.

21. I classified the post office data from *Shina* into the nine categories described by Skinner ("Cities and the Hierarchy of Local Systems," p. 348). I then

made cross-tabulations of the post office ranking and the other two variables. In both cross-tabulations, post office categories 3 and 4 (second-class post office with two or more services including fifty *yuan* postal orders and express delivery and second-class post office with two or more services not including express delivery) do not discriminate on any of the values of the other variables. Both classes 7 and 8 (third-class post office and postal agencies) also do not discriminate. These two categories were thus collapsed. Both classes 1 and 9 clearly discriminate on the variables, but the number of centers with these classes is so small that keeping them distinct or joining them with contiguous classes would make no difference in the end result. Class 1 was thus joined to class 2; class 9, to classes 7 and 8. In this way, postal categories were collapsed from nine to four. Appendix B shows the new classification.

22. I derived this four-zone approach in 1978, without reference to Skinner's later four-zone refinement of his *CLIC* model seen in "Social Ecology and the Forces of Repression" (1979).

The zonal designations apply with the same scale of indicators to both the Lower Yangzi and the Southeast Coast regions. Skinner's regional ranking ("Regional Urbanization," p. 229) and my descriptions of the inner core in both regions indicate that the Southeast Coast inner core was less urbanized than the Lower Yangzi inner core. Nevertheless, statistical development indicators for the Southeast Coast inner core, though in the low range, are consistent with those for the Lower Yangzi inner core; similarly, indicators for the Lower Yangzi outer periphery, though in the high range, are consistent with those for the Southeast Coast outer periphery. This consistency in the range of indicators for all zones across the two regions invalidates any consideration of an asymmetrical model of zonal equivalencies (such that, for example, the Southeast Coast inner core would generally be equivalent in terms of indicators to the Lower Yangzi outer core, and so forth).

Further study should show whether this four-zone framework is applicable to other regions of China. It is certain that specific variable values for zones in less developed regions would have to be readjusted to meet the lower degree of development.

The determined demarcations were further supported by scattered county data on total annual business volume and number of retail stores and by qualitative evidence from the geographical and economic gazetteers of Lin Chuanjia and Wei Songtang. See Wei, *Zhejiang jingji jilüe* (Shanghai, 1929), passim.

ZS has data on each county's imports and exports (2:88–122), but these are given in weights (which varied from county to county) or in rounded *yuan*. Furthermore, for many counties there is no data. Of greater use are the nine county studies undertaken by the government in 1930 and published under the title *Zhejiang jingji diaocha*. These studies provide information on annual volume of business, number of retail stores with general dates of establishment, imports and exports, and taxes. The counties covered with their zonal classification are inner core, Yuyao; outer core, Fuyang; inner periphery, Shouchang, Qingtian, and Qunan; and outer periphery, Songyang, Linan, and Yunhe.

23. Tilly, "Western State-Making," p. 620.

24. The terminology that I use in discussing urban centers (here, for example,

"highest level central places") was developed by G. William Skinner to discuss the urban hierarchy of central places in his elaboration of central place theory for China and his derivation of the macroregional model. See especially his "Cities and the Hierarchy of Local Systems" in *CLIC*.

25. Only the county of Chongde (known before 1912 as Shimen) is not in the inner core: its low zonal classification is a statistical artifact stemming from its having only a postal agency. The inner core had a population of over 8.8 million out of a total provincial population of over 19.8 million.

26. See Murphey, *Shanghai*, pp. 106–109; and Susan Mann Jones, "The Ningpo *Pang* and Financial Power at Shanghai" in *The Chinese City between Two Worlds*, ed. Mark Elvin and G. William Skinner (Stanford, 1974), pp. 73–96.

27. The portion of the Shanghai-Hangchow-Ningpo railway between Hangchow and the Cao-e River was not completed until the 1930s.

28. James H. Cole, "Shaohsing: Studies in Ch'ing Social History" (Ph.D. diss., Stanford University, 1975), pp. 15–17.

29. *ZS*, 3:8–29.

30. *TR*, 1897, p. 332 and 1901, pp. 369–370.

31. *ZS*, 10:120–135. See also *DC*, pp. 113–116; *CEB*, 9 (November 6, 1926): 278; *CEB*, 9 (November 27, 1926): 321; and *TR*, 1913, p. 1008 and 1915, p. 911. Compare also the trade statistics for Wenchow and northern provincial ports in *ZS*, 2:80–81.

32. Modern economic development had distorted Southeast Coastal regional integrity. The Ou River, the Min in Fujian, and the Han in Guangdong share the same watershed, draining from rough coastal mountains into the sea. But by the twentieth century, Wenchow no longer "had stronger economic links with [other cities of the Southeast Coast region] than [it] had with cities outside the region" (Skinner, "Cities and the Hierarchy of Local Systems," p. 283). The rise of Shanghai had shifted Wenchow's orientation. The city was connected to both Shanghai and Ningpo by regular seagoing steamers; in contrast, there were only occasional ships from Amoy and Fuzhou. See *DC*, p. 114; and *Shina*, pp. 306–308.

33. *ZS*, 10:96–100.

34. Ibid., passim.

35. Ibid. In Xuanping (outer periphery) merchants from a different macroregion were found.

36. Ibid.; also Lin Chuanjia, *Dazhonghua Zhejiang*, pp. 171–320 passim.

37. Cao, *Wo*, pp. 56 and 104.

38. For description of Jiande, see Wei, *Zhejiang jingji*, pp. 391–398; for areal figures, note *ZS*, 1:7–11.

39. See *Zhejiang Qunan xian jingji diaocha* (Shanghai, 1931). Also note Wei's treatment, *Zhejiang jingji*, p. 403. In addition see the detailed geographical sketch that appears in Michel Cartier, *Une reforme locale en Chine au XVIe siècle: Hai Jui à Ch'ün-an, 1558–1562* (Paris, 1973).

40. Lin Chuanjia, *Da Zhonghua Zhejiang*, pp. 185–186, 283–284, 301–302, and 309–310.

41. Mlinar and Teune, eds., "Theory, Methodology, Research and Application: Assessment and Future Directions" in *Social Ecology*, p. 37.

42. *S*, 1913/8/23.

43. Tilly's study of the Vendée underscores the correlation between economic and political development in eighteenth-century France. See *The Vendée*, pp. 146-147.

44. *S*, XT 1/12/24. For an account of the antagonism, see *Xincheng Z*, 4:7a-8a.

45. *S*, XT 1/11/15 and 12/7.

46. *S*, XT 2/1/14. School construction was also stimulated by the railroad's presence in Wangdian. See *S*, XT 3/6I/19. ("I" designates intercalary month.)

47. *S*, XT 1/12/1 and 12/7.

3. Common Organizations in the Four Zhejiangs

1. Ho Ping-ti and others have described the various possible contributing factors to the development of such feelings. Ho Ping-ti, *Zhongguo huiguan shilun* (Taibei, 1966), pp. 1-9; Peter Golas, "Early Ch'ing Guilds" in *CLIC*, p. 564; and G. William Skinner, "Introduction: Urban Social Structure in Ch'ing China" in *CLIC*, pp. 541-548.

2. Cao Juren, *Wo*, p. 15. For roles of these ties in times of trouble, see *S*, 1913/3/4 and 1923/9/9.

3. Skinner, "Urban Social Structure in Ch'ing China," pp. 543 and 548.

4. Some counties in peripheral zones with native place associations were, for example, Xuanping, Suian, Shouchang, and Qunan.

5. Taizhou prefecture had two native place associations. In addition, three of its component outer-zone counties also had associations: Wenling, Ninghai, and Tiantai.

6. Skinner, "Urban Social Structure in Ch'ing China," p. 541.

7. *S*, XT 2/4/10-11; 1912/6/28, 6/30.

8. *S*, 1924/2/17-18.

9. *S*, 1913/7/3, 1924/7/24; *ZX*, 1917/5/28.

10. Elites established the Zhuji association in Hangchow in 1907. *ZG*, section "Zhuji shehui xianxiang," p. 71. In 1913 Xiangshan county merchants formed an association in Ningpo as did Jiangshan merchants in Quzhou. *Xiangshan X*, 16:36a; *Qu X*, 4:50b.

11. Compare the lists in Yang Zuochang, comp., *YuHang jilüe* (Hangchow, 1924), juan *xia:* 8b-9b and in Jianshe weiyuanhui diaocha Zhejiang jingji suo, comp., *Hangzhou shi jingji diaocha*, pp. 986-987, for the appearance of the new associations.

12. Jones, "The Ningpo *Pang*," p. 92. Note also the formation of a Huzhou association in Shanghai in 1924 to escape the wrangling between the Huzhou *huiguan* and the Huzhou *tongxianghui*. See Ling Songru, *Hushe cangsang lu* (Taibei, 1969), pp. 1-2.

13. By the mid-1920s students were forming their own associations in Hangchow, just as Shaoxing workers were forming their own native place association in Shanghai, as if in an effort to escape restrictive elite control. *S*, 1924/8/2. See also *ZG*, section "Wunian lai zhi da shiji," p. 9.

The number of men actively involved in associations is difficult to determine because of the sketchy evidence on membership and attendance at meetings. The weakly organized Huangyan association in Hangchow attracted over forty men in a special meeting in early 1910 (*S*, XT 2/4/10). More well-established associations were probably better attended. A regular 1918 meeting of the Ci-Yu association (Ciqi and Yuyao counties) in Shaoxing drew over one hundred forty members (*S*, 1918/5/11). An organizational meeting of the Society of Huzhou (*Hushe*) in Shanghai in 1924 drew over two hundred members of the two existing Huzhou associations (Ling, *Hushe*, p. 2).

14. Bernard Gallin and Rita S. Gallin, "The Integration of Village Migrants in Taipei" in Elvin and Skinner, *The Chinese City between Two Worlds*, pp. 351–358.

15. See, for example, accounts of the extensive help in local projects that Dinghai residents received from Dinghai sojourners in Tianjin: *Dinghai X*, 2:6a, 12a–13a. In addition, see the projects of the Huzhou Society in Shanghai: Ling, *Hushe*, pp. 11–13. For aid in disasters, see *S*, 1919/8/14, 21; 1922/8/9, 10; and 1924/2/17.

16. *ZG*, section "Zhuji gaiguan," pp. 117–120.

17. *S*, XT 2/4/10; 1912/6/28, 11/19; 1919/8/14, 21; 1920/1/8, 4/18.

18. *XF*, section "Fulu," pp. 6–11.

19. *S*, 1924/8/2.

20. For example, see *MLB*, XT 3/6/4; *S*, 1917/1/5–14 passim., 1924/4/13; and *SS*, 1921/1/25, 8/6, 8/28, 9/11, 9/22.

21. See chap. 11 for an extended discussion of this phenomenon.

22. See, for example, other accounts suggesting the compatibility of "primordial" group loyalties and nationalism or national goals: R. William Liddle, *Ethnicity, Party, and National Integration* (New Haven, 1970); and Heeger, "Politics of Integration," especially pp. 1–14 and 334–350.

23. Golas, "Guilds," p. 558.

24. *S*, 1920/2/13.

25. *ZG*, section "Zhengwen," p. 56. For more on this theme, see chap. 7.

26. Although guild organization was often linked with administrative native place, the underlying structure was probably from certain marketing regions of that administrative unit.

27. *S*, 1919/4/17. See also Lillian Li, "Kiangnan and the Silk Export Trade, 1842–1937" (Ph. D. diss., Harvard University, 1975), p. 302, for the origin of the organization.

28. *S*, 1918/3/23; 1919/5/7.

29. *S*, 1913/5/27; 1918/6/4; 1924/5/17.

30. *Shina*, pp. 769–770. See also *S*, 1913/5/19.

31. *S*, 1923/7/17.

32. *S*, 1923/8/30.

33. Wang Wei, ed., *Xiaofeng zhigao* (Taibei, 1974), p. 183.

34. *Daishan Z*, 5:8a–12a.

35. *S*, 1912/9/12; 1913/7/5; and *Wu-Qing Z*, 9:37b–38b.

36. See Philip A. Kuhn, "Local Self-Government Under the Republic: Problems of Control, Autonomy, and Mobilization" in *Conflict and Control in Late Imperial China*, ed. Frederic Wakeman, Jr. and Carolyn Grant (Berkeley, 1975),

pp. 274–277. See also the treatment of local self-government in R. Keith Schoppa, "Local Self-Government in Zhejiang, 1909–1927," *Modern China,* 2 (October 1976): 503–505.

37. *Haining zhou zhigao,* 41:1a–3b; *Shouchang X,* p. 224.

38. Listed in John Fincher, "The Chinese Self-Government Movement" (Ph. D. diss., University of Washington, 1969), p. 100.

39. See Richard A. Orb, "Chihli Academies and Other Schools in the Late Ch'ing: An Institutional Survey" in *Reform in Nineteenth-Century China,* p. 234. In addition, see *Haining zhou zhigao,* 41:3a and *Xuanping X,* reprint, vol. 3, p. 1278.

40. *Haining zhou zhigao,* 41:1a–3b.

41. *S,* XT 2/3/7, 7/13.

42. Some townships in peripheral counties (for example, Xindeng and Xuanping) did not have elected Qing bodies.

43. *Jingning xian xuzhi,* pp. 207–208.

44. The three counties were Zhenhai and Dinghai in the inner core and Lishui in the inner periphery. A perusal of newspaper coverage throughout the period indicates lack of board roles. See *S* and *MLB,* 1912–13, passim. For magistrate subordination, see *S,* 1912/1/14 and 1913/6/25.

45. See chap. 6.

46. *S,* 1913/10/30, 12/31 and 1914/1/12.

47. *Jingning xian xuzhi,* p. 209. These generalizations are made from information in the gazetteers of Zhenhai, Deqing, Xinchang, Changhua, Shouchang, Tangqi, Xindeng, Jiande, Songyang, Lishui, and Shuanglin.

48. *Jingning xian xuzhi,* p. 209. The ward deputy position was honorary, without stipend. For examples of the same elites serving in both positions, see *ZXB, shang* juan: 76b–80a and *Shuanglin Z,* 8:4b. Evidence indicates that the ward was actually the old township in new nomenclature. Kuhn, "Local Self-Government," p. 279.

49. Former Hang County Assembly members continued to meet to discuss local problems (*S,* 1914/2/22).

50. Examples are found in *S,* 1914/3/7, 12/20; 1915/1/18, 20, 26; 1915/3/2–3, 5, 18; 1915/11/28, 30; 1916/4/12; and *QXLW,* 3:28b and 61b.

51. *S,* 1916/8/27, 10/21. The assemblies were in Chongde, Haining, Hang, Jiaxing, Wenling, and Nantian counties.

52. The fact that the military governor, Lü Gongwang, had not taken a firm stand against the assemblies no doubt helped provoke Beijing's move in early 1917 to oust Lü and install Beiyang control.

53. *ZX,* 1917/5/30; *S,* 1919/4/23.

54. See Tung, *Political Institutions,* p. 86. A "Local Administrative Conference" that was convened in the late spring of 1920 drafted procedural and electoral rules for the new county assemblies. These regulations were not published until June 1921; they are reprinted in *DZ,* 18, no. 13, pp. 127–132.

55. *SS,* 1921/5/17.

56. *S,* 1924/7/14.

57. *Jingning xian xuzhi,* pp. 207 and 209.

58. *S*, 1924/5/10. The Jiaxing assembly met in regular seasonal sessions, and the board met weekly, taking the lead in major decisions. See *S*, 1923/7/22, 9/3; 1924/3/15; 1925/1/14; and *SB*, 1926/8/31.

59. For cases in Shaoxing, Wenling, Qunan, and Tiantai see *S*, 1924/3/30, 4/27; 1924/2/21; and 1925/5/4 and 22.

60. *S*, 1924/5/10.

61. Note the continuity in personnel from the county board and the nominal continuity of the posts of board secretary and treasurer to the public fund and property bureau (*guanchan hui*) from 1928 to 1930 and the self-government offices after 1930. *Wu-Qing Z*, 9:22b, 33b.

62. Quoted in Andrew J. Nathan, *Peking Politics, 1918–1923* (Berkeley, 1976), p. 13. For a general dicussion of *fatuan*, see pp. 13–18.

63. Brunnert and Hagelstrom, *Present Day Political Organizations*, pp. 358–359 and 408–410; Nathan, *Peking Politics*, pp. 13–14.

64. See, for example, accounts dealing with *fatuan* and proposed auxiliaries, *S*, XT 2/3/1, 6/9, 11/27 and XT 3/3/9. In addition, note the chamber of commerce regulations cited in Shirley S. Garrett, "The Chambers of Commerce and the YMCA" in *The Chinese City between Two Worlds*, pp. 220–221.

65. Garrett, "Chambers of Commerce," p. 220. There were to be thirty to forty on the board of a general chamber and fifteen to thirty in a regular chamber. See also Edward J. M. Rhoads, "Merchant Associations in Canton, 1895–1911" in *The Chinese City between Two Worlds*, pp. 97–117, for evidence of the linkage between guilds and chambers.

66. The modal date for the outer core would be 1907; for the inner periphery, 1909; and for the outer periphery, after 1917. Inner-core dates are based on seven counties; outer core, on six; inner periphery, on seven; and outer periphery, on six.

67. *Shina*, pp. 739–792.

68. The reports mixed numbers of businesses that paid dues and numbers of representatives from certain businesses.

69. For example, *S*, XT 2/8/11, 10/5; 1918/8/20; 1919/5/17, 11/5–6; *SS*, 1921/9/11.

70. For example, *S*, 1919/6/19, 11/6, 12/6.

71. For Qingtian chamber tax protest, see *S*, XT 2/1/7. For chamber activity in militia formation, see *S*, XT 3/9/9 and 1913/5/18.

72. Brunnert and Hagelstrom, *Present Day Political Organizations*, pp. 408–410.

73. *S*, XT 3/4/13; XT 3/5/7, 13, 27; 6/1, 19; 6I/11.

74. *ZG*, section "Zhuji shehui xianxiang," p. 42.

75. *S*, XT 2/3/5.

76. Gazetteers used were from Xuanping, Suian, Shouchang, Tangqi, Dinghai, Jiande, Xiangshan, Changhua, Xinchang, Deqing, Yuyao, Jingning, and Lishui.

77. *S*, 1914/6/21.

78. For example, *S*, 1917/9/4, 19; 1920/7/22; 1923/6/7, 7/5, 10/8; 1924/1/9, 8/3; 1925/6/12–13; *SS*, 1922/3/4. For involvement before 1911, see my "Politics and Society in Chekiang," chap. 2. See the importance of the education associa-

tion in Hunan in Angus McDonald, *The Urban Origins of Rural Revolution* (Berkeley, 1978).

79. See, for example, *ZG*, section "Zhuji shehui xianxiang," pp. 42–43; also see case of Pinghu, *S*, 1924/7/22. For the provincial leadership, see *SS*, 1922/3/4. Under student advocacy, the associations in larger centers set forth principles for student participation in the governance of higher-level schools (*S*, 1920/12/13).

80. See *S*, XT 2/3/15, 26; XT 3/3/9, 4/13.

81. *S*, 1918/9/24.

82. *S*, 1920/4/28.

83. See chap. 6.

84. See, for example, *Suian X*, p. 225 and *Xuanping X*, reprint, vol. 2, pp. 548–549.

85. *Dinghai X*, 2:11b; *Xindeng X*, p. 849.

86. *ZG*, section "Zhuji gaiguan," p. 112. *XF*, section "Lunshuo," pp. 55–57.

87. Zhou Qiwei, "Luoqing xinhai geming shiliao" in *XGH*, vol. 4, pp. 194–195.

88. *S*, 1920/4/20. Described here is the Hang county association whose elected leaders had no apparent links to agriculture or its problems.

4. Inner-Core Elite Career Bases and Patterns

1. *SXZ*, ce 16:201b–202b.

2. Maurice Freedman, "Introduction" in *Family and Kinship in Chinese Society*, ed. Maurice Freedman (Stanford, 1970), pp. 13–14. At times in this analysis, I will differentiate the lineage from the family (*jia* or *fang*).

3. Jack M. Potter, "Land and Lineage in Traditional China" in Freedman, *Family and Kinship*, pp. 132–135.

4. Pan Guangdan, *Ming-Qing liangdai Jiaxing de wangzu* (Shanghai, 1947), and Cole, "Shaohsing," pp. 104–105.

5. See the treatment of lineages in *Tangqi X* and *Longyu X*. The inner-periphery county is Yongkang. See Muramatsu Yuji, "Shindai no shinshi-jinushi ni okeru tochi to kanshoku: Sekkō-shō Ei-kō ken Go-shi shihi giden o megutte" in *Hototsubashi ronsō*, 44: 698–726.

6. *ZXB*, shang juan, 48b–49a. The last Xie lineage on the Yuyao list, for example, had a five thousand *yuan* fund. The Ye lineage of Zhenhai had a reserve cash fund of twenty thousand *yuan*.

7. *ZXB*, shang juan, passim. See the Chen, Zheng, Zhou, Fang, Xu, Hu, Li, Luo, Wang, and Yu lineages.

8. *Deqing X*, passim.

9. *ZXB*, shang juan: 61a; see biography of Xie Jinfu, *xia* juan: 8a–b. For Jiaxing lineages, see Pan, *Ming-Qing liangdai . . . de wangzu*, pp. 76–77 and *S*, 1910–1926, passim.

10. *SXZ*, ce 6, "Lihaisuo zhigao," 2b; 12a–b; and 16a. Other examples are the Ren in Dinghai, which held thirty-one mu, *Daishan Z*, 8:6a; and the Shi lineage in Zhenhai, which held thirty-plus mu, *ZXB*, shang juan, 59a and *xia* juan, 59a–b.

11. *SXZ*, "Lihaisuo zhigao," 12a–b.

12. Hui-chen Wang Liu, *The Traditional Chinese Clan Rules* (Locust Valley, N.Y., 1959), pp. 187–188.

13. *S,* XT 2/10/9.
14. *S,* 1920/5/1.
15. *Yuyao liucang zhi,* 16:8b.
16. *S,* 1920/11/28.
17. *Daishan Z,* 8:5b. These families were the Lius, Zhangs, Chens, Wangs, Nis, and Qians.
18. See Lillian Li, "Kiangnan and the Silk Export Trade," pp. 66, 210, 282–283. On Puyuan's economic decline, see *CEB* (January-June 1933): 157–158. On Wangdian's growth, see *S,* 1924/6/27. For similar effects of railroad, see Xiashi, *S,* XT 3/8/3.
19. Analysis of the local functional elites in the early Republic as compared to the late Qing period indicates this decline. *Puyuan zhi,* passim.
20. Hui-chen Wang Liu, *Traditional Chinese Clan Rules,* pp. 188–189.
21. Teune and Mlinar, "Development and Participation," pp. 142–150.
22. Tilly, *The Vendée,* pp. 59 and 65.
23. Chen Xunzheng, comp., *Yinxian tongzhi renwu bian* (1934), pp. 239–240 and 349.
24. Quoted in John Fincher, "Land Tenure in China: Preliminary Evidence from a 1930's Kwangtung Hillside," *Ch'ing-shih wen-t'i,* 3 (November 1978): fn. 8, p. 81.
25. *Xuanping X,* juan 10, passim.
26. *Zhenhai X,* juan 19, passim.
27. The lack of outer-core subcounty statistics from 1911 to 1914 precludes a definitive statement; it is, however, logical to assume that the same pattern applied to these years as to the outer-core county statistics from 1912 to 1927, statistics that fit the trend described.
28. Table 10 reveals interesting information on the small number of degree-holders in any county who were at all officially or politically involved.
29. See chaps. 7 through 9 for a more detailed description of this dependency.
30. *Suian X,* pp. 246–289, passim.
31. *Shuanglin Z,* 8:4b–5b; 30:36b–41a.
32. There were three such from Daishan in Dinghai self-government; four from Ganpu in Haiyan bodies; and four from Puyuan in Jiaxing. Respective gazetteers have been cited except for Ganpu. See *Ganzhi fulu* (1935).
33. See, for example, evidence from Yin in Chen Xunzheng, *Yinxian . . . renwu bian,* pp. 349, 608, 631–632. Zhenhai had four such men in county assemblies and six in subcounty bodies.
34. Ichiko Chūzō, "The Role of the Gentry: An Hypothesis" in *China in Revolution,* p. 302. To be certain about Ichiko's assertion, I would have to press him on what constitutes a "virtual monopoly."
35. Marianne Bastid, "The Social Context of Reform" in *Reform in Nineteenth Century China,* pp. 125–126. See Joseph W. Esherick, *Reform and Revolution in China* (Berkeley, 1976), pp. 109–112 for the "conservative local gentry" approach. Kuhn hypothesizes their relationship to the "local bullies and evil gentry" group. See his "Local Self-Government under the Republic," pp. 292–293.
36. See, for example, *MLB,* XT 3/4/7 and 8/1; *S,* XT 3/6I/9. See also the case

of Jin Yuheng of Deqing, *Deqing X*, pp. 98–99, 428, 430–431; and Zhang Yugao of Shaoxing, *SXZ*, ce 16:195b–196a.

37. *SXZ*, ce 16:197b. Cao Juren, *Wo*, pp. 102–103, gives an example of an uneducated shopkeeper who was a member of the social elite in his community. This was the type of person who became involved in the self-government movement.

38. *MLB*, XT 3/7/8.

39. *S*, XT 3/3/2.

40. See, for example, *MLB*, XT 3/1/28 and 8/12; and *S*, XT 3/2/28, 1912/6/12, 1913/2/12 and 11/24. The location of newspaper bureaus in the inner core led to greater coverage of the core zones.

41. This is after deducting Suian's figures to compensate for possible skewing due to full coverage of gazetteer.

42. Kuhn, "Local Self-Government under the Republic," p. 293.

43. See, for example, *S*, 1918/7/20, 9/13 and 1923/7/20.

44. Mary B. Rankin, "Local Reform Currents in Chekiang Before 1900," pp. 226–229.

45. Xiang Shiyuan, *Zhejiang xinwen shi* (n.p., 1930), pp. 36 and 79.

46. Tang Shouqian, distinguished official and soon to be famous as head of the Shanghai-Hangchow-Ningpo railway, played a leading role in establishing schools in his native central market town of Linpu in Shaoxing. *SXZ*, ce 6, "Tianyue zhi," 21b–23b. At an intermediate market town in Jiaxing, Tang Jixun, a *linggongsheng*, was involved in educational reform to seek to strengthen the nation. *Zhulin bayu zhi*, 6:35b–38a.

This picture of elite excitement in remaking China at the local level reflects that described for other provinces. See especially Edward J. M. Rhoads, *China's Republican Revolution* (Cambridge, Mass., 1975); Charlton M. Lewis, *Prologue to the Chinese Revolution* (Cambridge, Mass., 1976); and Joseph W. Esherick, *Reform and Revolution in China*.

47. *S*, 1910–1914, passim.

48. Men like Xie Yuanhong, a former secretary of the Board of Works, left local leadership posts to take positions outside the province. *SXZ*, ce 16:199b–200a. Preeminent prerevolutionary leaders left for Beijing and Parliament. See biographies of Chen Jingdi, Zheng Jiping, Jin Shangxian, and Chu Fucheng in Satō Saburō, *Minkoku no seika*.

49. Chen Xunzheng, *Yinxian . . . renwu bian*, pp. 630–631; *GS*, p. 873. As other examples, note careers of Zhang Shujiao in Chen Xunzheng, p. 630 and Xu Bingkun and Cai Huanwen in *Deqing X*, pp. 210–211, 418, 676–677; *S*, 1911/12/1.

50. *Deqing X*, pp. 432 and 677. See also careers of Zhenhai elites Gu Pengxiang and Li Jingdi in Chen Xunzheng, *Yinxian . . . renwu bian*, pp. 608–609; and *ZXB, shang* juan, 75b.

51. *SXZ*, ce 16:195a–b.

52. Andrew Nathan has suggested that the age cohort of the 1860s and 1870s differed sharply from that of the 1880s, the former being basically politically conservative though sometimes trained abroad in various fields, the latter being

the generation of May Fourth leadership and the oldest Chinese Communist Party leadership. See his *Peking Politics*, pp. 9–13.

53. See biography of Wu Shanqing, Shaoxing dye entrepreneur, in *SXZ*, ce 16:197a–b; and for Shen Wenhua of Jiaxing, see *S*, XT 2/4/2; 1911/12/3; 1912/5/2, 7; 1913/7/21; 1918/11/29; 1923/7/28, 8/3, 10/22; 1924/3/1 and 9/17. Other examples include Zhu Baojin (late 1850s) of Haiyan, Fan Yaowen (1858) of Hang, Jin Shanxian (1868) of Wenling, Liu Jingzhao (1862) of Zhenhai, Sheng Bingwei (1855) and Sheng Bingzhi (1859) of Zhenhai, and Wang Shizhao (1860s) of Yin.

54. A good example of the latter is Chu Fucheng. For summary of his roles see my "Politics and Society in Chekiang," chaps. 2 and 3. Outstanding elites of this cohort who had little to do with their native places include Ruan Xingcun (1873) of Yuyao, Tao Baolin (1872) and Shen Junru (1872) of Jiaxing, Chen Qingdi (1872) of Hang, and Wang Jiaxiang (1875) of Shaoxing.

55. The careers of Zheng Jiping (1881) of Huangyan, Jiang Mengtao (1881) and Lu Haiwang (1881) of Yuyao, and Qin Binghan (1885) and Shen Guang (1887) of Jiashan, for example, illustrate no specific roles in local development.

56. See my "Province and Nation: The Chekiang Provincial Autonomy Movement, 1917–1927," *JAS*, 36 (August 1977): 661–674.

57. Some returned students from 1912 on tried to direct their locality's development in a specialized way. For example, Wu Jiajing and Wu Qiujun of Yin returned from a Japanese agricultural school to set up a successful agricultural experiment station (*S*, 1913/6/24).

58. These generalizations come from Zhenhai, Yuyao, and Jiaxing counties and various inner-core towns. See, for example, *S*, 1924/1/9, 3/8 and 7/16. In many cases, the school boards were seizing jurisdiction once held by county assemblies.

59. *S*, 1924/5/10. Part of the assembly's action came also from the unwillingness of county bureaucrats to grant recognition to some assembly actions.

5. Inner-Core Elite Collectivities

1. See, for example, Hilary Beattie, *Land and Lineage in China* (Cambridge, 1979).

2. Chang Chung-li, *The Income of the Chinese Gentry* (Seattle, 1962), pp. 149–195.

3. *ZXB, xia juan*: 7a–b and 14b–15b.

4. In Deqing, for example, see the activities of Xu Shijun and Shi Han, *Deqing X*, pp. 85, 87, 91, 93, 210–211, 222, 423, and 677.

5. See, for example, *S*, 1913/12/5; 1917/8/12; and Xiang Shiyuan, *Zhejiang xinwen shi*, p. 117. Chang Chung-li has suggested that the phrase can refer to gentry-turned-merchant or merchant-turned-gentry. There has been debate over who should be included by this term. Chang, *Income of the Chinese Gentry*, pp. 150–151. See also Chan, *Merchants, Mandarins and Modern Enterprise*, p. 58 and pp. 255–256, n. 51.

6. This social phenomenon has been noted by Asian and Western researchers alike. See Cole, "Shaohsing," p. 9; Bastid, "Social Context," p. 118; Chan, *Mer-*

chants, Mandarins and Modern Enterprise, passim; and Tōa Dōbun Shoin, comp., *Shina keizai zensho,* vol. 1 (Osaka, 1907), p. 175.

7. See the biographical data in *Zhenhai X,* "Yuxiu xingshi": 1a–5b and *ZXB, shang* juan: 12a–27b, passim, *xia* juan: 17a–18a; and *SXZ,* ce 16: 196b–197a.

8. *Yuyao liucang zhi,* 34:12a–b. See other biographical examples in *SXZ,* ce 16:182b, 197a–b.

9. See *ZXB, shang* juan: 21a; *xia* juan: 16b. There is no evidence of other involvement on Zhou's part. Note discussion of compradorial elites in Hao Yen-p'ing, *The Comprador in Nineteenth Century China* (Cambridge, Mass., 1970) and Albert Feuerwerker, *China's Early Industrialization* (Cambridge, Mass., 1958), pp. 16–17 and 108–123.

10. See G. William Skinner, "Mobility Strategies in Late Imperial China: A Regional Systems Analysis," in Smith, *Regional Analysis,* vol. 1: *Economic Systems,* pp. 327–364, where Skinner describes the phenomenon of sojourning.

11. Shopkeepers in the inner core were becoming increasingly politically involved. See the political protest of Wuxing meat sellers, *S,* XT 2/1/7.

12. The gentry-merchants were Zhang Shouyi, Jiang Laixian, Jiang Shifang, Gao Zhonglai, Lu Chujue, Shen Kairu, Shen Wenhua, Sheng Liangzhou, Tao Xianjin, Wang Yijun, and Yao Mulian. The merchants were Qian Jingren, Jin Minlan, Gao Ruxiang, Shen Zhaoyuan, Jin Licai, and Sheng Banghe. Information on these men comes from day-by-day reading of *S* from 1909 to 1927.

13. For defense, see *Wu-Qing Z,* 9:16b and *Shuanglin Z,* 32:18b–25b.

14. See Bastid, "Social Context." This picture also emerges from Mary Rankin's works, "Local Reform Currents in Chekiang" and "Rural-Urban Continuities," although Rankin does not use the phrase.

15. See *S,* XT 2/2/27, 12/23, and XT 3/3/9. Information on the men is scattered throughout the *S.* I have been unable to find the total number of members.

16. *MLB,* XT 3/6/5. For reemergence of the debate, *S,* 1914/7/6 and 9.

17. *MLB,* XT 3/6I/9.

18. *S,* XT 3/7/21 and 22.

19. *S,* XT 3/6I/10.

20. *MLB,* XT 3/7/7.

21. For this kind of arrangement, see Feuerwerker, *China's Early Industrialization,* pp. 16–26.

22. For the names of these men, see *S,* XT 1/12/14; XT 2/4/10, 4/17, 7/17, and 8/4.

23. *S,* XT 2/3/24 and XT 3/6I/24.

24. *S,* XT 1912/5/16–27, 5/27 and 9/12. For a clear statement noting the changes wrought by the revolution in this regard, see *Xiaoshan Xianghu zhi,* 3:8b.

25. *S,* 1913/5/6.

26. *S,* 1913/2/17.

27. *S,* 1913/4/16, 4/24, 5/12, 6/25, 7/7, 7/19–20, 9/20, 10/14 and 11/4.

28. For these episodes, see *S,* XT 3/4–7 passim; *S,* 1912/5/7, 6/5, and 6/26; *S,* 1916/9/12; and 1924/2/19, 3/1–2, 3/11, and 4/28.

29. *S,* 1920/10/17 and 1924/4/18.

30. My impression is that newspaper sources and gazetteers, by the 1920s and 1930s, respectively, tended to use *shenshang* to mean only two different groups. If

this is correct, it reflects a significant social development—the rise of a merchant stratum in local affairs divorced from gentry credentials and roles.

31. *S*, 1912/5/8. See also, as a probable indication of these bodies' interests in business, their action against a monopolistic night-soil collecting firm (*S*, 1912/11/20).

32. *S*, 1913/1/25. For more on these men, see *S*, XT 3/7/5 and 1914/6/13.

33. *MLB*, 1912/2/3. For the general condemnation, *TR*, 1912, p. 366.

34. See *S*, 1914/4/3 for one instance of Ningpo merchant irritation over local taxation.

35. See, for example, lists of board members and accounts of stockholders' meetings, *S*, XT 2/9/2.

36. For the story of the railroad nationalization and subsequent financial disputes, see *S*, 1914/5/2–3, 5, 8, 15, and 19; and *NCH*, 1914/3/7, p. 704; 3/28, p. 969; 4/4, p. 52; 4/18, p. 230 and 5/9, pp. 485–486.
Merchant ire was raised against gentry Tang Shouqian, company chairman, for his acceptance of a 20,000 cash bonus from the government and his subsequent pushing for nationalization. To many merchants, the bonus looked like a bribe; the affair turned even more sour when it became known that he used the bonus to help compensate for an 80,000 cash deficit in a Hangchow native bank of which he was the largest stockholder (*S*, 1914/5/2–5). Even though the 1914 affair has a provincial background, its major leaders were inner-core elites.

37. See Li, "Kiangnan and the Silk Export Trade," pp. 284–302. In addition, see *S*, XT 2/3/11; 1919/6/4, 8/1 and 8/5. The chamber of commerce in 1919 seemed strongly in favor of restrictions.

38. *S*, 1918/3/24, 5/4, 5/13. In addition, see 1919/12/22, 1920/3/3, 3/11, and 3/23.

39. They were four Hangchow merchants, an Anhui merchant, and one from Jiaxing (who was a tobacco and wine tax farmer). *S*, 1914/8/17 and 8/24.

40. *S*, 1918/4/6 and 5/14.

41. *S*, 1924/1/22.

42. *CEJ*, 8 (May 1931): 520–521. See also *Dinghai X*, 3:9a–b.

43. *S*, 1920/3/12 and 14; 9/23.

44. *S*, 1919/4/24.

45. There had already been complaints in 1913 about branches of foreign insurance companies (*S*, 1913/7/7). See the description of insurance companies in *ZS*, 8:22–30. Chinese insurance firms became significant in the 1920s; all those existing in the early 1930s were located in the inner core. See also *CEB*, 9 (October 2, 1926): 203. For real estate companies, see *CEB*, 11 (March 26, 1927): 168.

46. For examples of the external involvement, see *S*, 1920/4/6 and *CEB*, 8 (March 6, 1926): 127–128 and *CEB*, 8 (April 17, 1926): 212–213.

47. *S*, 1917/11/24 and 1920/12/9.

48. *S*, 1923/8/1 ff. passim.

49. *S*, 1924/9/24.

50. See, for example, *S*, 1924/1/1, 2/11, 5/17, 8/3, and 8/16. Local chambers were in the vanguard of nationalistic opposition to the Japanese and other foreigners and of the peace and constitutional movements of the early 1920s (*S*,

1919/5/17, 7/11 and *SS*, 1923/6/12). For the important role of the local chambers in the May Fourth Movement, see *Santō Mondai ni kansuru hai–Nichi jōkyō*, vol. 2 (Shanghai, n.d.), pp. 455–479 and vol. 3, pp. 786–822.

51. *S*, 1920/12/10.

52. *S*, 1923/9/25 ff. Chambers were generally the most outspoken opponents of increased local taxation. In the mid-1920s, attacks on the infamous cigarette tax became as vehement as the earlier condemnation of the *tongjuan* (*S*, 1924/7/22).

53. *S*, 1925/5/19.

54. *S*, 1924/2/28.

55. *NCH*, 1922/8/5, p. 374.

56. *S*, 1923/8/1 and *Wu-Qing Z*, 40:13a–b.

57. *S*, 1925/8/9. Merchant protests over such action (1925/8/24) were apparently futile; at least no further reference to these unions appeared.

58. *S*, 1919/4/25, 7/11 and 1920/4/24.

59. *S*, 1919/6/15.

60. *S*, 1920/11/27.

61. The chief stockholders of the Hefeng paper mill in Jiaxing and of the Jiaxing electric company (see lists *S*, 1923/9/22 and 1924/4/18) were mainly merchants whose chief roles were as chamber of commerce or guild leaders. They were frequently brought for advice (*S*, 1923–1926, passim).

62. These lists were compiled from Fang Zhaoying, *Qingmo minchu yangxue xuesheng timinglu chuji* (Taibei, 1962) and an unpublished register from Baoding Military Academy, *Baoding junxiao tongxunlu*. I am grateful to Ernest Young for allowing me to use his copy.

63. See *ZXB, shang* juan: 80a–85b, *Wu-Qing Z*, 26:40a–43b, and *Puyuan zhi*, 17:19a–b for lists of graduates. The statistics on origins are based on my studies of each area's elites.

64. This model remains hypothetical since definitive statements are made impossible by the spotty coverage. It is based upon impressions from detailed research in gazetteers and newspapers (and supported by detailed information from Fenghua [outer core]). For the Fenghua data, see chap. 7.

65. The list is from those studying in the United States under the auspices of Qinghua University. See "Directory of American Returned Students" in *Who's Who in China* (Shanghai, 1925). Because native place is not available, these men are not divided into zonal groups.

66. Diplomas from the private middle schools in Hangchow—Anding and Congwen—generally carried graduates to a higher career sphere than public middle schools.

67. This generalization is based on study of all gazetteers and newspapers.

68. Cole, "Shaohsing," pp. 4–7 and 72–80.

69. *S*, XT 2/4/17.

70. *S*, 1913/4/24 and 7/21.

71. *S*, 1913/10/19.

72. *S*, 1913/6/22. For the new *fatuan* regulations, see Nathan, *Peking Politics*, pp. 13–14.

73. See proceedings in *Hang xian lüshi gonghui baogao lu* (Hangchow, 1919).

74. Compare the lists of members in *Hang xian lüshi gonghui baogao lu,* passim, with later Guomindang supporters in *S* and *SB,* 1924–1927 passim.

75. *S,* 1912/11/20.

76. *S,* 1924/2/28.

77. *S,* XT 3/1/9 and 1913/5/21.

78. See, for example, *S,* XT 2/2/2, XT 3/8/16, 1917/4/22 and especially 1918/12/12 and 12/23.

79. Complaints of this sort are scattered throughout the sources. See, for example, *S,* 1916/12/1 and *ZG,* "Zhuji gaiguan," pp. 138–140.

80. Military graduates did not often gravitate to the smaller urban centers.

81. *S,* 1923/8/5.

82. *S,* 1924/12/1.

83. *S,* 1923/11/17.

84. See, for example, *S,* XT 3/1/6, 6I/19, 12/2; 1913/4/11; 1914/3/6, 3/25; 1916/8/4; and 1924/7/16.

85. See the following as examples: *S,* 1923/12/4 for reforestation; for the entomologists, see chap. 6; and for the engineers, see 1924/1/12, 1/18, 3/2, 3/10.

86. *S,* 1924/7/9. The remainder were either not employed, employed in other fields, or deceased.

87. This discussion is largely based on Xiang's rich study of journalism, *Zhejiang xinwen shi,* which contains important information on elites and social developments as well.

88. The peripheries were involved only in the telegrams and organizations of a few middle-school students in prefectural capitals. See statements of support from students in Jinhua, Quzhou, Yanzhou, and Chuzhou in Mobei, *Jiang-Zhetielu fengzhao,* p. 144.

89. *S,* XT 2/7/30 and 8/1.

90. *S,* XT 3/6/7, 6/13, 6/25, 6/28, 6I/9; and *MLB,* 6/26 and 7/6. The Shanghai representative to Jiaxing was Chen Qimei.

91. *MLB,* XT 3/6I/20 and *S,* XT 3/6I/28.

92. *S,* XT 2/4/2.

93. See accounts of meetings in note 90.

94. *S,* XT 3/6/25.

95. *S,* XT 3/6I/26, 7/19 and *MLB,* XT 3/6I/15.

96. *S,* XT 2/6/9, 11/27; XT 3/3/9, 6I/26; *MLB,* XT 3/6/28, 6I/15.

97. The phrase is from *S,* 1912/1/22.

98. See *S,* 1912/1/22, 2/4, 4/2, 4/21, 4/23, 5/2 and *MLB,* 1912/2/25 and 6/20.

99. *S,* 1912/4/21, 23; and 1913/6/25.

100. *S,* 1912/11/22–24.

101. *S,* 1912/5/7, 6/5, and 6/26.

102. *S,* 1912/7/14; *MLB,* 1912/8/31 and 1913/3/1.

103. *S,* 1912/1/29, 5/24, 7/15; 1913/4/12, 12/11; 1914/2/7; *MLB,* 1912/1/18, 2/25, 3/26, and 6/20.

104. *S,* 1912/2/26.

105. *S,* 1912/4/2.

106. *S*, 1913/7/21 and 12/15.

107. *S*, 1913/7/5 and 12/18.

108. *S*, 1913/1/9 and 3/6.

109. *MLB*, 1912/8/5.

110. *MLB*, 1912/3/2 and *S*, 1912/7/18.

111. *S*, 1914/6/29: the founding of the federation of education associations.

112. *S*, 1915/5/16.

113. See, for example, *S*, 1917/12/26, 1918/4/9, 10/24; 1919/4/16; 1920/7/12, 14, 16; and 1924/8/9.

114. See, for example, the very large contributions of Kong and Zhang lineage elites in Nanxun, *S*, 1920/4/15 and 4/21.

115. *S*, 1919/6/20, 11/5, 12/6, and 1920/3/3.

116. For example, see *S*, 1923/7/1, 16, 18, 25, 31; 1923/10/21, 11/20; and 1924/9/9.

117. See *S*, 1917/1/7; 1919/5/24, 6/30, 12/7–8, 10; 1920/2/15, 4/15; 1923/1/20, 7/24, 7/30, 10/11; 1924/2/10 and 5/2.

118. See, for example, the demonstrations in Chongde county, *S*, XT 2/12/26.

119. In the case of Hangchow, demonstrations were often held in an area near West Lake cleared since the 1911 revolution.

120. *S*, 1917/5/21; 1918/4/1, 4/16, 5/17, 9/17, and 9/24.

121. See, for example, *S*, 1919/5/25.

122. In 1916 and 1917 several elite parapolitical associations had formed to study national and provincial problems. Though they were short-lived, most of their leaders were connected to the Guomindang in the 1920s. They were the 1916 Association in Jiaxing (*S*, 1916/9/12); the Zhejiang Political Consultative Association (*Zhejiang zhengwu shangchuan hui*) (*S*, 1916/12/1 and 5; 1917/4/24, 5/16, 5/22; and *ZX*, 1917/4/20); and the Qiushi Society, named for the famous late Qing academy in Hangchow (*S*, 1917/5/1).

123. *S*, 1920/6/28. See also the report in *Shishi xinbao*, 1925/2/23 concerning interest in this Zhejiang-Jiangsu area (which in very early China formed the state of Wu) for a new political unit. Reported in Zhang Qiyun, "Lun Ningpo jianshe shenghui zhi xiwang," *Shidi xuebao*, 3 (May 1925): 5.

124. See chap. 11.

125. *SB*, 1925/6/2.

126. *S*, 1923/7/4, 7/7, 8/18, 10/27, 11/3 and 6; 1924/3/21; 1924/8/3. The last details their visit to the grave of the martyr Qiu Jin.

127. *S*, 1923/9/4; 1924/1/4, 9, 29; 2/11; and 7/21. Examples of groups devoted to discussing theory are the He society of Jiaxing, the Study Society of Wuxing, and the Yuyao society. Those considering practical matters were, for example, the Jiujiu society (named for Double Nine, September 9, 1921, the date of the promulgation of Zhejiang's first constitution) and the Xinyu society (named for the branch and stem for 1921). *S*, 1916/10/22; 1918/12/4, 12/6; 1919/6/16; 1920/4/15, 5/26, 8/14; 1923/7/12, 14, 16–17; 1924/3/22 and 8/10.

128. *S*, 1920/1/17, 3/5, 6/6; 1923/7/24, 6/11, and 7/2.

129. *S*, 1919/3/21, 24; 5/9–10; 1920/1/12; 1923/12/10; 1924/2/18. Occupational groups continued guild establishment and began modern union formation.

130. *S*, 1923/7/5 and 12/4.

131. Dewey was in Hangchow in 1919; Tagore in 1924. For the Korean speaker, see *S*, 1920/1/13 in the account of his Jiaxing visit.

132. *S*, 1918/12/6; 1920/10/17; 1924/4/18. Red Cross branches appeared during the September 1924 war and the Northern Expedition.

133. Xiang, *Zhejiang xinwen shi*, pp. 107–128; *S*, 1924/12/17; 1925/12/29; and *SB*, 1926/3/12.

134. See the range of organizations prompted by party bureaucrats in *Shouchang X*, for example. Such a policy considerably reduced local initiative.

6. Inner-Core Elites and Decision Making

1. For comments on the importance of decision-making analysis for elite studies, see David C. Hammack, "Problems in the Historical Study of Power in the Cities and Towns of the United States, 1800–1960," *American Historical Review*, 83 (April 1978): 323–349.

2. John R. Watt, *The District Magistrate in Late Imperial China* (New York, 1972), pp. 11–14, 85–87 and Ch'ü T'ung-tsu, *Local Government in China under the Ch'ing* (Cambridge, Mass., 1962), pp. 14–35.

3. *S*, 1912/1/14 and 1913/6/25.

4. See, for example, *S*, 1917/10/5, 11/5; 1918/4/18, 8/2; 1920/11/13; 1924/1/14, 12/19; and 1925/9/8.

5. See He Bingsong, "Zhejiang xiaoxue jiaoyude xianguang ji qi zuiren," *Jiaoyu zazhi*, 16 (September 1924): 1–2.

6. See, for example, *S*, 1920/1/18 and 10/21.

7. County courts were reestablished by 1922 in Shaoxing, Jiaxing, Wuxing, Linhai, Lishui, Jiande, and Qu.

8. *S*, 1916/7/13.

9. See, for example, *S*, 1917/4/18.

10. For the winter defense leadership, see *S*, 1915/11/18.

11. *S*, 1918/12/22 and 12/23.

12. See Xia Chao's orders, *S*, 1925/4/23 and 8/5 and a subsequent description, *SB*, 1926/8/30. Individual magistrates also established additional defense corps at times of crisis. *S*, 1917/4/22.

13. *S*, 1923/8/27, 31 and 9/13.

14. *S*, 1923/10/24.

15. *S*, XT 3/4/16.

16. *S*, 1913/1/13 and 10/24.

17. See, for example, scattered requests in *S*, 1920/4/18–7/16 and lack of response.

18. *MLB*, XT 3/7/7.

19. See Kojima Yoshio, "Shinmatsu minkoku shoki ni okeru Sekkō-shō Kakō fu shūhen no nōson shakai" *Yamazaki Sensei Taikan Kinen Tōyōshigaku Ronshū*, ed. Tokyo Kyōiku Daigaku Tōyōshi Kenkyushitsu (Tokyo, 1966), pp. 186–188; also Kojima Yoshio, "Shinmatsu minkoku shoki konan no nōmin undo," *Rekishi Kyōiku*, 16 (1968): 121–123.

20. *S*, XT 2/12/26.

21. See, for example, *S*, 1913/12/23; 1916/4/22; *MLB*, 1912/12/25; and *NCH*, 1912/12/14, p. 734.

22. *S*, 1913/1/9 and 2/13.

23. *S*, 1913/1/9, 3/6; 1914/1/7; 1916/4/22; 1917/12/7; 1924/8/12; *SB*, 1926/3/5.

24. *S*, 1924/8/12.

25. *S*, 1920/1/15, 20.

26. *Dinghai X*, 2:6a; *S*, 1913/11/17. Cf. Skinner's interpretation of elite informal governance, "Cities and the Hierarchy of Local Systems," pp. 336–344.

27. According to late Qing self-government regulations, towns (*zhen*) were nonadministrative centers with a population greater than fifty thousand, and townships were areas with less than fifty thousand. Brunnert and Hagelstrom, *Present Day Political Organizations*, p. 178. For disputes see *S*, XT 2/8/11, 10/12 and XT 3/5/10.

28. *MLB*, XT 3/3/9 and 8/12. The latter indicates the city's disdain for elected West Lake representatives.

29. *Shuanglin Z*, 32:18b–19b. Shuanglin needed the population of this township to qualify as a town (*zhen*).

30. The following information comes from *SXZ*, ce 11:6a–8a.

31. With regulations specifying only a population under fifty thousand, the guidelines for townships were vague. As Philip Kuhn has pointed out (Kuhn, "Local Self-Government," pp. 279–280), sizes of townships and numbers per county varied greatly. In most counties of all zones in Zhejiang, the number ranged from five to twelve. However, Yuyao county with twenty-one and Shaoxing county (at that time, divided into Shanyin and Guiji counties) with forty-two altogether based their townships initially on the old *du* division of multiplex defense associations.

32. Shanyin became part of Shaoxing county after the revolution.

33. See, for example, the concern for the drawing of self-government districts evidenced by a Yin county board member (*S*, 1913/5/10).

34. *MLB*, XT 3/6/8.

35. *Wu-Qing Z*, 23:6a.

36. *S*, XT 2/12/14; XT 3/4/11, 6I/10. For similar taxes levied for new schools, see Nakamura Tsune, "Shinmatsu gakudō setsuritsu o meguru Kōsetsu nōson shakai no ichi danmen," *Rekishi Kyōiku*, 10 (1962):77–79. For typical projects, see *S*, XT 3/2/18, 25; 3/11, 21, 23; 6/4; and *MLB*, XT 3/7/29. See also *Yuyao liucang zhi*, 34:13b–14a.

37. *S*, XT 3/7/1, 8/22 and 8/24.

38. *S*, XT 3/3/21.

39. *Ganzhi fulu*, 2a. It was reported that those who started the serious disturbance in Ganpu in 1910 were from Shanghai (*S*, XT 2/4/2).

40. *S*, XT 3/2/18 for Hangchow's action.

41. See *S*, 1912/4/16; 1913/6/7, 7/20–21, 8/7, 10/2, 10/13; and 1914/1/19.

42. *Shuanglin Z*, 32:18b–19b.

43. See, for example, *S*, 1913/6/7, 7/30, 8/8 and 9/21.

44. See, for example, *S*, 1913/9/15.

45. *MLB*, 1913/6/29; *S*, 1913/4/17.

46. *S*, 1913/12/18.

47. *NCH*, 1913/5/17, p. 505.

48. The main example here is the Fenghua County Assembly (outer-core), which was forbidden to continue discussions of this subject by the provincial government (*S*, 1913/12/31).

49. See, for example, *S*, 1917/9/26, 10/3, 10/22, 12/20; 1918/10/24; 1919/8/30, 10/20, 12/1; 1920/3/3, 8/1, 8/4 and 10/25.

50. See *S*, 1918/8/20, 10/8; 1920/1/22 and 4/15.

51. For example, see *S*, 1923/10/29, 11/24; 1924/4/28, 6/14, 7/15; and *SB*, 1925/12/19; 1926/7/2 and 7/27.

52. Examples are from *S*, 1924/1/11, 5/15; 1925/1/14; *SB*, 1926/5/8, 7/6; and 1926/8/31.

53. *S*, 1923/8/13, 12/18; 1924/1/9, 2/21, 3/8; and 1926/11/6, 13.

54. *S*, 1923/10/11 and *SB*, 1925/6/7–13. Although it is impossible to trace the number of county assembly members in the 1920s who had participated in the 911 coups, of twenty-five assemblymen in Yin county, three had been involved in 1911. Compare the list in *S*, 1924/4/25 with "Ningpo guomin shangwu fenhui xunbao pianduan," *JSZ*, I (1961):543–548.

55. This information comes from *S*, 1919/10/3; 1923/10/21, 10/30–31, 11/2 and 11/21. In 1918 the self-government system was the deputy system. Budgetary data on other zones are found in chaps. 7 and 9.

56. *Xuanping X*, p. 425, includes the percentage of the land tax surcharge allotted for various items. The amount of self-government funds for most counties was probably less than 20 percent of the total income of the county government. In addition to the land tax surcharge, counties took in miscellaneous taxes, interest revenue on public lands, and tuition from county schools. Details from Fenghua county, for example, show that of about 33,950 *yuan* collected in 1922, roughly 6,850 (about 20 percent) was spent on self-government. See *XF*, "diaocha," pp. 1–30.

57. By 1918 education associations were under the financial control of the education promotion office, and agriculture associations were supposedly self-supporting.

58. *S*, 1923/10/8.

59. *S*, 1918/9/24.

60. For price statistics indicating inflation, see *Dinghai X*, "Shihuo": 1b–5a and *ZG*, "Zhuji gaiguan," pp. 45–50.

61. *S*, 1923/9/25.

62. There was considerable bitterness on the part of self-government bodies against education organs because of their constant pleas for more money. See *S*, 1923/11/26.

63. *Wu-Qing Z*, 40:11a–12b; *Xincheng Z*, 4:7a–8a.

64. See *S*, XT 1/11/3, 17, 19 and 12/1; XT 3/3/15, 22 and 6I/16; 1912/5/14; 1913/3/26 and 4/21.

65. *S*, 1917/9/25; 1923/1/28; 1924/5/31 and 6/9.

66. *S*, 1912/10/22.

67. *S*, 1912/10/22.

68. *Meili beizhi,* 1:22a and *Dinghai X,* 3:4b–5a.

69. *Ganzhi fulu,* 2a, 21a–22b.

70. *QXLW,* 4:16a–18a.

71. *S,* 1913/7/14; *Shuanglin Z,* 32:20a. Control of outsiders, in fact, became the stated reason for the establishment of more militia units.

72. *S,* 1914/6/9. For the establishment in 1920, see "Telephone Scheme in Chekiang," *CEJ,* 8 (May 1931): 521.

73. *Puyuan zhi,* 14:17a.

74. The level of concern with outsiders probably was in part a function of the level of the economic hierarchy at which the situation existed: note the Shaoxing merchants who played an important role in Hangchow's economy.

75. *TR,* 1913, p. 1008.

76. See accounts of wealthy elites' involvement in dredging and dike building, *S,* XT 3/2/2; 1913/6/12; 1920/4/15, 4/21; *Ganzhi fulu,* 6a.

77. *S,* 1913/6/17–19.

78. *S,* 1913/10/19. As other examples, see *S,* 1916/9/23; 1917/3/7 and 4/30.

79. See my unpublished manuscript, "The Development of the Lake Xiang Region: Elite and Government Interaction, 1903–1926." See *Xiaoshan Xianghu zhi* (1925), *Xiaoshan Xianghu xu zhi* (1927), and *Xianghu diaocha baogao shu* (1927). This project also saw other trends mentioned above, including opposing elites and both government mediation and eventual intervention.

80. *S,* 1914/1/16 and 1924/3/2.

81. *S,* 1913/7/6. Also see *TR,* 1907, p. 381.

82. *S,* 1917/12/7, 10/12 and 19; 1918/1/21.

83. *S,* 1917/12/26 and 1918/1/6.

84. *S,* 1923/7/26 and 1924/3/2.

85. *S,* 1920/5/18. There were other important inner-core projects including the dredging of South Lake south of Hangchow (*S,* 1924/1/18 ff.) and Lake Tai. The latter suggests the importance of macroregional activity: Zhejiang and Jiangsu, in uneasy coalition, attempted to dredge the lake beginning in 1919. By 1926 the Lake Tai engineering committee was bankrupt with little to show for itself except considerable surveying (*S,* 1919/7/2; 1920/12/14; 1924/1/12, 2/16, 3/5, and 11/25). The scope of proposed action—beyond the locality, beyond provincial boundaries, to the region—is essential to note.

86. Gu Shijiang, *Xiaoshan xiangtu zhi* (n.p., 1933), pp. 10–12.

87. *S,* 1919/4/16 ff., 4/23, 28; 5/6, 5/8; and 7/11.

88. *S,* 1920/3/22; 5/16 ff.; 7/9, 7/21 and 11/27.

89. *S,* 1913/4/19; 1915/7/4. See also *QXLW,* juan 4, passim, for Qu's numerous calls for such an establishment.

90. *S,* 1916/11/17.

91. *S,* 1924/6/14.

92. *S,* 1912/11/11 and 1913/11/6.

93. *S,* 1913/4/19.

94. *S,* 1923/11/2.

95. See chap. 3; *S,* 1923/8/14.

96. See *S,* 1920/10/17. *Wu-Qing Z,* 6:9a.

97. *S*, XT 3/6I/10; 1912/1/10; 1917/11/10; 1920/9/17; 1924/3/5.

98. Much of the following account is based upon *CEB*, 8 (January 16, 1926): 29–30 and *CEB*, 9 (Octobert 30, 1926):249–252.

99. *CEB*, 9 (October 30, 1926):251.

100. S, 1924/2/19, 2/25, 3/1–2, 3/11, 4/28 and 5/3.

101. *CEB*, 9 (October 30, 1926):251–252. See also Fei Guxiang, "Zhexi zhiming gaiguang ji jinxing fangzhen," *Zhonghua nongxuehui bao*, 15 (March 1926):13–27.

7. Outer-Core Political and Elite Structures

1. *XF*, "Lunshuo," pp. 53–54.

2. *S*, 1923/8/10.

3. A reasonable hypothesis is that late Qing outer-core data would evidence the same relational pattern to other zones seen in the Republican data: more degree-holders, slightly fewer graduates, and fewer lineage-based elites than in the inner core.

4. See, for example, the biographies of Wu Zhonghuai and Lou Shouyu of Zhuji; Ou Renheng of Xiangshan; and Kong Xiantan of Qu. *ZG*, "Renwu xiaozhi," pp. 17–18 and "Zhuji shehui xianxiang," pp. 127–128; *Xiangshan X*, 26:16b–17b; and *Qu X*, 13:33a and 44b; 12:34a; and 3:26b.

5. Of the men cited above only Lou left his native county permanently.

6. *S*, 1913/12/6; 1914/3/29.

7. *XF*, section "diaocha," pp. 38–43.

8. For Tonglu, see *S*, 1920/5/1; the Qu case is in *Qu X*, 6:30b.

9. *ZG*, "Wunian lai zhi da shiji," pp. 11–12 and "Zhuji gaiguan," pp. 108–109.

10. *XF*, section "diaocha," p. 55.

11. *XF*, section "diaocha," pp. 55–56. The Fenghua figures are differentiated from the inner core by relatively more of both types serving on the local scene. It is also probably atypical in the number of returned officials.

12. See chap. 11.

13. See the biographies of Gao Chensheng, Kong Qingyi, Ye Rujang, and Xiang Gui in *Qu X*, 3:30b, 35a; 6:30b–31a; 23:61b, 63b–64a; and 24:23b.

14. *ZG*, "Zhuji gaiguan," pp. 110–114. Also "Wunian lai zhi da shiji," p. 3.

15. *S*, 1920/2/2.

16. See *S*, 1919/5/9 and Ruan Yicheng, *Ruan Xunbo xiansheng yiji* (Taibei, 1970), 1:28.

17. *ZG*, "Zhuji gaiguan," p. 135.

18. Xiang, *Zhejiang xinwen shi*, pp. 40 and 98.

19. *S*, 1913/12/1.

20. Xiang, *Zhejiang xinwen shi*, p. 98.

21. Ibid., p. 88.

22. Ibid., pp. 171–172.

23. See *S*, XT 2/11/16; 1917/3/4, 8/4; 1920/3/9; and *SB*, 1926/6/18.

24. *ZG*, "Zhuji gaiguan," pp. 75–79. Bureaus were located in the county seat and five market towns, with sixty-three men in the county seat bureau and eighty-five in the towns.

25. *ZG*, "Zhuji shehui xianxiang," p. 97.

26. See, for example, Zhu Rende, Xu Jie, and Wang Zhongting of Qu.

27. *ZG*, "Zhuji shehui xianxiang," pp. 71 and 96.

28. *ZG*, "Zhuji gaiguan," pp. 135–138.

29. *S*, 1923/2/11; 1924/3/19 and 5/31.

30. See the characterization of these counties in QXLW, 4:74a–75b, 81a–83a; and 84a–86b. See also *S*, 1924/7/18 and *ZG*, "Wunian lai zhi da shiji," p. 6.

31. *S*, 1924/9/24.

32. See the account of Qu county, *S*, 1924/12/19; and of Lanqi county, Xiang, *Zhejiang xinwen shi*, pp. 157–158.

33. *S*, 1912/6/20 and *MLB*, 1912/2/12.

34. *S*, 1919/3/25.

35. *ZG*, "Wunian lai zhi da shiji," p. 5; *Xiangshan X*, 14:38b; *XF*, passim. The Yan society was the editor and publisher of *XF*.

36. *S*, 1920/12/16 and *ZG*, "Wunian lai zhi da shiji," pp. 1–11.

37. *S*, 1924/5/16. *XF*, "diaocha," p. 54 and "lunshuo," pp. 33–35.

38. *ZG*, "Zhuji gaiguan," pp. 131–135; *Qu X*, 3:28a.

39. *S*, 1913/9/15.

40. *ZG*, "Zhuji gaiguan," p. 119. It remained under the council's control until 1914 when it reverted to private hands under a board of directors, which received a county subsidy.

41. *ZG*, "Zhuji shehui xianxiang," p. 81.

42. *ZG*, "Zhengwen," p. 56.

43. See the evaluation in *Qu X*, 3:28b; note the range of assembly issues delineated in *XF*, "diaocha," p. 52.

44. *ZG*, "Zhuji gaiguan," p. 56. For Zhuji's budget, see "Zhuji gaiguan," pp. 75–79; for Fenghua's budget, see *XF*, "diaocha," pp. 1–29.

45. *ZG*, "Zhuji gaiguan," pp. 56, 75, and 79–80; and "Zhuji shehui xianxiang," pp. 34, 68, and 104. The editors do admit to assembly roles in certain areas, and they call the self-government deputies (1914–1922) the actual county administration. Since the magistrate appointed these deputies, he probably named those from his inner circle.

46. Outer-core elites obviously initiated some public works. For example, when floods destroyed a Zhuji dike in 1915 and 1916, two hundred representatives of eighty-four villages met on their own at the Yu lineage ancestral hall to discuss the dike's immediate reconstruction. Work was divided among the villages and finished in eight months (*ZG*, "Zhuji gaiguan," p. 103).

47. *Qu X*, 3:30b.

48. *ZG*, "Zhuji gaiguan," p. 117 and "Liushinian zhanggu," pp. 22–27.

49. The account that follows is based on *OG*, 1:128–130.

50. *S*, 1913/8/24. I have no record of how the scheme worked.

51. *ZG*, "Zhuji shehui xianxiang,' pp. 96–97.

52. These impeachments are scattered through *S* from 1912 to 1926.

53. *ZG*, "Zhuji gaiguan," pp. 138–139.

54. Because of the specified division of the land tax surcharge for self-government and education in all three counties, the proportions are almost identical for these two expenses.

55. This computation excludes Zhuji's police expenditure to make the sums comparable.

56. *QXLW*, 4:60a–62a and 74a–75b.

57. *QXLW*, 4:60a–65a; 74a–75b, 81a–86b; 102a–103b; 128a–130a; 141a–144a; 147a–150a. Other reports in the late 1910s and 1920s suggest similar developments in the two other counties, Xinchang and Changshan. See Lin Chuanjia, *Da Zhonghua Zhejiang* pp. 237–238 and 273–274; and Wei Songtang, *Zhejiang jingji jilüe*, pp. 248–255 and 378–387.

58. *ZS*, 6:8–185 passim.

59. *ZG*, "Zhuji gaiguan," pp. 110–111.

60. *Qu X*, 6:35b.

61. This list comes from *S*, *ZS*, and *CEB*.

62. *S*, 1912/5/28.

63. *S*, 1913/2/17 and 12/11.

64. *OG*, 2:533–535.

65. *S*, 1920/2/27.

66. *Qu X*, 6:35b and *CEB*, 7 (September 12, 1925):157. See also the Shouchang merchant's effort to get permission for coal mining (*S*, 1919/3/30).

67. *S*, 1917/12/16.

68. See, for example, *S*, 1915/3/30; 1918/3/23, 5/28; and 1920/2/27.

69. For locally initiated projects, see modern sericulture farms in Xinchang and Cheng, *S*, 1918/3/23, and the Qu forestry station and county nursery, *Qu X*, 6:31a–b.

70. *S*, 1919/3/20.

71. *CEB*, 9 (September 18, 1926):165.

72. *S*, 1918/5/28.

73. *XF*, "diaocha," p. 55.

74. *Qu X*, 4:50b and 24:23a–b. Note also *S*, 1914/2/10; 1916/10/6; and 1917/10/22.

75. *ZG*, "Zhengwen," p. 56 and "Zhuji gaiguan," pp. 110–114.

76. *S*, 1918/3/7, 11/26; 1919/1/10.

77. Marshall Broomhall, ed., *The Chinese Empire: A General and Missionary Survey* (London, 1907), pp. 78–79.

78. See, for example, the disputes involving the missionary D. Duncan Main in Hangchow (*S*, 1918/12/29; 1919/1/3, 9/30; and 1920/7/27). See also the Zhapu affair of 1924 (*S*, 1924/3/14).

79. *Qu X*, 4:48b–50a.

80. *Qu X*, 9:36a–38a. See also Rankin, *Early Chinese Revolutionaries*, pp. 130–131.

81. *Xiangshan X*, 9:71b–73a.

82. *ZG*, "Liushinian zhanggu," pp. 18–20; "Zhuji gaiguan," pp. 122–124; and "Zhuji shehui xianxiang," p. 42.

83. Mobei, *Jiang-Zhe tielu fengzhao*, pp. 144, 386, 392, and 399.

84. *S*, 1919/5/27, 6/6, 7/18, and 8/12.

85. *S*, 1919/12/17 and 1920/9/17; and *ZG*, "Wunian lai zhi da shiji," pp. 1 and 3–4.

86. *ZG*, "Zhuji shehui xianxiang," p. 82.

87. *S*, 1919/12/17; *SB*, 1925/6/9–10, 13, and 17.

88. *S*, 1925/6/23.

89. *ZG,* "Wunian lai zhi da shiji," p. 1.

90. *SB,* 1925/6/8–10, 13, and 17. The counties were Lanqi, Zhuji, Jinhua, Xinchang, and Tonglu.

91. See, for example, *S,* 1925/4/29 on a provincial constitution issue and *SB,* 1925/6/10, 13, and 17 on the May Thirtieth tragedy.

8. Inner-Periphery Political and Elite Structures

1. *QXLW,* 4:13a–15a, 19a–21a, 48a–49a, 93a–101a, 111a–113b, 116a–127b, 131a–135b, and 138a–146b.

2. *Nantianshan zhi* (1935).

3. Muramatsu Yuji, *"Shindai no shinshi-jinushi,"* pp. 698–726.

4. Examples are the Fans of Houda, Dais and Wus of Lanyuan, Fengs of Huangtang, and Zhangs, Shaos, and Wangs of Waibei townships. The same trend is evident in Shouchang: Datong township (the Huangs and Wengs), the county seat (the Zhuges, Wengs, Yes, and Jiangs), and Changyue (Yes and Chens). The Changyue creek flows into Lanqi, a rich outer-core county; and the township area, a productive one, was probably incorporated into Shouchang to prevent additional orientation of wealth to Lanqi. In any case, Changyue, oriented naturally to Lanqi, produced important elites in Shouchang affairs.

5. These townships were Kaihua, Baisha, and Langye.

6. This phenomenon can be seen in Renfeng township, Shouchang (where the Ye family performed several functions but did not dominate); in Yangfou township, Tangqi; and Xiyi township, Lishui. This generalization is made from the respective gazetteers. For Lishui, also see *ZS,* 10:126–127.

7. The 3.9 percent listed in Table 7 includes those who had some experience outside throughout the period.

8. Mao Huhou, "Xinhai geming zai Lishui," p. 200.

9. *Lishui X,* 1:12b, 14a; 4:40a; 8:58b–59a.

10. See, for example, the careers of Feng Guitan in *Tangqi X,* 9:46a, 47a, 50a; and Xiang Hualong in *Lishui X,* 2:36b; 8:53a.

11. *Lishui X,* 8:53a, 59b; *OG,* 2:464–465.

12. These figures are garnered from newspapers and gazetteers. The eight were Fu Dianxiu (Dongyang), Xiao Jian (Wukang), Huang Zhifan (Pujiang), Mou Ruzi (Anji), Tang Xian (Lishui), Wang Binghao (Xindeng), Wang Bingyong (Qunan), and Ying Yigao (Yongkang).

13. See, for example, *Tangqi X,* 10:161b–163a.

14. Cao, *Wo,* pp. 106–107.

15. *S,* 1912/6/22.

16. Cao, *Wo,* pp. 56 and 104.

17. *Xindeng X,* pp. 912–943 passim and 1518.

18. *Xindeng X,* pp. 774, 849, 1179–1180, 1462, and 1502.

19. *Lishui X,* 4:39a–40b.

20. *Shouchang X,* p. 584.

21. *Xindeng X,* pp. 832, 911, 913, 916, 921, 931, 1382, 1387, 1462–1463, and 1502.

22. In a sense some inner-core counties saw control by a lineage oligarchy; but,

on the whole, inner-core structures allowed a much greater diversity of individual leadership.

23. These five were Hong Xicheng, Wu Xichang, Wu Renren, Wu Baosan, and Yuan Zhicheng. Since *Xindeng X* was published in 1922, there is no information on the political structure of the 1920s.

24. The multifunctional elites were Jiang Zhonghan, Jiang Zonggan, Fei Shoutian, and Weng Jiafu. The Anhui merchant was Cheng Bingpan. See *Shouchang X*, pp. 125, 221, 231, 367–370, 372, 374–375, 424, 442, 449, 495–496, 528, 532, 535, 582–586, 589–591, 787–789, and 1230.

25. *S*, 1914/1/7; see also 1913/12/27.

26. An exception to this narrow scope was Liu Tingxuan, whose range of activity is cited above.

27. See, for example, *S*, 1913/2/23, 3/29, 4/14, 5/8, 10/7, 12/6, and 12/31.

28. *S*, 1923/12/23.

29. *S*, 1925/5/22.

30. See *S*, 1923/9/14, 12/23; 1924/5/2, 5/17, 5/22; and 1925/5/4. In Tangqi, magistrate and elites puzzled over assembly procedure in replacing the resigned assembly chairman (*S*, 1925/4/5). In some cases, as in Yongkang, the question of regulations was initiated by the magistrate (*S*, 1924/6/29).

31. See *S*, 1924/3/20, 5/17, 5/24, 7/14, and 7/17. For the outer core, see 5/24 and for the outer periphery, 4/13 and 7/14.

32. *Lishui X*, 2:34a–b; (reprint), vol. 1, p. 241; and *S*, 1920/12/2 and 12/23.

33. These impeachments are scattered throughout *S* from 1912 to 1926.

34. *S*, 1919/12/29.

35. It joined other *fatuan* and assemblies in sending protest telegrams over taxes or, by 1925, on national affairs (*S*, 1920/12/2; 1924/4/13, 6/9; and *SB*, 1925/6/10, 12, and 13).

36. *Xindeng X*, p. 849.

37. *S*, 1920/4/12.

38. *S*, 1920/1/20, 3/2; 1923/12/25; 1924/3/20 and 6/18, 24.

39. *SB*, 1925/6/10, 12–14.

40. An alleged extortion by Qingtian officials in 1913 led to the founding of a Public Interest Federation (*gongyi lianhehui*) that was quickly suppressed by local officials and police (*S*, 1913/5/3). This ad hoc organization seems a notable exception in this zone.

41. *S*, 1923/12/6.

42. *S*, 1924/8/21.

43. *Shouchang X*, 4:11a–14a.

44. See citations in note 1.

45. Twenty-six of thirty-eight Shouchang militia leaders had served in late Qing subcounty self-government posts (*Shouchang X*, 6:30a–35a). Militia formation generally occurred in relatively commercialized townships. In Shouchang, slightly commercialized townships had as many as or more units than the most developed, mirroring the provincial scene where the partially developed middle zones were as frequent a bandit target as the inner core. See juan 4–6 for information on their location.

46. *ZG*, "Zhuji shehui xianxiang," p. 75.

47. *ZG*, "Liushinian zhanggu," pp. 22-27.

48. *S*, 1917/12/20.

49. Military Governor Zhu Rui put their number in late 1915 at about six thousand (*S*, 1915/11/13). He estimated twenty thousand men in the modern army.

50. *DC*, p. 99.

51. See the 1912 uprisings in Xianju and Tiantai and the 1915 disturbance in Changshan (*MLB*, 1912/11/9; *S*, 1915/6/6).

52. See also examples in *S*, 1917/8/5 and 1923/10/21.

53. Anti-Yuan organizers in 1913 contacted Zhou and received his promise to participate in the revolt against the president. For more on Zhou's campaign, see *S*, 1914/7/30, 9/9, and 12/23. Zhou was captured and executed in 1915 (*S*, 1915/3/17).

54. *OG*, 1:298-306.

55. *MLB*, 1913/1/19.

56. *NCH*, 1912/12/21, p. 804.

57. See the complaint from Jinyun that banditry was making commercial dealings difficult (*QXLW*, 3:133a-b).

58. *S*, 1917/10/19.

59. *S*, 1919/4/17.

60. *S*, 1923/11/29.

61. *S*, 1924/7/4.

62. *S*, 1917/12/27; 1920/9/20; and *OG*, 1:261-270.

63. See citations in note 1.

64. *S*, 1914/8/5, 14, 21-22, and 31.

65. *S*, 1919/8/3.

66. *S*, 1920/12/2.

67. *S*, 1920/11/20.

68. The *Tangqi X* county map has a special notation for villages and towns that had schools built by 1931.

69. *OG*, 2:538-556 and *QXLW*, 4:19a-21a.

70. The *yinli ju* of Tangqi existed for six years (*Tangqi X*, 4:17a-b).

71. *OG*, 2:593.

72. These leaders have been determined by surveying all relevant sources. They are as follows: inner core: Zhou Chengtan, Wu Siyu, Gao Erdeng, Zhu Rui, Wang E, Han Shaoji, Gu Naibin, Lai Weiliang; outer core: Jiang Zungui, Fu Qiyong, Zhou Fengqi, Zhang Zaiyang, Yu Wei, Yu Ding; inner periphery: Xu Zexun, Ye Songqing, Ye Huanhua, Lü Gongwang, Wang Guilin, Xia Chao, Liu Fengwei. Two of the twenty-four, Tong Baoxuan and Xu Liurao, were described only as from Taizhou and could have come from any one of the three zones represented in Taizhou's component counties.

73. *ZG*, "Zhuji shehui xianxiang," p. 83.

74. See, for example, *S*, 1923/10/18, 12/12; 1924/6/23, 11/18; 1925/1/3, 1/28, 2/4, 2/10, 11/9; 1926/2/7.

75. *QXLW*, 4:13a-18a; 48a-49a.

76. In every other county I have studied, the chamber of commerce was located at the county seat (*Tangqi X*, 9:46a-b).

77. *Shouchang X,* pp. 124–125, 368, 372, 374, 592, and 789.

78. Wei Songtang, *Zhejiang jingji jilüe,* p. 421. Shouchang had *huiguan* from Fujian and Jiangxi as well as Anhui (*Shouchang X,* 4:13b–14a).

79. *Tangqi X,* pp. 944–947.

9. Outer-Periphery Political and Elite Structures

1. See, for example, *OG,* 1:161–172.

2. See, for example, QXLW, 4:16a–18a, 22a–23b, 50a–52a, 66a–67b; and 3:139b–140a.

3. *SXZ,* ce 11:6b.

4. See chap. 8, note 5.

5. *S,* 1924/8/7.

6. See Lin Chuanjia, *Da Zhonghua Zhejiang,* p. 308. Lin suggests that the trade went to Tangqi. This was highly unlikely given the location of waterways and the nature of Tangqi's topography.

7. *Xuanping X,* vol. 2, p. 662.

8. Lin Chuanjia, *Da Zhonghua Zhejiang,* p. 308.

9. *Changhua X,* pp. 21–28.

10. *Xuanping X,* vol. 3, pp. 1275–1276.

11. *Xuanping X,* vol. 2, pp. 626–627.

12. In one provincial episode, local elites fought Hangchow to prevent the imposition of artificial boundaries on natural divisions. It involved the formation of the new county of Nantian (inner periphery) from poorly developed island territory originally under the control of Xiangshan (outer core). Long viewed as important for defense, the island was settled in the early Guangxu period. In 1912 the Hangchow government ordered that Nantian be made a separate county with Shipu, a market town on the Xiangshan peninsula, as its county seat. Both Xiangshan, which did not want to lose the flourishing town, and Nantian, which did not want to be governed by a town across the gulf, were upset. Ultimately, after much negotiation, Nantian became a county and its own island town became the county seat. The logic of natural separation won over the logic of Hangchow bureaucrats. See *Xiangshan X,* 9:73b–74a; *Nantian X,* pp. 367–370; and *S,* 1916/8/25, 10/15.

13. In Xuanping, these lineages and townships were the Tus of Guanghui, Pans of Zhenwu, Taos of Jinren, Chens of Chude; and in Suian, the Wus and Yus of Anyang, Lus and Yus of Hengyan, Wangs and Yus of Daye, and Hongs of Xiashe.

14. Examples are Lucun and Xiazhou of Suian; Lidao, Yongfeng, and Anliang of Xuanping; and Jingju and Tazhu in Songyang.

15. Examples are the Chens and Lis in Baohe, Xuanping; the Wangs of Guocun, Suian; the Shuais of Changbei, Changhua; and the Ques of Shicang, Songyang.

16. Potter, "Land and Lineage in Traditional China," p. 137.

17. *Xuanping X,* vol. 2, pp. 611, 616, 648, and 831.

18. *Jingning xian xuzhi,* pp. 126, 326, 414, and 425.

19. *Suian X,* pp. 281 and 286.

20. The following discussion is based on *Xiaofeng zhigao*.

21. The six were Zhou Shideng, Zhou Bi, He Wenlong, Xu Shufang, Cai Yufang, Ye Tongchi, and Ye Yulin (*Songyang X*, 8:48a, 50b, 55b; 9:99a-100b).

22. Scattered throughout the gazetteer is information on Chen Haoshu, Chen Nixin, Chen Fengkan, Qiu Zhaolin, Zhu Xingtan, He Xifan, Pan Hao, Tao Jianxun, and Cai Guozhen.

23. This is especially true of men who served in the governments of their native places immediately after 1912. Many left for other analogous posts shortly afterward. A few examples are Zheng Yongxi of Qu, Zhou Bin of Jiaxing, Lou Shouguang of Zhuji, and Bi Jinyuan of Jiande.

24. *Suian X*, vol. 1, pp. 66-67, 188, and 211.

25. *Songyang X*, 14:12b-14a.

26. *Xuanping X*, vol. 1, pp. 189-193, 279, 365; vol. 2, pp. 425, 540-541.

27. In the computation of graduates, the two categories of "school graduates" and "both degree and graduate" were combined.

28. *QXLW*, 4:16a-18a, 22a-23b, 50a-52a, and 3:124b.

29. R. H. Tawney, *Land and Labor in China* (Boston, 1966), p. 77.

30. See the citations in note 28. On the efforts to reconstruct the Longchuan pottery industry, see *S*, 1918/5/18 and *CEB*, 9 (September 25, 1926): 176.

31. *Xiaofeng zhigao*, p. 183.

32. *Xiaofeng zhigao*, p. 194.

33. For example, in Xuanping, the association lasted from 1915 to 1920; in Suian, from 1917 to 1925.

34. In Changhua, for example, the workhouse existed from 1915 to 1916 and 1919 to 1923.

35. The sources are the respective gazetteers. Pages for the other zonal counties have been given in previous chapter notes. The outer-periphery county pages are *Xuanping X*, vol. 2, pp. 423-424; *Jingning xian xuzhi*, pp. 170 ff.; and *Changhua X*, pp. 153-154.

36. The percentage of self-government expenditures designated as administrative expense was only 16.3 percent of the total in Xuanping.

37. *Suian X*, vol. 1, p. 210.

38. *Xuanping X*, vol. 2, pp. 635-636.

39. The following workhouse account comes from *Xuanping X*, vol. 2, pp. 545-546.

40. See, for example, *S*, XT 3/1/22; 1914/8/5; 1917/6/11; 1918/12/27; 1919/2/7; 1924/1/11; 1925/8/25. See also *OG*, 1:32 for an example of problems in Qingyuan county.

41. *OG*, 1:42-44 and 48.

42. *Xuanping X*, vol. 2, p. 649.

43. *SS*, 1922/8/17; *S*, 1924/10/25, 11/8; 1925/2/10; 1926/10/5; 1926/12/7.

44. *Suian X*, vol. 2, pp. 715-716.

45. *Jingning xian xuzhi*, pp. 342-350.

46. *Xiaofeng zhigao*, p. 18.

47. The first three counties received many immigrants following the Taiping Rebellion. Yu Lie, *Yuqian xianggong dili dagang chugao* (1934), p. 74; *Xiaofeng*

zhigao, pp. 228–237; and *Changhua X,* pp. 21–24. Large numbers of She people, immigrants from Guangdong in the late seventeenth century, settled in mountainous counties of Chuzhou prefecture (*Songyang X,* 6:22a).

48. *Suian X,* vol. 1, pp. 31, 225.

49. *Suian X,* vol. 1, p. 224.

50. *Xiaofeng zhigao,* pp. 186–187.

51. *Xuanping X,* vol. 1, pp. 279, 288, 365–366; vol. 2, pp. 551, 650, 833. This situation is similar to the role of Cheng Bingpan, Anhui outsider involved in Shouchang's (inner periphery) political oligarchy.

52. Men like the outsider Wus and Gans of Xuanping were gentry merchants: merchants in occupation, gentry in scope. In Songyang several gentry-merchants were evident: see, for example, Xu Shufang and Zhou Shideng, *Songyang X,* 8:48a, 50b, and 55b.

53. This is 22 percent, close to the percentage of second assembly men who had had experience beyond their county.

54. *Xuanping X,* vol. 2, pp. 506–507: the first came in 1907; *Suian X,* vol. 1, p. 220: the first Catholics came in the Guangxu period; the first Protestants at the end of the Qing dynasty.

55. *Suian X,* vol. 2, p. 715.

56. *Xuanping X,* vol. 2, pp. 762–763. See also *OG,* 1:274–286 and 2:464, 513–515.

57. *Xuanping X,* vol. 2, pp. 616, 621, 730, 818, and 827.

58. *Changhua X,* pp. 1332–1341.

59. Yu Lie, *Yuqian xianggong dili dagang chugao,* pp. 27–28.

60. *S,* 1923/9/1, 12/6; 1924/5/5.

61. *Xiaofeng zhigao,* p. 126.

62. *Xiaofeng zhigao,* pp. 126 and 148. See also *S,* 1924/2/29.

63. *S,* 1924/4/13 and 7/14.

64. *SB,* 1925/6/8 and 6/12.

10. The 1911 Revolution

1. See the bibliographical essay on the revolution in Joseph W. Esherick, "1911: A Review," *Modern China,* 2 (April 1976): 141–184.

2. See the "Comments from Authors Reviewed," *Modern China,* 2 (April 1976): 185–220, especially the comments of Mark Elvin and Michael Gasster. Esherick's treatment in *Reform and Revolution in China: The 1911 Revolution in Hunan and Hubei* (Berkeley, 1976) of the "urban reformist elite" speaks directly to the nature of leadership, but does not adequately delineate the spatial context.

3. Mary Wright, "Introduction: The Rising Tide of Change" in *China in Revolution,* pp. 1–63.

4. The Beijing government in 1903 ordered each province to organize and train New Army units.

5. Xiao Xingyuan, a Hunanese, was a graduate of the Japan Army Officers Academy and Zhu Rui and Xu Zexun, of the Nanjing Military Academy. For specific accounts of Jiang's success at building the New Army units and for their histories after his 1909 transfer, see Si Daoqing, "Zhejun shibanian de huiyilu,"

JSZ, 2 (1957): 78–79; Ge Jingen, "Xinhai geming zai Zhejiang," *XGH*, vol. 4, pp. 94–95; Zhou Yawei, "Guangfu hui jianwen zayi," *XGH*, vol. 1, pp. 624–626, 633; and Lü Gongwang, "Xinhai geming Zhejiang guangfu jishi," *JSZ*, 1 (1954): 109.

6. Zhang Xiaoxun, "Zhejiang xinhai geming guangfu jishi," *JSZ*, 1 (1954): 119; Ge, "Xinhai geming," p. 98; and Lü, "Xinhai geming," p. 112.

7. Zhang, "Zhejiang xinhai geming," p. 121; Lü, "Xinhai geming," p. 112. See also Zhejiang jun sishijiu lü siling bu, "Zhejun Hangzhou guangfu ji," *GG*, vol. 2, pp. 132–145.

8. See Ruan Yicheng, "Ji Chu Fucheng xiansheng," *ZW*, 16 (June 1970): 37–38; Shen Yiyun, "Yiyun huiyi," *ZW*, 4 (December 1964): 31; Wang Ziliang, "Jincui sangzide Chu Fucheng xiansheng," *ZY*, 2 (1969): 11; and Wang Ziliang, "Bainian beihuan hua Jiaxing," *ZY*, 1 (1969): 10–11.

9. Chu Fucheng, "Zhejiang xinhai geming jishi," *GG*, vol. 2, pp. 117–121. See also Shen Junru, "Xinhai geming zayi," *XGH*, vol. 1, pp. 139–140.

10. *S*, XT 3/8/30 and 9/3. See also Clarence Burton Day, *Hangchow University* (New York, 1955), pp. 28–29.

11. Lü, "Xinhai geming," p. 112. The agents were Lü Gongwang to Jinyun and Wang Jinfa to Shaoxing. See also the account of this stillborn alliance in Rankin, *Early Chinese Revolutionaries*.

12. Zhejiang jun sishijiu lü, "Zhejun Hangzhou guangfu ji," pp. 136–143; Ge, "Xinhai geming," pp. 100–101.

13. Lü, "Xinhai geming," pp. 112–114; Ge, "Xinhai geming," p. 100.

14. Zhong Liyu, "Guangfu Hangzhou huiyilu," *JSZ*, 1 (1954): 99.

15. Wang hotheadedly withdrew to Shaoxing to set up his own government.

16. *S*, XT 3/9/18.

17. Rankin, *Early Chinese Revolutionaries*, p. 217.

18. *S*, XT 1/12/15; XT 2/8/12.

19. Zhang Xiaoxun, "Zhejiang xinhai geming," p. 123 and Shen, "Xinhai geming zayi," p. 140.

20. *S*, XT 3/9/19.

21. After the successful seizure of Nanjing from the loyalist forces of Zhang Xun, the Zhejiang contingent, commanded by Zhu Rui and his deputy Lü Gongwang, had become dissatisfied that key positions in the Zhejiang government were going to the "imported goods." Tang had sent Zhou Chengtan to Nanjing to quiet the dissatisfaction, but he was completely unsuccessful. (Ge, "Xinhai geming," pp. 122–23).

22. Ma Xulun, "Wo zai xinhai zheyinian," *XGH*, vol. 1, p. 178.

23. Zhang Huangqi, "Guangfu hui lingxiu Tao Chengzhang geming shi," *XG*, vol. 1, pp. 527–528. See also Rankin, *Early Chinese Revolutionaries*, pp. 104–105, 148–149, and 218.

24. *S*, 1912/1/8 and *MLB*, 1912/1/9.

25. *S*, 1912/1/11.

26. *S*, XT 3/10/9.

27. *S*, 1912/1/11.

28. The committee was composed of representatives from each of the eleven prefectures, five army officers (all Tongmeng hui members or associates), and, for the appearance of balance, six Restoration Society members (*S*, 1912/1/13). I

have been unable to find information about these six either before or after the events of 1911; perhaps their main qualification was that they would support Jiang.

29. *S*, 1912/1/14.

30. Zhang Huangqi, "Guangfu hui lingxiu Tao Chengzhang," p. 528; Ma Xulun, "Tao Chengzhang zhi si," *XG*, vol. 1, p. 520. *S*, 1912/1/16; *MLB*, 1912/6/4.

31. *S*, 1912/3/28-29, 31; 4/1; *MLB*, 1912/3/28-29, 31; *S*, 1912/3/19.

32. *MLB*, 1912/2/11, 2/27; *S*, 1912/2/12, 2/22.

33. Ge, "Xinhai geming," p. 123.

34. See *S*, XT 3/5/7, 6/4, 6/7, 6/13, 6/25, and 7/19.

35. The Martial Association (see chap. 5) served as revolutionary front in Huzhou and Jiaxing. For Huzhou, see Qiu Shouming, "Huzhou guangfu huiyi," *XGH*, vol. 4, p. 168. For Ningbo, see "Ningbo guoming shangwu fenhui xunbao pianduan," *JSZ*, 1 (1961): 543-548; and Lin Duanfu, "Ningbo guangfu qinli ji," *XGH*, vol. 4, pp. 174-182.

36. Lin Duanfu, "Ningbo guangfu," pp. 180-181. The council was composed of six instead of seven because of the uncertain status of Nantian county, which had been formed only with the coup. For a detailed description of the administrative confusion between Nantian and Xiangshan counties, see *Nantian X*, pp. 387-442.

37. Chen Shouyong, "Wenzhou xiangying Wuchang qiyi de jinshen jingli," *XGH*, vol. 4, p. 185.

38. Lai Weiliang, "Zhejun guangfu Hangzhou he chiyuan Nanjing qinli ji," *XGH*, vol. 4, p. 152. See also the biography of Chen in Howard L. Boorman, ed., *Biographical Dictionary of Republican China* (New York, 1967), vol. 1, pp. 163-165.

39. *Deqing X*, vol. 2, pp. 676-678. Cheng Sen, the emissary, visited only Deqing and Wukang counties.

40. Qiu, "Huzhou guangfu huiyi," p. 168.

41. The following account comes from *Shuanglin Z*, 32:18b-24b.

42. See *Luqiao zhilüe* (1935), 5:7b and *NCH*, 1911/10/7, p. 26; 10/28, p. 208; 11/11, p. 363; 11/18, p. 433; 11/25, p. 517; 12/30, p. 866; and 1912/1/20, p. 178. To compound the already violent situation, the two main lineages in Linhai were reportedly destroying the city in their fight for control.

43. The Deqing county revolution, for example, was brought about both in the county seat and the local city of Xinshi by lineage-based gentry, gentry-merchants, and educators (*Deqing X*, vol. 2, pp. 676-678).

44. Wright, "Introduction" in *China in Revolution*, p. 30.

45. *S*, 1911/12/4.

46. *Qu X*, 9:38a-39a.

47. The provincial troops in mid-1911 numbered approximately 13,800. Scattered throughout the province in administrative centers (but comparatively stronger in the outer zones), they often handled problems of unrest that militia units could not deal with (H. G. W. Woodhead, ed., *The China Year Book 1913* [Tientsin, 1913], p. 287). Militia units had been formed and disbanded sporadically since the mid-nineteenth century; their existence and number by 1911 var-

ied from county to county. See, for example, *Xindeng X*, pp. 1461–1462 and *Jiande X*, p. 291.

48. *S*, XT 3/10/9.

49. *Xiangshan X*, 9:74b.

50. *Longyu X*, vol. 1, p. 35.

51. *S*, 1911/12/4.

52. *Xinchang X*, vol. 2, pp. 736–738.

53. Zhou Qiwei, "Luoqing xinhai geming," p. 192.

54. Ti Wei, "Guangfu Tangyi xiaoshi," *XG*, vol. 7, pp. 159–160.

55. *Shouchang X*, vol. 3, pp. 1227–1228. See also *MLB*, 1911/12/20.

56. *MLB*, 1912/7/8.

57. Wang Wei, ed., *Xiaofeng zhigao*, p. 14.

58. *MLB*, 1911/12/1.

59. Biographical information is gained by perusal of various sections of gazetteers from Deqing, Xindeng, and Shouchang.

60. Lü Gongwang, "Xinhai geming," p. 116.

61. Lishui's status as prefectural capital accounts for an inner-periphery county's having several returned students.

62. For details on this group, see *S*, 1913/12/27. The Songyang group of ten had three returned students from Japan, four degree-holders, six men in local self-government, and two provincial assemblymen.

63. Jiang Tianwei, "Xinhai geming hou Songyang de yici jianbian douzheng," *XGH*, vol. 4, pp. 203–204.

64. See *S*, 1913/12/27.

65. *S*, XT 3/10/4; *MLB*, 1911/12/17.

66. The clause "there is no king's law" comes from a report in *S*, 1912/1/22.

67. From the viewpoint of nonelites, the revolution was scarcely a "success." A Western reporter noted that within less than a decade, the 1911 revolution had acquired among the populace a rather dubious reputation: word spread that canals in the province were clogged with certain types of weeds that "were never known till sown by the revolutionaries of 1911" (*NCH*, 1919/8/9, p. 340).

68. See chap. 5.

69. See *S*, XT 3/4/2 and his reappointment, *S*, 1915/11/12.

70. *ZG*, section "Zhuji shehui xianxiang," p. 75.

71. *MLB*, 1912/2/12.

72. *S*, 1914/3/7.

73. For most of the outer periphery, nothing happened: in local affairs, there was little meaning in the revolution. Only one of the five complete gazetteers extant from outer-peripheral counties even mentions it. *Xuanping X*, for example, says not a thing about the revolution whereas it lists even the names of caves to which people fled during the Taiping Rebellion (vol. 1, pp. 166–167).

74. Seen in this light, the resolution of the debate between Mary Wright and Ichiko Chūzō over the nature and motivation of local revolutionary leadership may not be so much a case of *either* progressive leadership bringing social and political change *or* conservative elites bolstering their own power, as it is a situation of *both-and*. See Wright's description of her differences with Ichiko in Wright, "Introduction," p. 40. For Ichiko's position, see "The Role of the Gentry:

An Hypothesis" in *China in Revolution,* pp. 297–313. See also related comments in Esherick, "1911: A Review," pp. 162–168.

11. Patterns of Nonofficial Elite Provincial Politics

1. *S,* 1920/5/26.

2. For the Qing assembly, there were to be 114 men in all; Zhang's list contains 111. I have located one additional member in *Linan X.*

3. Zhang Pengyuan has suggested on the basis of five provinces studied in detail (not including Zhejiang) that close to 90 percent of the elected Qing assemblymen held traditional degrees (*Lixian pai,* p. 27).

4. Zhang Pengyuan determined the average age of Qing assemblymen from five other provinces to be forty-one (*Lixian pai,* p. 39). Zhang's sample is from the assemblies of Fengtian, Sichuan, and Heilongjiang plus the National Consultative Assembly.

5. Lists of key figures from various prefectures involved in the railway movement are found in Mobei, *Jiang-Zhe tielu fengzhao,* pp. 39–40.

6. Ho Ping-ti, *Studies on the Population of China, 1368–1953* (Cambridge, Mass., 1959), p. 241.

7. *NCH,* 1914/8/1, p. 336.

8. See, for example, Shen Yiyun, *Yiyun huiyi* (Taibei, 1968), vol. 1, p. 1; Cao, *Wo,* p. 13; and Chiang Monlin, *Tides from the West* (New Haven, 1947), pp. 6–10. Biographical accounts in *ZY* also include numerous references to the Taiping Rebellion and its effects.

9. *S,* XT 3/9/3. For additional material on Chen Fuchen and his ideas, see "Chen Jieshi xiansheng nianpu," *Oufeng zazhi,* no. 6 (n.d., n.p.).

10. The performance of the Qing assembly compared very favorably with other province's assemblies. In diligence (measured in willingness to stay on past the regular forty-day session and ten-day extension without pay) and in accomplishment (measured in number of definite resolutions—twenty-seven of fifty-six), the Zhejiang assembly ranked near the top of the list of the provincial roster (Fincher, "The Chinese Self-Government Movement," pp. 132, 138–139).

11. *MLB,* XT 3/11/24.

12. Yanzhou, Quzhou, Hangzhou, Taizhou, Ningbo, and Jinhua prefectures sent four representatives; Huzhou, Jiaxing, Shaoxing, and Chuzhou sent three; and Wenzhou sent two.

13. In speaking of Great Britain's persistent claims of the right to import opium into China on its own terms, the assembly wrote to Beijing that "the Board [of Foreign Affairs] can be afraid of her, but not we the Chekiang people" (*NCH,* 1912/7/20, p. 240).

In an assertively nationalistic mood, the Zhejiang civil commissioner Chu Fucheng in August 1912 cancelled forthcoming elections for a permanent provincial assembly. Supported by the PPA, this defiant action was undertaken because the central government had not yet announced uniform election laws for the nation. Chu and his supporters claimed that provincial laws were subordinate to national laws and that a provincial election could not be held until clear regulations had been set down by the central government. In an ironic twist, these men in the name of nationalism were denouncing and invalidating orders from the national government (*S,* 1912/8/15, 17).

14. See, for example, the agenda in *S,* 1912/12/6.

15. *DC,* p. 74; *S,* 1912/12/7. The commuted tax was called the *dibujin.* Although Beijing disapproved of this latter action, it was the first step toward the levy's commutation and toward shifting the burden to the whole province.

16. Names in Mobei were cross-checked against assembly elites.

17. The extant fragmentary records of votes cast in elections suggest in the core zones, at least, that the elite electorate expanded during the early Republic and that it took voting rights quite seriously. Republican suffrage qualifications substantially relaxed the Qing regulations, reducing the ten-year residency requirement to two years, the 5,000 *yuan* real estate requirement to 500 *yuan,* and the voting age from twenty-five to twenty-one. In addition, one had to pay two *yuan* per year in taxes and be a school graduate or the equivalent (*S,* 1917/10/6). Although no county-level voting records exist for the Qing assembly, it is quite obvious that the electorate had expanded by the first Republican assembly election. In Zhuji county, the recorded number of voters in late 1912 was 30,254 (about 5 or 6 percent of the estimated population); in the 1918 elections, 62,518 (about 12 to 14 percent); and in the 1921 elections, 147,921 (about 28 percent). *ZG,* "Zhuji gaiguan," pp. 79–80. The population figures come from *ZS,* 1:13. Such figures, even if overstated, reflect a substantial increase in elite political involvement.

Assembly elections had two phases: a primary election and the actual election. The only statistics I have discovered of the percentage of qualified voters actually voting came in the 1912 primary election in Jiaxing when, of about eighteen thousand eligible voters, only eight thousand (about 44 percent) cast ballots. The number for the actual election may have been larger. In one electoral district, the primary election was halted when one more vote was cast than there were eligible voters and when one of the candidates chosen was discovered to be head of a branch *tongjuan* office. These cases prompted telegrams to Hangchow authorities, who ordered another election (*S,* 1912/7/30).

The seriousness with which elites took voting rights was noteworthy also in April 1912 when Jiaxing prefectural representatives elected a replacement to the sitting provisional assembly. Because Tongxiang county had not had representatives present, its county assembly called for a reelection on the grounds that 170,000 people had not been represented (*S,* 1912/4/30). Although there was no reelection, the demand illustrates elite concerns for participation in choosing their representatives. No voting information is available from later elections; but the continual censuses in preparation for elections, discussions over delimiting electoral districts, and elections for county and provincial positions indicate continuing politicization of elites.

18. *S,* 1913/8/9, 14.

19. *S,* 1918/5/4.

20. *S,* 1925/5/13 and 24. The tax also applied for foreign billboards. The Shanghai Consul-General decried the action, noting that "particularly attractive are these signboards for. . . Sun Maid Raisins, Old Mill Cigarettes, and Royal Baking Powder" (NA 893.00/6767).

21. *S,* 1924/5/21, 23; and 6/4.

22. See *S,* 1919/5/10–13, 15 and 22–27; and *NCH,* 1919/5/31, p. 558.

23. *S*, 1923/7/30.

24. For battles with Qi, see *S*, 1917/4/15, 1918/5/13 and 30. In 1914 local courts of law (*shenjiansuo*), established in the late Qing dynasty, were abolished, and the legal administration of the counties returned to the magistrate. The county courts were reestablished during late 1916 by Lü Gongwang, with the tacit consent of Beijing. In March 1917, Qi abolished them, charging they were obstructionary, corrupt, expensive, and inefficient. Zhejiang's chief prosecutor (*gaodeng jiancha ting jianchazhang*) ordered magistrates to reestablish the courts. The confrontation was joined by the first RPA, which impeached Qi. Beijing eventually ordered the courts abolished and ordered counties to wait for the organization of a new system of local courts (*difang fenting*). *S*, 1917/3/18, 23, 28, 31; 4/1, 3, 7, 9; and *ZX*, 1917/3/25, 26; 4/4 and 8. For the final impeachment fight, see *S*, 1920/6/9–11, 13, 15, 17.

25. *S*, 1924/11/17; 12/3, 11, 18–19.

26. See, for example, *S*, 1917/5, 6 passim; 1918/12/19–22; 1919/5/2; 1920/5/21; and 1923/11/22.

27. *NCH*, 1923/4/14, p. 93; 1919/12/20, p. 752; 1920/12/4, p. 666; and *S*, 1916/9/19.

28. *ZX*, 1917/11/8; *S*, 1918/5/1, 17; 1918/12/29; 1919/12/12; 1923/11/18; and *NCH*, 1920/5/29, p. 511 and 1919/11/29, p. 554.

29. *S*, 1917/2/25; 1912/12/21 and 22; and 1923/7/13.

30. *S*, 1923/10/24 and 1925/4/29.

31. *SS*, 1922/11/6, 12/20; 1923/2/28; *S*, 1923/7/1 and 10/18.

32. Of nineteen county assembly representatives whom I can identify, all but four came from the inner core (*S*, 1923/10–1924/10 passim). Recognition of the federation by the government came in early 1924. (*S*, 1924/3/6).

33. *S*, 1923/7/25.

34. *S*, 1924/9/7.

35. *S*, 1923/10/26.

36. *S*, 1923/10/27.

37. *S*, 1924/1/5 and 2/26.

38. *S*, 1925/12/14–16.

39. *S*, 1923/10/21.

40. *S*, 1923/7/1, 16, 18, 25; 10/21; and *SS*, 1922/11/6, 12/21.

41. *S*, 1923/7/30.

42. *S*, 1923/7/1 and 4.

43. Earlier chapters have shown that county and township administrative boundaries were often of lesser importance than natural borders in local political affairs. In provincial affairs, administrative boundaries provided the political framework of state bureaucratic units and election districts. Native place associations took the names of these same administrative units. See Appendix A.

44. An article by Zhang Qiyun sets forth the basis for Ningpo's hopes to replace Hangchow. See "Lun Ningpo jianshe shenghui zhi xiwang," *Shidi xuebao*, 3 (May 1925): 1–17.

45. For opposition to the *tongjuan*, *S*, 1912/3/26, 30; for opposition to equalizing the *dibujin* (on which Zhexi paid a heavier rate than the rest of the province), *S*, 1917/4/8; for opposition to lowering the land tax surcharge in Zhexi, Xiang, *Zhejiang xinwen shi*, p. 95.

46. See my account in "Province and Nation."

47. Rankin, "Local Reform Currents in Chekiang before 1900," p. 226. Another key provincial leader from Wenchow was Xu Banhou, a nationalist of moderate political views, who became head of the Yongjia military government following the revolution (*GS*, p. 833).

48. Xiang Shiyuan *Zhejiang xinwen shi*, (p. 98) comments on Wenzhou's greater traditionalism especially as it related to the development of modern journalism and education. The influence of new ideas apparently becomes important only in the May Fourth period. *S*, 1920/3/6 and Huang Qinglu, *OG*, 1:137–140, 160 provide examples.

Yongjia county was a less developed inner-core county; in fact, by the mid-1920s, it reportedly was being challenged for economic leadership in the area by Ruian (*CEB*, 9 [November 6, 1926]: 278).

49. *Shina*, pp. 310–313.

50. Both counties had prerevolution associations and established modern newspapers in the early Republic, Xiang, *Zhejiang xinwen shi*, pp. 79–80.

51. *S*, 1920/5/26.

52. *DC*, p. 77; Ge Suicheng, *Zhejiang* (Shanghai, 1939), pp. 63–65.

53. Ge Jingen, "Xinhai geming," p. 106; Fei Jingzhong, *Dangdai mingren xiaozhuan* (Shanghai, 1926), p. 136. For an excellent summary of important traditional Chinese connections, see Nathan, *Peking Politics*, pp. 47–58.

54. *S*, 1912/6/19; 8/19; and 8/20.

55. *NCH*, 1913/6/7, p. 705.

56. *S*, 1919/8/26.

57. *S*, 1919/7/30.

58. *S*, 1918/1/23. Investigations revealed the use of a number of fraudulent techniques. Many of the electorate in forty-eight counties did not have proper educational or economic qualifications; in certain places dead men were registered. In Taishun county, in the outer periphery of Wenzhou, the registered number was originally over sixty-seven thousand whereas the actual electors should have been only about twenty-four thousand (*S*, 1918/3/6, 6/9 and 11).

59. Except, that is, as objects of inner-core mining entrepreneurs.

60. In the early 1930s, these three prefectures had an overall population of 3,319,461 compared with Taizhou's 2,266,899. According to Taizhou's proportion of the total population (which is only suggestive of what representation should have been), it should have had between eighteen and twenty representatives.

61. *S*, 1918/6/15. The phrase is Nathan's, *Peking Politics*, p. 97.

62. Nathan, *Peking Politics*, pp. 97–103.

63. *S*, 1918/10/14.

64. *S*, 1918/10/27, 30.

65. For the elections, *S*, 1918/11/3 and 10; for the Chenglu Club, *S*, 1918/11/28 and 12/4.

66. Jiang stated that he had spoken in Beijing with the respected official and former diplomat Sun Baoqi, a native of Hangchow, who urged the establishment of a political party without ties to national politics.

67. *S*, 1918/11/28 and 12/4.

68. *S*, 1919/4/29.

69. *S,* 1919/5/10, 15-16, 23, 25, and 28; 1920/6/11, 14, 30; 7/1, 3, 5, 27; 1925/1/7.

70. Joseph Esherick has contended that many Qing assemblymen in Hunan and Hubei were probably permanent residents of the provincial capitals rather than of counties from which they were elected. Whether Esherick's hypothesis applies to Zhejiang's Qing assembly is difficult to say; it does not apparently apply to the second and third RPAs. Esherick, *Reform and Revolution in China,* p. 101.

71. *S,* 1918/4/13, 6/15; 1923/12/23.

72. *S,* 1924/9/28. At least three of the fewer than forty represented Hang county in the assembly.

73. This material is scattered throughout the years 1918-1920 and 1923-1926. See, for example, *S,* 1918/12/22; 1919/5/3; 1920/6/3; 10/16; 1923/12/23 and for the Shaoxing incident, see *S,* 1924/5/17.

Much of the later assemblies' local and provincial concerns may well have come from distaste for what was occurring on the national scene.

74. Charles Tilly has described how political development brings new themes to older local rivalries (*The Vendée,* p. 64). See also Henry Teune's assertion that "non-political factors dominate the behavior of local units under conditions of low development, but with ... developmental change, macro-political factors, including the values of political leaders, will emerge [on the local scene]." See "The Developmental Ecology of Political Intervention," p. 158.

75. For these local political factions, see *S,* 1918/7/17 (Hang); Xiang, *Zhejiang xinwen shi,* pp. 88-90, 97-100 (Pinghu, Zhuji, and Linhai); *SB,* 1925/9/8 (Yongjia, Yiwu, Yongkang, Taishun, and Changhua); *Xiaofeng zhigao,* p. 126 (Xiaofeng). At least Pinghu, Zhuji, Linhai, and Xiaofeng had faction-sponsored newspapers.

76. *S,* 1918/8/21.

77. *S,* 1919/6/9 and 9/17.

78. *S,* 1920/7/26.

79. *S,* 1919/11/17. The title was the *Two Zhejiangs Daily* (*LiangZhe ribao*), explicitly pointing to the traditional twofold provincial division. Xiang, *Zhejiang xinwen shi* (p. 85), says that the paper was called the "news" (*xinwen*) rather than the "daily" (*ribao*).

80. *S,* 1920/11/8.

81. *S,* 1920/5/21.

82. The Taizhou group had become tied to the project through its connection to Yun Shao, the provincial industrial commissioner whom they successfully defended against impeachment by Jin-Qu-Yan and HJHNS bloc elites (*S,* 1920/5/18, 31; 7/27; 10/9; 11/2, 17; and 12/4, 7). The project, to be controlled by returned and returning overseas Chinese (*huaqiao*), upset inner-core elites who believed that extraprovincials were being treated with partiality (*S,* 1920/5/31). See also Ruan Xingcun, "Ruan Xingcun yigao," 5:22-24 in *Ruan Xunbo xiansheng yiji,* ed. Ruan Yicheng, vol. 1 (Taibei, 1970). Despite gaining a favorable charter, the interest of the overseas Chinese never translated itself into practice. For the charter, see *S,* 1920/11/4, 18 and 23. For subsequent attempts to revive it,

see *S*, 1923/10/18; *S*, 1925/3/17; 1926/12/16; and *CEB*, 19 (July–December 1931): 214.

83. Xiang, *Zhejiang xinwen shi*, pp. 88–89.

84. The man was Qin Binghan of Jiaxing, who was a leader in the Chenglu Club.

85. Although the substantial coalitional membership whose native place cannot be determined (twenty-four of the Peace Society and twenty-one of the Weekly Association) may in reality indicate greater factional identification with prefectures than the listed statistics could suggest, my conclusions, I believe, would not ultimately be affected.

At least 66 percent of the assembly belonged to a faction, with the number almost evenly divided between the factions. The members of each faction are garnered from the day-by-day reading of *S*, from July 1923 until mid-1925.

86. *S*, 1923/11/21.

87. *S*, 1923/11/25 and 1924/5/8.

12. The Emergence of Outer-Zone Elites in Provincial Politics

1. *S*, 1919/5/13.

2. *S*, 1918/11/17 reveals action by these elites but no mention of the organization. Sources indicate that a meeting in October 1920 was the fourteenth association meeting. The association convened twice annually, in the spring and fall, for regular meetings; but there is evidence that there were frequent other meetings, coming as closely as every other month in 1920. See *S*, 1920/10/31; 1920/10–12 for meetings. See also spring meeting, 1920/5/15.

3. Yang Zuochang, *Yu-Hang jilüe, xia* juan, 9a.

4. In Shanghai, of course, there was the well-known joint Ning-Shao native place association. See chap. 3.

5. *S*, 1913/7/6. Although continually dogged by funding problems and the formation of personal cliques, the council, many of whose leaders were provincial assembly members, remained a significant organization in Hangchow affairs into the mid-1920s. Its two major projects, the dredging of Lake Tai and of South Lake (Nanhu) in Yuhang county, took substantial specialized engineering expertise and organization and required additional funding. See, for example, *S*, 1917/7/20, 8/11, 12/7; 1918/9/29; 1920/5/18; 1923/7/15, 10/21; 1924/1/12, 18, 30; 2/16, 18, 19; 3/11 and 11/25.

6. *S*, 1917/12/26 and 1918/1/6.

7. *S*, 1917/12/26 and 1918/8/20.

8. *S*, 1917/12/7 and 1918/4/22. This convoluted method of allocation frequently brought local protest. In May 1920, elites from the market center of Nanxun in Wuxing county threatened to collect conservancy taxes and use the money themselves instead of turning it over to Hangchow. Their ire came when the town's river needed dredging; but Hangchow's response was that all conservancy association funds were already depleted for the year (*S*, 1920/5/18).

9. See Lin Chuanjia, *Da Zhonghua Zhejiang*, pp. 278, 280; *S*, 1920/7/16.

10. *S*, 1918/4/22 and 1920/7/16.

11. *S*, 1920/12/4.

12. *S*, 1920/6/2.

13. *S*, 1920/12/9.

14. *S*, 1920/12/13.

15. See, for example, *S*, 1923/12/21 and 1925/5/23.

16. *S*, 1923/12/14–15, 27.

17. *S*, 1924/6/9.

18. *S*, 1924/7/6.

19. *S*, 1919/11/17. There were eighteen signers altogether.

20. *S*, 1923/11/2.

21. *S*, 1924/5/1 and 19.

22. Schoppa, "Province and Nation."

23. *S*, 1923/12/20. The opponents of a new attempt contended that the Hunan constitution had not saved that province from suffering military takeover.

24. Regulations for the 1921 convention, set down by the provincial assembly, had originally excluded professional associations, which had been most vociferously opposed to the assembly. Instead, the convention was to include only fifty-five assemblymen and one nominated per county. In the early summer, the federation of professional associations began an intense campaign to be included. Two weeks into its sessions, the original 130-man convention agreed that associations from each former prefecture could name seven representatives for a total of seventy-seven, a surprisingly high total and therefore an immense concession to association pressure. Ruan Yicheng, *Zheng Yan* (Taibei, 1955), p. 6. The episode had underlined the increasing political power of these associations.

25. Ruan, *Zheng Yan*, p. 15.

26. Details of composition are included on Table 17. Social and functional backgrounds can be determined for 96 (64.4 percent) of the 149 members. Of these 96, 17.7 percent (17) held traditional degrees and 30.2 percent (29) were modern-school graduates. Fully 26 percent (25) had served in an official post either in or outside Zhejiang during their careers. Eight of the Qing provincial assembly members were representatives—more than in any Republican assembly. Thirty-five (23.5 percent of the total 149) had served in one or more of the four Republican assemblies. The percentages of new professional elite representatives were comparable to those of the third RPA. Women also attended the convention, but there is no indication of the number.

27. *S*, 1924/8/3. Provincial assembly cliques, the Peace Society and Weekly Association, hosted the welcoming of the convention representatives. Notably, the main speaker, Lin Muxiu of the Weekly Association, was from Jinhua (*S*, 1924/8/6).

28. *S*, 1924/8/7 and 12.

29. *S*, 1924/8/9 and 23.

30. *S*, 1924/8/18 and 21. The following arguments in the text are from this source.

31. *S*, 1924/8/21.

32. This argument is a modification of my *JAS* article (1977). The zonal classification has allowed me to trace the spokesmen of the positions and to put in proper perspective the arguments that they made. In cases, the surface provincialist thrust is misleading; for when one sees that inner-core elites were making

the strongest arguments for autonomy, the complex of inner-core ideals must be brought into play for a proper interpretation.

33. *S*, 1924/10/1.

34. Tung, *The Political Institutions of Modern China*, pp. 70–72 and 341.

35. The third Zhejiang constitution, promulgated on January 1, 1926, is in *DZ*, 22 (January 25, 1926): 129–138.

36. *S*, 1924/8/14, 24 and 30.

37. *S*, 1924/9/4.

38. The 1926 draft produced a substantial local elite victory: it vested all local power in the hands of a county assembly and five self-government deputies chosen by that assembly. The magistrate and executive board were to be ousted; the civil governor could no longer name leaders. See *DZ*, 22 (January 25, 1926): 135–136.

39. Article 5, Section 55 states the details: if more than one thousand of the electorate in each of at least 10 percent of the counties supported a proposal, it could be sent to the provincial assembly. If the assembly could not agree, the civil governor could send the matter to county and special municipal assemblies. If more than half agreed, the civil governor could declare it in effect. See *DZ*, 22 (January 25, 1926): 131. Also see Ruan, *Zheng Yan*, p. 15.

40. *S*, 1924/4/24. For biographical information on Shen Dingyi, see Gu Shijiang, *Xiaoshan xiangtu zhi* (n.p., 1933), pp. 101–103; Chang Kuo-t'ao, *The Rise of the Chinese Communist Party, 1921–1927* (Lawrence, Kansas, 1971), vol. 1, pp. 103–104, 108, 128, and 342–343; Chow Tse-tung, *The May Fourth Movement* (Stanford, 1967), pp. 248–249, 306, 321–322, and fn. a on 343; and Xiang, *Zhejiang xinwen shi*, pp. 91–93.

41. Xiang, *Zhejiang xinwen shi*, pp. 98–99 and 124. In Shaoxing by late 1925, the Guomindang bureau was playing an active political role (*S*, 1925/12/29).

42. *SB*, 1926/3/12.

43. *Shouchang X*, 4:12b–13a and *Suian X*, p. 229.

44. For the establishment of the office by Shen, see Xiang, *Zhejiang xinwen shi*, pp. 98–99. For the Consultative Society see *S*, 1916/12/1 and 5; 1917/4/24, 5/16 and 22; *ZX*, 1917/4/20; for the hostile reception by local elites, see chap. 5.

45. Chang Kuo-t'ao notes that a Socialist Youth corps unit was formed in Hangchow in October 1920, one month after formation of such a unit in Shanghai. Members included some of the 1926 elected left-wing leaders. Chang, *Rise of the Chinese Communist Party*, vol. 1, p. 128. It should be noted that Shen Dingyi was involved in early Communist party activity, but he moved to the right by 1924.

46. Xiang, *Zhejiang xinwen shi*, pp. 98–99.

47. *S*, 1926/10/21, 27 and 28.

48. *S*, 1924/4/20 and 5/15.

49. *S*, 1924/7/6.

50. *S*, 1924/5/2.

51. *Shouchang X*, 4:12b.

52. *Xuanping X*, vol. 2, p. 551.

53. *Xuanping X*, vol. 2, pp. 551, 621, 824, 834.

54. It is also unclear whether the description of a "union" of Dongyang work-

ers in Huzhou in 1925 refers to the Workers' Association branch or to a differently structured union (*CEB*, 7 [October 17, 1925]:226).

55. Jean Chesneaux, *The Chinese Labor Movement, 1919–1927* (Stanford, 1968), pp. 364–366.

56. Xiang, *Zhejiang xinwen shi*, p. 154.

57. The registration of the Dongyang workers' native place association, around which the Workers' Association was structured, had been rejected by the party's Workers' Bureau. Presumably this rejection came because of its control by employers. Because of this rejection, it needed little prodding to join the movement.

58. Xiang, *Zhejiang xinwen shi*, p. 165; *S*, 1927/4/1–2, 6.

59. *ZY*, 8 (September 6, 1976): 6.

60. See *S*, 1927/4/1–2, 6, 11, 13, and 17.

61. *S*, 1927/4/17–5/16 passim; see for Xu, *Who's Who in China* (Shanghai, 1936), p. 97.

62. An example of the kind of local reform-minded elite who was expelled from the circles of leadership was Song Yunpin of Xiashi in Haining, a left-wing Guomindang member and member of Haining's county assembly in the early 1920s. He was purged in April 1927. See Xiang, *Zhejiang xinwen shi*, p. 123.

63. For an interpretation of the post-1927 years, see Lloyd Eastman, *The Abortive Revolution* (Cambridge, Mass., 1974).

Conclusion

1. For a theoretical view of development and social structure, see the essay by Carol A. Smith, "Exchange Systems and the Spatial Distribution of Elites: The Organization of Stratification in Agrarian Societies" in Smith, ed., *Regional Analysis*, vol. 2: *Social Systems*, pp. 309–370.

2. Immanuel Wallerstein, *The Modern World-System* (New York, 1976); Michael Hechter, *Internal Colonialism: The Celtic Fringe in British National Development 1536–1966* (Berkeley, 1975). See also the discussion of these issues in Carol A. Smith, "Regional Economic Systems: Linking Geographical Models and Socioeconomic Problems" in Smith, ed., *Regional Analysis*, vol. 1: *Economic Systems*, pp. 51–58.

Appendix A. The Units of Analysis

1. Marwyn S. Samuels, "Review Article: *The City in Late Imperial China*," *Journal of Asian Studies*, 37 (August 1978): 713–723.

Appendix C. Methodological and Source-Related Problems

1. The counties involved were Zhenhai, Deqing, Yuyao, Qu, and Xiangshan and the market towns (in other counties) of Puyuan, Shuanglin, Xincheng, and Wu-Qing.

2. The counties involved were Lishui, Xuanping, Shouchang, Xindeng, Suian, Songyang, Tangqi, and Changhua.

3. *Xiangshan X, shou* juan: 2b; 14:38a; see also *S*, 1913/12/23.

4. *Qu X*, 23:63b–64a.

5. *Xinchang X, tongju timing:* 3a; 5:62b.

Bibliography

Major collections, including *Xinhai geming*, *Xinhai geming huiyilu*, *Geming renwu zhi*, *Geming wenxian*, and *Gesheng guangfu*, are entered alphabetically by title rather than by compiler or editor for the reader's convenience. In addition, collections of the Zhongguo Guomindang zhongyang weiyuanhui dangshi shiliao bianzuan weiyuanhui 中国国民党中央委員会党史史料編纂委員会 (Party Archives Commission of the Guomindang under the Guomindang Central Committee) will be listed as published or compiled by the Dangshi hui 党史会 for the sake of brevity.

Alapuro, Risto. "Statemaking and Political Ecology in Finland." In *The Social Ecology of Change*, ed. Zdravko Mlinar and Henry Teune. Beverly Hills, Calif.: Sage Publications, 1978.

Baoding junxiao tongxunlu 保定軍校通訊錄 (Graduates of the Baoding Military Academy). 1922.

Bastid, Marianne. "The Social Context of Reform." In *Reform in Nineteenth Century China*, ed. Paul Cohen and John Schrecker. Cambridge, Mass.: Harvard University Press, 1976.

Beattie, Hilary. *Land and Lineage in China*. Cambridge: Cambridge University Press, 1979.

Bergère, Marie-Claire. *La bourgeoisie chinoise et la revolution de 1911*. Paris: Mouton and Co., 1968.

——— "The Role of the Bourgeoisie." In *China in Revolution: The First Phase, 1900–1913*, ed. Mary Wright. New Haven, Conn.: Yale University Press, 1968.

Boorman, Howard L., ed. *Biographical Dictionary of Republican China*. 4 vols. New York: Columbia University Press, 1970.

Broomhall, Marshall, ed. *The Chinese Empire: A General and Missionary Survey*. London: Morgan and Scott, 1907.

Brunnert, H. H. and V. V. Hagelstrom. *Present Day Political Organization of China*. Shanghai: Kelly and Walsh, 1912.

Cao Juren 曹聚仁. *Wo yu wode shijie* 我與我的世界 (My world and I). Hong Kong, 1971.

Cartier, Michael. *Une reforme locale en Chine au XVIe siècle: Hai Jui à Ch'ün-an, 1558–1562.* Paris: Mouton and Co., 1973.

Chan, Wellington K. K. *Merchants, Mandarins, and Modern Enterprise in Late Ch'ing China.* Cambridge, Mass.: Harvard University Press, 1977.

Chang Chung-li. *The Income of the Chinese Gentry.* Seattle: University of Washington Press, 1962.

Chang Hao. *Liang Ch'i-ch'ao and Intellectual Transition in China.* Cambridge, Mass.: Harvard University Press, 1971.

Chang Kuo-t'ao. *The Rise of the Chinese Communist Party, 1921–1927.* 2 vols. Lawrence, Kan.: University of Kansas Press, 1971.

Changhua xianzhi 昌化縣志 (Gazetteer of Changhua County). 1924.

"Chen Jieshi xiansheng nianpu" 陳介石先生年譜 (A chronological biography of Chen Fuchen). In *Oufeng zazhi*, no. 6.

Chen Shouyong 陳守庸. "Wenzhou xiangying Wuchang qiyi de qinshen jingli" 溫州響應武昌起義的親身經歷 (Personal experiences during the response to the Wuchang uprising in Wenzhou). In *Xinhai geming huiyilu*, vol. 4, pp. 183–187.

Chen Xieshu 陳燮樞. "Shaoxing guangfu shi jianwen" 紹興光復時見聞 (Experiences at the time of the revolution in Shaoxing). In *Jindai shi ziliao*, 1958, vol. 1, pp. 105–108.

Chen Xunzheng 陳訓正, comp. *Yinxian tongzhi renwu bian* 鄞縣通志人物編 (A biographical compendium from Yin county). 1934.

Cheng xianzhi 嵊縣志 (Gazetteer of Cheng county). 1934.

Chesneaux, Jean. *The Chinese Labor Movement, 1919–1927.* Stanford: Stanford University Press, 1968.

Chi, Madeleine. "Shanghai-Hangchow-Ningpo Railway Loan: A Case Study of the Rights Recovery Movement." *Modern Asian Studies*, 7 (January 1973): 85–106.

Ch'i Hsi-sheng. *Warlord Politics in China, 1916–1928.* Stanford: Stanford University Press, 1976.

Chiang Monlin. *Tides from the West.* New Haven: Yale University Press, 1947.

Chow Tse-tsung. *The May Fourth Movement.* Stanford: Stanford University Press, 1960.

Chu Fucheng 褚輔成. "Zhejiang xinhai geming jishi" 浙江辛亥革命紀實 (An account of the 1911 revolution in Zhejiang). *Gesheng guangfu*, vol. 2, pp. 114–121.

Ch'u T'ung-tsu. *Local Government in China under the Ch'ing.* Cambridge, Mass.: Harvard University Press, 1962.

Cole, James H. "Shaohsing: Studies in Ch'ing Social History." Ph. D. diss., Stanford University, 1975.

"Comments from Authors Reviewed." *Modern China*, 2 (April 1976): 185–220.

Cressey, George B. "The Land Forms of Chekiang, China." *Annals of the Association of American Geographers*, 28 (1938): 259–276.

Crissman, Lawrence W. "Specific Central-Place Models for an Evolving System of Market Towns on the Changhua Plain, Taiwan." In *Regional Analysis*, vol. 1, *Economic Systems*, ed. Carol A. Smith. New York: Academic Press, 1976.

Dahl, Robert A. "Power." In the *International Encyclopedia of the Social Sciences*. New York: Macmillan, 1968.

Daishan zhenzhi 岱山鎮志 (A gazetteer of Daishan town). 1919.

Day, Clarence Burton. *Hangchow University*. New York: United Board for Christian Colleges in China, 1955.

Decennial Reports, 1912–1921. Shanghai: Inspectorate General of the Maritime Customs, 1921.

Deqing xianzhi 德清縣志 (Gazetteer of Deqing county). 1923. Reprint, Taibei, 1970.

Dinghai xianzhi 定海縣志 (Gazetteer of Dinghai county). 1924.

"Directory of American Returned Students." *Who's Who in China*, 3rd ed. Shanghai: The China Weekly Review, 1925.

Dongfang zazhi 東方雜誌 (The Eastern Miscellany). Shanghai, 1904–1927.

Eastman, Lloyd. *The Abortive Revolution*. Cambridge, Mass.: Harvard University Press, 1974.

Edinger, Lewis J. "The Comparative Analysis of Political Leadership." *Comparative Politics*, 7 (January 1975): 253–269.

"Editorial Foreword." *Comparative Studies in Society and History*, 20 (April 1978): 175–176.

Eisenstadt, S. N. "Political Modernization: Some Comparative Notes." *International Journal of Comparative Sociology*, 7 (March 1964): 3–24.

Elvin, Mark. "Market Towns and Waterways: The County of Shanghai from 1480 to 1910." In *The City in Late Imperial China*, ed. G. William Skinner. Stanford: Stanford University Press, 1977.

Esherick, Joseph W. "1911: A Review." *Modern China*, 2 (April 1976): 141–184.

——— *Reform and Revolution in China*. Berkeley: University of California Press, 1976.

Fang Zhaoying 房兆楹. *Qingmo minchu yangxue xuesheng timinglu chuji* 清末民初洋學學生題名錄初輯 (A preliminary summary of Chinese students abroad during the late Qing and early Republic). Taibei, 1962.

Fei Guxiang 費穀祥. "Zhexi zhiming gaiguang ji jinxing fangzhen" 浙西治螟概況及進行方針 (A description of Northern Zhejiang's insect control and movement toward progress). *Zhonghua nongxuehui bao*, 15 (March 1926): 13–27.

Fei Jingzhong 費敬仲 (Pseud. Wuqiu zhongzi 沃丘仲子). *Dangdai mingren xiaozhuan* 當代名人小傳 (Brief biographies of contemporary famous men). 2 vols. Shanghai, 1926. Reprint, Hong Kong, 1973.

Fenghua xianzhi 奉化縣志 (Gazetteer of Fenghua country). 1908.

Feuerwerker, Albert. *China's Early Industrialization*. Cambridge, Mass.: Harvard University Press, 1958.

Fincher, John. "The Chinese Self-Government Movement, 1900–1912." Ph. D. diss., University of Washington, 1969.

——— "Land Tenure in China: Preliminary Evidence from a 1930s Kwangtung Hillside." *Ch'ing-shih wen-t'i*, 3 (November 1978): 69–81.

Freedman, Maurice. "Introduction." In *Family and Kinship in Chinese Society*, ed. Maurice Freedman. Stanford: Stanford University Press, 1970.

Friedman, Edward. *Backward toward Revolution*. Berkeley: University of

California Press, 1974.

Fujii Masao 藤井正夫. "Shinmatsu Kōsetsu ni okeru tetsudō mondai to burujawa seiryoku no ichi sokumen" 清末江浙における鐵路問題とブルジョア勢力の一側面 (One aspect of bourgeois power and the question of the Jiangsu-Zhejiang railroad in the late Qing). *Rekishigaku kenkyū*, 183 (1955): 22–30.

Gallin, Bernard and Rita S. Gallin. "The Integration of Village Migrants in Taipei." In *The Chinese City between Two Worlds*, ed. Mark Elvin and G. William Skinner. Stanford: Stanford University Press, 1974.

Ganzhi fulu 澉誌補錄 (A continuation of the Ganpu town gazetteer). 1935.

Gao Yuetian 高越天. "Shen Dingyi xianshengde yisheng" 沈定一先生的一生 (The life of Shen Dingyi). *Zhejiang yuekan*, 4, no. 3 (1972): 5–8 and ibid., 4, no. 4 (1972): 8–13.

Garrett, Shirley S. "The Chambers of Commerce and the YMCA." In *The Chinese City between Two Worlds*, ed. Mark Elvin and G. William Skinner. Stanford: Stanford University Press, 1974.

Ge Jingen 葛敬恩. "Xinhai geming zai Zhejiang" 辛亥革命在浙江 (The 1911 revolution in Zhejiang). In *Xinhai geming huiyilu*, vol. 4, pp. 91–126.

Ge Suicheng 葛綏成. *Zhejiang* 浙江. Shanghai, 1939.

Geertz, Clifford. "The Integrative Revolution." In *Old Societies and New States*, ed. Clifford Geertz. New York: Free Press, 1963.

Geming renwu zhi 革命人物誌 (Records of revolutionary personalities). Ed. Dangshi hui. Taibei, 1969– .

Geming wenxian 革命文献 (Documents on the revolution). Ed. Dangshi hui. Taibei, 1953– .

Gendai Shina jimmeikan 現代支那人名鑑 (Biographical dictionary of contemporary Chinese), comp. Gaimushō jōhōbu 外務省情報部 (Public Information Bureau, Ministry of Foreign Affairs). Tokyo, 1928.

Gendai Shina jimmeiroku 現代支那人名錄 (Biographical directory of contemporary Chinese), comp. Gaimushō jōhōbu 外務省情報部 (Public Information Bureau, Ministry of Foreign Affairs). November 1912, SP 47. Microfilmed archives of the Japanese Ministry of Foreign Affairs, Library of Congress, Washington, D.C. Reel SP 10, pp. 89–543 passim.

Gesheng guangfu 各省光復 (The revolution in the provinces). In *Zhonghua minguo kaiguo wushinian wenxian* 中華民国開国五十年文献 (Documents on the fiftieth anniversary of the founding of the Republic of China). Ed. Zhonghua minguo kaiguo wushinian wenxian bianzuan weiyuanhui 中華民国開国五十年文献編纂委員会 (Committee on the compilation of documents on the fiftieth anniversary of the founding of the Republic). 3 vols. Taibei, 1962.

Golas, Peter. "Early Ch'ing Guilds." In *The City in Late Imperial China*, ed. G. William Skinner. Stanford: Stanford University Press, 1977.

Gu Shijiang 顧士江. *Xiaoshan xiangtu zhi* 蕭山鄉土誌 (A gazetteer of Xiaoshan). 1933.

Guan Weilan, comp. 官蔚藍. *Zhonghua minguo xingzheng quhua ji tudi renkou tongji biao* 中華民国行政區劃及土地人口統計表 (Statistical tables of population by administrative division and land area). Taibei, 1956.

Guoli Beijing daxue jiniankan 国立北京大學紀念刊 (A commemorative publication for National Beijing University). 2 vols. 1917. Reprint, Taibei, 1971.

Haining zhou zhigao 海寧州志稿 (Draft gazetteer of Haining zhou). 1917.

Hammack, David C. "Problems in the Historical Study of Power in the Cities and Towns of the United States, 1800–1960." *American Historical Review*, 83 (April 1978): 323–349.

Hang xian lüshi gonghui baogao lu 杭縣律師公會報告錄 (Reports of the Hang county lawyers' association). 1919.

Hangzhou fuzhi 杭州府志 (Gazetteer of Hangzhou prefecture). 1911.

Hao Yen-p'ing. *The Comprador in Nineteenth Century China*. Cambridge, Mass.: Harvard University Press, 1970.

Hatano Yoshihiro 波多野善大. "Shingai kakumei chokuzen ni okeru nōmin ikki" 辛亥革命直前に於ける農民一揆 (Peasant uprisings in the years prior to the 1911 revolution). *Tōyōshi kenkyū*, 13, no. 1–2 (1954): 77–106.

He Bingsong 何炳松. "Zhejiang xiaoxue jiaoyude xian guang ji qi zuiren" 浙江小學教育的現狀及其罪人 (Elementary education in Zhejiang and its detractors). *Jiaoyu zazhi*, 16 (September 1924): 1–6.

Heaphey, James J. "Spatial Aspects of Development Administration." In *Spatial Dimensions of Development Administration*, ed. James J. Heaphey. Durham, N.C.: Duke University Press, 1971.

Hechter, Michael. *Internal Colonialism: The Celtic Fringe in British National Development, 1536–1966*. Berkeley: University of California Press, 1975.

Heeger, Gerald A. "The Politics of Integration: Community, Party, and Integration in Punjab." Ph. D. diss., University of Chicago, 1971.

——— *The Politics of Underdevelopment*. New York: St. Martin's Press, 1974.

Ho Ping-ti 何炳棣. *Studies on the Population of China, 1368–1953*. Cambridge, Mass.: Harvard University Press, 1959.

———*Zhungguo huiguan shilun* 中国會舘史論 (A historical survey of *Landsmannschaften* in China). Taibei, 1966.

Hua Lu 化魯. "Difang zizhi yu xiangcun yundong" 地方自治與鄉村運動 (Local self-government and the village movement). *Dongfang zazhi*, 19 (March 25, 1922): 1–2.

Ichiko Chūzō 市古宙三. "The Role of the Gentry: An Hypothesis." In *China in Revolution: The First Phase, 1900–1913*, ed. Mary Wright. New Haven, Conn.: Yale University Press, 1968.

——— *Kindai Chūgoku no seiji to shakai* 近代中国の政治と社会 (Modern Chinese government and society). Tokyo, 1971.

——— "Kyōshin to Shingai kakumei" 鄉紳と辛亥革命 (Rural elite and the revolution of 1911). In *Kindai Chūgoku no seiji to shakai*, pp. 331–360.

Jiande xianzhi 建德縣志 (Gazetteer of Jiande county). 1919.

Jiang Tianwei 江天蔚. "Xinhai geming hou Songyang de yici jianbian douzheng" 辛亥革命後松陽的一次剪辮闘爭 (A fight over queue-cutting in Songyang after the 1911 revolution). In *Xinhai geming huiyilu*, vol. 4, pp. 203–204.

Jianshe weiyuanhui diaocha Zhejiang jingji suo 建設委員會調查浙江經濟所 (Office of the reconstruction commission to investigate Zhejiang's economy), comp. *Hangzhou shi jingji diaocha* 杭州市經濟調查 (An investigation of the economy in the municipality of Hangchow). 2 vols. Hangchow, 1932. Reprint,

Taipei, 1971.

Jiaxing xinzhi 嘉興新志 (A new gazetteer of Jiaxing county). 1929. Reprint, Taibei, 1970.

Jindai shi ziliao 近代史資料 (Materials on modern Chinese history). Compiled by Zhongguo kexue yuan lishi yanjiusuo disan suo 中国科學院歷史研究所第三所 (The third bureau of the history research bureau of the Chinese Academy of Science). Beijing, 1954–1961.

Jingning xianxuzhi 景寧縣續志 (Continuation of the gazetteer of Jingning county). 1933. Reprint, Taibei, 1970.

Jones, Susan Mann. "The Ningpo *Pang* and Financial Power at Shanghai." In *The Chinese City between Two Worlds*, ed. Mark Elvin and G. William Skinner. Stanford: Stanford University Press, 1974.

Jones, Susan M. and Philip A. Kuhn. "Dynastic Decline and the Roots of Rebellion." In *The Cambridge History of China*, vol. 10, *Late Ch'ing, 1800–1911, Part 1*, ed. John K. Fairbank. Cambridge University Press, 1978.

Kenworthy, Eldon, "Coalitions in the Political Development of Latin America." In *The Study of Coalitional Behavior*, ed. Sven Groennings, E. W. Kelley, and Michael Leiserson. New York: Holt, Rinehart, and Winston, 1970.

Kojima Yoshio 小島淑男. "Shinmatsu minkoku shoki ni okeru Sekkō shō Kakō fu shūhen no nōson shakai" 清末民国初期における浙江省嘉興府周遊の農村運動 (The rural society in the vicinity of Jiaxing prefecture, Zhejiang province in the late Qing and early Republic). In Tokyo Kyōiku Daigaku Tōyōshi Kenkyūshitsu 東京教育大學東洋史研究室 (Tokyo Education University Oriental Seminar), ed. *Yamazaki Sensei Taikan Kinen Tōyōshigaku Ronshū* 山崎先生浪官記念東洋史學論集 (Oriental Seminar essays in commemoration of Professor Yamazaki). Tokyo, 1966.

——— "Shinmatsu minkoku shoki Kōnan no nōmin undō" 清末民国初期江南の農民運動 (The peasant movement in Jiangnan in the late Qing and early Republic). *Rekishi kyōiku*, 16, no. 1.2 (1968): 116–124.

Kuhn, Philip A. *Rebellion and Its Enemies in Late Imperial China*. Cambridge, Mass.: Harvard University Press, 1970.

——— "Local Self-Government under the Republic: Problems of Control, Autonomy, and Mobilization." In *Conflict and Control in Late Imperial China*, ed. Frederic Wakeman, Jr. and Carolyn Grant. Berkeley: University of California Press, 1975.

Lai Weiliang 來偉良. "Zhejun guangfu Hangzhou he chiyuan Nanjing qinli ji" 浙軍光復杭州和馳援南京親歷記 (A personal account of the Zhejiang army at Hangchow in the 1911 revolution and the rapid assistance at Nanjing). In *Xinhai geming huiyilu*, vol. 4, pp. 152–160.

Levy, Marion J. Jr. "Patterns (Structures) of Modernization and Political Development." *Annals of the American Academy of Political and Social Science*, 358 (March 1965): 30–40.

Lewis, Charlton M. *Prologue to the Chinese Revolution*. Cambridge, Mass.: Harvard University Press, 1976.

Li Chien-nung. *The Political History of China, 1840–1928*, trans. Teng Ssu-yu and Jeremy Ingalls. Princeton, N. J.: Van Nostrand, 1956.

Li, Lillian. "Kiangnan and the Silk Export Trade, 1842–1937." Ph. D. diss., Harvard University, 1975.

Liddle, William R. *Ethnicity, Party, and National Integration.* New Haven: Yale University Press, 1970.

Lin Chuanjia 林傳甲. *Da Zhonghua Zhejiang sheng dili zhi* 大中華浙江省地理志 (A gazetteer of Zhejiang province). Shanghai, 1918.

Lin Duanfu 林端輔. "Ningpo guangfu qinli ji" 寧波光復親歷記 (A personal account of the revolution in Ningpo). In *Xinhai geming huiyilu*, vol. 4, pp. 174–182.

Linan xianzhi 臨安縣志 (Gazetteer of Linan county). 1910.

Ling Songru 凌頌如. *Hushe cangsang lu* 湖社滄桑錄 (A record of major changes in the Huzhou society). Taibei, 1969.

Linhai xianzhi 臨海縣志 (Gazetteer of Linhai county). 1935.

Linz, Juan J. and DeMiguel Amando. "Within-Nation Differences and Comparisons: The Eight Spains." In *Comparing Nations: The Use of Quantitative Data in Cross-National Research*, ed. Richard Merritt and Stein Rokkan. New Haven: Yale University Press, 1966.

Lishui xianzhi 麗水縣志 (Gazetteer of Lishui county). 1926.

Liu, Hui-chen Wang. *The Traditional Chinese Clan Rules.* Locust Valley, N.Y.: Association for Asian Studies, 1959.

Liu Kwang-ching. "Nineteenth-Century China: The Disintegration of the Old Order and the Impact of the West." In *China in Crisis*, ed. Ho Ping-ti and Tsou Tang. 2 vols. Chicago: University of Chicago Press, 1968.

Liu Shoulin 劉壽林. *Xinhai yihou shiqinian zhiguan nianbiao* 辛亥一後十七年職官年表 (A list of officials from 1912 to 1928). Beijing, 1966.

Longyu xianzhi 龍游縣志 (Gazetteer of Longyu county). 1925. Reprint, Taibei, 1970.

Luqiao zhilüe 路橋志略 (Annals of Luqiao). 1935.

Lü Gongwang 呂公望. "Xinhai geming Zhejiang guangfu jishi" 辛亥革命浙江光復紀實 (An account of the 1911 revolution in Zhejiang). In *Jindai shi ziliao*, 1954, vol. 1, pp. 114–117.

Lü Yueping 呂月屏. "Huiyi xinhai geming shiqide jijian shi he Chuzhou guangfu jingguo" 回憶辛亥革命時其的幾件事和處州光復經過 (Recollections of a few things in the period of the 1911 revolution and experiences during the revolution in Chuzhou). In *Xinhai geming huiyilu*, vol. 4, pp. 196–199.

Ma Jisheng 馬濟生 as told to Dong Sunguan 董巽觀. "Jiaxing guangfu jilüe" 嘉興光復記略 (A brief summary of the revolution in Jiaxing). In *Jindai shi ziliao*, 1958, vol. 2, pp. 67–68.

Ma Xulun 馬叙倫. "Tao Chengzhang zhi si" 陶成章之死 (The death of Tao Chengzhang). In *Xinhai geming*, vol. 1, p. 520.

——— "Guanyu xinhai geming Zhejiang shengcheng guangfu jishide buchong ziliao" 關於辛亥革命浙江省城光復記事的補充資料 (Supplementary material on the 1911 revolution in the provincial capital of Zhejiang). In *Jindai shi ziliao*, 1957, vol. 1, pp. 47–57.

——— "Wo zai xinhai zheyinian" 我在辛亥這一年 (My activities in 1911). In *Xinhai geming huiyilu*, vol. 1, pp. 170–179.

Mao Huhou 毛虎侯. "Xinhai geming zai Lishui" 辛亥革命在麗水 (The 1911 revolution in Lishui). In *Xinhai geming huiyilu*, vol. 4, pp. 200–202.

McDonald, Angus. *The Urban Origins of Rural Revolution*. Berkeley: University of California Press, 1978.

Meili beizhi 梅里備志 (A prepared gazetteer from Wangdian town [Jiaxing county]). 1922.

Minli Bao 民立報 (The People's Stand). Shanghai, 1911–1913. Reprint, Taibei, 1969.

Mlinar, Zdravko. "A Theoretical Transformation of Social Ecology: From Equilibrium to Development." In *The Social Ecology of Change*, ed. Zdravko Mlinar and Henry Teune. Beverly Hills, Calif.: Sage Publications, 1978.

Mlinar, Zdravko and Henry Teune, eds. *The Social Ecology of Change*. Beverly Hills, Calif.: Sage Publications, 1978.

———— "Theory, Methodology, Research, and Application: Assessment and Future Directions." In *The Social Ecology of Change*, ed. Mlinar and Teune. Beverly Hills, Calif.: Sage Publications, 1978.

Mobei 黑悲, ed. *Jiang-Zhe tielu fengzhao* 江浙鐵路風潮 (Agitation over the Jiangsu-Zhejiang railroad). Shanghai, 1907. Reprint, Taibei, 1958.

Muramatsu Yuji, "Shindai no shinshi-jinushi ni okeru tochi to Kanshoku: Sekkō-shō Ei-kō ken Go-shi shihi giden o megutte" 清代の紳士地主における土地と官職: 浙江省永康縣胡氏試費義田をめぐって (Land and office in the case of a Qing gentry-landlord: concerning the estate of the Hu lineage in Yongkang county, Zhejiang). *Hitotsubashi ronsō*, 44 (December 1960): 698–726.

———— "A Documentary Study of Chinese Landlordism in the late Ch'ing and early Republican Kiangnan." *Bulletin of the School of Oriental and African Studies*, 29, part 3 (1966): 566–599.

Murphey, Rhoads. *Shanghai: Key to Modern China*. Cambridge, Mass.: Harvard University Press, 1953.

Nakamura Tsune 中村恒. "Shinmatsu gakudō setsuritsu o meguru Kōsetsu nōson shakai no ichi danmen" 清末學當設立を回繞る江浙農村社会の一斷面 (The movement against the establishment of new schools in villages of Jiangsu and Zhejiang at the end of the Qing). *Rekishi kyōiku*, 10, no. 11 (1962): 72–85.

Nantian xianzhi 南田縣志 (Gazetteer of Nantian county). 1930. Reprint, Taibei, 1970.

Nantianshan zhi 南田山志 (Gazetteer of Nantianshan). 1935.

Nanxun zhi 南潯志 (Gazetteer of Nanxun city). 1922.

Nathan, Andrew J. *Peking Politics, 1918–1923*. Berkeley: University of California Press, 1976.

National Archives. United States Department of State. "Decimal File, 1910–1929: China, Internal Affairs." Microfilm publications, M-329.

"Ningbo guomin shangwu fenhui xunbao pianduan" 寧波國民伵武分会旬报片斷 (Selections from the newspaper of the Ningbo Citizens' Martial Society). In *Jindai shi ziliao*, 1961, vol. 1, pp. 543–548.

North China Herald and Supreme Court and Consular Gazette. Shanghai, 1907–1927.

Orb, Richard A. "Chihli Academies and Other Schools in the Late Ch'ing: An Institutional Survey." In *Reform in Nineteenth Century China*, ed. Paul Cohen and John Schrecker. Cambridge, Mass.: Harvard University Press, 1976.

Ouhai guanzheng lu 甌海觀政錄 (A record of governmental matters in Ouhai circuit) by Huang Qinglan 黃慶瀾. 1921. Reprint, Taibei, n.d.

Pan Guangdan 潘光旦. *Ming-Qing liangdai Jiaxing de wangzu* 明清兩代嘉興的 望族 (Notable lineages in Jiaxing during the Ming and Qing periods). Shanghai, 1947.

Pingyang xianzhi 平陽縣志 (Gazetteer of Pingyang county). 1925. Reprint, Taibei, 1970.

Playfair, G. M. H. *The Cities and Towns of China*, 2nd ed. Shanghai: Kelly and Walsh, 1910.

Potter, Jack M. "Land and Lineage in Traditional China." In *Family and Kinship in Chinese Society*, ed. Maurice Freedman. Stanford: Stanford University Press, 1970.

Putnam, Robert D. *The Comparative Study of Political Elites*. Englewood Cliffs, N.J.: Prentice Hall, 1976.

Puyuan zhi 濮院志 (Gazetteer of town of Puyuan). 1927.

Qiu Shouming 邱壽銘. "Huzhou guangfu huiyi" 湖州光復回憶 (Recollections of the restoration at Huzhou). In *Xinhai geming huiyilu*, vol. 4, pp. 167–169.

Qu xianzhi 衢縣志 (Gazetteer of Qu county). 1929.

Qu xunanshi xunshi liang Zhe wengao 屈巡按使巡視兩浙文告 (Reports of inspection trips of Civil Governor Qu through Zhejiang) by Qu Yingguang 屈映光. 4 juan.

Quanguo yinhang nianqian 全国銀行年鑑 (National banking yearbook). Shanghai, 1935.

Rankin, Mary Backus. "The Revolutionary Movement in Chekiang: A Study in the Tenacity of Tradition." In *China in Revolution: The First Phase, 1900–1913*, ed. Mary Wright. New Haven: Yale University Press, 1968.

——— *Early Chinese Revolutionaries, Radical Intellectuals in Shanghai and Chekiang, 1902–1911*. Cambridge, Mass.: Harvard University Press, 1971.

——— "Local Reform Currents in Chekiang before 1900." In *Reform in Nineteenth Century China*. ed. Paul Cohen and John Schrecker. Cambridge, Mass.: Harvard University Press, 1976.

——— "Rural-Urban Continuities: Leading Families of Two Chekiang Market Towns." *Ch'ing-shih wen-t'i*, 3 (November 1977): 67–104.

Returns of Trade and Trade Reports. Shanghai: Inspectorate General of the Maritime Customs, 1896–1927.

Rhoads, Edward J. M. "Merchant Associations in Canton, 1895–1911." In *The Chinese City between Two Worlds*, ed. Mark Elvin and G. William Skinner. Stanford: Stanford University Press, 1974.

——— *China's Republican Revolution*. Cambridge, Mass.: Harvard University Press, 1975.

Ruan Xingcun 阮性存. "Ruan Xingcun yigao" 阮性存遺稿 (A draft of the writings of Ruan Xincun). 4 juan. In *Ruan Xunbo xiansheng yiji* 阮荀伯先生遺集 (The works of Ruan Xunbo), ed. Ruan Yicheng 阮毅成. 2 vols. Taibei, 1970.

Ruan Yicheng 阮毅成. "Du Zhejiang zhixian shi" 讀浙江制憲史 (Studying a history of Zhejiang constitutions). *Shengliu banyuekan*, 4 (November 16, 1946).
—— *Zheng Yan* 政言 (Political Essays). Taibei, 1955.
—— "Ji Chu Fucheng xiansheng" 記褚輔成先生 (Remembering Chu Fucheng). *Zhuanji wenxue*, 16, no. 6 (1970): 37–40.
Rudolph, Lloyd I. and Susanne H. Rudolph. *The Modernity of Tradition*. Chicago: University of Chicago Press, 1967.
Samuels, Marwyn S. "Review Article: *The City in Late Imperial China*." *Journal cf Asian Studies*, 37 (August 1978): 713–723.
Santō Mondai ni kansuru hai-Nichi jōkyō 山東問題に關する排日狀況 (The situation regarding the anti-Japanese movement in the wake of the Shandong problem). Vols. 2 and 3. Shanghai, n.d.
Satō Saburō 佐藤三郎, comp. *Minkoku no seika* 民国之精華 (Biographies of members of the National Assembly, 1912–1913). Reprint, Taipei, n.d.
Schnore, Leo F. "Social Morphology and Human Ecology." *American Journal of Sociology*, 63 (May 1958): 620–634.
Schoppa, R. Keith. "The Composition and Functions of the Local Elite in Szechwan, 1851–1874." *Ch'ing-shih wen-t'i*, 2 (November 1973): 7–23.
—— "Politics and Society in Chekiang, 1907–1927: Elite Power, Social Control, and the Making of a Province." Ph. D. diss., University of Michigan, 1975.
—— "Local Self-Government in Zhejiang, 1909–1927." *Modern China*, 2 (October 1976): 503–530.
—— "Province and Nation: The Chekiang Provincial Autonomy Movement, 1917–1927." *Journal of Asian Studies*, 36 (August 1977): 661–674.
—— "The Development of the Lake Xiang Region: Elite and Government Interaction, 1903–1926." Unpublished manuscript.
Shanghai Hongwen tushuguan 上海宏文圖書館, comp. *Jiang Zhe zhan shi* 江浙戰史 (A history of the war between Jiangsu and Zhejiang). Vol. 1. Shanghai, 1924.
Shaoxing xianzhi ziliao diyi ji 紹興縣志資料第一輯 (A compilation of materials for a gazetteer of Shaoxing county). 1937.
Shen Bao 申報. Shanghai, 1923–1949 (microfilm).
Shen Junru 沈鈞儒. "Xinhai geming zayi" 辛亥革命杂忆 (Miscellaneous recollections of the 1911 revolution). In *Xinhai geming huiyilu*, vol. 1, pp. 138–143.
Shen Yiyun 沈衣雲. "Yiyun huiyi" 衣雲回憶 (Remembrances of Shen Yiyun). *Zhuanji wenxue*, 4, no. 6 (1964): 29–34.
—— *Yiyun huiyi* 衣雲回憶 (Remembrances of Shen Yiyun). 2 vols. Taibei, 1968.
Shen Zonghan 沈宗瀚. *Kenan kuxue ji* 克難苦學記 (An account of overcoming hardship through diligent study). Taibei, 1954.
Sheridan, James. *Chinese Warlord: The Career of Feng Yu-hsiang*. Stanford: Stanford University Press, 1966.
—— *China in Disintegration*. New York: Free Press, 1975.
Shi Bao 時報 (The Eastern Times). Shanghai, 1909–1937 (microfilm).
Shiba Yoshinobu. "Ningpo and Its Hinterland." In *The City in Late Imperial*

China, ed. G. William Skinner. Stanford: Stanford University Press, 1977.

Shina Shōbetsu zenshi: Sekkō-shō 支那省別全誌: 浙江省 (A gazetteer of all provinces of China), comp. Tōa Dōbunkai 東亞同文会. Vol. 13. Tokyo, 1919. 18 vols.

Shouchang xianzhi 壽昌縣志 (Gazetteer of Shouchang county). 1930. Reprint, Taibei, 1970.

Shuanglin zhenzhi 雙林鎮志 (Gazetteer of Shuanglin town). 1917.

Shuntian Shibao 順天時報 (The Shuntian Times). Beijing, 1920–1923.

Si Daoqing 斯道卿. "Zhejun shibanian de huiyilu" 浙軍十八年的回憶錄 (Recollections of eighteen years in the Zhejiang army). In *Jindai shi ziliao*, 1957, vol. 2, pp. 76–93.

Sills, David. "Voluntary Associations: Sociological Aspects." In the *International Encyclopedia of the Social Sciences*. New York: Macmillan, 1968.

Skinner, G. William. "Marketing and Social Structure in Rural China." *Journal of Asian Studies*, 24 (November 1964) and 24 (February 1965).

——— "Mobility Strategies in Late Imperial China: A Regional Systems Analysis." In *Regional Analysis*, vol. 1, *Economic Systems*, ed. Carol A. Smith. New York: Academic Press, 1976.

——— "Cities and the Hierarchy of Local Systems." In *The City in Late Imperial China*, ed. G. William Skinner. Stanford: Stanford University Press, 1977.

——— "Introduction: Urban Social Structure in Ch'ing China." In *The City in Late Imperial China*, ed. G. William Skinner. Stanford: Stanford University Press, 1977.

——— "Regional Urbanization in Nineteenth Century China." In *The City in Late Imperial China*, ed. G. William Skinner. Stanford: Stanford University Press, 1977.

——— "Social Ecology and the Forces of Repression in North China." Unpublished conference paper, 1979.

Smith, Carol A. "Analyzing Regional Social Systems." In *Regional Analysis*, vol. 2, *Social Systems*, ed. Carol A. Smith. New York: Academic Press, 1976.

———"Exchange Systems and the Spatial Distribution of Elites: The Organization of Stratification in Agrarian Societies." In *Regional Analysis*, vol. 2, *Social Systems*, ed. Carol A. Smith. New York: Academic Press, 1976.

——— "Regional Economic Systems: Linking Geographical Models and Socioeconomic Problems." In *Regional Analysis*, vol. 1, *Economic Systems*, ed. Carol A. Smith. New York: Academic Press, 1976.

Songyang xianzhi 松陽縣志 (Gazetteer of Songyang county). 1926.

Suian xianzhi 遂安縣志 (Gazetteer of Suian county). 1930. Reprint, Taibei, 1974.

Sun E-tu Zen. "The Shanghai–Hangchow–Ningpo Railway Loan of 1908." *Far Eastern Quarterly*, 10 (1950–51): 136–150.

Tangqi xianzhi 湯溪縣志 (Gazetteer of Tangqi county). 1931.

Tawney, R. H. *Land and Labor in China*. Reprint, Boston: Beacon Press, 1966.

Teraki Tokuko 寺木德子. "Shinmatsu minkoku shonen no chihō jiji" 清末民国初年の地方自治 (Local self-government in late Qing and the early Republic).

Ochanomizu Shigaku, 5 (1962): 14–30.

Teune, Henry. "Development and Territorial Political Systems." *International Review of Community Development*, r.o. 33–34 (1975): 159–172.

—— "The Developmental Ecology of Political Intervention." In *The Social Ecology of Change*, ed. Zdravko Mlinar and Henry Teune. Beverly Hills, Calif.: Sage Publications, 1978.

Teune, Henry and Zdravko Mlinar. "Development and Participation." In *Local Politics, Development and Participation*, ed. F.C. Bruhns, Franco Cazzola, and Jerzy Wiatr. Pittsburgh: University Center for International Studies, 1974.

—— *The Developmental Logic of Social Systems*. Beverly Hills, Calif.: Sage Publications, 1978.

Ti Wei 惕微. "Guangfu Tangyi xiaoshi" 光復湯邑小史 (A brief account of the revolution in Tangqi city). In *Xinhai geming*, vol. 7, pp. 159–160.

Tilly, Charles. *The Vendée*. Cambridge, Mass.: Harvard University Press, 1964.

—— "Western State-Making and Theories of Political Transformation." In *The Formation of National States in Western Europe*, ed. Charles Tilly. Princeton: Princeton University Press, 1975.

Tipps, Dean C. "Modernization Theory and the Comparative Study of Societies: A Critical Perspective." *Comparative Studies in Society and History*, 15 (March 1973): 199–226.

Tōa Dōbun Shoin 東亞同文書院 (East Asian Language School), comp. *Shina keizai zensho* 支那經濟全書 (Complete studies of the economy of China). 4 vols. Osaka, 1907.

Ts'ai Ching-huai. "Telephone Scheme in Chekiang." *Chinese Economic Journal*, 8 (May 1931): 520–521.

Tung, William L. *The Political Institutions of Modern China*. The Hague: Martinus Nijhoff, 1968.

Wakeman, Frederic, Jr. *The Fall of Imperial China*. New York: Free Press, 1975.

Wallerstein, Immanuel. *The Modern World-System*. New York: Academic Press, 1976.

Wang Wei 王微, ed. *Xiaofeng zhigao* 孝豐志稿 (A draft gazetteer of Xiaofeng county). Taibei, 1974.

Wang Ziliang 王梓良. "Jiashu geming xianjin renshi ji gexian guangfu qingxing" 嘉屬革命先進人士及各縣光復情形 (The leaders of the revolution around Jiaxing and the situation of "restoration" in each county in Jiaxing). *Zhejiang yuekan*, 2, no. 2 (1969): 12–13.

—— "Jincui sangzide Chu Fucheng xiansheng" 蓋瘁桑梓的褚輔成先生 (The incessantly active career of our local Mr. Chu Fucheng). *Zhejiang yuekan*, 2, no. 3 (1969): 11.

—— "Bainian beihuan hua Jiaxing" 百年悲歡話嘉興 (Speaking of a century of sorrow and joy at Jiaxing). *Zhejiang yuekan*, 1, no. 7 (1969): 10–11.

—— *Zhexi kangzhan jilüe* 浙西抗戰紀略 (An account of northern Zhejiang in the war against Japan). Taibei, 1973.

Watt, John R. *The District Magistrate in Late Imperial China*. New York: Columbia University Press, 1972.

Wei Songtang 魏頌唐, ed. *Zhejiang jingji jilüe* 浙江經紀略 (An account of the Zhejiang economy). Shanghai, 1929.

Wen Gongzhi 文公直. *Zuijin sanshinian Zhongguo junshishi* 最近三十年中国軍事史 (A history of Chinese military affairs in the last thirty years). 2 vols. Taibei, 1962.

Who's Who in China, 5th ed. Shanghai: The China Weekly Review, 1936.

Woodhead, H. G. W., ed. *The China Year Book*. Tientsin: Tientsin Press, 1912–1922.

Wright, Mary C. "Introduction: The Rising Tide of Change." In *China in Revolution: The First Phase, 1900–1913*, ed. Mary C. Wright. New Haven: Yale University Press, 1968.

Wu-Qing zhenzhi 烏青鎮志 (Gazetteer of Wu-Qing town). 1936.

Wusi shiqi qikan jieshao 五四時期期刊介紹 (Introduction to the periodicals of the May Fourth period). 3 vols. Beijing, 1958–59.

Xiang Shiyuan 項士元. *Zhejiang xinwen shi* 浙江新聞史 (A history of journalism in Zhejiang). 1930.

Xianghu diaocha baogao shu 湘湖調查報告書 (Report of the investigation of Lake Xiang). 1927.

Xiangshan xianzhi 象山縣志 (Gazetteer of Xiangshan county). 1926.

Xiaoshan Xianghu xuzhi 蕭山湘湖續志 (A continuation of the Lake Xiang gazetteer from Xiaoshan county). 1927.

Xiaoshan Xianghu zhi 蕭山湘湖志 (Gazetteer of Lake Xiang in Xiaoshan county). 1925.

Xiaoshan xianzhi gao 蕭山縣志稿 (Draft gazetteer of Xiaoshan county). 1935.

Xin Fenghua 新奉化 (New Fenghua). 1922.

Xinchang xianzhi 新昌縣志 (Gazetteer of Xinchang county). 1919. Reprint, Taibei, 1970.

Xincheng zhenzhi 新塍鎮志 (Gazetteer of Xincheng town). 1916.

Xindeng xianzhi 新登縣志 (Gazetteer of Xindeng county). 1922. Reprint, Taibei, 1970.

Xinhai geming 辛亥革命 (The revolution of 1911), ed. Zhongguo shixue hui 中国史學会 (Chinese Historical Association). Compiled by Chai Degeng 柴德賡, et al. 8 vols. Shanghai, 1956.

Xinhai geming huiyilu 辛亥革命回憶錄 (Recorded recollections of the revolution of 1911), ed. Zhongguo renmin zhengzhi xieshang huiyi quanguo weiyuanhui 中国人民政治協商會議全国委員會文史資料研究委員會 (Committee on written historical materials of the National Committee of Chinese People's Political Consultative Conference). 5 vols. Beijing, 1961–1963.

Xu Baoshan 徐寶山. *Zhejiang sheng* 浙江省 (Zhejiang province). Shanghai, 1933.

Xu Bingkun 許炳堃. "Hangzhou guangfu zhi yede yici guanshen jinji huiyi" 杭州光復之夜的一次官紳緊急會議 (An urgent meeting of officials and gentry on the eve of the Hangchow revolution). In *Xinhai geming huiyilu*, vol. 4, pp. 165–166.

Xu Helin 徐鶴林. "Jiangshan shehui zhuangtai" 江山社會狀態 (Social conditions in Jiangshan county). *Xuesheng zazhi*, 9 (April 1922): 64–68.

Xuanping xianzhi 宣平縣志 (Gazetteer of Xuanping county). 1934. Reprint, Taibei, 1974.

Yang Zuochang 楊祚昌, comp. *Yu-Hang jilüe* 遊杭紀略 (A sketch for traveling to Hangchow). Hangchow, 1924.

Young, Ernest. *The Presidency of Yuan Shih-k'ai.* Ann Arbor: University of Michigan Press, 1977.

Yu Da 於達. "Yang Shande ru Zhe gushi" 楊善德入浙故事 (The account of the entrance of Yang Shande into Zhejiang). *Zhejiang yuekan*, 2, no. 10 (1970): 16.

Yu Lie 余烈. *Yuqian xianggong dili dagang chugao* 於潛鄉工地理大綱初稿 (Major elements of an initial draft of a gazetteer of Yuqian county). 1934.

Yui, Stewart and Harold S. Quigley, trans. "The Provincial Constitution of Chekiang." *Chinese Social and Political Science Review*, 6 (1921–1923): 114–142.

Yuyao Lantang xiang Qianjinhu xuanken zhilüe 餘姚蘭堓鄉千金湖濬墾志略 (An account of the dredging and development of Qianjin Lake in Lantang township, Yuyao county).

Yuyao liucang zhi 餘姚六倉志 (Gazetteer of Yuyao county). 1920.

Zhang Huangqi 張篁溪. "Guangfu hui lingxiu Tao Chengzhang geming shi" 光復會領袖陶成章革命史 (The revolutionary activities of Restoration Society leader Tao Chengzhang). In *Xinhai geming*, vol. 1, pp. 521–529.

Zhang Pengyuan 張朋園. *Lixian pai yu xinhai geming* 立憲派與辛亥革命 (The constitutionalists and the 1911 revolution). Taibei, 1969.

Zhang Qiyun 張其昀. *Zhejiang sheng shidi jiyao* 浙江省史地紀要 (Historical geography of Zhejiang province). Shanghai, 1925.

——— "Lun Ningpo jianshe shenghui zhi xiwang" 論寧波建設省會之希望 (On the hopes of Ningpo's becoming provincial capital). *Shidi xuebao*, 3 (May 1925): 1–17.

Zhang Xiaoxun 張效巡. "Zhejiang xinhai geming guangfu jishi" 浙江辛亥革命光復記事 (An account of the 1911 revolution in Zhejiang). In *Jindai shi ziliao*, 1954, vol. 1, pp. 118–124.

Zhao Jinyu 趙金鈺. "SuHangYong tielu jie kuan he JiangZhe renminde jukuan yundong" 蘇杭甬鐵路借款和江浙人民的拒款運動 (The Shanghai–Hangchow–Ningpo Railway loan and the opposition to the loan by the people). *Lishi yanjiu* 9 (1959): 51–60.

Zhejiang caizheng yuekan 浙江財政月刊 (Zhejiang Financial Monthly). July 1917–December 1918.

Zhejiang chao 浙江潮 (Tides of Zhejiang). Tokyo, 1903. Reprint, Taibei, 1968. 5 vols.

Zhejiang jun sishijiu lü siling bu 浙江軍四十九旅司令部 (Headquarters of the Forty-ninth Brigade of the Zhejiang army). "Zhejun Hangzhou guangfu ji" 浙軍杭州光復記 (An account of the Zhejiang army at the Hangchow revolution). In *Gesheng guangfu*, vol. 2, pp. 131–145.

Zhejiang xinzhi 浙江新志 (New gazetteer of Zhejiang). 1936.

Zhejiang yuekan 浙江月刊 (Zhejiang Monthly). 1968–.

Zhenhai xianzhi 鎮海縣志 (Gazetteer of Zhenhai county). 1931.

Zhenhai xinzhi beigao 鎮海新志備稿 (A prepared draft of a new gazetteer of

Zhenhai county). 1924.

Zhong Liyu 鍾豐玉. "Guangfu Hangzhou huiyilu" 光復杭州回憶錄 (Recollections of the revolution in Hangchow). In *Jindai shi ziliao*, 1954, vol. 1, pp 89–103.

Zhongguo shiye zhi, vol. 2, *Zhejiang sheng* 中国實業誌—浙江省 (Gazetteer of Chinese Industry—Zhejiang province), comp. Shiyebu guoji maoyi ju 實業 部国際貿易局 (Office for International Trade of the Ministry of Industry). Shanghai, 1933.

Zhonghua Xinbao 中華新報 (The China News). Shanghai, 1917. Reprint, Taibei, 1970.

Zhou Qiwei 周起渭. "Luoqing xinhai geming shiliao" 樂青辛亥革命史料 (Historical materials on the 1911 revolution in Luoqing). In *Xinhai geming huiyilu*, vol. 4, pp. 188–195.

Zhou Yawei 周亞例. "Guangfu hui jianwen zayi" 光復會見聞雜憶 (Miscellaneous recollections of the Restoration Society). In *Xinhai geming huiyilu*, vol. 1, pp. 624–636.

Zhuanji wenxue 傳記文學 (Biographical literature). Taibei, 1963– .

Zhuji gaiguan 諸暨概觀 (Views of Zhuji county), ed. Zhuji minbao she 諸暨民報社 (Office of the Zhuji minbao). 1925.

Zhulin bayu zhi 竹林八圩志 (A gazetteer of the town of Zhulin [Jiaxing county]). 1932.

Zuijin guanshen lili huilu 最近官紳履歷彙錄 (A directory of recent gentry and officials). Beijing, 1920. Reprint, Taibei, 1971.

Glossary

This character glossary contains names and phrases found in the text. It excludes the names of well-known personages, names of provinces, and persons who authored works cited in the bibliography.

Anchang 安昌
Anji 安吉

Baiguan 百官
bang 帮
bao quanguoquan hui 保全国權会
Baoding sucheng xuetang 保定速成
　學堂
Baohe 保和
baojia 保甲
baxiang huiguan 八鄉会館
bendi ren 本地人
bolaipin 舶來品

canshihui 參事会
canyihui 參議会
Cao-e 曹娥
caonanmi 漕南米
cehui xuetang 測絵學堂
Cha Renwei 査人偉
Changbei 昌北
Changhua 昌化
Changshan 常山
Changxing 長興
Changyue 常樂
Chen Fuchen 陳黻宸
Chen Huang 陳梡

Chen Qicai 陳其采
Chen Qimei 陳其美
Chen Shanying 陳善瑛
Chen Shixia 陳時夏
Chen Xihao 陳希豪
Chen Xiong 陳雄
Chen Yi 陳儀
Chen Zaiyan 陳宰埏
Chen Zihao 陳滋鎬
Cheng 嵊
Cheng Bingpan 程秉泙
Chenglu julebu 澄廬俱樂部
Chongde 崇德
chuming hui 除螟会
Chuzhou 處州
Ciqi 慈谿
Cong Nengshu 宗能述
conggonghui 總工会
cun zizhi zhi 村自治制

Dai Yan 戴彦
Daishan 岱山
dangren 黨人
daoyin 道尹
dapo quyu zhuyi 打破區域主義
Deqing 德清
dibujin 抵補金

267

difang zizhi 地方自治
Ding Meisun 丁眉孫
Dinghai 定海
Dongting 東亭
Dongyang 東陽
Dongyang gongjie tongxiang hui
　東陽工界同鄉會
du 都
Duan Qirui 段祺瑞

fangzu 房租
Fenghua 奉化
Fengqiao 楓橋
Fenshui 分水
Fu Tinggui 傅廷佺
fuguo 富國
fumu guan 父母官
fushen 富紳
Fuyang 富陽

Gan Shixin 甘詩信
Ganpu 澉浦
Gao Erdeng 高爾登
gaoyao 膏藥
gejie lianhehui 固界聯合会
gongcheng shiwusuo 工程事務所
gonghui 工会
gongjie xiehui 工界協会
gongmin 公民
gongso 公所
gongye xuexiao 工業學校
gongyu 公寓
gu 股
Gu Naibin 顧乃斌
Gu Songqing 顧松慶
guangfu 光復
guanshen 官紳
guanzhi 官治
Guiji 會稽
Guilin 貴林
guomin dahui 国民大会
guomin shangwuhui 国民尚武会
Gushi 古市

Haimen 海門
Haining 海寧

Haiyan 海鹽
Han Baohua 韓寶华
Hang 杭
Hangzhou 杭州
hao 豪
Hong Chenglu 洪承魯
Hong Dao 洪燾
Hong Weiguang 洪煒光
Hong Xicheng 洪錫承
Hu Bingliu 胡炳旒
huahui 花会
Huang Weishi 黃維時
Huangyan 黃巖
huiguan 会館
Huizhou 徽州
hujunshi 護軍使
Huzhou 湖州

Jiande 建德
Jiang Banyan 蔣邦彥
Jiang Menglin 蔣夢麟
Jiang Ruiqi 蔣瑞麒
Jiang Zungui 蔣尊簋
Jiangshan 江山
jiaoyu hui 教育会
jiaoyu hui lianhehui 教育会聯合会
jiaoyu ju 教育局
Jiashan 嘉善
Jiaxing 嘉興
jin 金
Jin-Qu-Yan-Chu tongxiang hui
　金衢嚴處同鄉会
Jin Yuanao 金元熬
jingbeidui 警備隊
Jingning 景寧
jingshi fazheng xuetang 京師法政學堂
jingzuo 警佐
Jinhua 金華
Jinyun 縉雲
Jiqi 績溪
ju 局
junzheng fenfu 軍政分府

Kaihua 開化
keren 客人

Kong Qingyi 孔慶儀

Lanqi 蘭谿
li 里
Li Kangguang 李康光
liang she 良社
lieshen 劣紳
Lihaisuo 瀝海所
lijia 里甲
Lin Yonghuai 林永懷
Linan 臨安
Ling 嶺
Linghu 菱湖
Linhai 臨海
Linpu 臨浦
linshi canyihui 臨時參議会
linshi jingcha 臨時警察
linshi shengyihui 臨時省議会
linshi yihui 臨時議会
Liu Tingxuan 劉廷煊
liuxing gonghi 六姓公会
liuyi gonghui 六邑公会
Longchuan 龍泉
Longyu 龍游
Lu Chongyue 盧鍾嶽
Lu Yongxiang 盧永祥
Lufu 路富
Luofou 羅埠
Luoqing 樂清
Lü Fengqiao 呂逢樵
lü Hang tongxianghui 旅杭同鄉会
lüshihui 律師会

minbao 民報
minbing 民兵
minglun tang 明倫堂
minyi 民意
minzheng 民政
minzhi 民治
Mo Yongzhen 莫永貞
Moganshan 莫干山
mu 畝
mufu 幕府
muyou 幕友

Nantian 南田

Nantianshan 南田山
Nanxun 南潯
nayuan 納員
Ningbo 寧波
Ningguo 寧国
Ninghai 寧海
nonghui 農会
nongmin 農民
nongwuhui 農務会
nongye shiwusuo 農業事務所

Ou 甌
Ouhai 甌海

pai 派
Pan Guanlan 潘觀瀾
Peng Zuling 彭祖齡
pineryuan 貧兒院
Pinghu 平湖
pingshe 平社
Pingyang 平陽
pinmin xiyisuo 貧民習藝所
Pujiang 浦江
Puyuan 濮院

qingnian tuan 青年団
Qingshan 青山
Qingtian 青田
qingxiang 清鄉
Qingyuan 慶元
Qingzhen 青鎮
Qiu Jin 秋瑾
qu 區
Qu 衢
quansheng daibiao dahui
 全省代表大会
quanxuesuo 勸學所
qun 群
Qunan 淳安
Quzhou 衢州

rikugun shikan gakkō 陸軍士官學校
Ruian 瑞安

Sanjiang 三江
Sanmenwan 三門灣

shang 上
shang 商
shanghui 商会
shangjie lianhehui 商界聯合会
Shangrao 上饒
shangyi tuan 尚義団
Shangyu 上虞
Shaoxing 紹興
shemiao 社廟
shen 紳
Shen Dingyi 沈定一
Shen Jinjian 沈金鑑
Shen Wenhua 沈文華
shendong 紳董
Sheng Bangbian 盛邦采
Sheng Bingwei 盛炳緯
shengji 生計
Shengze 盛澤
shenqi 紳耆
shenshang 紳商
shenshi 紳士
Shimen 石門
Shipu 石浦
shishen 士紳
Shouchang 壽昌
Shuanglin 雙林
shuili weiyuanhui 水利委員会
shuyuan 書院
sifa jingcha 司法警察
sifa xiehui 司法協会
Siming 四明
Songyang 松陽
Suian 遂安
Suichang 遂昌
Sun Chuanfang 孫傳芳
Sun Shouzhi 孫壽芝
suo 所

Taihu 太湖
Taiping 太平
Taishun 泰順
Taizhou 台州
Tang Ermin 唐爾民
Tang Shouqian 湯壽潛
Tangqi 湯溪
Tao Chengzhang 陶成章

Teng Huajin 滕華欽
Tiantai 天台
tianye lianhehui 田業聯合会
Tianyue 天樂
tiyu hui 体育会
Tong 桐
tongjiji 同濟集
tongjuan 統捐
Tonglu 桐廬
Tōyō Daigaku 東洋大學
Tu Chenxiang 杜震鄉
Tu Tihua 杜棣华
tuanlian 団練
tufei 土匪
tuhuangdi 土皇帝
tumin 土民
tuzaishui 屠宰税

Waibei 外北
Wan He 萬和
Wang Dexing 王德星
Wang Jinfa 王金發
Wang Lisan 王立三
Wang Shengsan 王省三
Wang Tingyang 王廷揚
Wang Xitong 王錫彤
Wangjiangjing 王江涇
Wangdian 王店
weiyuan 委員
wenhua weiyuanhui 文話委員会
Wenling 温嶺
Wenzhou 温州
Wu 吳
Wu Baosan 吳寶三
Wu Daonan 吳道南
Wu Zhiying 吳之英
wubei xuetang 武備學堂
Wukang 武康
Wuqiangqi 武強溪
Wu-Qing 烏青
Wuxi 無錫
Wuxing 吳興
Wuyi 武義

Xi Bingyuan 嵇炳元
xia 下

Xia Chao 夏超
xian 縣
xiang 鄉
Xianghu 湘湖
xiangmin 鄉民
xiangdong 鄉董
Xianju 仙居
xianyihui 縣議会
xianyihui lianhehui 縣議会聯合会
Xiaofeng 孝豐
Xiaoli 垓里
Xiaoshan 蕭山
Xiashi 硤石
Xin Bao 新報
Xin Jinhua xunkan 新金華旬刊
Xinan 新安
Xinchang 新昌
Xincheng 新際
Xindeng 新登
Xingqihui 星期会
Xinhuang 新篁
Xinshi 新市
Xu Baiyuan 徐柏園
Xu Xilin 徐錫麟
Xu Zexun 徐則恂
Xu Zuqian 許祖謙
Xuan Zhonghua 宣中华
Xuanping 宣平
xuequ 學區
xunfangdui 巡防隊
xunzheng xuetang 巡政學堂

Yan she 剡社
Yang Shande 楊善德
Yangwang 楊望
Yanzhou 嚴州
Ye Huanhua 葉煥華
Ye Xiangyang 葉向陽
Ye Zhengrong 葉正榮
Yi 黑
yihui 議会
Yin 鄞
yinliju 因利局
Yiwu 義鳥
Yiwu ribao 一鳥日報
Yiyanglu 怡養廬

yizhuang 義莊
Yongfeng 永豐
Yongjia 永嘉
Yongkang 永康
Yu Linsen 郁林森
Yu Ruchang 俞汝昌
Yu she 愚社
Yu Shichang 俞師昌
yuan 圓
Yuan Zhicheng 袁志成
Yue 越
Yuhang 餘杭
Yuhuan 玉環
yumin 愚民
Yun Shao 雲淄
Yunhe 雲和
Yuyao 餘姚
yuyingtang 育嬰堂

zao 裹
Zhang Hao 張浩
Zhang Renjie 張人傑
Zhang Xiaojin 張小金
Zhang Yinhua 張殷華
Zhang Zaiyang 張載陽
Zhao Baisu 趙伯素
Zhedong 浙東
Zhedong shuili yishihui
    浙東水利議事会
Zhejiang ge fatuan lianhehui
    浙江固法团聯合会
zhen 鎮
Zheng Baolin 鄭寶琳
zheng shendong 正紳董
Zhenhai 鎮海
Zhenwu 振武
Zhexi 浙西
Zhexi shuili yishihui 浙西水利議事会
zhong 中
Zhonghua minguo gonghe
    中華民国共和
Zhou Chengtan 周承炎
Zhou Jirong 周繼溁
Zhou Shiying 周士溏
Zhou Shu 周書
Zhou Wenfu 周文富

Zhou Yongguang 周永廣
Zhuang Jingzhong 莊景仲
zhuanmen xuexiao 專門學校

zongban 總辦
zu 族
zuoli 佐理

HARVARD EAST ASIAN SERIES

1. *China's Early Industrialization: Sheng Hsuan-huai (1884-1916) and Mandarin Enterprise.* Albert Feuerwerker.
2. *Intellectual Trends in the Ch'ing Period.* Liang Ch'i-ch'ao. Trans. Immanuel C. Y. Hsu.
3. *Reform in Sung China: Wang An-shih (1021-1086) and His New Policies.* James T. C. Liu.
4. *Studies on the Population of China, 1368-1953.* Ping-ti Ho.
5. *China's Entrance into the Family of Nations: The Diplomatic Phase, 1858-1880.* Immanuel C. Y. Hsu.
6. *The May Fourth Movement: Intellectual Revolution in Modern China.* Chow Tse-tsung.
7. *Ch'ing Administrative Terms: A Translation of the Terminology of the Six Boards with Explanatory Notes.* Trans. and ed. E-tu Zen Sun.
8. *Anglo-American Steamship Rivalry in China, 1862-1874.* Kwang-Ching Liu.
9. *Local Government in China under the Ch'ing.* T'ung-tsu Ch'u.
10. *Communist China, 1955-1959: Policy Documents with Analysis.* Foreword by Robert R. Bowie and John K. Fairbank. (Prepared at Harvard University under the joint auspices of the Center for International Affairs and the East Asian Research Center.)
11. *China and Christianity: The Missionary Movement and the Growth of Chinese Antiforeignism, 1860-1870.* Paul A. Cohen.
12. *China and the Helping Hand, 1937-1945.* Arthur N. Young.
13. *Research Guide to the May Fourth Movement: Intellectual Revolution in Modern China, 1915-1924.* Chow Tse-tsung.
14. *The United States and the Far Eastern Crisis of 1933-1938: From the Manchurian Incident through the Initial Stage of the Undeclared Sino-Japanese War.* Dorothy Borg.
15. *China and the West, 1858-1861: The Origins of the Tsungli Yamen.* Masataka Banno.
16. *In Search of Wealth and Power: Yen Fu and the West.* Benjamin Schwartz.
17. *The Origins of Entrepreneurship in Meiji Japan.* Johannes Hirschmeier.
18. *Commissioner Lin and the Opium War.* Hsin-pao Chang.
19. *Money and Monetary Policy in China, 1845-1895.* Frank H. H. King.
20. *China's Wartime Finance and Inflation, 1937-1945.* Arthur N. Young.
21. *Foreign Investment and Economic Development in China, 1840-1937.* Chi-ming Hou.
22. *After Imperialism: The Search for a New Order in the Far East, 1921-1931.* Akira Iriye.

76. *A Study of Samurai Income and Entrepreneurship: Quantitative Analyses of Economic and Social Aspects of the Samurai in Tokugawa and Meiji Japan.* Kozo Yamamura.
77. *Between Tradition and Modernity: Wang T'ao and Reform in Late Ch'ing China.* Paul A. Cohen.
78. *The Abortive Revolution: China under Nationalist Rule, 1927–1937.* Lloyd E. Eastman.
79. *Russia and the Roots of the Chinese Revolution, 1896–1911.* Don C. Price.
80. *Toward Industrial Democracy: Management and Workers in Modern Japan.* Kunio Odaka.
81. *China's Republican Revolution: The Case of Kwangtung, 1895–1913.* Edward J. M. Rhoads.
82. *Politics and Policy in Traditional Korea.* James B. Palais.
83. *Folk Buddhist Religion: Dissenting Sects in Late Traditional China.* Daniel L. Overmyer.
84. *The Limits of Change: Essays on Conservative Alternatives in Republican China.* Ed. Charlotte Furth.
85. *Yenching University and Sino-Western Relations, 1916–1952.* Philip West.
86. *Japanese Marxist: A Portrait of Kawakami Hajime, 1876–1946.* Gail Lee Bernstein.
87. *China's Forty Millions: Minority Nationalities and National Integration in the People's Republic of China.* June Teufel Dreyer.
88. *Japanese Colonial Education in Taiwan, 1895–1945.* E. Patricia Tsurumi.
89. *Modern Chinese Literature in the May Fourth Era.* Ed. Merle Goldman.
90. *The Broken Wave: The Chinese Communist Peasant Movement, 1922–1928.* Roy Hofheinz, Jr.
91. *Passage to Power: K'ang-hsi and His Heir Apparent, 1661–1722.* Silas H. L. Wu.
92. *Chinese Communism and the Rise of Mao.* Benjamin I. Schwartz.
93. *China's Development Experience in Comparative Perspective.* Ed. Robert F. Dernberger.
94. *The Chinese Vernacular Story.* Patrick Hanan.
95. *Chinese Village Politics in the Malaysian State.* Judith Strauch.
96. *Chinese Elites and Political Change: Zhejiang Province in the Early Twentieth Century.* R. Keith Schoppa.

(Some of these titles may be out of print in a given year. Write to Harvard University Press for information and ordering.)